memorabile ipermoda
edited by Maria Luisa Frisa

Marsilio Arte   MA XXI

memorabile
ipermoda

edited by Maria Luisa Frisa

MINISTERO
DELLA
CULTURA

REGIONE
LAZIO

enel

CAMERA NAZIONALE DELLA
MODA ITALIANA

Camera Nazionale
della Moda Italiana

President
Carlo Capasa

Honorary President
Mario Boselli

Vice President
Patrizio Bertelli

Management Board
Pierre-Emmanuel Angeloglu
Roberta Benaglia
Patrizio Bertelli
Alfonso Dolce
Massimo Ferretti
Marco Gobbetti
Luigi Maramotti
Angela Missoni
Jean-François Palus
Renzo Rosso
Remo Ruffini
Carla Sozzani
Jacopo Venturini
Ermenegildo Zegna

TEAM
*Head of Sustainability
and New Brands Projects*
Paola Arosio

*Head of Members &
Corporate Affairs*
Barbara Beghin

Production Specialist
Agata Bigi

Front Office
Federica Borsotti

Partnerships Coordinator
Ludovica Casilli

*Head of International
Relations & Buyers Projects*
Paola Ciolina

Partnerships Coordinator
Alessia Di Bari

Communication Junior Specialist
Martina Guicciardi

Accounting Manager
Alessandro Levati

Sustainability Projects Manager
Chiara Luisi

Digital Communication Coordinator
Matteo Miranda

Executive Assistant to Chairman
Susanna Molon

*Senior Digital Communication
Specialist*
Nicolò Montori

Graphic Designer Specialist
Andrea Morelli

Head of Fashion Week Calendar
Alessandra Panico

Finance Director
Silvia Pellegrini

*Facility Manager &
Associates Service Officer*
Tina Redaelli

Head of PR
Beatrice Rossaro

*Senior Fashion Week
Calendar Specialist*
Elena Tedesco

*Head of Content &
Digital Communication*
Andrea Vigneri

Production Manager
Carlotta Villa

Creative Manager
Alice Egle Volontè

Accountant
Valentina Vozza

New Brands Coordinator
Jovana Vukoje

EXHIBITION

Rome, MAXXI – National Museum of 21st Century Arts
November 27, 2024–March 23, 2025

Curated by
Maria Luisa Frisa

Consultant at Large
Gabriele Monti

General Coordination
Anne Palopoli

Assistant Curator
Dylan Colussi

Research Coordination
Alessandra Varisco

Exhibition Setup Project
Supervoid

Technical Coordination
Dolores Lettieri

Registrar
Roberta Magagnini
Eleonora Turli *(Intern)*

Conservation and Restoration
Simona Brunetti
Livia Marinelli

Licensing Video
Giulia Pedace

Lighting Coordination
Paola Mastracci

Technical Office
Elisabetta Virdia
Cristina Andreassi

Safety Coordination
Livio Della Seta

Marketing and Development
Maria Carolina Profilo
Camilla Fidenti
Giulia Zappone

Press Office
Flaminia Persichetti
Ilaria Mulas

Communication
Prisca Cupellini
Giulia Chiapparelli
Eleonora Colizzi
Cecilia Fiorenza
Olivia Salmistrari

*Public Programs
and Film Screening*
Irene de Vico Fallani
Carolina Latour

Educational Programs
Marta Morelli
Giovanna Cozzi

Opening Events
Viola Porfirio
Ludovica Persichetti

Public Service Quality
Laura Neto
Stefania Calandriello

Graphic Design
bruno — Andrea Codolo
e Giacomo Covacich

English Translations
Lost in translation

Insurance
Willis Towers Watson

Shipping and Handling
Arteria

Mannequinage
Simona Fulceri
Opera Laboratori Fiorentini S.p.a.

Exhibition Setup
Artigiana Design

Audiovideo
Informasistemi

Mannequin
Bonaveri

Electrical Wiring and Lighting
Sater4show
Natuna

CAMERA NAZIONALE DELLA MODA ITALIANA

General Coordination
Andrea Vigneri

Marketing and Development
Ludovica Casilli
Alessia Di Bari

Press Office
Karla Otto

Communication
Beatrice Rossaro
Andrea Vigneri
Alice Egle Volontè
Matteo Miranda
Nicolò Montori
Martina Guicciardi

Legal Affairs
Barbara Beghin

Main Sponsor

FONDAZIONE BVLGARI

Sponsor

♪ TikTok

Sponsor

Spotify®

Technical Sponsor

NEWMAT.
THE NEW STANDARD IN STRETCH CEILINGS

Technical Sponsor

≡ informasistemi

CATALOGUE

Edited by
Maria Luisa Frisa

Consultant at Large
Gabriele Monti

Head of Publishing
Flavia De Sanctis Mangelli

Graphic Design and Layout
bruno — Andrea Codolo
e Giacomo Covacich
with Alessandro Durighello

General Coordination
Maria Pia Verzillo

Assistant Curator
Dylan Colussi

Research Coordination
Alessandra Varisco

Research
Chiara Braidotti
Chiara Cottone

Still Video
Furio Ganz

Translations
Huw Evans

Copy Editing
Riccardo Dirindin

Editorial Consultancy
Richard Sadleir

Licensing
Valeria Dellino

Memorabile: Ipermoda is a project that examines the role of fashion as a discipline able to respond to the social, political, economic, and cultural pressures of our time. It is the second exhibition on the theme hosted by the MAXXI, curated like the previous one by Maria Luisa Frisa with the intent of presenting this complex and porous system in a museum setting, tracing the course of its evolution in the production of a collective imagery.

The exhibition explores fashion's ability to be at once extraordinary and at the same time rooted in everyday life, where its images are pervasive. The growing interaction between fashion and new technologies is breaking down established canons and leading people to wonder about the emergence of a new cultural awareness. In analyzing these questions, *Memorabile* makes clear the role of curatorial practices in fashion, actions that require structure and development, especially in a country that still does not have a museum dedicated to the subject.

The exhibition project has found inspiration in the ideas of the anthropologist Carlo Severi, and in particular his theory of "visual belief" and the consequent notion of "memorability." While the traditional approach of the art historian focuses on the physicality of the work and its historical contextualization, *Memorabile* highlights the importance of the "figural mystery" inherent in the artwork and in fashion, revealing an approach that has taken on, with discretion, an impure configuration, always ready to resurface. Maria Luisa Frisa is proposing a critical vision of contemporary fashion, reflecting on such topical questions as gender, ethics, cultural appropriation, and sustainability. Through a mixture of works of art, clothing, virtual reality, professional ethics, influencers, and celebrities emerge multiple perspectives and innovative proposals in the making of fashion, with a particular emphasis on the role of collective memory and the ability of even the most common images to persist in time.

Memorabile is an exploration of the phenomenon of fashion that goes beyond its traditional confines, with reference to the concept of the "language of dress," which holds that clothes do not have fixed meanings but are involved in a process of continual redefinition. Fashion is not just a matter of aesthetics. It is a means of expression that is constantly reflecting and renegotiating social and cultural values. The exhibition also looks at the effects of the pandemic, an event that has altered the rhythms of the fashion system, driving many creators to rethink the dynamics of production and venture into new territories, like the digital, artificial intelligence, and the metaverse. This has given new luster to the concept of the past, turning over the course of the years the archive of fashion into an experimental laboratory, in which historical materials are reinterpreted and reactivated.

The exhibition is organized around a series of installations that offer the public a fragmented vision, prompting the visitor to explore the various themes in a critical and personal way and emphasizing the importance of the curator in the construction of a visual narration that can make the experience of fashion *memorable* and that invites us to see this work as a starting point for further critical reflections.

So we are honored to have investigated, over the course of these months, the challenges that fashion faces and the scenarios that lie ahead. An important catalogue, enriched by the contributions of scholars, philosophers, and writers, adds further polyphonic value to a discipline that should be understood not just as an art form, but also as a physical and cultural substance.

Francesco Stocchi
Fondazione MAXXI, Artistic Director

For some years now exhibitions of fashion have come to be eagerly awaited and extremely popular events on the busy calendar of a system characterized by a rapid succession of shows and other occasions. They are invaluable means of carrying out analyses of the complex and multilayered phenomenon that is fashion, stimulating reflections and proposing critical interpretations.

The Camera Nazionale della Moda Italiana has long been conducting a multifaceted project for the promotion of fashion as a fundamental expression of contemporary society, reflecting its spirit and at the same time contributing to the process of transforming society itself. Exhibitions have proved a fundamental way of encouraging participation and dialogue not only with those involved in the industry, but also and above all with an ever broader and more enthusiastic swathe of the public.

Memorabile: Ipermoda presents a many-sided and critical vision of the aspirations of fashion in the present day and the profound changes that it is undergoing, and draws an accurate picture of a lively system in which many forces are at play. Space is found for the visions of established designers and up-and-coming talents, heritage is married with innovation, a dialogue is established between cultures and sensibilities, and new scenarios are outlined for the industry and the business in the light of the demands of environmental and social sustainability and in relation to the new means of communication and promotion through which the image and icons of our time are forged. There are many forms of creativity at the beating heart of fashion, and the vast range of clothes, objects, and videos presented by *Memorabile: Ipermoda* celebrates and represents its multiple facets. At the same time it draws attention to the fundamental and seminal contribution made by Italian fashion to the system through the brands, creative directors, entrepreneurs, and gifted designers that underpin the Made in Italy label.

We are happy that the exhibition is being held in Rome, one of the cities symbolic of the history of fashion as well as home to some of the most important players of the present day. It is the place that saw the establishment, at the Grand Hotel on Via Vittorio Emanuele Orlando on June 11, 1958, of the Camera Sindacale della Moda Italiana, precursor of what would come to be known as the Camera Nazionale della Moda Italiana, based in Rome up until 1987.

Memorabile: Ipermoda is a product of the memorandum of understanding signed between the Fondazione MAXXI (National Museum of 21st Century Arts) and the Camera Nazionale della Moda Italiana: a three-year-long collaboration in view of their joint organization of activities around the country devoted to the themes of the culture and narration of fashion, of sustainability, and of the promotion of the Italian industry. Convinced that connections and strategic alliances are more fundamental than ever today, we would like to express our gratitude to the Fondazione MAXXI for sharing the vision and the work required to stage this ambitious project.

Special thanks go to the curator Maria Luisa Frisa—with whom the Camera Nazionale della Moda Italiana has been conducting for years a fertile dialogue on the realization of initiatives for the cultural promotion of fashion—as well as to the brands that have participated with enthusiasm and the team at the Camera Nazionale della Moda Italiana. And our thanks go too to the partners who have made possible the realization of this project, embracing its spirit.

Carlo Capasa
Chairman of the Camera Nazionale della Moda Italiana

What is it that defines, then and now, the concept of "memorable"? The exhibition *Memorabile: Ipermoda* is not simply an exploration of contemporary fashion, but a deep dive into the complex system of concepts, forms of expression, and cultural phenomena that have helped shape the inexorable evolution of the world of fashion and luxury. A project curated by Maria Luisa Frisa that sees the Fondazione Bvlgari in the role of official sponsor of an exhibition for the first time, ten years after *Bellissima: Italy and High Fashion 1945–1968* was staged at the MAXXI with Bvlgari's support.

Set up at the beginning of 2024, the foundation perpetuates and amplifies a mission that was already an integral part of Bvlgari's vision: the commitment to building a magnificent future and creating long-term value for the environment and society in the fields of art and patronage, education, philanthropy and inclusiveness, and the handing on of knowhow.

From actions aimed at conserving the artistic and cultural heritage, in particular of the city of Rome, to the promotion of initiatives of contemporary art, through collaborations with cultural institutions like the MAXXI, the Fondazione Bvlgari is supporting the art of the past, present, and future. Art as a priceless source of beauty and upliftment, but also as a precious resource to be preserved and strengthened for the generations to come. For it is precisely the infinite metamorphoses of the artistic and cultural heritage that have been constantly fueling Bvlgari's creative vision since 1884. Driven therefore by a determination to give something back to the community, the house first and the Fondazione Bvlgari today are contributing with their activity to this process of enrichment and preservation.

With a history stretching back 140 years, Bvlgari too views the evolution of the concept of memorability as a stimulating challenge. In a continual tension between its own identity and the requirements of the modern world, and with the need to preserve know-how by projecting it into the future, the house has continued to affirm its iconic style while embracing ever new languages. All the while remaining faithful to an idea of excellence in craftsmanship and creative daring, indispensable for a fine jewelry brand.

To trace the link between Bvlgari and the fashion world, space has been found in the exhibition for some emblematic creations, including Francesco Vezzoli's work *Tortue de Soirée*, studded with magnificent gems, two *Serpenti* pieces from the Bvlgari Heritage Collection, and a selection of bags arising from a collaboration with the designer Mary Katrantzou, examples of how the different languages of creativity can inspire and enrich each other, without eroding their individual identities.

Jean-Christophe Babin
Bvlgari CEO and Fondazione Bvlgari President

First Edition November 2024
ISBN 979-12-5463-232-1

Available through ARTBOOK | D.A.P. 75 Broad Street, Suite 630 New York, NY 10004
www.artbook.com

Table of Contents

memorabile
ipermoda

Over the fractured time that, as with all projects, it has taken to develop *Memorabile: Ipermoda* as complementary exhibition and book, I was always guided by the desire to present a vision of the fashion of the present day whose confines would be as supple and porous as possible.[1] I wanted *Memorabile* to take shape in a space that would be at once dense and nuanced, to be traversed in order to explore critically a discipline that today is more capable than ever of reflecting many of the material and immaterial questions of our time. And that in its end product, clothing, acts somewhere between what we might call the search for an architectural synthesis of the item of apparel and the visual and imaginative hyperbole in which, in an age of exponential multiplication of images, is framed fashion's aspiration to become, to be *memorabile*, memorable.[2]

The fact of having enriched and clarified its vocabulary with words that have crossed over from many areas of activism; of having adapted to the wide variety of bodies and many ideas of beauty; of having tackled such now inescapable themes as the ones relating to gender, cultural appropriation, and an ethics poised between ecology and politics: all this has led fashion to overcome prejudices and customs, to question canons and rules, and to become aware of the responsibility that stems from offering models of reference to what is now a definitively global public.

Thus *Memorabile* is a sort of exploration of the questions that are raised today by fashion through its ability to react to any impulse, be it social, political, economic, or cultural. At the same time, it is a recognition of fashion's vocation for the extraordinary,

I've always wanted to have a big album and to be able to portray myself in it as I have changed with age and in the clothes I was wearing at the time. So great was my desire to commemorate myself day by day . . .
Paola Masino, *Album di vestiti*

Provisional Maps
Maria Luisa Frisa

the extravagant; of its effort to be something that is nevertheless impossible without its opposite: "When we neglect the ordinary, the option for the extraordinary vanishes. If we ignore the quotidian and commercial, we are doomed to speak only of the venerable and awesome."[3] So *Memorabile* attempts to act from a critical perspective, starting out from the wardrobe of everyday attire and taking up the notion of the "language of clothing," according to which garments are not objects with immutable meanings but participate in a process in which meanings are continually renegotiated.[4]

Some parts of the anthropologist Carlo Severi's book *Capturing Imagination: A Proposal for an Anthropology of Thought* have made me think about the extent to which the act of dressing or choosing a garment has assumed a significance in our society which transcends the individual, becoming more often than not something that does not match the latter's personality and desires. The performativity of an article of clothing can be independent of that of the body. Thus I started to think of clothes as "object-persons," as structures that are not casts or mirrors of the individual: "Within a ritual context, it [the object] becomes more complex than a mirror image or a 'double.' It resembles more a crystal. . . . If we decipher the complexity of the bond of belief created between objects and persons, the very idea of a 'living object' appears in a completely different light."[5]

The word *ipermoda*, "hyperfashion," is a mode of emphasis that derives from ideas inspired by the title and philosophical and ecological arguments out forward in Timothy Morton's book *Hyperobjects*: "Hyperobjects . . . are 'hyper' in relation to some other entity, whether they are directly manufactured by humans or not."[6] *Ipermoda* makes clear the meaning of *Memorabile*. It expresses the need of fashion in all its manifestations to extend beyond its limits, to occupy spaces that can give it the greatest visibility, to be an expanded body that invades the screens of our devices and installs itself in our imagination; its need to gain control of the territories of pleasure, leisure, and beauty. And of the city.

Fashion is an increasingly complex system that underpins our daily lives—from the private dimension of us standing in front of the mirror in our homes to the public one of the cities in which we move[7]—and in which, between silence and clamor, euphoria and disenchantment, creativity, authoriality, culture, communication, the market, and engagement confront one another and are intertwined.

Memorabile: Ipermoda is also a sequel to and development of *Memos: On Fashion in This Millennium*, the exhibition that I curated in 2020 at the Museo Poldi Pezzoli in Milan and that was intended as a reflection on the design paradigms of contemporary fashion.[8] Inaugurated on February 20 of that year, the exhibition was forced to close almost immediately because of the pandemic. The clothes remained frozen inside that house-museum until the fading of a calamity that had us living in one of the dystopian futures imagined by Philip K. Dick. When the museum was finally able to reopen,

1   I have taken the expression "fractured time" from Lara Conte's essay "An Ever-Going Adventure," in *Io dico Io – I say I*, catalogue of the exhibition at the Galleria Nazionale d'Arte Moderna e Contemporanea, Rome, March 1–June 5, 2021 (Cinisello Balsamo: Silvana, 2021), 78.

2   *Memorabile*: "Worthy of being remembered; said in general of facts, events, periods of time, or even words, that have something grand or glorious about them, or are for some reason famous." *Treccani: Vocabolario on line*, s.v. "Memorabile," accessed September 7, 2024, https://www.treccani.it/vocabolario/memorabile/.

3   Richard Martin, "Addressing the Dress," in *The Crisis of Criticism*, ed. Maurice Berger (New York: New Press, 1998), 70.

4   See Efrat Tseëlon, "Erving Goffman: Social Science as an Art of Cultural Observation," in *Thinking through Fashion: A Guide to Key Theorists*, ed. Agnès Rocamora and Anneke Smelik, (London: I.B. Tauris, 2016), 149–64.

5   Carlo Severi, *Capturing Imagination: A Proposal for an Anthropology of Thought* (Chicago: Hau Books, 2018), 5. The connection with Severi's book stems from a suggestion made by Dylan Colussi.

6   Timothy Morton, *Hyperobjects: Philosophy and Ecology after the End of the World* (Minneapolis: University of Minnesota Press, 2013), 1.

7   See Deborah Acosta and Kate King, "You Know LVMH for Its Luxury Bags. It's Also a Titan of Real Estate," *Wall Street Journal*, April 26, 2024, https://www.wsj.com/real-estate/commercial/louis-vuitton-lvmh-real-estate-communities-47aa1d55.

8   The project arose out of a reappraisal of *Six Memos for the Next Millennium*, the notes left by Italo Calvino for the series of Charles Eliot Norton Poetry Lectures that he was due to give at Harvard University in the fall of 1985 and that he was preparing when he died unexpectedly in the month of September. A translation of the notes was published in English in 1988 and the original texts published in Italy in 1988 under the title *Lezioni americane: Sei proposte per il prossimo millennio*. See Maria Luisa Frisa, ed., *Memos: On Fashion in This Millennium*, catalogue of the exhibition at the Museo Poldi Pezzoli, Milan, February 21–September 28, 2020 (Venice: Marsilio, 2020).

memorabile ipermoda

its time was already up. Everything had to be dismantled and the clothes sent back to the lenders. The current exhibition starts out from that rupture, from a discontinuity. For *Memorabile* I have steeped myself in a here and now that is a desire to observe things at the moment in which they appear, but it is still a here and now affected by the temporal distortion caused by the pandemic. And so, in the selection of the pieces for the exhibition and in the tracing of their genealogy, the present has been pushed back by a handful of years.

In those strange months of the pandemic, in that time for which nothing had prepared us, factories and stores were shut and all the events on the tight schedule of the fashion system had been canceled. The pandemic required the censorship of our public body, of the clothed body, and also led to the realization by some creators of the need to transform the rituality of fashion and give a new rhythm to their work. The sudden possibility of having and making space became an occasion for self-awareness and a reappraisal of the discipline. There was a lot of talk of the opportunity provided by a violent and unforeseen event to look again at the frenetic pace at which the system operated.[9]

Viktor&Rolf, *Late Stage Capitalism Waltz*, haute couture Spring/Summer 2023 show, InterContinental Paris le Grand Hotel, Paris, January 2023. Photo Giovanni Giannoni/WWD/via Getty Images.
Carlo Severi, *Capturing Imagination: A Proposal for an Anthropology of Thought* (Chicago: Hau Books, 2018).   Carlo Severi, *L'oggetto-persona: Rito memoria immagine* (Turin: Einaudi, 2018).   Timothy Morton, *Iperoggetti: Filosofia ed ecologia dopo la fine del mondo* (Rome: NERO, 2018).
Memos: A proposito della moda in questo millennio, catalogue of the exhibition curated by Maria Luisa Frisa at the Museo Poldi Pezzoli in Milan, 2020 (Venice: Marsilio, 2020). Photo Andrea Pertoldeo. Courtesy private collection, Venice.

At the time of the pandemic everything had to take place in the immaterial and viscous realm of the web and fashion put itself on show in a virtual space, exploring its potentialities even more thoroughly than before. After occupying the metaverse and expanding its presence in the varied world of gaming, so full of possibilities, fashion participated in the great acceleration in the use of artificial intelligence, which established itself controversially as a means of generating images and products as well and has led to a new reassessment of the relationship of clothes with our bodies. However, the landscapes of the digital have also become a way of reasserting the forms of fashion's heritage, suggesting sophisticated actions of reverse engineering capable of decoding and relaunching the archives.

In the visions of the various designers who succeed one another in the creative direction of a brand, the archive is a workshop in which the materials that have accumulated over the course of its history are continually reactivated and given new meanings. The fashion archive transcends its chronological organization to take on the character of an archipelago in which the different periods coexist in the creative director's imagination. I am reminded of Anna Piaggi's double-page spreads, a sort of Warburgian atlas, of mood board, of mobile archive, that used the lens of the present to revitalize forgotten materials: "Over the years, I have chosen to express myself synthetically. To associate the fashion of the moment with the ideas of the past."[10]

Every exhibition inevitably presents the personal perspective of whoever has imagined and constructed it. According to Harald Szeemann, an indispensable point of reference for many curators, an exhibition takes on the outlines of a new work, in which all the objects selected, in the relations that are established between them under a title which sums up and conveys the intentions of its curator, become part of a dialogue that offers a visual account in 3D in which the viewer feels involved. Fashion and above all its display can become means of viewing themes and materials at once from a distance and from close-up through the objects and their relationships. Thus *Memorabile* also sets out to make clear the capacity of the curatorial project/act to "make history," in this case to render "memorable" the way in which fashion and its forms are able to represent the contemporary world and the themes that pervade it. In this sense the proliferation of exhibitions of fashion all over the world in recent years has stimulated a new awareness of its value and given rise to a different attitude toward the discipline and its players.[11]

The making of an exhibition provides an extraordinary opportunity to put intuitions and ideas to the test. A process of verification that does not necessarily have to lead to a definitive outcome, but serves rather to indicate new points of action on a sort of map that is constantly being redrawn.

The points of action that in my notes I have sometimes referred to as "stages," and at others as "halts" are listed below, even though in the exhibition they have not become the visible themes around which the objects are organized, since I wanted to retain the possibility of finding new modes of display right up until the end. I would like these titles, these provisional definitions, to be viewed in the same way as one might read a forgotten memo in a notebook that has

9   The fashion designers who commented on the calendar of shows during the pandemic and declared their intention to reexamine the rate at which they took part in them were Alessandro Michele, creative director of Gucci at the time, and Anthony Vaccarello, who still has the same role at Saint Laurent, while Dries Van Noten, Giorgio Armani, and Michael Kors expressed some other ideas about the system. In particular, in the July of 2020 *WWD* published an open letter from Giorgio Armani in which the Italian designer reflected on the opportunities offered by the pause due to the pandemic to look again at the processes of the fashion industry and its times, declared his intention to reconsider the model on which his shows were based and reflected on the impact of cruise shows.

10   Anna Piaggi, *Anna Piaggi's Fashion Algebra: D.P. in Vogue* (London: Thames & Hudson, 1998), 27.

11   Fashion takes on different forms, each with characteristics of its own, that have to be taken into consideration when reflecting on its multifaceted nature. Richard Martin, a critic and a curator (first at The Museum at FIT in New York and then at the Costume Institute of the Metropolitan Museum of Art in the same city), spoke of the need to imagine more models with which to interpret, put on show, and collect fashion in its many different expressions.

been rediscovered by chance, an annotation in the margin of a book, a reminder of things to be done.

Memorabile: Unexpected combinations make images memorable, according to Carlo Severi's principle of the "chimera." Metamorphoses. Anachronisms. Imperfect eternal recurrence. The imperfect times and rhythms of fashion. Variations on the heritage. *Ordinary/Extraordinary*: The project as reflection on the structural elements of fashion. *Fashion and Staging*: Fashion and interpretation as presentation. Creating memorable settings. Continually restaging fashion. *The Repetition of Canons. The Bending of Canons*: Originals and copies. References and repetitions. Reactivations. Ruptures. Rules. *Out of Scale*: Big-big. Small-small. *Collaborations*: The new authoriality. The collective. Participatory fashion. *Double Identity*: Makeup as mask. Makeup as performative element of the face that fits into the styling of the persona. *Hyperpersonalities. Hypershows. Fashioning AI*: The project of the celebrity stylists. The red carpet. The Met Gala. The design frontiers of AI. *Independent Fashion, Reflective Fashion. Craftsmanship. Future Manifestos*: Alternative forms of fashion to the mainstream. Design spaces as

a place for reflection on twin transitions. The new landscapes of production that identify a responsible approach to fashion.

This sort of list is intended to indicate a series of questions from a perspective of militant criticism (if I may be allowed to use this term) of the forms that the fashion system produces. Not considering only the products as such and not examining them solely in terms of their hypothetical novelty or their material and structural quality. Roland Barthes pointed out that, taken by itself, the item of clothing means nothing and that the vision needs to be broadened to take in the ambition which has shaped it, the poetics and the intentions that have generated its content and its communicative impact.

Every single piece in this exhibition is a representation, a reflection of a precise line of research, a declaration of poetics, the expression of a desire to play an active part in a story that is set in the present—but a present embedded in a time whose progression is not necessarily linear. Each object in the exhibition is an expression of itself, but at the same time it is the fruit of personal and collective memories, feelings, intentions, and visions. It is a work in its own right in dialogue with others, one in which visitors will be able to find a fragment, an indication of something that is part of their own lives.

Thus the exhibition is laid out in a way that does not aim to create a coherent overall vision, but seeks expression through isolated appearances and revelations (semicircles that turn into miniature theaters, each oriented in a different way), in order to get the visitor to concentrate on one segment at a time. Each scene is organized around focuses, expressions of a point of view that at times relies on contrast. For example Francesco Vezzoli's turtle made by Bvlgari not far away from the IKEA bag designed by Virgil Abloh: objects lightyears apart but expressions of the same desire to intervene not so much in forms in themselves as in what they represent.

Francesco Vezzoli, *Tortue de Soirée*, 2019, carapace in bronze and brass with Greek silver coins, topaz, rubellite, citrine, peridot, amethysts, and diamonds, 40 × 66 × 70 cm, Bvlgari Heritage Collection. Made in collaboration with Bvlgari for the exhibition *Huysmans: De Degas à Grünewald, sous le regard de Francesco Vezzoli*, Musée d'Orsay, Paris, 2019-20. Installation view. Courtesy Bvlgari Historical Archives.
"Sculpture" bag from the limited edition collection *MARKERAD*, produced by IKEA in collaboration with Virgil Abloh, 2019. Photo Andrea Pertoldeo. Courtesy private collection, Venice.

For similar reasons, you will find texts in this book that differ widely from one another, in which each author takes a very personal approach. Some contributions have not turned out as I had requested and imagined, but then I realized I didn't mind that the book would be something different from my expectations, taking another road and leading me to revise the sequence of the essays and broaden the critical perspectives with treatments I had not foreseen.

From the outset I had also thought about a book whose graphic layout would reflect the way in which many of us come into contact with images, and with texts too, i.e. on the screen of our smartphones. The versatility of the graphic design has made it possible to move freely between texts and images, without fear of making the reader aware of the gaps, of the iconographic absences due to the difficulties which you're faced with when you want to make use of images in publishing.

Memorabile is a project that through the variety of the materials of which it is composed throws open a series of windows onto what fashion is today, in the messages of which it is a vehicle and in the forms that it assumes. An open-ended, deliberately unfinished project, full of contradictions like any work that is not intended to be exhaustive or definitive. A point of departure, not of arrival.

The project arose from a series of conversations with Judith Clark, exhibition maker and professor of museology at the London College of Fashion. Without the continual exchange of ideas with her *Memorabile: Ipermoda* would not have taken shape. So I would like to express my gratitude to Judith, with whom I have long enjoyed a friendship rooted in esteem and affection.

For many years I have taught Curatorial Practices in Fashion in the master's degree course of Visual Arts and Fashion at the Università Iuav di Venezia. In this teaching experience I have sought to apply with my students the critical approach to which bell hooks devoted the book *Teaching Critical Thinking*, the last part of a trilogy that also included *Teaching to Transgress* and *Teaching Community*. In this dimension, one in which I have always laid claim to the need to break down disciplinary boundaries, I have proposed to the students every year a project that, starting out from fashion curating, could provide an opportunity for continual trespasses into other fields, for moments of comparison that raised more questions than offered answers, for an abandonment of a systematic approach in favor of the impulses of militant criticism (drawing for inspiration on such an artist of criticism as Francesca Alinovi, whose activity was molded by her militancy).

This work of mine is dedicated to my students.

Maria Luisa Frisa in the lecture hall, Iuav Moda, Università Iuav di Venezia, 2017. Photo and courtesy Mattia Balsamini.

I collect. It is part of who I am. It has always been something that has attracted me, the amassing of the individually alike into a collective body. As a child, toys; then books, records, magazines. Finally, most significantly, clothes. Clothes I once wore, clothes I could never. There is no divide between the two, although certain pieces are purchased with the intention of actually inhabiting, and other purely as *objets d'art*, for consideration. Nevertheless, there is always an idea of posterity and permanence, a notion of the future even when considering the present. I find the idea of a future history fascinating, that what we create today may be remembered by subsequent generations. Of course, not everything is of significance—so in collecting for a perceived tomorrow, you make a value judgement. I may like this, truly, but does it matter? Will it matter?

The psychology of collecting has long fascinated me; as has the aforementioned consideration for the forthcoming, a collision of my own habit with my career as a fashion critic, an observer and analyzer of fashion. It is the opposite of Christopher Isherwood's assertion—"I am a camera with its shutter open, quite passive, recording, not thinking." There is nothing passive in a critic's observation of their subject matter, opinions always forming, forever contrasting one example with others, historic and contemporary. And in my head, there is a deep connection between the motivations behind my criticism and my collecting—a love for fashion. I collect what I admire, both in terms of individual designers and the attributes of their clothes. It is a material reflection of my ideological belief in what is great in fashion: craftsmanship, complexity, originality. And a sense of history, not only in the cherishing of clothes drawn from the past, albeit a recent one, but in their own sartorial quotations.

Every passion borders on the chaotic, but the collector's passion borders on the chaos of memories. More than that: the chance, the fate, that suffuse the past before my eyes are conspicuously present in the accustomed confusion.
Walter Benjamin, *Unpacking My Library: A Speech on Collecting*, 1931

Dead Dreams in Living Memory:
A Psychology of Collecting
Alexander Fury

Collecting has often been seen as a way to accumulate knowledge. The *Wunderkammern* or cabinets of curiosities that emerged in Europe in the mid-sixteenth century were devised to excite a thirst for knowledge, through their amalgamation of strange and unseen objects. Precursors to the museum, they were theatrical displays of objects precious and unusual, curation as a work of art in and of itself. When the Flemish scholar Samuel Quiccheberg wrote of the *Wunderkammern* in his 1565 text *Inscriptiones vel tituli theatri amplissimi*, he defined them as more than an expression of wealth or might. Rather, in his eyes, the act of collecting objects proved a practical means of understanding the material world, a way to make culture intelligible. The study of disparate object could, he argued, produce practical knowledge that would aid in governance — and termed the ideal *Wunderkammer* a *theatrum sapientiae*, a theatre of wisdom.

The clothes I collect are clothes embedded with a knowledge, a history, a deeper meaning. Not just in and of themselves, as objects of innovative design, although they unquestionably function as such, but as a moment on a wider scope of culture. A mapping of the past through design of the present is something I have always been drawn to, to clothes that embrace echoes, that have an awareness and understanding of their own antecedents. Vivienne Westwood, Christian Lacroix, John Galliano — all excavate history for ideas, telescoping and juxtaposing references to create a fusion that reflects the contemporary, informed always by that which has gone before. Miuccia Prada, too, has an awareness of history as a lesson to be learned — for

Dress by Stephen Sprouse, Spring/Summer 1984. Hat by Prada, Spring/Summer 2005. Scarf by Prada, Fall/Winter 2017-18. Sleeves by Vivienne Westwood, Fall/Winter 1988–89. Beret by Stephen Jones, for Marc Jacobs for Louis Vuitton, Fall/Winter 2007-8.

her, histories connect with lives, ways of living, meaningful fragments not just raiments of forgotten times, synthesized into the indisputably modern.

Beyond their histories, the study of physical objects surrenders new and unexpected understanding. Their construction, for instance, often hidden in imagery, obscured by the motion of the runway show, can be fully appreciated as a three-dimensional object—the consideration of a dart spiraling a torso to blossom into a pocket, the swell of a padded breast inside a tailored jacket, a network of seams intricately engineered to create the image of a flower against the skin. And I'm fascinated by a "fourth dimension" of clothing—which, to me, is the interior. To get inside a garment is to not only comprehend its architecture but its spatial qualities, how it feels around a body and how a body feels within it. The sinuous hug of a bias-cut dress, like a second skin; the extraneous space created by a hooped skirt, the distance it places between yourself and others. That is an idea of import to many designers: Rei Kawakubo's earliest Comme des Garçons shops eschewed mirrors, in an attempt to force wearers to focus on how clothes felt as opposed to how they looked.

The cardboard archival boxes used to store garments are habitually—somewhat morbidly—referred to as "coffins," but to me there is something alive about clothes. Some bear the imprint of specific humans that have inhabited them, somehow magically absorbing their essence, as if engaged in some form of spiritual enfleurage. I'm always reminded of the story of Patrick Süskind's *Perfume* when I consider this,

Belt by Karl Lagerfeld for Chanel, Spring/Summer 1993. Waistcoat by Nicolas Ghesquière for Balenciaga, Spring/Summer 2007. Shoes by Stefano Pilati for Yves Saint Laurent, Spring/Summer 2008.
Hooded jacket and *Saddle* bag by John Galliano for Christian Dior, Spring/Summer 2000. Trench coat by John Galliano for Christian Dior, Fall/Winter 2000-2001.

of cloth somehow taking on the traces of the human being it once wrapped. And it explains the fervor excited by humdrum garments that once had the closest possible proximity to greatness — a bodice worn by Marie Antoinette, a dress worn by Marilyn Monroe. Nothing is nearer to the body than clothing — the ultimate act of honor, in the court of Louis XIV, was to pass the king his undershirt, the garment that would be worn against his skin, touching flesh. That notion still sticks in our collective craw: somehow, to procure these clothes is to invert ownership — these garments that were once possessed by another, in turn can become our way of possessing them, their memory, their quintessence. It explains our fetish for clothes "once owned by" — and indeed, the word *fetish*, derived from the Portuguese *feitiço*, meaning "spell," was originally applied to a talisman imbued with a supernatural force, something man-made that could hold an inexplicable power over others.

That idea, however, doesn't attract me. I am not interested in clothes "worn by," where the power is in the association rather than the garment itself. For me, clothes are mementoes of moments rather than of people, sometimes cultural but, honestly, often embedded in the artifice of the fashion show, a garment as a material reflection of the magic of an image. The clothes of John Galliano, for instance, seem forever part of a larger narrative, a greater body of work — Galliano's view of fashion is as a living, breathing fantasy, the clothes themselves perhaps the one physical thing we can take away from the magic of a mise-en-scène. And there is a heady dose of nostalgia to that, for me — as a child with a nose pressed to the metaphorical window of fashion, watching and yearning at a formidable distance, through blurry newspaper photographs, glossy magazine pages, and sporadic television broadcasts, I longed for these clothes. Not necessarily to own them, but to be part of the universe of creativity that they represented. The clothes were the tangible takeaway, the one thing you could grab and touch and get close to the magic of the image. Which, in a sense, is the same as buying Marilyn Monroe's old dress: you can never be there, those moments will never be replayed, but you can touch something that bore witness to those extraordinary times. It's the same with these clothes, for me. The logic in me reasons that collecting these clothes warrants an accumulation of some of the greatest pieces

of design of the past half century, which have shifted not only the way we dress, but our considerations of beauty. The emotion in me, however, connects with an isolated child escaping, through fashion, into another world, a metaphorical Narnia accessed, of course, through a wardrobe. The emotion — the memory — holds the power.

Boots by John Galliano for Christian Dior, Fall/Winter 2000–2001. Corset by Vivienne Westwood, Fall/Winter 1990–91. Skirt by Azzedine Alaïa, Spring/Summer 1991. Gloves by Stefano Pilati for Yves Saint Laurent, Fall/Winter 2009–10.

Dead Dreams in Living Memory

Hence, the examples that make my teeth rattle, that make my hair stand on end with exhilaration, are those worn in a fashion show—the ones present for that sublime moment. Fashion uses dull nomenclature to designate these extraordinary items—"sample," or "prototype". Neither goes any way to expressing the power, for me, of holding a piece in my hand that was worn when a design first appeared, worked on by a designer themselves, the first projection of their new vision of the world. The original. Some are even shorn of that traditional signifier of status, the designer label—replaced instead with a hand-written *bolduc* in cotton that describe, perhaps, their origins, the atelier that painstakingly worked on the piece, the name of the model that first wore it. At the Musée Yves Saint Laurent in Paris, these are even more magical—Saint Laurent himself wrote the designation "museum" in his slightly shaky, instantly recognizable hand, to denote the pieces to be preserved for the museum he and his partner Pierre Bergé were assembling, even as his life's work was still unfolding. I have a few examples—pieces from Christian Lacroix's final collection for the house of Jean Patou, never commercially produced, each example one of one. A few surviving examples from John Galliano collections: an organza frock coat with degraded aluminum foil sandwiched between layers, from a collection inspired by Empress Josephine and Lolita, a whiplash of silk chiffon with "Amphetamine" sleeves inspired by the styles of the 1830s, worn by Shalom Harlow for an American *Vogue* editorial. The hem is torn, where a stiletto, at some point, pierced the fabric. There's a dress from Galliano's first haute couture collection for Christian Dior, in lilac bias-cut chiffon and, secreted inside a side seam, a cotton tag handwritten with the name "Eva," for Eva Herzigová. I remember watching this dress on television—not just a dress like this dress, but this exact dress. There's something about that recollection, that memory, that gives it additional gravitas. The idea of not

Hat by Prada, Fall/Winter 2007-8. Shirt and skirt by Prada, Spring/Summer 2011. Jacket by Miu Miu, Spring/Summer 2011. Shoes by Prada, Spring/Summer 2012.

Alexander Fury

only dreaming, but obtaining a part of that dream, a physical manifestation of a former desire. Of course, this isn't unique to fashion — but, to me, fashion is almost uniquely democratic, egalitarian. Of course, the objects are largely unobtainable, undeniably elitist by their nature, but the imagery fashion creates — and which, one could argue, is its most powerful creation — can be consumed by many, or any.

When people ask me why I collect, they underestimate the impact of memory, and of emotion. They anticipate a simple answer, a direct and quantifiable motivation. A straightforward assumption is that one accumulates to disperse, presumably for profit. Or, perhaps, that there is the urge to collect and then to donate to a museum body, properly accredited, as a means towards some form of immortality. A name affixed to a public collection, allowed to molder and gather dust. There is a certain attraction in both those eventualities — not least because it relieves the collector of a dual role they automatically assume, as caretaker to their possessions. To collect is to be a custodian — inevitably, if a collector does their job properly, their pieces will outlive them, be passed to another collector to take care of them again.

Dress by Christian Lacroix for Jean Patou Haute Couture, Spring/Summer 1987. Shoes by Stefano Pilati for Yves Saint Laurent, Spring/Summer 2008. Handbag and scarf by Versace, Fall/Winter 2018-19.

And yet, unlike say artworks, fashion has an inherent fragility, exacerbated by its design for purpose. Fashion is created to be worn, and that proximity to the body is its inherent vice, the essential quality to its being that could ultimately destroy it. The human body destroys that which it touches, especially in terms of fabric. It sweats and secretes, and those secretions bind with garments and attract pestilence. It's all very biblical. Never mind the notion of motion, wear, and tear. But also, there is something Walter Benjamin speaks of, in his 1931 essay on the notion of collecting — which he sees as something distinct from a collection in its psychology, its compulsion. As Benjamin states, "The most profound enchantment for the collector is the locking of individual items within a magic circle in which they are fixed as the final thrill, the thrill of acquisition, passes over them." I also sometimes quote the Duchess of Windsor, who once stated, simply, "The possession of beautiful things is thrilling to me." That is reason enough to acquire — to have and to hold, to allow something exceptional to pass through your ownership for at least some of its life. So a collection is the result

Alexander Fury

of the action of collecting, for many, as opposed to collecting being the way to achieve a final goal. Again, that divides between institutional bodies, who seem to amass specific types of objects for set purposes, and the individual, who collects what they can, as they can. They seek, for sure, but without system, often without reason.

Benjamin speaks of the "chaos of memories" within a collection — he collected books, which are far more passive than clothes. A spine of a book surrenders little, while a garment hanging holds a promise, an immediate reminder of its past lives. It can be immediately read through its textile, its color and shape, even inanimate. Those hidden in boxes, of course, are more difficult to decipher. Chaos is a true term — the more I speak to individual collectors, the more I recog-

Dress by Antony Price, custom-made for Paula Yates, 1980. Gauntlets by Azzedine Alaïa par Lavabre Cadet, Fall/Winter 1981–82.

Bra by Azzedine Alaïa, Spring/Summer 1991. Jacket by Prada, Fall/Winter 2014–15.

nize a shared sense of chaos and impulse, the spontaneous and unfettered. Few collect with the mindset of a museum, with a method or distance from their pieces. Every piece is embedded with those memories, memories of acquisition, of first encounter—which could be very different, of course. I have a Galliano dress I first saw aged twelve, an image in a magazine seared into the mind's eye of a white gown with a black flower magically unfurling across it. The model stood on a rooftop, pretending to be in Spain, and it seemed to be snowing. That image haunted me, an expression of fashion not as cloth dressing bodies but as a way of weaving something magical, a narrative embedded with meaning and nuance, of which the clothes are only part. To be able to own that dress seemed unbelievable, impossible. There's still something impossible about it today, even when it's surrendered into a coffin, patiently waiting to be reactivated.

All the images: garments and accessories Alexander Fury's archive; photographies Louie Banks; model Jazzelle Zanaughtti; styling Rúben Moreira; hair Ali Pirzadeh using AP Wigs; makeup Terry Barber using MAC; photographic assistant Melissa Arras; styling assistant Ruairi Horan; hair assistant Grace Hatcher. From C✮NDY Transversal, no. 12 (2019). Thanks to Luis Venegas.

Dead Dreams in Living Memory

The miniature is at once a recreation and representation of a section of a relief panel hanging in Palazzo Altemps in Rome. The section, which was a seventeenth-century plaster restoration by Alessandro Algardi of a Roman (130–50 CE) narrative panel dedicated to the myth of the judgement of Paris, is now missing. It was removed and destroyed at the beginning of the twentieth century due to contemporary museological standards, leaving only the original section of the panel. The remaining fragment, currently on display in the museum, depicts the central scene of the judgement: it represents all three goddesses and Paris, Oenone, Eros, and an oak tree representing Mount Ida. By recreating the section of the scene that depicts the "occasional" characters or onlookers—the river gods and nymphs grouped at the margins of the composition—the ring privileges (and records as its essential souvenir) an absence. Why create a souvenir of a missing fragment if the fragment is not apparently integral to the story?

> The history of those unusual objects which vanish from the "canon," vanish, indeed, from view, but are restored after long periods of neglect, struck me as a good way to enter the discussion.   Frank Kermode[1]

I met Frank Kermode almost exactly twenty years ago, whilst I was working on a project for the ModeMuseum in Antwerp. The exhibition I was working on, entitled *Malign Muses: When Fashion Turns Back*, was about patterns of reference and recovery in fashion; the ways in which fashion asks us to pay attention to aspects of its own history whilst momentarily ignoring others, and how these patterns might be translated into exhibition design.

Making Fashion Memorable—After Warburg
Judith Clark

1   Frank Kermode, *Forms of Attention: Botticelli and* Hamlet (Chicago: University of Chicago Press, 2011), xiii.

2   The *Atlas* in its last version, which was left unfinished at the time of Warburg's death in 1929, was made up of sixty-three panels.

The idea of the cyclical (a well-rehearsed concept in fashion history) means that a reference never fully disappears but lies dormant; the labyrinth simply takes it on an extended journey, sometimes out of sight, and sometimes perhaps with its back to us; a fragment on the other hand makes the links to its source precarious whilst multiplying its possibilities, and so on. Kermode, a literary scholar, whose work was so alert to textual patterns, was unusually and dynamically engaged with the proposition that these might be *staged*, and in particular that it could be dress to perform the task of illustrating the rhetorical devices. What was never cited during that exchange was the key common ground we shared: an interest and affiliation with the work and legacy of Aby Warburg, and the traditions of the eponymous research institute in London.

Aby Warburg (1866–1929) was a cultural historian, perhaps most renowned for his role in establishing the discipline of "iconology." The ambivalence towards this particular discipline within the broader umbrella of art history contributed, for a long time, to a resistance within academia to his restless and idiosyncratic ideas within it. His increasingly studied and celebrated project, the *Bilderatlas Mnemosyne*, was a visual "map in progress" dedicated to cultural memory. It took the form of a series of themed screens, mobile panels covered in black cloth, upon which Warburg would pin genealogies of images: black and white photographic copies of artworks cropped at different scales, with which he could plot (and rehearse his thoughts about) the "afterlife of antiquity," by looking, for example, at the imagery, for the survival of gestural expression.[2]

Fashion exhibition making is the subject of this essay and the ways we might extend the uses of Warburg's porous art history-without-words, to look at its structural eloquence, its forms of attention, and the particular ways it asks a visitor to remember and therefore also to forget, beyond the analogy of a curatorial mood board. The vital nature of the afterlife of Dionysian passions that Warburg so insistently pursued might seem at odds with the frequently remarked-upon deathliness of the museum exhibit, and in particular regarding exhibitions of dress—surrogates doing too little

Judith Clark, *Two-Finger Ring "Research Souvenir 002,"* 2024, gold-plated bronze cast. 3D scanned from a wax carving by Jim Patrick commissioned by Clark. © Judith Clark Studio.

to offset the absence of the body. But how might we use the rhythm of the space, intervals, omissions, scale, relays, doublings—the devices that the *Atlas* as a *method* uses to draw our attention across the panels, distracting us from an unfolding story associated with temporal or even contextual clarity, and instead investing the experience of associative looking and thinking with dynamic ruptures and movement? And what might we learn from another kind of movement that, at the very beginning of his own research, Warburg located in details that surrounded the painted, static body via its "accessories" (such as agitated drapery or windswept hair)? And how might it help our own three-dimensional surrogates?

Cesare Ripa's *Iconologia* (1593), the first of many editions of which is still to be found in the rare books section of the Warburg Institute library, was a manual used by artists for allegorical depictions and personifications in which meaning was ascribed through codified accessories; "Antiquaries . . . had long speculated that attributes might be indicators of a 'survival' of ancient, primitive meaning"[3] opening up a place and a cultural reference for a new kind of exhibition "prop." Often situated to the side of the protagonist, it was invested in the essential clue to the story: Athena's shield, Hera's peacock, for example. Could contemporary practice look to these references for a different kind of model of how to delegate part of the story to exhibition ephemera? If fashion exhibition making is, amongst other things, about making fashion memorable, in order for

3   Hans C. Hönes, *Tangled Paths: A Life of Aby Warburg* (London: Reaktion Books, 2024), 39.

Vionnet, catalogue of the exhibition held at the Judith Clark Costume Gallery, London, 2001.

it to take its place within our collective memory, it is also about building a bridge between theory and practice, and a bridge between the archive (often analogous with objects lying dormant) and the exhibition, when the object and its identifying motifs, be they gestural or via its "ornaments," are again put into circulation.

Fashion exhibition making might also sit—if we persist with Warburg's preoccupations that concentrate predominantly on Renaissance art's anachronic agility—somewhere between historic pageants that were early choreographed instances of life as art, and the spatial illusion and attributes of portraiture; aligning it with ideas of reenactment and a more narrative version of prop making. It might be here that we find and can think about the shift between "fashion show" and "exhibition."

Warburg had studied the work of the extraordinary Italian theatre designer Buontalenti's *Intermedi* (in particular the pageants he staged in Florence in 1589 on the occasion of the marriage of the Grand Duke Ferdinand I of Tuscany to Christine of Lorraine). For the spectacles of 1589, Buontalenti redesigned the old theatre of the Uffizi. He installed machines, adapted the infrastructure to the production of unusual special effects, a veritable memory theatre that included every element that Renaissance rhetoricians were taught might commit a scene to memory. (It is easy to make comparisons with the fashion show, harnessing stagecraft, to make the event memorable.) Warburg's attention was drawn to those costumes' accessories and associated props that were designed to evoke the antique: how to build a "nymph" from gauze and plaster. Like Ghirlandaio's Nympha who walked across the Tornabuoni Chapel disturbing its spatiotemporal continuity, Buontalenti was able to stage otherworldly figures in real time. Cultural transmission was therefore not only represented but could be reenacted.

If the fashion show is the moment a designer reveals their idea, shows are akin to a themed series, or indeed the pageant: the essential "reference" or memorable identifier is built up over often twenty-thirty silhouettes within a built or carefully selected environment—a contemporary

Malign Muses: When Fashion Turns Back, exhibition held at the MoMu, Antwerp, 2004–5, and then at the Victoria and Albert Museum in London in 2005 under the title *Spectres: When Fashion Turns Back*. The "Labyrinth" section shown here illustrates historic relays within fashion's history. Photo © Tim Stoops.

THE
JUDGEMENT
OF PARIS —

*

16 FEBRUARY – 2 APRIL 2011 / JUDITH CLARK / JOURNAL No.3

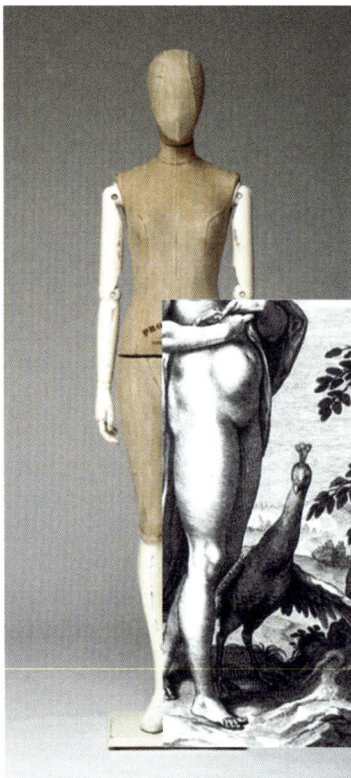

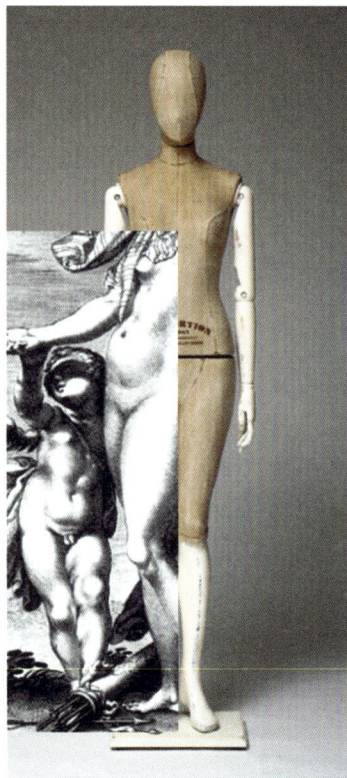

Judith Clark, *The Judgement of Paris*, exhibition catalogue, 2011. The exhibition held at the Fashion Space Gallery at the UAL, University of the Arts London, was the first in the series of practice-based research projects dedicated to the theme of the judgement of Paris. The exhibition looked at the identifiers associated with the three goddesses in the myth and the uses of "attributes" in experimental fashion exhibition making.

theatrum mundi. It is through the insistence of a motif, or a mood—repeated and reimagined—that we *learn* what to look out for what is being made fashionable during the span of twenty minutes. The avant-garde not only raids fashion's memory to make it new, but newly memorable—harnessing the past (often heavily disguised of course) for a new cause. To isolate only one of those garments for an exhibition is to present an unstable object, already belonging to at least two histories. The exhibition maker needs to attend to this. *Malign Muses: When Fashion Turns Back* twenty years ago in Antwerp was about imagining and building the fashion system's routes to and from the past with fashion itself as the subject, to illustrate its role as a vehicle of rhetorical virtuosity.

There is, however, a more contemporary balance to be established, between recognition and singularity; the narrative efficiency needs to be heightened, and the temporal frame shortened. We need to zoom in, so to speak, to the individual figures and their ornaments, and be more attentive to which histories have been omitted.

Rome Again

> Warburg . . . combined a perpetual interest in the recurrent transformations of ancient symbols with minute research into the social and pictorial circumstances of their reappearances. . . . He could, for example, compare Manet's *Déjeuner sur l'herbe* with the sarcophagus that, through Renaissance intermediaries, is its source.
> Frank Kermode[4]

The ring included in this exhibition and catalogue is intended as an experimental proposition following a long period of research under the umbrella title *The Judgement of Paris*, and a direct reference to Aby Warburg's work in Rome. Warburg's research led him to trace Manet's controversial *Déjeuner*

sur l'herbe back to a Roman sarcophagus (via Johannes Riepenhausen, via Alessandro Algardi, via Marcantonio Raimondi, the most memorable of all representations of the myth, itself after a lost drawing by Raphael, and back again: we never know which reference comes first).

My point of "entry" was an encounter with the fragment cited above in Palazzo Altemps and the discovery of its inclusion on a mobile panel mounted in Warburg's hotel room in Rome in 1929. By the final version of his *Mnemosyne Atlas* panel 55 that he dedicated to the judgement of Paris, it was no longer there. Why? We know that it represented the scene of the judgement. Warburg's change of heart was due to the discovery of the link between Marcantonio Raimondi's print of 1515–20 and Édouard Manet's *Déjeuner sur l'herbe* that caused such a sensation in 1863. Manet's recovery of the group of river gods as a new iteration of the judgement of Paris becomes one of Warburg's clearest examples of classical transmission reaching modernity. By the time Warburg worked on his final version of the panel, the restored lower half of our Altemps relief had been removed. By commissioning (re)carving the missing section, I was not engaged with restoration (indeed the scale was altered), but recording a turning point in Warburg's thought, and reenacting the essential link in Warburg's thesis; in gold, asserting its value,

Aby Warburg, *Picture Atlas Mnemosyne*, panel 55, dedicated to the myth of the judgement of Paris. The last version of the panel, created by Warburg in October 1929, illustrates the representations and recoveries of the myth from a Roman relief at Villa Medici to Manet's infamous *Déjeuner sur l'herbe*, which signaled such a seismic shift in art whilst remaining faithful to the grouping of the river gods from Marcantonio Raimondi's print of the judgement, itself after Raphael. Photo The Warburg Institute.

the double ring makes it current, fashionable even. The souvenir will always be about what we "take away" from the museum, and ultimately what we remember.

Fashion designers can now preempt the museum or gallery display, conjuring the garment, styling, ornament, and prop into one object; efficient signifiers populate fashion show sets, themselves ready for museum loans with greater prescience of their place in history: but like the Roman relief of the judgement of Paris, the apparent consistency of the attributes, the coerced looking, may not be the point

Remembering Martin Kamer (1943–2023)

The exhibition that this publication documents, amongst other things, is about making fashion memorable. It is an opportunity, requested by its curator Maria Luisa Frisa, to remember a beloved colleague who devoted an enormous part of his life to collecting historic dress, researching, documenting, and significantly lending the most important examples of fashion from his own collection to exhibitions worldwide. Kamer trained as a costume and set designer in London, going on to work with, amongst others, Rudolf Nureyev; but as early as the 1970s he started collecting (presciently) what was then affordable: vintage journals, photographs, eighteenth- and nineteenth-century menswear, and eventually the most exquisite couture. By cross-referencing his own collection he could spot the idiosyncrasies of a designer's details, identifying not only the designer and the date of the work, but when it might have been altered. Working closely with museum conservators and dress historians Rita Brown, Jan Reeder, and Annette Soumilas, who shared his background in the theatre, to name a few constant collaborators and interlocutors, he seamlessly became part of temporary museum teams whilst setting up exhibitions, always accompanying his loans in person—his joyous enthusiasm for making fashion visible in new ways a constant inspiration to everyone involved. Whilst installing Kamer's collection with him for *Diana Vreeland after Diana Vreeland*, an exhibition curated by Maria Luisa Frisa and me at the Museo Fortuny in Venice in 2012, it transpired that he had lent pieces to Vreeland's own *Eighteenth-Century Woman* exhibition (1981–82): these were the kind of anecdotes we came to expect, his extraordinary experience across fashion history but also fashion exhibition history. It was perhaps due to his training in the theatre that he believed so adamantly in the possibilities for restaging and in doing so reimagining dress, without hesitation allowing us to use his objects to do so.

Large relief (from the front of a sarcophagus?) depicting the judgment of Paris, ca. 130–50 CE, RA (Reperto Archeologico) entry, inv. no. 8563. Ludovisi Collection, Museo Nazionale Romano. Courtesy the Ministry of Culture–Museo Nazionale Romano, photo Archivio del Catalogo.

It is not merely an updated form or contemporary expression of the fact—present in every human culture and in all periods of history—of wearing clothes. What has been dubbed the "fashion system" ever since the publication of a celebrated and problematic work by Roland Barthes has in fact bestowed on clothes a totally different cultural status from the one they have had for centuries, in every latitude. From artifacts characterized by their immediate and specific climatic and social utility, they have turned into open experimental laboratories in which life shows itself to be amenable to the constantly renewed invention of an identity that is never fixed in advance, and art becomes a spiritual exercise that does not set out to manipulate the world alone but also and above all the impalpable and yet sensible material of the human spirit.

For this reason, the roots of the fashion system are not purely social and technological. It is nothing but the final outcome of the need that drove the *Kunstwollen* of the European artistic avant-gardes. As Peter Bürger put it in his most celebrated work, "The European avant-garde movements can be defined as an attack on the status of art in bourgeois society. What is negated is not an earlier form of art (a style) but art as an institution that is unassociated with the life praxis of men." This is not just a question of art's claim (an extremely trivial one today) to political and social significance, but also of an attention to "the way art functions in society, a process that does as much to determine the effect that works have as does the particular content," and to "its dissociation from the praxis of life as the dominant characteristic of art in bourgeois society." Art "was not to be simply destroyed, but transferred to the praxis of life where it would

New Bodies
Emanuele Coccia

be preserved, albeit in a changed form." Behind this lay "the attempt to organize a new life praxis from a basis in art."[1]

Clothing has proved to be the most suitable means of achieving this aim for at least two reasons: its social and geographical universality and the fact that it requires a different kind of relationship with and mode of use of the work of art. In fact whoever, without distinction of age, gender, ethnic and racial identity, geographical origin, culture, and wealth, wears clothing, does so every day and all day. And, unlike what happens with a film or a novel, a painting or a sculpture, there is nothing purely contemplative about the relationship between a human being and an item of clothing: wearing something signifies making skin-to-skin contact with it and asking its size and its color, its texture and its silhouette to serve as our identity. It is due to its anthropological universality and closeness to the body that clothing has become the Trojan horse that has allowed art to enter everyone's life, to cast the magic spell that has turned it into the concrete form of the relationship that all human beings have with themselves, with others, and with the world. Art, through fashion, has not only escaped from the white box of galleries and museum, but become the set of gestures through which each individual incessantly molds and redesigns his or her own appearance.

The consequences of this twofold transfiguration are still far from being understood. For the fashion system is not just a new mode of existence of art: it embodies a genuine anthropological revolution. No one and nothing has made this clearer than the show Hussein Chalayan staged to present his Fall/Winter 2000–2001 collection at Sadler's Wells Theatre in London, under the title of *After Words*. At a particularly moving moment of the event, four models removed the covers from the same number of armchairs and turned them into clothing. A few instants later, Natalia Semanova entered wearing an asymmetrical blue top and a long gray skirt. She walked up to a low round table, removed the panel at its center and stepped into the opening. With a delicate gesture she lifted two handles on the edge of the hole and the table was transformed into a long and sculptural skirt. The collection turned on the theme of refugee families, of their mobility, their need to carry their possessions, their home, around with them. And yet, above and beyond the immediate message, it is hard not to see in this fragment a sort of metalinguistic statement on the very nature of fashion: fashion is the art that transforms objects and the skin of the world's material and the appearance of human beings. To the philosophical and moral tradition that has always contrasted freedom and alienation, and that has viewed emancipation as a liberation from the burden of objects and therefore of the world, fashion seems to oppose the idea that freedom and a sense of identity can only be attained in relation to things, and inside them: there is no life outside the relationship with the world. Fashion is nothing but the effort to say "me" at the heart of things, to get the self and the world to coincide at least for a moment. To the idea of spirit as a purely immaterial and fundamentally acosmic essence, fashion opposes the evidence that the mental dwells in all the colors and materials of the world:

1   Peter Bürger, *Theory of the Avant-Garde* (Minneapolis: University of Minnesota Press, 1984), 49.

Cephalophore Bishop, 1476–1500, limestone with traces of polychromy, 78 × 32 × 24 cm, Musée des Augustins, Toulouse.

it has a sensible nature, an aesthetic substance, and for this very reason can only be experienced through a practice of artistic manipulation.

It is in this way that fashion embodies the most radical anthropology of modernity. In an essay that lies at the heart of his reflection on money, Simmel showed that modernity has allowed the ego to be freed from any form of preestablished identity, obliging individuals to construct themselves and constantly reinvent themselves in an independent way. To construct the self, however, modern people are compelled to delegate to objects the task of bringing their psychological (and not just social) identity into existence: "It is as if the ego could really no longer carry itself."[2] By surrounding themselves with objects, making them their skin, modern individuals offload onto things a means of establishing an identity that would otherwise be impossible. In this way, identity also becomes a cosmic fact. We can be a certain "self" only by binding ourselves to particular things, coexisting with and in them. From this point of view the self is always a cyborg.

One contemporary collection seems to have placed a particularly significant emphasis on this aspect: the one for the Fall/Winter of 2018–19 that Alessandro Michele designed for Gucci. Like Chalayan's *After Words* and some other shows of Michele's — it suffices to think of the *Carte de tendre* (Spring/Summer 2016) or *Twinsburg* (Spring/Summer 2023) collections — *Cyborg* was a "discourse on method" that tried to explain what fashion is.

2   Georg Simmel, "The Problem of Style", *Theory, Culture & Society* 8, no. 3 (August 1991): 69.

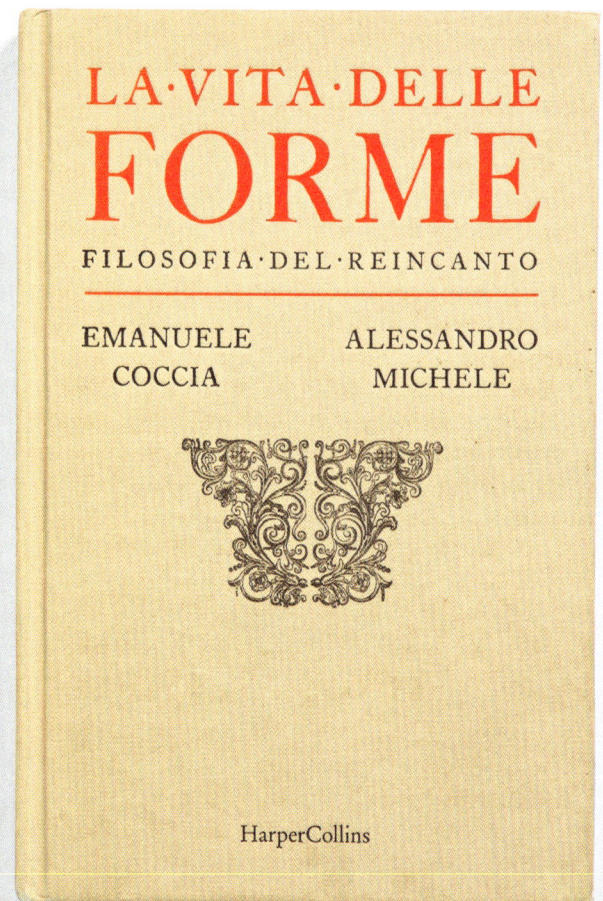

Emanuele Coccia and Alessandro Michele, *La vita delle forme: Filosofia del reincanto* (Milan: HarperCollins, 2024). Photo Andrea Pertoldeo. Courtesy private collection, Venice.

As the preparatory notes for the show declare, fashion is what makes it possible to resist and combat the tendency of disciplinary power to "impose a precise identity on the subject," placing it "inside binary fixed categories, [such] as the normal/abnormal one, with the specific intent of classifying, controlling and regulating the subject." It does so with strategies "so alluring that the subject voluntarily chooses to stick to that particular categorization, claiming its positioning inside a given social structure." In contrast to this tropism every article of clothing asserts that identity "is neither a natural matter nor a preset category, which can be imposed with violence. It's not an immutable and fixed fact, rather a social and cultural construction and, as such, it's a matter of choice, joining, invention. Identity, thus, is a never ending process, keen on new determinations each time." This is why every garment turns the human being into a cyborg, "a paradoxical creature keeping together nature and culture, masculine and feminine, normal and alien, psyche and matter" and blending "different evolving identities. Hybrid and shifting identities, built on multiple belongings, that transgress the normative discipline." Hybrid identities and posthuman identities, with "eyes on [their] hands, faun horns, dragon's puppies and doubling heads."[3] The reference is, obviously, to Donna Haraway's *A Cyborg Manifesto*, that in 1985 revolutionized feminist debate in America and Europe. But to grasp the profundity of the collection's theoretical proposal it is necessary to go back to the origin of the word, coined by the American scientists Manfred E. Clynes and Nathan S. Kline in 1960. In the article in which they proposed the neologism the questions at stake were the possibility of space travel and the technological advances that would "permit man's existence in environments which differ radically from those provided by nature as we know it." If "in the past evolution brought about the altering of bodily functions to suit different environments," now, explained the authors, it was possible to achieve this by making "suitable biochemical, physiological, and electronic modifications of man's existing modus vivendi." The article offered the example of a fish that wished to live on land: "If . . . a particularly intelligent and resourceful fish could be found, who had studied a good deal of biochemistry and physiology, was a master engineer and

3   Alessandro Michele and Giovanni Attili, "Cyborg," press release, February 21, 2018.
4   Manfred E. Clynes and Nathan S. Kline, "Cyborgs and Space," *Astronautics*, September 1960, 26, https://web.mit.edu/digitalapollo/Documents/Chapter1/cyborgs.pdf.
5   Clynes and Kline, 27.

cyberneticist, and had excellent lab facilities available to him, this fish could conceivably have the ability to design an instrument which would allow him to live on land and breathe air quite readily."[4] This is precisely what a cyborg is: the modification of an organic body to allow it to survive in an environment that we are unable to modify. It is this that will permit the human being to go into space without "insisting on carrying his whole environment along with him."[5] We never think about it, but you don't need a chip implanted under your skin to become a cyborg. A garment is sufficient: and it was an item of apparel that allowed the human being to survive, for a few hours at least, on the Moon.

One of the most incisive examples of clothing able to turn the human body into a cyborg is provided by two of the looks in Alessandro Michele's collection in which the models carried under their arm an accessory that was a replica of their head. It was, literally, a variation on the iconological theme

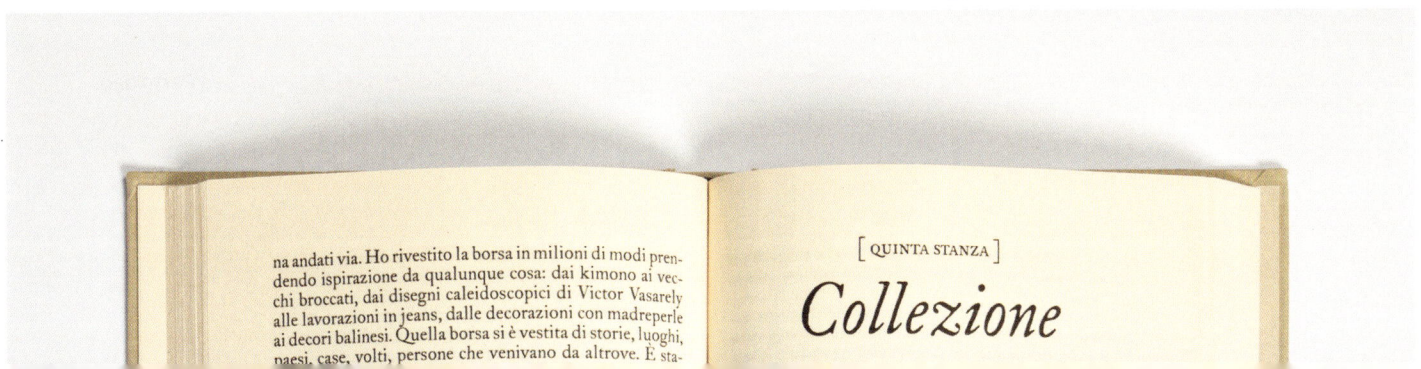

na andati via. Ho rivestito la borsa in milioni di modi prendendo ispirazione da qualunque cosa: dai kimono ai vecchi broccati, dai disegni caleidoscopici di Victor Vasarely alle lavorazioni in jeans, dalle decorazioni con madreperle ai decori balinesi. Quella borsa si è vestita di storie, luoghi, naesi, case, volti, persone che venivano da altrove. E sta-

[QUINTA STANZA]

Collezione

ancestrale: è quel nucleo archetipico che rappresenta il destino primigenio di ogni essere umano. La sua urgenza espressiva e immaginativa.

❋

Non è mai facile parlare di sé. Si rischia sempre di dire troppo o troppo poco. Per secoli abbiamo creduto che bastasse confezionare una lista esaustiva degli eventi che abbiamo attraversato: siamo quello che ci è accaduto, pensiamo, ed è l'importanza e la risonanza di questi accadimenti a far brillare il nostro volto. Eppure quando cerchiamo di capire chi sia la persona che amiamo non riflettiamo su cosa le è successo. Osserviamo i suoi gesti più insignificanti, passiamo in rassegna i dettagli più nascosti del suo viso. Un racconto biografico non è una cronaca: la nostra personalità si esprime spesso in momenti inaspettati e non è detto che sia la sequenza cronologica di quanto ci è successo a tratteggiare il nostro volto con più accuratezza. È stato Plutarco, filosofo e sacerdote del tempio di Apollo a Delfi, vissuto nel I secolo della nostra era, ad averlo intuito per primo: raccontare una vita non significa soffermarsi con prolissità sulle grandi imprese compiute nell'arco dell'esistenza anche quando sono molto celebri. "Non è nelle azioni più rumorose che si manifestano la virtù o il vizio" scrisse nella prefazione alla sua biografia di Alessandro Magno. "Spesso" continuava, "un'azione ordinaria, una parola, una battuta rivelano molto di più sul carattere di un uomo rispetto a battaglie sanguinose, assedi e gesta memorabili. Perciò, come i pittori usano per i loro ritratti le sembianze del volto e le linee in cui il carattere e l'indole sono più evidenti, e prestano poca attenzione al resto, così a noi dovrebbe essere con-

---

☞ La moda non è la sola apparenza di vita: è l'insieme delle idee e delle pratiche di trasformazione di sé e del mondo che permettono a una vita desiderata di diventare reale, sensibile. Di farsi esperienza. È l'evidenza che l'Io è il luogo di un incessante esercizio insieme spirituale e materiale su di sé.

meno parlante di un qualsiasi utensile da cucina. Un vestito aspetta solo di essere indossato e rendere così possibile la vita per cui è stato immaginato. Un abito abbandonato, che nessuno ha mai messo, dimenticato in un negozio vintage, somiglia quasi all'incarnazione sensibile del mistero e del dolore di una esperienza che avrebbe dovuto aver luogo e non ha potuto realizzarsi.

Per questo è impossibile pensare astrattamente alle silhouette: le forme e i volumi cominciano a materializzarsi solo quando si inizia a incarnarli. È impossibile parlare di abiti senza raccontare una storia o definire i dettagli della vita delle persone che li indosseranno. L'immaginazione della moda è sempre biografica.

Quando ho cominciato a immaginare lo show "Love Parade" ho visualizzato, come in un film, una protagonista eccentrica: una donna texana, forse lesbica, che aveva un rapporto maniacale con i vestiti che metteva. Da lì ho cominciato a disegnare ogni singolo pezzo, dal cappello agli zoccoli di legno. Era una donna improbabile che poteva scegliere di indossare sfarzosi abiti della vecchia Hollywood, come riesumati da un armadio polveroso. Oppure coltivare la sua ossessione per ricercati indumenti maschili, costruiti con sofisticati tessuti gessati rigorosamente grigi e vistosissimi principi di Galles. Non era chiaro se

sceglie di pettinare in una certa maniera una persona, di metterle o toglierle le calze, di usare quelle scarpe con o senza tacco, che si preferisce quel colore o quel materiale. Un abito che si astrae dalla vita per la quale è stato pensato non significa nulla: è

---

questi ultimi abiti fossero davvero suoi o ereditati da chissà quale ambigua relazione avuta nel passato, forse con un designer con una passione a tratti rigida per lo stile. Il film si stava componendo nella mia testa, sovrapponendo indizi minimi ed evanescenti. Quello che stava emergendo era la biografia di una donna che non avrei mai conosciuto ma che, lo intuivo, era capace di portare dentro di sé lo spirito libertario di una Los Angeles magnetica.

Solo quando la sceneggiatura si compone in maniera così dettagliata inizia una sorta di rituale di vestizione. È un viaggio collettivo che percorro insieme alle persone con cui da anni lavoro. È con loro che approfondisco ulteriori sfumature. Entriamo letteralmente nella vita di questo personaggio immaginario e ci chiediamo se siano più adatti fiori di seta o di rame dipinto. Cominciamo a decorarne il corpo disegnando la sua vita. Scegliere il paio di scarpe che indosserà per una particolare cena significa precisare il suo passato. Capire il colore della sua camicia significa diventare i rabdomanti e gli speleologi della sua personalità: ci si immerge in un universo cercando di divinarne le forme. A poco a poco non emergono solo la silhouette, la natura dei tessuti, i colori, gli accessori. È una biografia che si disegna.

Tutto nasce da questo tipo di visioni. Fare vestiti significa scrivere la sceneggiatura di vite possibili in cui possiamo entrare (e uscire) ogni giorno. Un abito non è uno spettacolo, è un portale: un corridoio che conduce il nostro corpo altrove. La moda è il cinema naturale dell'esistenza umana. Ci si cuce addosso ogni volta un carattere, lo si assimila, lo si anima: indossare un vestito non significa giocare con le apparenze, ma sperimentare la trasformazione del no-

☞ Più che uno specifico materiale o una classe di materiali, il tessuto è la materia in quanto è capace di accogliere la vita, di abbracciarla nel suo seno, di farla esistere diversamente, di darle la forma della felicità.

Emanuele Coccia and Alessandro Michele, *La vita delle forme: Filosofia del reincanto* (Milan: HarperCollins, 2024), inside pages. Photos Andrea Pertoldeo. Courtesy private collection, Venice.

of the cephalophore, the legend from late antiquity and the Middle Ages of the severed head of a saint that continues to speak and is carried in the hands of the saint himself as he walks to the place where he has chosen to be buried.[6] In modern painting it is often the artist who depicts him or herself as a cephalophore, as if to declare a status of sanctity or melancholic authority. In the case of Michele's collection, however, the theme was taken up with at least two fundamental differences. In the first place the head was not present as the result of decapitation but out of a sort of superfluity: as if to say that fashion is always a multiplication of faces, an excess of identities. On the other hand, this excess of identities transforms, literally, our face into the equivalent of a bag, an accessory. In this case too it is hard not to discern a metalinguistic statement: fashion is what turns our head, our face, our identity into an accessory that is in our hands, into something we can modify, change, transform. Everything is accessory, but this is exactly why the accessory becomes a mark of identity: the almost axiomatic consistency of this principle was underlined by the fact that in one of the two looks the blouse worn by the model was a modification of the famous Gucci *Flora* foulard that Vittorio Accornero had designed for Grace Kelly in the 1960s.

The collection also made numerous references to Leigh Bowery, the Australian performer and fashion designer, friend of Lucian Freud and Boy George. And, to underline the transformative aspect, the venue of the show contained an operating table, as if to declare that every garment is a sort of operation of anatomical restructuring that we carry out on our body and its appearance. This is what Michele himself stressed in a statement quoted by Vanessa Friedman: "'We are all the Dr. Frankenstein of our lives.' . . . 'Inventing, assembling, experimenting' with identity as expressed through clothes, which 'can accompany you while you develop an idea of yourself.'"[7] In this case too, however, the at once literary and iconological theme is radically transformed: thanks to clothing, in fact, we are both Victor Frankenstein and his creature. And, unlike the character in Mary Shelley's novel, the new body that fashion constructs does not kill but gives us a new and more intense life.

6 On this see Pierre Saintyves, "Les saints céphalophores: Étude de folklore hagiographique," *Revue de la histoire des religions* 99 (1929): 158–231; Maurice Coens, "Nouvelles recherches sur un thème hagiographique: La céphalophorie," in *Recueil d'études bollandiennes* (Brussels: Société des Bollandistes, 1963), 9–31; Philippe Gabet, "Recherches sur les saintes 'céphalophores,'" *Bulletin de la Société de mythologie française*, no. 119 (October–December 1980): 131–49; Gabet, "La céphalophorie," *Bulletin de la Société de mythologie française*, no. 140 (January–March 1986): 1–24; Edina Bozoky, "Têtes coupées des saints au Moyen Âge: Martyrs, miracles, reliques," in "Le chief tranché," ed. Carine Giovénal and Alain Corbellari, special issue, *Babel: Littératures plurielles*, no. 42 (2020): 133–68, https://doi.org/10.4000/babel.11516.

7 Vanessa Friedman, "At Gucci, Dressing for the Post-human World," *New York Times*, February 22, 2018, https://www.nytimes.com/2018/02/22/style/gucci-alessandro-michele-milan-fashion-week.html.

I've been asked to write a text for this book about my own personal experience as a creative director . . . and even if I've claimed that role for myself during my career, lately I doubt whether it's a precise description of what I do. Am I a creative person? I think so, I hope so and I'm happy some people I deeply respect and some unknowns have been kind enough to praise my creativity in different fields. Do I like to direct people, teams, concepts, budgets, everything? Yes, I love it!

Sooo voilà: a creative person who likes to direct and uses those skills professionally = creative director, yes? That's it? Just like that? Well, after recalibrating my own impulses, interests, and skills I've came up with a new—more precise—title, one I've never read, seen or heard applied to any professional before: I'm a Creative Communicator.

The main goal in everything I do is based on the need to communicate.

For the last twenty-something years I've developed my career mostly in the field of fashion. I studied fashion design because I fell in love with the dreamy images printed in magazines. Fashion universities in the late 1990s were really focused on the garments, the making of clothes—or at least the one where I studied in Barcelona was—so that's what I had to learn to reach my dream and enter the world that was calling me. As a child I loved the mythically elusive Spanish designer Sybilla. One day the fashion history teacher asked us to do a little homework about a favorite designer; everybody did some short two-to-three-page text sticking in four to five pics cut out from magazines . . . But for some reason I felt like I had to do an extensive 150-page study about Sybilla, filled with some 200 images and some 30 pages of text. It was a challenge and I surpassed

I Am a Creative Communicator
Luis Venegas

everyone's expectations, including my own. I felt so proud that I photocopied the whole thing and sent that copy to Sybilla's studio in Madrid. She called me two weeks later quite astonished, and a month or so later I was hired and started my new life in Madrid. Long story short: in fact that was the first time I edited a publication, thinking of the content but also about making it a seductive, exciting book. I wanted to communicate. I wanted Sybilla to know how much I liked her. And that's how I got my first job. It was the wish to communicate and finding a way to do it creatively. I worked there for the next five years and to this day Sybilla and I still have a very friendly relationship.

If I know something about editing and designing publications, I've learned it by looking at books and magazines. Good and bad ones, everything. If I've loved magazines since so long ago, what stopped me from starting my own? After looking at printed matter since forever I felt ready: I wanted to join the publisher's club. That simple idea is what made me start this arty publication of mine called *Fanzine137* in 2004. I was deeply impressed by the legendary American publication *Visionaire*, which had the best contributors, changed its format every new issue — always in a flamboyant, luxurious way — and was a limited edition. So deeply inspired by all that, my first issue was in an atypical format humble at the time: an envelope filled with loose sheets, all done by artist friends of mine and printed in only 1137 numbered copies. I decided to ask Dior Homme's team — the hottest brand then, led by Hedi

9.137. UNFORGETTABLE FACES

Fanzine137, no. 13.137 (June 2008), "Ladies & Gentlemen (Vol. 1)." Carmen Dell'Orefice photographed by Xevi Muntané. Published by Luis Venegas.
Fanzine137, no. 9.137 (April 2007), "Unforgettable Faces." Amy Wesson photographed by Steven Klein. Published by Luis Venegas.

Fanzine137, no. 23.137 (June 2018), "Never Too Late." Leo Rydell Jost's rugs photographed by Luis Venegas. Published by Luis Venegas.

Slimane—to put their advertising campaign on the back of the envelope, and they agreed. That was the cherry on top of the cake, lighting up my little personal project. Colette in Paris was also the best store for selling any fashion-related product, and its owner Sarah was the first to order copies of my magazine. The freshness of my ideas and that Dior advertisement on the back cover sent a message of credibility. That's how I started communicating, being part of the conversation in a world I had only seen from the outside until then, and making new connections. I did it my way, creating without really knowing but definitely by following my instincts.

Having a first printed issue enabled me to ask other creatives whom I had always admired to get involved in the following issues of *Fanzine137*, to contribute. It was—and still is—the most exciting thing to get people whose work I like to contribute to my projects. That's how I was able to communicate with some of my idols in the worlds of art, fashion, photography, and writing. And since I had this pretty cool list of people willing to be involved in my independent projects, I felt I had to keep on trying to go deeper into my own published profile and try to do other new publications.

Fanzine137 is an art publication that often features in-depth interviews with creatives. So I wanted to explore quite the opposite, and start a very light sexy splash pages, young tabloid magazine, quite the opposite of *Fanzine137* but also "very me." I definitely wanted to communicate with a younger queer audience and that's how I started the magazine *Electric Youth!*—mostly known as *EY!*—with a title quite obviously inspired by the homonymous song by Debbie Gibson (go check it on YouTube). Again, creativity and communication. As an independent publisher, I felt it sent a daring message to have not just one but two publications.

So I decided to try the "even most difficult," and do not just two, but three magazines. I wanted to start a fashion magazine, but one whose content could be as important and relevant as it was to see—for example—black models in fashion magazines in the late 1960s and early 1970s. In a world oversaturated with maaany fashion magazines

that were often just a collection of allegedly pretty images, I wanted mine to transcend, to add something else to how we see the world. Something ideally never seen or done before. That's how I developed what I think is my best professional idea ever and certainly the most influential.

I decided to do the first fashion and style magazine fully focused on celebrating everything transversal, an adjective that I use to evoke all identities that are beyond the old, outdated rules of gender: trans people, transvestism, drag queens, gender-bending, non-binary people, androgyny, and a long etc.—all the identities that had been part of fashion forever, but for some reason there was never a magazine focused on that spectrum. There was always so much inspiration coming from the transversal world, and fashion hadn't given proper credit in return.

I decided to name it C☆NDY, first as a tribute to the legendary, gorgeous, stylish actress Candy Darling, but mostly because *candy* is a catchy word, kind of playful but also sweet and sexy—all the qualities I wanted to convey in the publication. (Naming is fundamental in creative communication!)

EY!, no. 11 (Summer 2021), "The Aussie Issue!" Oliver Moyne and Gumnut the koala photographed by Zac Bayly. Published by Luis Venegas.
EY!, no. 2 (Fall 2008), "UK Is Burning Up!" Ashley Stymest photographed by Alasdair McLellan. Published by Luis Venegas.

51

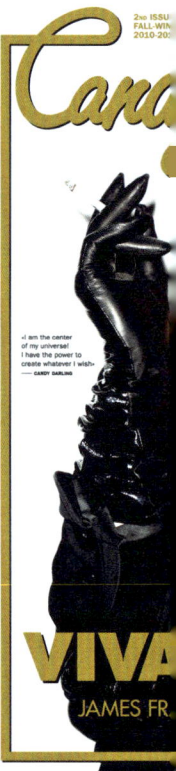

C★NDY

• THE FIRST TRANSVERSAL STYLE MAGAZINE •

LADY GAGA

ART + FASHION + TRANSGRESSION

C★NDY Transversal, no. 7 (Winter 2013–14). Lady Gaga photographed by Steven Klein. Published by Luis Venegas.

This was in 2009—in a climate of severe worldwide economic recession, by the way—and to this day it remains the only fashion and style magazine focused on transversal identities. Until then there were some occasional underground zines, and maybe an article about some trans person here and there but that was all. Six months after C☆NDY was published, the fabulous Brazilian trans model Lea T was featured in a Givenchy campaign, and also Andreja Pejić did H&M and was a regular model at Gaultier shows, among others. Maybe it was a coincidence, could be . . . but most fashion insiders would agree C☆NDY started a new trend then that is now here to stay. You know when you throw a pebble into a peaceful lake? It sets up little ripples that spread across its surface. People start to take note. C☆NDY did that. Now fifteen years later it's not news—for example—to have transgender models on the fashion week runways or campaigns, fortunately.

It wasn't a political statement originally, it was all about celebrating fashion and creativity, but at the same time making such a bold move in 2009 also became a political thing. My goal with C☆NDY is to show the newest people in the transversal world but also to "bring back to life" some forgotten, almost unknown figures who are or have been pioneers, the brave personalities who opened doors sometimes just by living their lives. And I also regularly have transversal contributors creating the contents of each new issue. To me all those things are fundamental in order to create the proper messages, to reinforce the cultural statements made by the magazine. That kind of strong, proper communication is what ensures C☆NDY remains a relevant publication. Creative choices.

Later on the most beautiful thing happened in my life, the most incredible creature came to me: a little French bulldog named Perrillo. That's how I discovered a new world of feelings and experiences related to the amazing bond between humans and dogs, so almost immediately I felt the need to create another new magazine to explore those symbiotic love relationships. That's how I started the least commercial of my publications, called The Printed Dog, but probably the one that is the closest to my heart. I see the only two issues that I published and all the many amazing dogs that we featured, and great contributors who collaborated, and I'm so happy I did it. Once again, the urge to communicate! Maybe I should start my publishing projects with a specific marketing plan in my head, something I've never done before. Someone whose opinion I deeply respect told me, "Your publications are so much more. They are Art projects in fact." When I heard that I realized it was 100% accurate.

I mention all these personal projects because yes, I've always found a way to make them financially sustainable, but at the same time they've been my professional portfolio. All the collaborations that I've done as creative director for brands have happened because they've thought of me after seeing and appreciating my personal publishing projects, my magazines. And that's quite a fortunate strategy for me, I have to admit. Brands often have a strong DNA and it's unusual for them to want to be flexible and try new paths. In my case, I know for sure that most often, when they con-

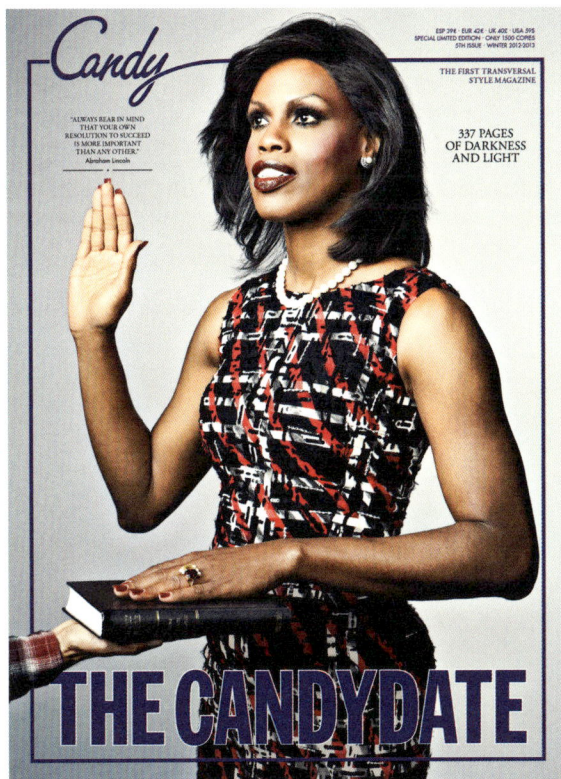

C☆NDY Transversal, no. 2 (Fall-Winter 2010–11). James Franco photographed by Terry Richardson. Published by Luis Venegas.
C☆NDY Transversal, no. 5 (Winter 2012–13). Connie Fleming photographed by Danielle Levitt. Published by Luis Venegas.

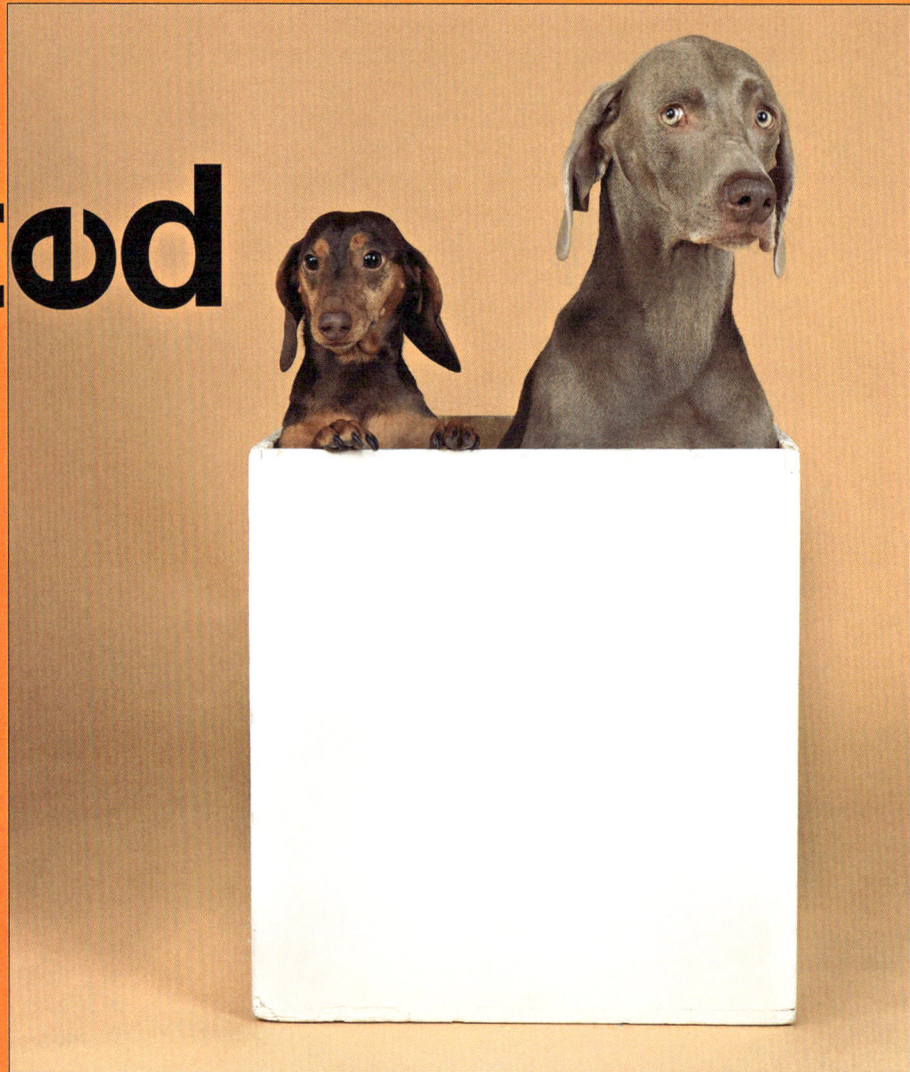

The Printed Dog

2

ESP 25€
EUR 27€
UK 25£
USA $45

tacted me for a commercial job, that's precisely what they expected. They want me to "shake" their foundations a bit, in order to come up with a new, much more modern, progressive, edgy, and cool take on their own perception. Yes, once again: to shift the communication.

When I collaborate with a brand, I usually prefer to understand their boundaries: the audience, the format, the message, the goals. In fact I really enjoy getting the picture. Once I know them, the challenge is to come up with an idea that fits into those parameters but at the same time skips over all of them in unexpected, hopefully exciting ways. And I've found the best formula to try that is precisely to focus on myself: to work in an idea that fundamentally pleases me, to try creating something that actually I'd like to see as a member of the public. After all, if a brand has called me in to bring my ideas, my duty is mix my own salad. For some reason I'm quite confident about my skills and I've been lucky enough to work always with clients who trusted me. To this day I've never worked on a project that has been rejected. Sometimes there might be a little struggle at the beginning, but remaining flexible and open-minded has always worked. Of course that often means a lot of emails,

The Printed Dog, no. 2 (2016). Rupert and Flo photographed by William Wegman. Published by Luis Venegas.

Zooms, phone calls . . . so yes, lots of interaction and guess what again? Communication!

One of the commercial projects that I did with a brand that I'm most proud of is a six hundred-page book I did for Loewe in 2016. Jonathan Anderson became creative director of the — originally Spanish — brand and commissioned me to create a book about Loewe. This was one of the rare times when a client just gave me total freedom to come up with a strong personal idea. The only goal was to make a book like no other before, and it had to convey the idea of a modern, edgy cultural foundation for the brand. It was like a reset, a new take on what at the time was a rather dusty fashion house. I spent a couple of months visiting the Loewe archives almost daily and — once again — doing my own mix, my own edit of what was exciting to me. Sometimes the older Loewe team had their own ideas about what was relevant and what was insignificant and I always listened carefully, but quite often I had to go my own way and ignore their advice. That's how I decided the book was going to be the same as all my other personal publications: a deeply personal art project. In this case, a book about myself and my relationship with Loewe, a brand that — as a Spaniard — I had known since I was a child. There are many contents in that book that are so beyond Loewe — for example personal holidays photos or my dog Perrillo — but somehow they add a certain balance of playfulness and mystery that add new layers to the "official" Loewe imagery and by extension to the brand too. Loewe probably thought it was about them, as they requested . . . Well, think twice, that whole book is in fact mostly about me. Jonathan was happy and the book sold out almost immediately. Now it is a rare collector's item. Try to find one online and — if you're lucky — you'll see how much it costs.

It can be a big book project or online content or a shirts collection or a film or a little zine or a fifteen-second TikTok . . . it can be anything, and as long as it's somehow a reflection of part of your personality it ought to be good, relevant. Try to have fun in the process and that'll make all projects worthwhile. Creative direction and communication, or whatever you call it, makes an impact in the world, so the choices we make matter.

Now, in rereading all this, I wonder whether maybe this text is very much "me! me! me!" Should it have been a much more conceptual/abstract one about the world of ideas and the many complexities of creativity? The thing is, I'm also a quite pragmatic person and feel like the best tool I can use for saying things is my own experience. So hopefully there's a chance that you — dear reader — will find a connection between us. See? It's again about communication. Or is it simply plain self-promotion done in an allegedly creative way? Well, that's a secret I'll never tell. XOXO

Perrillo with a vintage Loewe scarf photographed by Luis Venegas, Barcelona, April 27, 2016. Unpublished.

Moving image is an integral part of the promotional imagery produced by the fashion industry. In today's platform economy, in which film, TV, and video are constantly remediated via the Internet, entertainment has become a central pivot in the communications strategies of the global luxury/fashion brands. In my book *Fashion Film: Art and Advertising in the Digital Age*, published in 2018,[1] I described how the creative impulses behind forms of postdigital filmmaking (cinema in the most extended sense) are invariably in tension with the commercial dynamics of marketing and promotion. One question animating my research is: Exactly how do culture and commerce intersect differently now through the example of digital fashion moving image? If fashion film is more than simply a type of motion imagery for the fashion industry, rather if we consider it as a type of digital postcinema, then do we presume to know its contours in advance? Understood by those within the fashion industry simply to refer to the production of spreadable media content, today's fashion film, at least in its purely commercial guise, consists of online video content and branded entertainment commissioned by designer labels and fashion houses as a promotional tool. In subsequent research published in the *Journal of Visual Culture* in 2020,[2] I pushed my analysis further by positioning fashion film predominantly as a shape-shifting form of content through dissemination on social media platforms, in which the dynamic of the feed (of marketing and data) could be said to be superseding the framework of cinema (of narrative and drama). Rather than situating it predominantly as part of film history, I repositioned the contemporary fashion moving image at the intersection of digital interactivity, fashion branding, and celebrity influence. The migration of promotional fashion film to

Those Indelible Moments:
Fashion and Cinema after Digital Culture
Nick Rees-Roberts

social media platforms therefore calls into question the relevance of the category in today's digital media economy. Online image-sharing culture (particularly across Instagram, TikTok, and YouTube) has locked the fashion/luxury industry into a commercial relationship with the platform economy, with entertainment and tech, both Hollywood and Silicon Valley. With the increased online consumption of video since the 2000s, fashion houses have morphed into hybrid studios that produce both material objects *and* digital content. As the launch in 2023 of Saint Laurent Productions would indicate, no longer content to operate as cultural brokers, fashion brands are now also extending their domain by repositioning themselves as producers, thereby stamping film nominally with the brand's identity: Saint Laurent by Anthony Vaccarello. This territorial move into prestige auteur cinema therefore allows the brand to compete with the traditional financial stakeholders of the film and entertainment industry.

This transformation of fashion into a type of cross-platform media entertainment business has been driven by the rapid integration over the last decade of film and video into fashion promotion and communications, from the addition of video to Instagram in 2013, which was followed by wides-

1   Nick Rees-Roberts, *Fashion Film: Art and Advertising in the Digital Age* (London: Bloomsbury Visual Arts, 2018).
2   Nick Rees-Roberts, "After Fashion Film: Social Video and Brand Content in the Influencer Economy," in "Archaeologies of Fashion Film," special issue, *Journal of Visual Culture* 19, no. 3 (December 2020): 405–21, https://doi.org/10.1177/1470412920964907.
3   Anna Kornbluh, *Immediacy: Or, The Style of Too Late Capitalism* (London: Verso, 2023), 115.

creen in 2015, stories in 2016 (allowing users to post ephemeral moving image), and reels in 2020 (enabling users to post fifteen-second video clips set to music). Cultural theorist Anna Kornbluh has described the dominant style of our postdigital epoch as involving a form of "disintermediation" in which the core aesthetic and economic values of immediacy (instantaneity, transparency, flow, circulation, insatiability, excess) conjoin in the continuous stream of images produced and consumed across entertainment platforms. Kornbluh describes how in the case of moving image, "immediacy eddies 'the stream' of increasingly homogenized customized content in a continuous loop of deformatted genre-fluid absorption."[3] Accordingly, the stream style of fashion would include a range of hybrid digital texts from traditional short promotional films and series to visual experimentation with live-streamed narratives. In practice, different formats coexist and, at times, overlap. For example, at the Milano Digital Fashion Week in July 2020, held online due to the Covid-19 pandemic, Prada invited five fashion photographers to make films to embody a collection called *The Show That Never Happened*. Meanwhile Gucci unveiled a twelve-hour live-streamed video titled *Epilogue* that sought to comment on the tedium of lockdown by going behind the scenes with Alessandro Michele's design team as they shot and modelled the garments they had created — a durational staging of labour in which the production process was curated and exhibited online. In contrast, other brands opt to communicate using more traditional cinematic formats: independent designer Marine Serre, for example, has been using short films in recent years to evoke the distinct sensibility and aesthetic territory of her label — the apocalyptic future in *OSTAL 24* (Spring/Summer 2022) and the edgy party vibe in *HEARTBEAT* (Spring/Summer 2024).

Similarly, serial narratives in traditional televisual and web formats coexist: alongside the recent proliferation of mainstream miniseries about the lives of famous designers made for the major streamers (in 2024 alone, *Cristóbal Balenciaga* and *Becoming Karl Lagerfeld* for Disney+ and *The New Look* on Christian Dior for Apple TV+), one of the most innovative remediations has been jewellery and accessories designer Alexis Bittar's award-winning Instagram miniseries *Margeaux and "Jules"* (2023 onwards) that uses a telenovela format to tell the story of a rich, abusive employer and her put-upon assistant. This longing for narrative (in whatever format) rather than confining fashion film to the early twenty-first-century history of digital cinema,[4] actually illustrates how film and TV are constantly being commercially reconfigured and revitalized by the proliferation of fashion narratives. Fashion film (in its extended mode of multiplatform cinema, TV, and digital moving image) is therefore a useful heuristic to understand the ways in which cinema is constantly being remodulated postdigital as an integral part of a hypermodern media culture rather than simply as a genre, mode, or period of filmmaking.[5]

However, going on the evidence of Chanel's nostalgic black and white tribute to Claude Lelouch's 1966 film *A Man and a Woman* for its Fall/Winter 2024–25 ready-to-wear collection, a promo staring Penélope Cruz and Brad Pitt and directed by Inez & Vinoodh, the aptly titled *A Cinematic Story*, the iconic trace of analogue film and the memory of classic mid-twentieth century European art cinema would still seem to be a high-cultural reference point for mainstream fashion branding. The commercial appropriation of art cinema potentially elevates luxury brands above their status as "mere" businesses, thereby inscribing them in artistic tradition and cultural history rather than the ephemeral cycles of consumer fashion—in the now, the immediate, and the disposable. Cinematic memory is about the trace or the sediment of the past lodged in the minds of viewers. Like the fine arts with their institutionally prestigious spaces of exhibition, cinema too can make fashion memorable. The paradox is that in an era in which industry professionals continually evoke the extinction of cinema after digital, the fashion industry lucratively exploits its symbolic value as a shared cultural language.[6] Fashion's longing for art cinema (exhibited through its constant retrovision of famous movie stars, directors, and moments from the twentieth-century history) is thus intended to boost the cultural capital of luxury brands as a means of imbibing them with a deeper sense of history. Cinema—at least in its artistic iteration—is important therefore not just for reasons of prestige (the institutional importance of events such as film festivals like Cannes and Venice and the PR display value of the red carpet) but also for its iconicity, for how it routinely works through advertising as encoded shorthand to convey (among other things) sophistication, taste, cultivation, elegance, and wealth. Paradoxically, one might wonder why luxury fashion brands so persistently reproduce the sheen of art cinema quite so willingly if not to mask their own status anxiety or lack of lustre.

This supposition is no doubt troubled by those instances in which the brand's visual identity is self-consciously articulated through a disjunctive aesthetic of intentionally bad taste. Take Alessandro Michele's designs for Gucci (2015–

4   Rather than situating fashion film within the broader cross-platform proliferation of digital moving images of fashion, Louise Wallenberg argues on the contrary that digital fashion film emerged between 2000 and 2016 and that the wave (a moment rather than a movement) of "new" fashion films that lasted for a decade and a half is now over. Louise Wallenberg, "Films with a Vengeance: Lesbian Desire and Hyper-Violence in the Fashion Film, 2009–12," in *Fashion, Performance & Performativity: The Complex Spaces of Fashion*, ed. Andrea Kollnitz and Marco Pecorari (London: Bloomsbury Visual Arts, 2022), 182–98.

5   For an excellent overview of fashion's digital hypermodernity, see Marco Pecorari, "Fashion and Hypermodernity," in *The Cambridge Global History of Fashion*, ed. Christopher Breward, Beverly Lemire, and Giorgio Riello (Cambridge: Cambridge University Press, 2023), vol. 2, *From the Nineteenth Century to the Present*, 994–1020.

6   On the cultural discourses of extinction in relation to cinema and fashion, see Hilary Radner, "The Ghost of Cultures Past: Fashion, Hollywood and the End of Everything," *Film, Fashion & Consumption* 3, no. 2 (June 2014): 83–91, https://doi.org/10.1386/ffc.3.2.83_1.

22) by way of illustration. The advertising campaigns were noted for their innovative ways of engaging with film/video content to rejuvenate the brand's visual codes by tailoring imagery more specifically to social media consumption. If Michele's tenure at Gucci was marked by the brand operating as media, evolving from a traditional design-led business into a production studio pumping out content across platforms, his imagery nonetheless drew inspiration from the analogue history of cinema. The designer referenced his baroque style as a form of costume design expressing a desire both to direct and design for the cinema, emphasizing the importance of narrative to his creative process.[7] The *Gucci Love Parade* collection staged on Hollywood Boulevard in November 2021 was conceived as a love letter to the film industry and Michele's final collection for the house, *Exquisite Gucci* (Fall/Winter 2022–23), was a full-blown homage to the cinema of Stanley Kubrick, recreating memorable scenes from his movies. Beyond Hollywood, Michele also collaborated with US indie director Gus Van Sant, codirecting *Ouverture of Something That Never Ended* (2020), an episodic miniseries, the aim of which was to piggyback off the director's signature style—Christopher Doyle's cinematography reproduces the roaming camera and the series is thematically on-brand focusing on youth, sexuality, and identity, supported by the casting of queer performance artist Silvia Calderoni alongside a cameo from trans theorist Paul B. Preciado, who provides a meta-commentary on the technologies of gender dissidence. The series is a prime example of hyperfashion in which an overload of codes, references, and messages submerges the artistry in a self-conscious post-postmodern style, illustrative of how contemporary pop culture endlessly devours itself through quotation, curation, and recycling.[8] (In parallel, Ridley Scott's sensational schlock bio-film, *House of Gucci* in 2021, although not commissioned by the brand, literalized and vulgarized this hyperaesthetic through its mode of excess, incarnated by brand ambassador Jared Leto's distinctly overripe performance.) The intersection of high fashion and celebrity was also consolidated by the appearance of pop stars and brand ambassadors Harry Styles and Billie Eilish in *Ouverture*, a feature aimed to ensure the series' viral potential going on comments made by fans on the brand's YouTube channel ("Who's here for Harry and Billie?" and so on). Michele's own renown was clearly a factor in the brand's commercial success during his years at the creative helm, making the appointment of an unknown successor a PR challenge for Gucci. The quirky documentary, ironically titled *Who Is Sabato De Sarno?* (2024), directed by Ariel Schulman and Henry Joost, narrated by actor and ambassador Paul Mescal, and streamed on MUBI (the art-film streamer, producer, and distributor), was humorously intended to present the designer and extend his profile beyond the world of fashion.

The strategic role played by streamers such as MUBI in promoting international art cinema is also relevant to the recognition and success of Italian filmmaker Luca Guadagnino. In 2019, Pierpaolo Piccioli, then creative director of Valentino, collaborated with the director on a thirty-seven-minute film, *The Staggering Girl*, featuring the Hollywood star Julianne Moore. Portraying different episodes in a woman's relationship with her mother, the

7   See Rebecca Mead, "Gucci's Renaissance Man," *New Yorker*, September 12, 2016, https://www.newyorker.com/magazine/2016/09/19/guccis-renaissance-man; and Jessica Michault, "Alessandro Michele's Exclusive Interview: 'I'm a Fetishist,'" *Antidote*, March 15, 2016, http://magazineantidotecom/english/alessandro-michele-exclusive-interview.

8   On Michele's hyperaesthetic and fashion after postmodernism, see Nigel Lezama, "Intensified: Alessandro Michele's Hyperaesthetic at Gucci," in *Fashion, Dress, and Post-postmodernism*, ed. José Blanco F. and Andrew Reilly (London: Bloomsbury Visual Arts, 2021), 75–98.

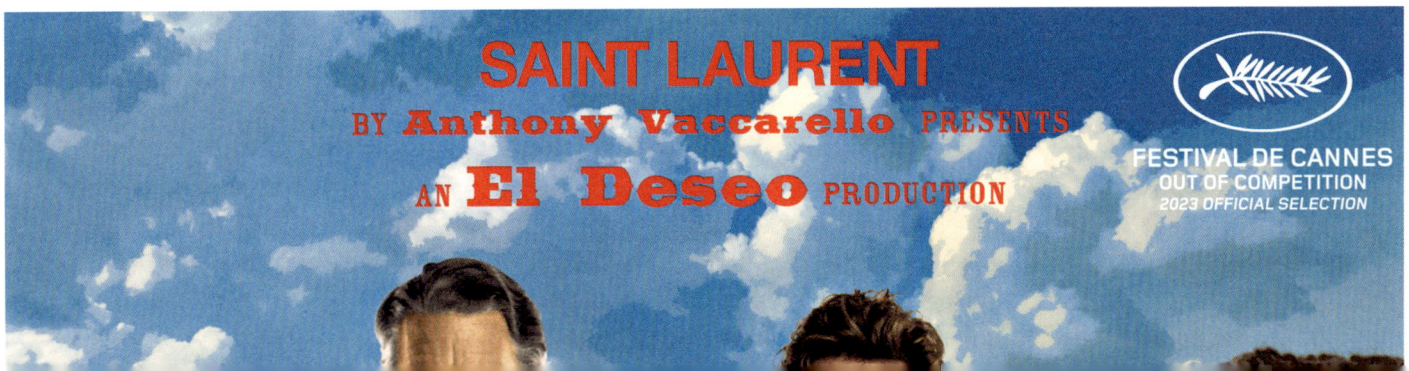

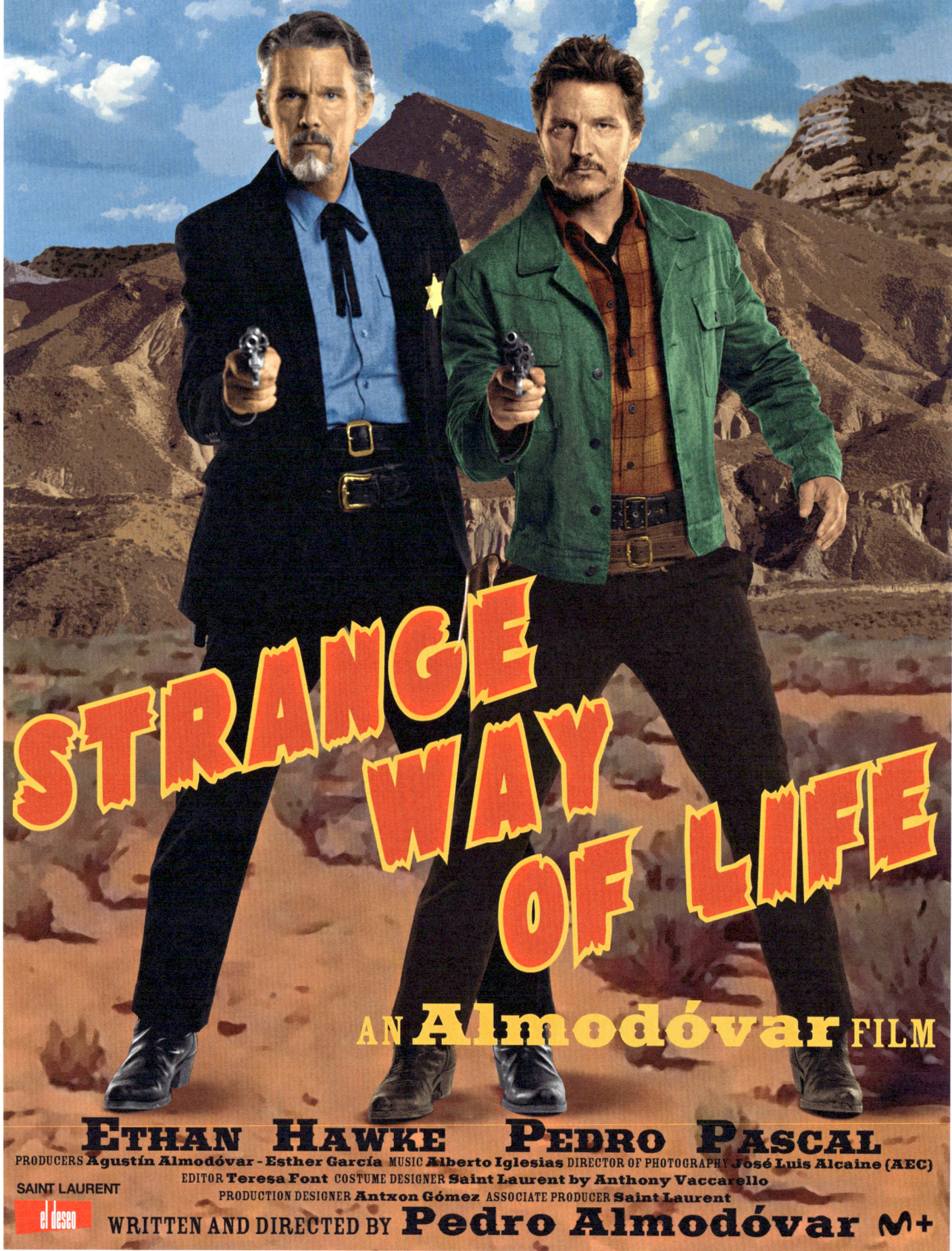

Strange Way of Life, directed by Pedro Almodóvar (Saint Laurent Productions, 2023), film poster. Graphic design by Studio Gatti. © El Deseo.

project was conceived and packaged as a short art film, in which the *alta moda* tradition was woven into the story by displaying the brand's entire Fall/Winter 2018–19 collection. Despite its function as motion content that blended narrative art with promotional display, the project was not apparently intended simply as a straightforward ad for Valentino, although it certainly works better as promotion than as drama. The languid camerawork by cinematographer Sayombhu Mukdeeprom beautifully showcases the outfits at the expense of narrative tension and cohesion. Guadagnino has been celebrated principally for a type of middlebrow cinema like the Oscar-winning gay romance *Call Me by Your Name* (2017), the success of which owed much to its vintage sensibility consisting of nostalgic quotations from 1980s styles. Working as film director, producer, and TV showrunner (for the HBO / Sky Atlantic coming-of-age drama series *We Are Who We Are* in 2020), Guadagnino straddles film and fashion, talking in interview of the "marriage" between a form that tells a story and another that conveys identity.[9] He has also made a documentary on Ferragamo (*Salvatore: Shoemaker of Dreams*), first shown at the Venice Film Festival in 2020 while in parallel shooting a campaign film for the house, a homage to Alfred Hitchcock's *Marnie* (1964) for creative director Paul Andrew's Spring/Summer 2021 collection. He has worked on film projects through his production company, Frenesy, commissioned by luxury brands such as Armani, Cartier, DKNY, and Pomellato—his commercial work in advertising acting as the experimental ground for some of the formal ideas developed through the feature films. The costumes for his tennis-set movie *Challengers* (2024) were designed by Jonathan Anderson, the designer for both Loewe and JW Anderson. Coproduced by Guadagnino with the film's star Zendaya, the big-budget project for Amazon MGM Studios, which resembles a hypersexualized workout video contained within a love-triangle plot, included pieces from the Loewe tie-in collection, *I TOLD YA*, branded merch worn as a sartorial message by the film's protagonists. The film's preppy normcore styling also included sportswear brand inclusion for Nike, Adidas, and UNIQLO, as well as luxury product placements for Chanel and Aston Martin. Anderson's mastery of the vernacular of digital culture ensured the film's broader inscription within pop culture. The digital strategy for his eponymous label has included humorous online promos, JWA TV, parodying the generic for-

9   Luca Guadagnino quoted by Stella Bruzzi in her discussion of his narrativization of style. Stella Bruzzi, "Hollywood and Beyond: Fashion and the Fiction Film," in Breward, Lemire, and Riello, *Cambridge Global History of Fashion*, 2:966.

mat of teleshopping channels and his 3D designed pigeon clutch went viral as part of the digital "weirdcore" aesthetic after it adorned Sarah Jessica Parker in the second series of the *Sex and the City* spin-off, *And Just like That...*, in 2023.

These examples of integrated branded entertainment blending product, design, and media (across film, TV, and digital) illustrate how the commercial and creative territories of fashion and entertainment intersect in today's platform economy. If the logic of the feed and style of the stream could now be said to dominate the production contexts for fashion film and moving image, the more formal questions of aesthetics and narrative still remain, however. As Caroline Evans and Jussi Parikka point out, beyond the interplay of surface and sensation that marks out the more avant-garde end of the spectrum, "narrative still features as a constant reference point at least in industry discussions about cultural attraction and (re)production as to what is the definition of film in fashion film."[10] The fashion industry's territorialization of film production is therefore partially motivated by the need to go beyond the commercial limitations of the short film project (conceived by the industry as digital marketing content) and move into cinema production proper, to shape the narratives and aesthetics produced by the film industry from the inside. In 2023, Anthony Vaccarello, creative director at Saint Laurent, consolidated his in-house film initiative by launching a production studio, a registered subsidiary of the brand and the first to count film production among its principal activities.

In 2023, the studio produced Pedro Almodóvar's short film *Strange Way of Life*, starring Ethan Hawke and Pedro Pascal, with costumes designed by Vaccarello. The film was shown out of competition at the Cannes Film Festival in May

10   Caroline Evans and Jussi Parikka, "Introduction: Touch, Click and Motion; Archaeologies of Fashion Film after Digital Culture," in "Archaeologies of Fashion Film": 332, https://doi.org/10.1177/1470412920966015.

Strange Way of Life, directed by Pedro Almodóvar (Saint Laurent Productions, 2023). Photo Iglesias Más. © El Deseo.

2023 before a limited theatrical release. Promoted as the director's homage to early Hollywood Westerns, the thirty-minute narrative breathes new life into a tired (heteronormative) genre, queered here through the melancholic reunion after twenty-five years of two gunslingers and former lovers, one a sheriff (Hawke) and the other a rancher (Pascal). Almodóvar is a good fit for fashion since his back catalogue of films includes immersive, entertaining narratives that celebrate melodramatic excess, surface style, and intermedial borrowings from pop culture, TV, and genre cinema.[11] Expressive, flamboyant, colourful, and maximalist are the constant queer aesthetic reference points used to describe his cinema. Shot in Almería in Spain on sets first mounted for Sergio Leone's 1960s spaghetti Westerns, *Strange Way of Life* juxtaposes the barren ochre desert landscape with the sexy American workwear (colourful plaid and denim shirts; cowboy neckties and leather boots) designed by Vaccarello for the attractive leads—the moustachioed, middle-aged Pedro Pascal, star of the postapocalyptic TV drama *The Last of Us*, has been singled out on TikTok as a "zaddy", a charismatic, sexy protector figure.

This equation of (white, male) seniority and artistry in the film industry is problematically reinscribed in Vaccarello's auteur selection: Saint Laurent's Spring/Summer 2023 *Director's Cut* campaign consisted of fifteen-second short films made by David Sims to celebrate a number of senior directors of international cinema, including Jim Jarmusch, who made a star-studded campaign film *French Water* for Spring/Summer 2021, and David Cronenberg, whose subsequent thriller *The Shrouds* was one of three SL coproductions in official competition at the 2024 Cannes Film

11 On fashion in Almodóvar's cinema, see Gerard Dapena, "Making Spain Fashionable: Fashion and Design in Pedro Almodóvar's Cinema," in *A Companion to Pedro Almodóvar*, ed. Marvin D'Lugo and Kathleen M. Vernon (Malden, MA: Wiley Blackwell, 2013), 495–523; Jorge Pérez, "Significant Outfits: Almodóvar Wears Chanel," *MLN* 133, no. 2 (March 2018): 336–56, https://doi.org/10.1353/mln.2018.0022; and Sarah Gilligan and Jacky Collins, "Suits and Subcultures: Costuming and Masculinities in the Films of Pedro Almodóvar," *Film, Fashion & Consumption* 8, no. 2 (October 2019): 147–69, https://doi.org/10.1386/ffc_00004_1.

Festival. The other two were Paolo Sorrentino's *Parthenope*, which received a tepid reaction, criticised for its luxurious settings and slick advertising aesthetic, and Jacques Audiard's hybrid musical crime drama, *Emilia Pérez*, in which the designer's style contributes to the film's antirealist aesthetic—the film makes nods to Almodóvar's poignant melodramatic stories of transition and gender reassignment. Vaccarello's seductive eveningwear complements the plot in which the struggling lawyer Rita Moro Castro (Zoë Saldaña) is handsomely rewarded for arranging gender reassignment surgery for a Mexican cartel leader, who becomes the eponymous heroine (Karla Sofía Gascón). Rita's new-found wealth and status allow her to move to an affluent London, interior shots of which resemble a chic fashion editorial. From the commercial perspective of the brand, the film also includes fleeting product placements and brand integration: Selena Gomez wears a Rive Gauche T-shirt in a semiotic nod to the fashion house; she is filmed in a karaoke-style music video sequence as a pop star and when she returns home after partying, her stilettos are given their own luminescent close-up.

The advent of the brand as production studio marks a shift from fashion's previous role as artistic philanthropist or cultural broker, the historical model for which is Miuccia Prada, who has for years been supporting cinema through initiatives like the *Women's Tales* film series. The example of Saint Laurent Productions raises a number of industrial questions of importance for both fashion and cinema. First, the house of Saint Laurent is credible given the founder's close links with film, particularly the famous costumes designed for *Belle de Jour* (Buñuel, 1967) that are referenced as part of Vaccarello's cinematic runway presentations (Fall/Winter 2024–25, for example). Second, international auteurs increasingly struggle to finance their projects and so now accept fashion as a viable commercial partner. Third, a fashion house can be present at the inception of a film project without necessarily appearing egregiously promotional or swamping the film with an advertorial aesthetic (the problem with Gucci's collab with Gus Van Sant). Lastly, the red-carpet events in Hollywood or at festivals like Cannes and Venice are clearly valuable for their relaying of images to billions of consumers on social media platforms. In our so-called attention economy, the red carpet is, in purely marketing terms, a highly competitive commercial space for the visibility of fashion. Coproducing the products that are being promoted for awards and negotiated for distribution deals is a logical next step for the fashion industry to create meanings beyond the purely mercantile, to go beyond its role as a communications platform or cultural broker for cinema. To compete with the Kering group's move into film production, its rival LVMH announced in early 2024 the launch of 22 Montaigne Entertainment, founded to tell the stories of the group's houses through audiovisual formats, a clear sign of the territorial expansion of luxury into the world of digital film and entertainment. The indelible trace of twentieth-century film aesthetics and narrative tradition remains a central feature of this new industrial reconfiguration of fashion and cinema after digital.

At once fragile and monumental, Juergen Teller's solo exhibition *i need to live*, first staged at the Grand Palais Éphémère in December 2023 and then at the Triennale di Milano in January 2024,[1] raises a series of questions that appear crucial to me when talking of photography and, in particular, of the way that images of fashion circulate.

Teller was assisted in the planning of the exhibition by the curator Thomas Weski and by his wife Dovile Drizyte — his professional partner, muse, and obsession — as well as by the studio 6a architects, responsible for the display design at both venues. In fact *i need to live* is a retrospective that, in addition to bringing together for the first time a thousand or so works produced since the 1980s, comprises, without distinction, personal projects and commercial ones, portraits and self-portraits conceived for exhibition spaces, and photographic features produced for double-page spreads in magazines, especially fashion magazines. They include photographs that have lodged in the collective imagination, like the ones of Victoria Beckham in an advertising campaign for Marc Jacobs in 2008[2] or that portrayed Vivienne Westwood completely nude in 2012, made up into a book five years later by the OK-RM studio: *Vivienne Westwood, Andreas Kronthaler, Juergen Teller*.[3]

The surgical layout of the exhibition at the Grand Palais Éphémère, which cut the space into four parts by means of two wooden structures, each about a hundred meters long, that were arranged in a cross, lost its cohesion and efficacy at the Triennale di Milano, where the fragmentation of the spaces resulted in a feeling of chaos and where the subdivision of their perception inevitably led

Another Form of Life:
Notes on Fashion Images Today
Saul Marcadent

to more confusion. What remained the same, however, and makes the show a good starting point for the arguments put forward here, was the handling of the images, in particular the multiplicity of supports, printing methods, and formats, as well as the range of quality, in the sense of definition. Moving around the exhibition, in fact, you might come across the same photograph three or four times — I'm thinking for instance of the one of the singer and songwriter Björk with her son Sindri in Iceland in 1993 — printed first in a postcard format of 10 × 15 cm and presented along with a galaxy of other images, then on a large scale and isolated on a wall, mounted in a museum-style frame and glass, and, yet again, printed on a letter-size sheet pinned to the wall with thumbtacks. And, looking at photographs of a large format, you might instantly become aware of the presence of pixels, as in the case of the image chosen by Teller as vehicle of the exhibition and cover for the book that accompanies it,[4] in which he is portrayed lying on a mattress wearing nothing but a pair of boxers and socks and holding a bunch of balloons. In this case, the self-portrait was taken with an iPhone in 2017 and its low information content means that it is unable to guarantee the quality of the reproduction in the exhibition. Teller seems uninterested in this aspect, or rather, he seems interested in challenging it, taking it almost to breaking point.

In keeping with the practice that has made his work so recognizable — the use of direct flash even in full daylight, resulting in overexposed photographs — Teller has included low-definition images in the exhibition, produced on all sorts of devices and even including screenshots. In doing so he removes the aura of myth surrounding the image — breaking it down in order to monumentalize it and reproducing it ad infinitum — and updates the concept of authoriality, raising questions about his relationship with photography today (and inevitably ours as well).

On the Qualities of Fashion Images
The encounter with the exhibition *i need to live* and, more generally, with the authoriality of Juergen Teller necessarily leads to a wider reflection on fashion images and their visual and graphic qualities. A fixed point is the lack of any critical literature on the subject: notwithstanding the central role of fashion photography, from both the commercial and the cultural viewpoint, there are few probing theoretical analyses capable of throwing light on the mechanisms by which it functions. At the same time there is an abundance of photographic books that arrange images or their creators chronologically or pigeonhole them on the basis of standardized categories or too narrow themes, such as the relationship with technological experimentation.

Eugénie Shinkle describes fashion photography as a cultural assimilator that absorbs, connects, and reimagines the past and the present, uniting the commercial sphere with the cultural one, fusing aesthetic dimension and political dimension. In her work, Shinkle looks at the image as both product and process and, especially where the latter aspect is concerned, stresses its connective power, its relational dimension.[5] An image of fashion, in fact, is never the result of a single person's work but always of a collective effort that, in

1 The exhibition was held in Paris from December 16, 2023, to January 9, 2024, and in Milan from January 27 to April 1, 2024.

2 The campaign was so iconic that Teller restaged it ten years later, in 2018, for Victoria Beckham's homonymous brand. It was a sort of reenactment in which the new images, however, did not have the radical character, rejection of celebrity, and brazenness of the originals.

3 Designed by the duo of Oliver Knight and Rory McGrath, it was brought out by their publishing house InOtherWords. The book, which focuses on the creative partnership between Vivienne Westwood and Andreas Kronthaler, contains pictures taken by Juergen Teller between 1993 and 2017.

4 Published by Steidl, it has been produced in collaboration with Grand Palais Éphémère and the Triennale di Milano and its graphic design is by Teller himself, together with Dovile Drizyte.

5 See Eugénie Shinkle, *Fashion Photography: The Story in 180 Pictures* (London: Thames & Hudson, 2017). See too Shinkle, ed., *Fashion as Photograph: Viewing and Reviewing Images of Fashion* (London: I.B. Tauris, 2008).

addition to the photographer, involves the fashion designer, art director, models, makeup artists, and hairstylists: a whole set of professionals with different skills that are directed toward a common goal. The process, therefore, is always characterized by a multiplicity of connections, and this plurality of eyes and hands means that fashion photography has much in common with the performing arts: "We should grasp the photographic act as one that results from the interaction of all the figures around the camera and as being essentially defined by observing and acting."[6]

Lining up the properties of images of fashion necessarily signifies facing up to the fact that they are often produced on commission and for rapid consumption: it suffices to think of their seductive power and the relations they have with the realm of desire and the world of advertising. In addition, they traditionally find full expression in their layout on the page,[7] in sequentiality and intertextuality, and are open to the possibilities of the digital, which are shaping new modes of production, circulation, and fruition. It is significant, in fact, that people working in the area of fashion photography have been among the first to carry out experiments of this kind. Since the end of the 1990s Nick Knight, founder of the SHOWstudio platform, has not only brought the possibilities of technological innovation to bear but

Viviane Sassen, *Self Portrait*, 1998, C-print. © Viviane Sassen.
Juergen Teller: i need to live, exhibition view, Grand Palais Éphémère, Paris, 2023–24. Exhibition design and photo 6a architects.

produced works in which such innovation is intrinsic to the image itself: this is the case with photographic series like *Sister Honey* (1999), which presents bodies transfigured by digital processing, or *Sweet* (2000), in which computerized tomography is used.

Observing the contemporary situation, in the light of these considerations, obliges us to look at the opposing forces at work and the diversity of cultural propensities and aesthetic characteristics, which I view as a sign of richness, in as much as it is the lifeblood of the language's evolution. In contrast to those who are embracing the possibilities of the digital and seeking a high-tech aesthetic in their work, there are photographers who prefer an analog approach and the feel of low-tech images on film. Together, they form a generation of practitioners that moves freely within the system of fashion and that of art, in the pages of magazines and the spaces of galleries, without making distinctions between personal projects and commercial ones, bringing their own keen vision to bear on the latter too. Emblematic, in this sense, is the work of Viviane Sassen, recently celebrated in a wide-ranging retrospective at the Maison Européenne de la Photographie in Paris[8] that offers a reflection on the surface of the fashion image, partly through experimentation with collage, photomontage and interaction with painting. The attention to materiality seems to find a point of contact with the renewed taste for printed magazines, especially

6   Jule Hillgärtner, "Displaying the Gaze: On Fashion Photography as Photography," in *Not in Fashion: Photography and Fashion in the 90s*, ed. Susanne Gaensheimer and Sophie von Olfers, catalogue of the exhibition at the Museum für Moderne Kunst, Frankfurt, September 25, 2010–January 9, 2011 (Bielefeld: Kerber, 2010), 49.

7   See in this connection Vince Aletti, *Issues: A History of Photography in Fashion Magazines* (London: Phaidon, 2019).

8   *Phosphor: Art & Fashion 1990–2023*, staged from October 18, 2023, to February 11, 2024, presented more than two hundred works produced over the course of thirty years and was accompanied by a volume published by Prestel.

avant-garde and self-initiated ones, independent of a publisher or publishing group, which have different characteristics to periodicals with a high circulation. Curiously, these forms of small-scale publishing, aimed at a niche readership and dealing with niche genres and subjects, often suggest a broadening of the gaze from a Eurocentric and Western focus to a more widespread and rarefied geography.

Printed Images

In recent times brands like Loewe, Gucci, and Bottega Veneta, through the intuition and sensitivity of their creative directors, have established significant relationships with the publishing world and with experimental photography, partly by investing money in niche magazines and in publications produced in close collaboration with key image makers on the contemporary scene.

The case of Jonathan Anderson, founder of the JW Anderson brand in 2008 and creative director of Loewe since 2013, is exemplary. Between 2017 and 2018 he worked in parallel on three projects on paper that reflected his interest in print publishing, to which he assigns a profound cultural value: the book *Your Picture / Our Future*,[9] in which he connected up the work of fifty male and female photographers who had never previously been published, going on to involve them in the Fall/Winter 2018-19 campaign of his own brand; the series of timeless works of literature entitled Loewe Classics, which comprises cult novels by writers like Emily Brontë, Oscar Wilde, and Gustave Flaubert,

Juergen Teller: i need to live, exhibition view, Grand Palais Éphémère, Paris, 2023–24. Exhibition design and photo 6a architects.

republished in limited editions illustrated with archive pictures by Steven Meisel, a photographer who has worked on many of Loewe's advertising campaigns; and the volume *Disobedient Bodies*, brought out by the independent publishing company InOtherWords, which accompanied the exhibition of the same name curated by Anderson in the spaces of the Hepworth Wakefield in West Yorkshire.[10] In the same period and with the same intensity, Alessandro Michele, creative director of Gucci at the time, brought out in collaboration with the independent publisher and distributor IDEA, a series of photographic volumes with a run of a thousand copies, each with its own visual identity and specific physical characteristics, that accompanied the brand's collections. Michele's work for Gucci from 2016 to 2019 was interpreted by photographers and filmmakers like Ari Marcopoulos, Martin Parr, Harmony Korine, and Yorgos Lanthimos, invited to create books in which they had complete freedom of action and whose content was reflected in the design of the object, from the choice of paper to the typographic characteristics and the packaging.

Matthieu Blazy, creative director of Bottega Veneta since 2021, is probably the figure who is showing the most interest in innovative forms of publishing today. Less than a year after taking up the post he chose to boost the brand's investment in publishing, with a particular emphasis on independent publications with a low circulation and high degree of experimentation. *Air Afrique*, with a focus on African arts and the cultures of the African diaspora, and *Magma*, inspired by the avant-garde periodicals of the twentieth century, both founded in 2023, are two contemporary niche publications produced with the support of Bottega Veneta. However, the reactivation of *BUTT* in the February of 2022, something strongly desired by Blazy, is the case that I would like to examine at greater length in this context. A Dutch magazine that became a cult for the international queer community, with twenty-nine issues published from 2001 to 2011, *BUTT* has had the ability to speak to that community, with an ever greater geographical and cultural spread, in an authentic and explicit language.[11] The publication of the thirtieth issue in alliance with Bottega Veneta, after a hiatus of over a decade, attests to the appeal that this space of production has for the fashion industry. Matthieu Blazy, who took over from Daniel Lee after three years of creative direction characterized by nonconformist strategies of communication,[12] is interested in establishing a lasting dialogue with the founders of *BUTT*, the duo Gert Jonkers and Jop van Bennekom. It is not, in fact, a question of positioning the brand in the magazine through traditional forms of advertising but of constructing a true relationship, in which Bottega Veneta is the only commercial player involved and *BUTT* guarantees the legitimation of the brand's cultural value among its own community of readers. We can see Blazy's engagement as being in tune with what Hedi Slimane did ten years earlier during his creative direction of Saint Laurent, with a substantial investment by the brand in advertising in the independent press. The relaunch of *BUTT* is paradigmatic on the one hand of the ability of niche magazines to take an active position and, as a consequence, to lay down new rules, even in their relationship with the mainstream, and on the other of their capacity to reinvent themselves, by being receptive and open, adapting to the context that is changing around them.

9   Produced by the JW Anderson brand with a run of a thousand copies and designed by M/M (Paris), it accompanied the exhibition of the same name held in London in May 2018. The book and exhibition were preceded by an international call for submissions.

10   Running from March 18 to June 18, 2017, the exhibition offered a reflection on the body, establishing a dialogue between some of the sculptures in the gallery's permanent collection and a selection of items of clothing and objects, with a display design by 6a architects.

11   The interruption of its publication in 2011 did not stop numerous authors from continuing to talk about it afterwards: emblematic examples are the anthology *Forever BUTT* brought out by Taschen and the installation *After BUTT* at the Chelsea College of Arts, accompanied by Ian Giles's documentary of the same name that, as well as drawing attention to the qualities of the magazine, highlighted some of its flaws, such as the Eurocentric point of view.

12   The brand abandoned social media platforms, including Instagram, and launched *Issued by Bottega*, a digital magazine that expanded its range of imagery and established new kinds of relationship with its followers.

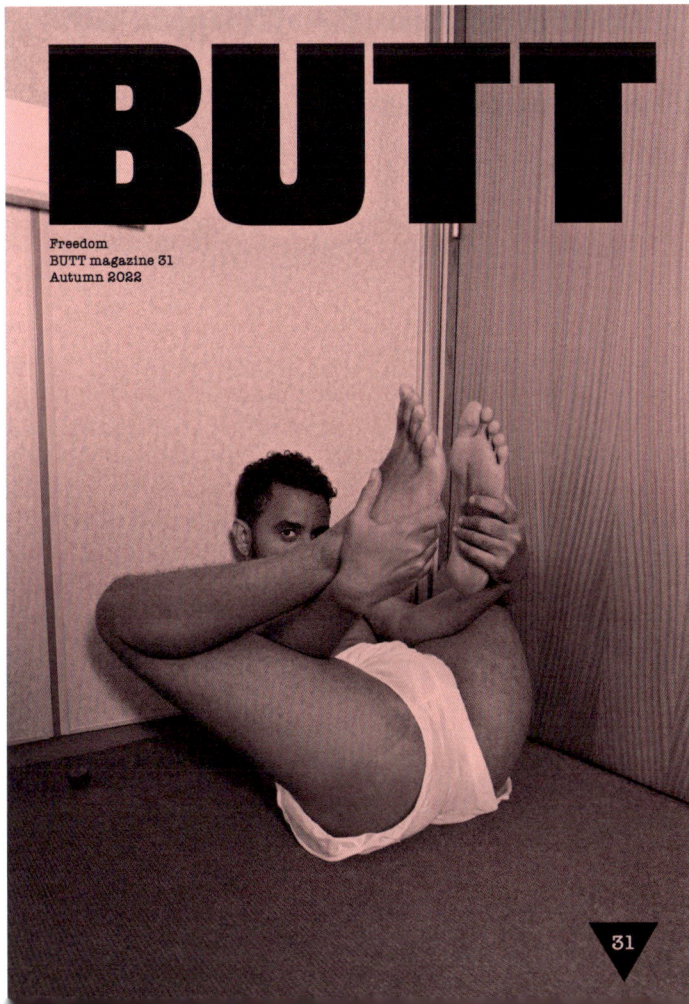

BUTT, no. 31 (Fall 2022).

On Virality and Hybridization

In 2020, in the midst of the pandemic, Adrián González-Cohen and David Uzquiza, founders in 2011 of the magazine *Buffalo Zine*, brought out its thirteenth issue, with the title "Viral." Traditionally characterized by continual changes in dimensions, binding, and graphic layout—its motto is "Serious fashion mags are over"—the magazine in this case had a 29 × 21 cm format and a large number of pages held together by a plastic spiral. Apparently free from any kind of scheme, the layout simulates the act of scrolling, with fragmentary images that are only completed when you turn the page. The scanty typographical experimentation on the texts, which look as if they were made up in Word with elements in a blue color to mimic hypertextual links, is balanced by the efficacy of the images, in some cases disproportionately large and in others as small as postage stamps, that float across the double-page spread. Images conceived expressly for the magazine by a generation of photographers who move freely between the independent scene and the mainstream: I am thinking of people like Reto Schmid and Annie Collinge. The content of the issue explores the possibilities and contradictions of the digital, the aesthetics of memes and filters, avatars and NFTs, makeup tutorials and the bionic body. Pervaded by a more or less explicit sense of irony, "Viral" connects celebrities on a small and large scale and images created by digital and visual artists with contributions from writers, thinkers, and activists, experimenting with forms of hybridization between reality and fiction; or rather between real and hyperreal, to draw on the ideas of Jean Baudrillard, who seems to have guided the work of González-Cohen and Uzquiza throughout the design of the issue, although this is not openly declaredly.

The encounter with *Buffalo Zine* has allowed me, in these days, to go back to the work of Nick Knight, mentioned earlier on, which in my view is still crucial today to an understanding of the ability of fashion photography to question its own qualities and to anticipate, grasp, and amplify a wide range of propensities, expressions, and practices. Photographic series like the aforementioned *Sister Honey* and *Sweet* are certainly examples of Knight's pioneering interest in experimenting with a mixture of the analog and digital and the production of hybrid images. We could also point to photographs like the one of Devon Aoki wearing a dress from Alexander McQueen's 1997 Spring/Summer collection, taken for issue no. 20 of the magazine *Visionaire*:[13] the model looks like a cyborg geisha, with cherry blossom emerging from her pierced forehead. Or, again, the series *Fashion-Able*, published the following year in *Dazed & Confused*, in which the protagonists are the disabled bodies fitted with prostheses of athletes like Aimee Mullins and dancers like David Toole.

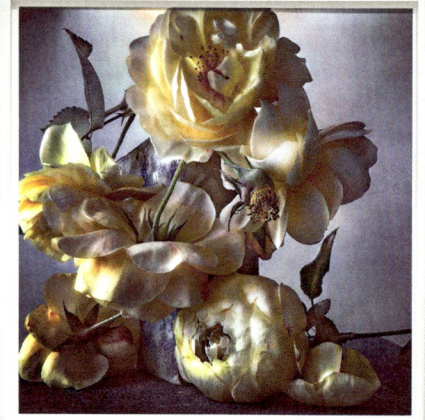

But it is on Knight's most recent works that I intend to dwell, in conclusion of this essay. In 2010 the photographer paid tribute to Alexander McQueen in the issue of *i-D* marking the magazine's thirtieth anniversary. To McQueen, who had taken his own life on February 11 of that year, Knight devoted an image spread across two pages—a composition of red, pink, and maroon roses—accompanied by the phrase, tucked away in the bottom right corner, "To Lee, With Love."

For a decade Knight went on producing series of photographs dedicated to roses, designing and choreographing still lifes with flowers grown in his garden. Unlike his works for the fashion industry, in which the photographer had the support of a team, he acted here in complete independence and solitude. In *Roses from My Garden* — a series shown for the first time in 2019 — he photographed the flower arrangements with his iPhone, uploading them to Instagram and intervening with the filters and other tools available on the app. Subsequently he experimented with artificial intelligence to augment the definition of the images, which he often presents as large-format prints. The contribution of AI to the original image accentuates the dimension of suspense and the photographs look slightly unreal. The textures that derive from this resemble neither the brushwork of a painting nor the grain of a photograph: the result of the interaction between the original photograph and the AI generates, in fact, a hybrid quality, which retains the initial connotations while emphasizing the details. Thanks to an algorithm trained on millions of photographs of roses, the gaps in the initial image are eliminated and high definition is restored, to the point of creating an odd sensation of unreality or hyperreality.[14]

Alongside these experiments relying on the aid of technological innovation, Knight has not renounced, in recent years, more physical actions. He chooses, for example, to print some of his pictures on photographic paper inserted into the printer the wrong way up — so that the surface does not absorb the ink and what look almost like drips of paint are generated — showing us, once again, the urge to carry out research and experimentation on the part of image makers working with fashion today. And the extent to which this distinctive photographic language plays a part in shaping a complex visual and cultural landscape that comprises both possibilities and contradictions.

13   The issue was put together by the magazine's editors, Stephen Gan, Cecilia Dean, and James Kaliardos, with Rei Kawakubo, founder of Comme des Garçons, and was intended as an exploration of the brand's archives. Kawakubo, in the capacity of guest editor, involved the photographers Mario Sorrenti, Philip-Lorca diCorcia, and Nick Knight, who was invited to blend the imagery of Comme des Garçons with Alexander McQueen's.

14   See in this connection Alexander Fury, "Nick Knight's Unreal, Surreal Images of Roses," *AnOther Magazine*, June 21, 2019, https://www.anothermag.com/art-photography/11779/nick-knight-roses-interview-albion-barn-exhibition-alexander-fury.

Nick Knight: Roses, exhibition view, Albion Barn & Fields, Little Milton, 2019. Photo Todd-White Art Photography.

One term over which there has been much wrangling in the debate over the fashion of 2010s, in other words ever since the time when the Internet and its logic began to play a forceful part in the dynamics of the industry, is undoubtedly that of democratization. In those fundamental years fashion opened up, quite suddenly, and the small group of tastemakers that had long determined its course was at last expanded. In the meantime parallel trends in style, which have always existed and have to do with the way in which people dress around the world, arrived for the first time at the heart of European fashion, in the French and Italian houses, on the catwalks of Paris and Milan. The habits and customs of a small and highly influential sector were made accessible, digitally at least, to a public that had never been so vast and multifaceted, and its dynamics were for the first time subjected to public scrutiny. Taste could no longer be shaped exclusively by influence from the top down but needed to be globalized, to take on board ideas and suggestions that could bring together markets and logics often remote from one another. It was a momentous change, one that went hand in hand with what was happening in all the visual arts and more in general with the direction in which the culture of the time was moving. As digital platforms evolved, and with them the ways in which people interacted with them, fashion had to learn how to present itself and reach as many people as possible, and in the quickest and most effective manner. It would not be going too far to say that, like tech, fashion is one of the sectors that has undergone the most striking changes over the last fifteen years: in a certain sense it has burst out, reaching parts of society from which it was previously excluded. One of the most unpredictable and shocking

Memorable Fashion
Silvia Schirinzi

consequences of this was highlighted in 2018 by Christopher Wylie, the whistleblower who lifted the lid on the goings on at Cambridge Analytica, when he explained to the world the implications of our online behavior, even such innocuous activities as shopping, and revealed that that attempt to build political consensus had also entailed the analysis of data, including on people's tastes in clothing.[1] Fashion, and the consumption connected with it, helped to make visible to others the place we occupy in society and, along with the rest of our activity on social media, define how we behave as individuals within it. To speak of the importance — and danger — of online profiling seems almost to be taken for granted today, but that was not at all the case just a few years ago.

But what has all this to do with the presumed democratization of fashion? A great deal, in reality. When the social media appeared on the horizon, after blogs and YouTube had been the first to open the doors of fashion to a new generation of consumers, commentators, or simple enthusiasts, an entire system was brought into question. The central role played by the Internet, and thus by social media, and the consequent loss of cultural relevance on the part of traditional media, and in particular the specialist journals, which in the past had set the pace of the sector, changed not only the makeup of the front rows at the catwalks and even the ways in which a fashion show is put together and experienced, but also the people in charge and on the staff of the style and communication departments of the big brands and their marketing strategies. Since 2010 we have seen what could be described as one of the greatest efforts to redefine itself that fashion has ever made. An effort that, to be sure, is only natural, given that fashion has always been for everyone: in these years we have seen the processes of the setting and interpretation of trends, which had hitherto been strictly limited, spread out and involve many more people than in the past. The most glaring example is undoubtedly the way streetwear has caught on (it suffices to think of the long success that sneakers have enjoyed, something that was foreshadowed by the tracksuit and the T-shirt, already legitimized in the 1990s by the casualwear movement and the influence of hip-hop). It has emerged from its restricted niche to become a new category of clothing, subverting traditional business models by introducing the drop (the release of special collections outside the usual seasonal schedules), sanctioning collaborations between brands, and redefining, finally, the role of creative directors, who no longer utilize clothes alone to shape their universe of meaning around the label. The loss of centrality of clothing has in fact gone hand in hand with the rise of the personal brand, another product of the 2010s, which has contributed to altering the profile of those who end up guiding a fashion label today. Alongside such star designers as John Galliano, we have designers everywhere: especially in the social media. These processes, however, have not just been about boundary-spanning creatives like Virgil Abloh, Demna Gvasalia, and Alessandro Michele, but have also involved a host of "self-entrepreneurs" who throng digital spaces today.

Abloh, Gvasalia (who for some years now has dropped his surname and calls himself just Demna), and Michele

1 See Vikram Alexei Kansara, "Cambridge Analytica Weaponised Fashion Brands to Elect Trump, Says Christopher Wylie," *Business of Fashion*, November 29, 2018, https://www.businessoffashion.com/articles/news-analysis/cambridge-analytica-weaponised-fashion-brands-to-elect-trump-says-christopher-wylie/.

should certainly be considered the spearhead of a new generation of creative directors, of authors, who have re-written the rules of fashion, taking up the multiple cues — of a cultural, social, economic, or identity-based character — provided by the global society to which fashion wishes to speak today and incorporating them into their own visions. It has not been a straightforward process, but an incredibly uneven one, involving a series of shots in the dark, experiments, glaring mistakes, and misunderstandings due to the virulent and simplistic nature of the social media, but none-theless extremely interesting in its rapid advance. A process that has ended up affecting the way in which the big fashion brands look at their history and their archives, which in these years have come to life, as much in the continual reposts on Tumblr, Pinterest, Instagram, and more recent-ly TikTok as in the cultural operations in which they have played a leading part. To his first show as creative director of Louis Vuitton, in June 2018, Virgil Abloh (whose life came to a tragic end at the age of just forty-one in November 2021, carried off by a rare form of cancer) invited a thousand students from Parisian fashion schools, giving each of them a T-shirt that was at one and the same time a reminder, for him as well as for others, of the point of departure and that of arrival. Abloh was the first person of African-American origin to head a French fashion house and the first to come from a creative scene, the one that starting out from Chicago has defined the story of some of the most important and divi-sive musical figures of our time — yes, we're talking about Kanye West, who now calls himself Ye — and their growing influence on pop culture. In it there were music, clothes, the performing arts, a personality cult, and above all the idea of community, something that would profoundly change the dynamics of the fashion system. Inviting the students was a symbolic gesture, all the more so for Abloh, who found the title of fashion designer a tight fit (to start with, he had a de-gree in civil engineering and a master's in architecture) and had always preferred to describe himself as a creative with a multidisciplinary approach.[2] This is a trait shared with both Demna and Michele, who in those years were redefining the aesthetic worlds of Balenciaga and Gucci respectively.

Although very different from one another, what is evident in these projects is the attempt to tackle the grand themes of the present day in an unconventional manner (climate change and war for Demna, for instance, fluid identity and freedom of expression for Michele), where fashion in itself, understood as clothing alone, has become in a way second-

2   See Silvia Schirinzi and Giorgio Di Salvo, "Un'ora con Virgil Abloh," *Rivista Studio*, February 15, 2018, https://www.rivistastudio.com/virgil-abloh-workshop/.

ary to the construction of multiple signs and meanings able to reflect the stimuli and food for thought that the creative director wishes to incorporate into his work and then offer back to society. In this way, in the seminal work of these cre-atives, but not of them alone, a special relationship has been established on the one hand with the past and the need to be remembered, and on the other with the present, whose pressing issues continue to invade the spaces of fashion. Thus the latter has begun to talk about cultural appropria-tion, redefining the relationship between legitimate inspira-tion and copying, openly raising questions about the ethics of the supply chain, challenging the Eurocentric model of beauty that it has long championed, and, not least, looking with different eyes at its own history, indeed at the *histories* that have shaped its myth. All these impulses have often been bolstered by the disruptive force of the social media, which, before turning into the machines of programmed indignation they are today, truly brought about a rupture of a kind never known before. Not so much, as one might be tempted to think, by way of the possibility of commenting in real time on a show or on any kind of content published by a brand, as for the endless reproducibility that they permitted. A sounding board of almost infinite power that would pose, as we can see clearly today, a series of problems: it is no coincidence that in 2024 there is talk of a culture flattened, i.e. standardized by algorithms, to paraphrase the title of the excellent book *Filterworld: How Algorithms Flattened Culture*, recently published by the journalist of the *New Yorker* Kyle Chayka, also the author of an article that went viral in October 2023 with the self-explanatory title "Why the Internet Isn't Fun Anymore."[3]

On the other hand, when discussing the culture of the 2010s in all its ramifications, we cannot avoid the question of nostalgia. The perennial return of the past, in the eyes of many, is proof that the visual arts, and consequently the society that produces them, are caught in a sort of impasse, incapable of creating new imagery that is not rooted in something we have already seen. In the movies the superhero franchises, with their universes expressly constructed

3   Kyle Chayka, *Filterworld: How Algorithms Flattened Culture* (New York: Doubleday, 2024); Chayka, "Why the Internet Isn't Fun Anymore," *New Yorker*, October 9, 2023, https://www.newyorker.com/culture/infinite-scroll/why-the-internet-isnt-fun-anymore.

Eliza Douglas in *Faust* by Anne Imhof, German Pavilion, 57th International Art Exhibition, La Biennale di Venezia, Venice, 2017. Photos Nadine Fraczkowski. © Anne Imhof. Courtesy the artist, Sprüth Magers, and Galerie Buchholz.

in episodes in order to keep the money rolling in for as long as possible, are all the rage. As are reboots, i.e. remakes of films and TV series that have already had their moment of glory, in the absence of new ideas. Music is sounding more and more the same and, while still under the enduring cultural influence of hip-hop, seems to have now gelled — or flattened, to use the same expression as before — around a digestible and stereotyped formula, with songs that among other things are growing ever shorter. In the meantime our lives have moved progressively into the social media, where we have created alter egos and above all contributed to the endless repetition of images, sounds, and sentiments that have nothing in common except the fact they share a hashtag. In 2021, the critic Dean Kissick wrote in *Spike* that "lately artworks have begun to look more like memes, while memes have begun to look more like artworks. The memes look nicer, and offer more hope."[4] An ironic reflection on the extreme simplification of much of the more popular sort of contemporary art, which has overstepped the boundaries of galleries and the narrow market of traditional collectors to establish itself as a new point of reference, and often the only one, for the globalized taste of which we spoke at the beginning of this essay. Fashion too is prone to nostalgia, an

4   Dean Kissick, "Popular Things," *Spike*, March 10, 2021, https://www.spikeartmagazine.com/articles/the-downward-spiral-popular-things.

attachment that has often been reproached not only by the critics but also by the public, which in the social media ends up mercilessly juxtaposing images of the past with those of the present (more often than not in an arbitrary manner). And yet, if everything is *so* steeped in nostalgia, what does this tell us about the age we are living in? Why at the most technologically advanced moment in human history do we continue to look back? What are we seeking? What is fashion saying about itself when it reopens the doors of archives that have long only been accessible to insiders? Who is it trying to reach when it entrusts pieces of its history to new minds, new hands, new means?

In its continual attempt to establish a reputation and leave a mark through its elusive and deliberately ephemeral nature, two characteristics that, while closely linked, move in opposite directions, fashion has found in the fragmentation triggered by the Internet at once a stimulus — to its creativity — and a challenge — to its very survival. In years in which it is so easy to be cancelled or still worse to flop (in the sense the word has on the internet of "being ignored"), to make itself memorable fashion has become a multitude, immersing itself, multiplying, incorporating, and dispersing too, with a voracity that is at times obtuse but nonetheless astounding. It is precisely the relationship with time that is the linchpin around which all these new visions are shaped. This is as true for the big brands, which follow the commercial logic of the conglomerates of luxury and increasingly often end up by highlighting their idiosyncrasies and contradictions, as in the smaller ones, where more and more often designers are choosing antiestablishment narrations, stressing their ties with specific communities and setting about the extremely difficult task of making themselves visible in a world overflowing with images. In this determination — and need — to be in the time in which one lives lies perhaps the most romantic of the impulses that drive con-

temporary fashion. Here its touch can be beneficial, almost lifesaving, in turning the spotlight on a place, a craft technique, a culture, and at the same time predatory, in its appropriation of the new only to move on at once to the next challenge. Despite its many shadowy areas, it would be too facile to ascribe all the moves that fashion has made and is making in these difficult and intense years to mere nostalgia, as in fact it always succeeds in inducing short circuits and frictions that make us think: about fashion itself and the time it sets out to represent, about its desire for immortality in an age in which everything changes fast and new skepticisms emerge daily. It is true that fashion follows the algorithm, but so do we: and it is fashion's job to speak of us, even when we don't have time to listen.

Sylvie Fleury, *Insolence*, 2007, shopping bags with content, mixed media, 42.5 × 113 × 90 cm (dimensions variable). Photo Ingo Kniest. © Sylvie Fleury. Courtesy the artist and Sprüth Magers.

The model Eliza Douglas, dressed in a metallic suit of armor, climbs a crag and plants her sword in the ground, speeding up the flow of time. The shot moves past the figure and pans over the rocky landscape, before closing in on the sun, whose luminous disk turns into a pulsating interface that invites the player to breathe. These are the concluding scenes of *Afterworld: The Age of Tomorrow*, a video game launched by Balenciaga on December 6, 2020, to present its Fall/Winter collection 2021–22.[1] The game was set ten years in the future, in 2031, partly in a city in which messages could be read on material and digital billboards that suggested the planet was suffering the profound consequences of climate change. *Afterworld* is set in five "zones," the first of which is the interior of a Balenciaga store, a nonplace that could be located anywhere. The player follows a route through settings and scenery with unreal atmospheres. On a rainy street in Zone 2, a bus approaches the shelter of a stop, under which there is a young man wearing a pair of torn jeans through which metal shin guards can be glimpsed: the model takes his hands out of his pockets and turns them toward himself, when they start to emit flames, while the autobus moves on, hovering above the road and twisting around. At a rave in the middle of a forest in Zone 4, models and luminous figures dance, illuminated by stroboscopic lights. In each of these settings, fifty virtually recreated male and female models wear the clothes designed for Balenciaga by its creative director Demna. Accessible on any device, the video game, as well as serving as a substitute for the fashion show, allowed the player to interact in person not only with the French brand's products, but also with its protagonists and imagery.

Virtual Bodies, Digital Clothes, Synthetic Worlds
Dylan Colussi

Hans Ulrich Obrist, who in 2022 curated the exhibition *Worldbuilding: Gaming and Art in the Digital Age* at the Julia Stoschek Collection in Düsseldorf, has explained that video games are the biggest mass phenomenon of our time, with an impact similar to that of movies in the twentieth century and novels in the nineteenth.[2] Video games have provided the fashion system with a field in which to explore relations with new bodies, landscapes, and forms of narration. The impulse to explore the digital dimension came in 2020 with the Covid-19 pandemic, which induced the fashion industry to seek new channels to connect with the public. More in general, over the last ten years fashion has been involved in the changes that have made digital technologies, and the devices through which we access them, an integral part of contemporary phenomena, articulating the modes in which we interact with the world. Fashion has been able to find and reveal unexpected ways of making use of these processes and influencing them, demonstrating its ability to assume new forms that allow it to insert itself into every aspect of our time. The digitizing of products, activities, and creators, the use of gaming as a means of communication, the exploration of the metaverse, and even the integration of artificial intelligence into creative processes define an unprecedented relationship between the fashion system and the way that it responds to the contemporary world, blurring the confines of the material and the immaterial and making room for new spaces of imagination.

Nicolas Ghesquière, creative director of Louis Vuitton's women's collections since 2013, became involved in this interaction in 2016 when he chose to use Lightning, the protagonist of some chapters in the *Final Fantasy* saga of video games,[3] in the *Louis Vuitton Series 4* advertising campaign. In the campaign, realized in collaboration with the game

1   The project was carried out with the support of the Streamline Media Group, which oversaw the development of the game, and Dimension Studio, which digitized the human figures, with creative input from Substance & Inhalt. The in-game cinematic sequences were produced and animated by Builders Club.

2   Hans Ulrich Obrist, "Introduction," in *Worldbuilding: Gaming and Art in the Digital Age*, booklet of the exhibition at the Julia Stoschek Collection, Düsseldorf, June 5, 2022–February 4, 2024, https://www.jsfoundation.art/wp-content/uploads/2022/05/WORLDBUILDING_Booklet.pdf. The exhibition looked at the forms in which artists utilize the language of video games in their works.

3   This popular series has been developed by Square (now Square Enix) since 1987.

A scene from one of the cinematic sequences produced by Builders Club for the video game *Afterworld: The Age of Tomorrow*, released by Balenciaga to present its Fall/Winter collection 2021–22.

LIGHTNING
SERIES 4
A curated series of artwork by:
JUERGEN TELLER, BRUCE WEBER,
LIGHTNING by TETSUYA NOMURA & VW of SQUARE ENIX

Sold exclusively in Louis Vuitton stores. 866-VUITTON louisvuitton.com

LOUIS VUITTON

4   See Tim Blanks, "Past, Present and Future Fuse at Louis Vuitton," *Business of Fashion*, October 8, 2015, https://www.businessoffashion.com/reviews/fashion-week/past-present-and-future-fuse-at-louis-vuitton/.

5   The character appeared in images made by Core Design, developer of the video game in 1996, that were used to illustrate Miranda Sawyer's article "The Bit Girl" and the cover of the issue.

6   See Nick Remsen, "Riccardo Tisci Gives Japan's Biggest Virtual Virtuoso an Haute Couture Makeover," *Vogue*, May 2, 2016, https://www.vogue.com/article/riccardo-tisci-hatsune-miku-haute-couture-makeover-avatar. Hatsune Miku, created in 2007 by Crypton Future Media as a voice bank for the Vocaloid synthesizer software, has subsequently appeared on several platforms, in games, and in manga.

artist and designer Tetsuya Nomura and the Square Enix production company, the virtual character, with her distinctive pink hair, moves against a white background and reproduces the style of combat and spectacular poses that she assumes in the game while wearing some items of clothing and accessories from the Spring/Summer collection 2016. The character had been picked by Louis Vuitton's team because she was in line with the collection's atmosphere, inspired by, among other things, Wong Kar-Wai's movie *2046* and the *Neon Genesis Evangelion* anime series.[4] Lightning had already been used as a model, along with other characters from the *Final Fantasy* series, in a feature produced for issue no. 37 of the magazine *Arena Homme +*, wearing some looks from the Prada Spring/Summer collection 2012. A similar experiment had been made in 1997 in the British magazine *The Face*, when Lara Croft, protagonist of the *Tomb Raider* series of video games, had worn some outfits from recent Jean Colonna, Gucci, and Alexander McQueen collections.[5]

In 2016, in contrast, the hologram character Hatsune Miku was photographed in Givenchy's *real* atelier with its then creative director Riccardo Tisci, wearing a dress from the house's latest haute couture collection.[6] Like her, Noonoouri, Lil Miquela, and Rozy, models and influencers created by CGI (computer-generated imagery), interact IRL (in real life), sharing their imaginary lives on social media platforms, where they have millions of followers. The possibility of making real bodies virtual and immersing them in situations that go beyond reality has instead been explored by many designers, who have found another way of giving

Lightning, the protagonist of some chapters in the *Final Fantasy* series of video games, wears an outfit from the Spring/Summer 2016 collection for the *Louis Vuitton Series 4* photo campaign. Lightning by Tetsuya Nomura and visual works of Square Enix.

form to their imagination, getting their work to coexist with the ambiences and themes that have inspired it. This is what happened for example in the immersive digital experience WEARWEARE, created by Marni to present its Spring/Summer collection 2022.[7] Real male and female models were turned into the virtual inhabitants of the psychedelic world imagined by Francesco Risso, made up of iridescent hills and pearly subterranean lakes, where the bodies of the models were contorted along with the striped patterns of their clothes. The multimedia artist Frederik Heyman has taken the same free approach to the use and modification of replicated bodies, scanning the models in three dimensions so as to be able to alter them digitally. Heyman collaborated with the designer Glenn Martens on the creation of the advertising campaign for Y/Project's Spring/Summer collection 2019, in which human figures were piled up to construct sculptures of living flesh, or taken apart and given the connotations of cyborgs. As the literary critic Antonio Caronia wrote in his essay *Il corpo virtuale*, the possibility of inhabiting virtual worlds and taking on an appearance different from our usual one brings into play the primary means of our relationship with the world, the body, which is duplicated, multiplied, and acquires unlimited possibilities for disguise.[8] A particular perspective was presented by the American designer Hillary Taymour, founder of the Collina Strada brand, who in 2020 created the video game *Collina Land*, working with the Capture It in 3D company to recreate in three dimensions her friends and models wearing the Pre-Fall collection 2021.[9] In the video game, the twelve avatars, including that of the transgender and physically disabled model Aaron Rose Philip, complicate questions of representation, for in this imaginary domain the biases of the real world are replicated. The designer's choices led to an identification of the virtual as a realm in which to deal with the wide range of human bodies and identities.

While bodies become virtual in order to inhabit alternative realities, it can be asked whether clothes must necessarily possess a material form to be considered real. In recent years designers and creatives have come up with garments that only exist in digital form: the first solely digital item of clothing, called *Iridescence* and made by the Dutch studio The Fabricant to a design by its creative director Amber

7   Marni worked with the Future Corp creative studio and the metaverse platform AnamXR.

8   Antonio Caronia, *Il corpo virtuale: Dal corpo robotizzato al corpo disseminato nelle reti*, 2nd ed. (Brescia: Krisis, 2022), 28.

9   *Collina Land* was presented at GucciFest, the film and fashion festival organized by Gucci and held from November 16 to 22, 2020.

10   JW Anderson's cardigan had already become famous for having been worn by Harry Styles during rehearsals for his concert for the *Today Show* in 2021, giving rise on TikTok to the so-called #HarryStylesCardigan challenge between users who tried to reproduce it, to the point where the designer ended up sharing the instructions for making it (https://www.jwanderson.com/fr/cardigan-pattern).

Jae Slooten, was sold at auction in 2019. Worn by the model Johanna Jaskowska in an image made by Julien Boudet, it consists of a jumpsuit with drapery of a pearly transparency in front, which appears light because of the way it floats. The aim of The Fabricant, like that of other companies which have emerged in these years to produce, sell, or present the work of digital designers, is to propose solutions to problems faced by fashion houses linked to the sizes and wearability of clothes, to consumption, and to the waste of resources. Exploring the possibilities of the processes of digitization, in 2021 JW Anderson collaborated with xydrobe on the creation of NFTs of a patchwork cardigan presented in the Spring/Summer collection 2020.[10] It took over three hundred hours of work to model the object digitally, reproducing the yarn utilized to create the cardigan's many stitches in three dimensions. The project took the concept of digitizing

Model Aaron Rose Philip in the presentation video created by Collina Strada designer Hillary Taymour in collaboration with photographer Charlie Engman for the video game *Collina Land*. The video was presented as part of GucciFest, film and fashion festival promoted by Gucci in 2020. Video by Collina Strada.

fashion to an extreme, imitating not just the form of the garment but also the basic elements of which it was made and the techniques used to materially produce it.

All the experiences and operations that link fashion to digital worlds are being amplified and expanded by the introduction of artificial intelligence, which has established itself in this sector as a means of probing the boundaries between human design and that based on algorithms. The first experiments with these programs relied on a limited amount of data that was supplied to the AI to generate new images. In 2017, The Fabricant's *DEEP* collection experimented with an AI that utilized data and images taken from the collections presented during Paris Fashion Week to design new clothing that blended their characteristics. On one of the covers of issue zero of the magazine *Dazed Beauty*, published in February 2019, a photograph of the face of the model and businesswoman Kylie Jenner taken by Daniel Sannwald was submitted to the Beauty_GAN artificial intelligence system, which used the data from its analysis of seventeen thousand images downloaded from Instagram to rework Jenner's makeup and features to suit the resulting canons.[11]

Artificial intelligences like Google's Bard or OpenAI's ChatGPT and DALL-E, which draw on vast amounts of data and turn them into new materials and information, were put to work, in 2023, as an unprecedented tool for creators of fashion. Coperni's designers asked the DALL-E software, for example, to generate images of a robot and a lamb on the basis of Jean de la Fontaine's fable "The Wolf and the Lamb," which was the inspiration for the brand's Fall/Winter collection 2023–24, and then reproduced them on some of the garments.[12] The ability to create synthetic images in response to text prompts has also led to the emergence of a new category of creatives, the so-called AI artists, whose work, along with certain aspects of that of prompt designers, consists in formulating indications to guide the AI in its generation of original images. Together with the photographer Carlijn Jacobs and the stylist Imruh Asha, Chad Nelson produced the prompts used to create, with DALL-E, the surreal backdrops against which the model Bella Hadid posed for the feature "Ars Artificialis," published in the May 2023 issue of the Italian edition of *Vogue*. Marco De Vincenzo, creative director of Etro, has collaborated instead with the artist Silvia Badalotti to generate with an AI the images of the advertising campaign for *Nowhere: Out of Time, in Another Space*, its Spring/Summer collection 2024. The artist, in dialogue with De Vincenzo, has translated the creative director's vision into a series of scenes and pictures that combine the abstract references and imaginary worlds explored by De Vincenzo in his design of the collection. The dreamlike images mix up classical-style works of architecture, greenhouses, and still lifes composed of alien or naturalistic plants and animals, including male and female models — also generated by the AI — posing in the clothing of the collection, the only real elements in the scenes.

According to Francesco D'Abbraccio and Andrea Facchetti, AIs are a resource of fundamental value in interpreting the world and interacting with the vast amount of data architecture that fills it, occupying a key position in the contemporary

cultural ecosystem.[13] Given the way in which they appear able to analyze and interpret fashion and its codes, these tools also offer alternative prospects for the creation of new kinds of fashion image. Patric DiCaprio and Bryn Taubensee, founders of Vaquera, used AI to generate the clothing — covered with mud or made out of garbage bags — of some fake celebrities presented on the red carpet of the 2023 Met Gala. The photo of Pope Francis walking around in an oversized white puffer jacket, a version of the cassock that seems to belong to one of the collections of Moncler's Genius line, spread like wildfire online as soon as it was published in 2023. The photo was not real, nor was the pope wearing Moncler: it was a deepfake

11   Beauty_GAN is a project developed by the Selam X and ART404 design studios.
12   At the show of the collection the part of the wolf in the fable was played by canine robots from the American company Boston Dynamics.
13   Francesco D'Abbraccio and Andrea Facchetti, "Introduzione," in *AI & Conflicts*, ed. D'Abbraccio and Facchetti (Brescia: Krisis, 2021), 13.

created by a construction worker called Pablo Xavier with the Midjourney software, the same as the one that was used by somebody else to create a version of the characters in the series of Harry Potter movies in the style of Demna Gvasalia's Balenciaga. The rapid spread of these images through the Internet and its platforms stems as much from their absurdity as from their plausibility. Generated in milliseconds, they encapsulate the aesthetic and visual codes of fashion brands, events, places, and the personalities that inhabit them. These images, like many others that are produced and shared on a daily basis, are part of a new visual economy that is nurturing unprecedented forms of storytelling.

In his 1983 film *Sans soleil* Chris Marker says of the first video games that for one of their creators electronic objects are the only ones that can deal with sentiment, memory, and imagination. Moving between material and digital, real and imaginary, the processes explored by fashion through the digital medium are bolstering its forms of narration. Scrolling down a screen, in a field of possibilities that is constantly renewed, keeping pace with the advances in technology, the phenomena of fashion are being dematerialized in order to inhabit the realm of the virtual, clearing the way for solutions that challenge and redefine them and triggering processes that are becoming crucial to our understanding of the new landscapes in which fashion is designed and communicated.

An image from the advertising campaign for Etro's Spring/Summer 2024 collection *Nowhere: Out of Time, in Another Space*. The campaign was created with the aid of artificial intelligence by the artist Silvia Badalotti in collaboration with the house's creative director Marco De Vincenzo. Courtesy Etro.

When Charles Frederick Worth had the idea of inviting potential customers to his Paris salons to present his designs in the mid-nineteenth century, he had no idea that he was inventing one of the most important communication tools in what was to become a veritable fashion industry. The father of haute couture wanted to move beyond the role of artisan (or a simple service provider) to take on that of an inventor, one who not only made and sold clothes but also transformed the moment of presentation of his pieces into a memorable spectacle. Since then, the catwalk has become a language in itself, with its own grammar, inspiring the creative world beyond the confines of fashion. Federico Fellini famously ironized the ritualization of the catwalk in his 1972 film *Roma*, while theatre directors Jérôme Deschamps and Macha Makeïeff transformed the stage into a catwalk for their 1995 show *Vestiaire (et défilé)*. Now everyone seems to have their own catwalk show, including those who are not even involved in manufacturing fashionable clothes.

Certain questions regarding the fashion show still remain unanswered: what is its secret? How to account for its appeal? After all, it has been inspiring and attracting attention ever since the first clients of the fledgling milieu of haute couture watched Worth's designs almost religiously paraded around his Paris salons. And how does the catwalk still maintain this appeal despite competition from digital and the many attempts to replace it with virtual experiences?

The fashion show, that moment when the spotlight shines on the ephemeral, has consolidated itself over the course of its history as a communication and marketing tool. It sets the tone for the collection and the season, guides buyers,

Heterotopic Performance:
Atmosphere as Language in the Fashion Show
Silvano Mendes

and creates seasonality for accessory brands, whose sales of bags, shoes, and even cosmetics are all driven by the images presented on the catwalk and relayed by the press and digital influencers. But the success of this ritual does not depend solely on the collection presented. It also depends on the way the models embody the clothes, the staging of the presentation, and the narrative potential of the space in which the event takes place. Now filmed as much as photographed, fashion has become more than ever a matter of image.

In the 1960s, the theorist of mass media Marshall McLuhan already drew attention to the fact that clothing was beginning to be influenced by television and the way it appeared on screen.[1] From that time on, textures and sculptural shapes were favored because they facilitated the visual identification of products on screen. This phenomenon has only been reinforced by digital technology and social networks that rely on visuality to promote products. The more identifiable lines a garment has, the more it stands out visually on the screen. And brands are aware that, from this point of view, the fashion show experience is experienced both on site and via the mediation of mobile phones.

From the 2010s onwards, the catwalk setting has become an increasingly central motor in fashion communications, driven by the support of digital media for its dissemination. The example of the Jacquemus video made for the brand's Spring/Summer 2021 show, which took place in a wheat field, is highly emblematic in this respect. The event, both physical and digital as it was broadcast live on Instagram, made a huge impact online and was seen as a moment of reprieve from the ongoing Covid-19 pandemic. Even though the wheat field in the Parc naturel régional du Vexin français was a mere forty-five minutes from Paris, the feeling of escape from the oppressive context of urban life was deemed a success with a show that was streamed more than 2.5 million times on the brand's Instagram account alone, not counting the extracts broadcast separately and the images relayed by the press or by guests.

1 Marshall McLuhan, "Clothing: Our Extended Skin," chap. 12 in *Understanding Media: The Extensions of Man* (New York: McGraw-Hill, 1964).

Viral/Ephemeral

Simon Porte Jacquemus has become one of the most hyped designers of his generation in less than a decade. One of the reasons for his success is precisely his ability to stage fashion shows that mobilize the press and attract attention largely thanks to the choice of location and their "viral" potential for online mediation. The use of the viral metaphor is also relevant to discussions of fashion shows, ephemeral events par excellence, which are not intended to be reproduced but which, thanks to social media platforms, circulate freely between groups of individuals with

Jacquemus, *L'Amour*, prêt-à-porter Spring/Summer 2021 show, Parc naturel régional du Vexin français, July 2020. Courtesy Jacquemus.

an inherent logic of both contamination and mutation. Like a language, the fashion show is transformed, adapted, and resignified, with the reproduction of the catwalk ritual remodeled almost ad infinitum.

For the brands the stakes are high because the ritual of the catwalk show, depending as it is on scenography and staging, can echo far beyond the fashion industry and change the status of a label. This was the case with Coperni's Spring/Summer 2023 collection, for which the creative directors Sébastien Meyer and Arnaud Vaillant, in partnership with the designer Manel Torres, created a spray-on fabric dress directly on the body of model Bella Hadid. Although the image quite clearly brings to mind through its self-conscious pastiche Alexander McQueen's celebrated Spring/Summer 1999 show, for which Shalom Harlow's dress was spray-painted by robots, with the quantitative power of video dissemination on social media, Coperni's spray-on fabric dress has achieved the status of artistic performance with both media and economic impact. In the two days following the show, according to Launchmetrics, the Media Impact Value (MIV) of the event was measured at over $25 million.

Beyond its purely commercial dimension, the contemporary fashion show has become a communications tool with several different functions: it can, for example, be a symbol of soft power for certain brands, like those organized by Fendi on the Great Wall of China in 2007 or in front of the Trevi Fountain in Rome in 2016; by Louis Vuitton on the Pont Neuf in Paris in 2023; or by Moncler to celebrate the brand's seventieth anniversary in the Piazza del Duomo in Milan in

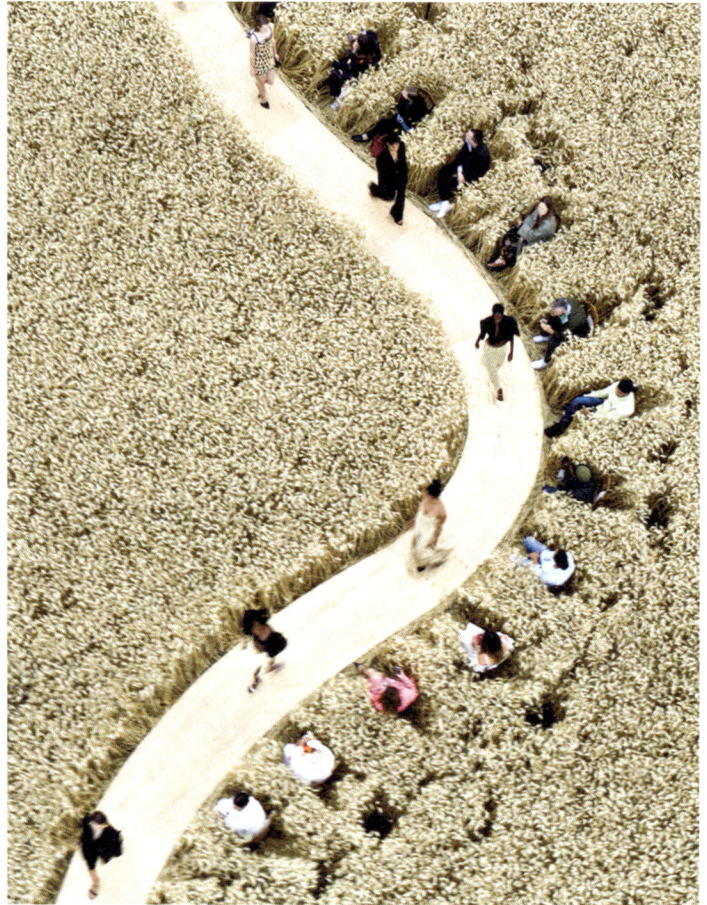

2022. However, it can also be an emblem for reaffirming the brand's identity either by highlighting the real places that embody the brand (such as the Balenciaga show in the form of a video in front of the company's historic building in Paris for the Spring/Summer 2024 collection) or by completely reconstructing these places.

For its return to haute couture with the Fall/Winter 2021-22 collection Balenciaga recreated from scratch the mid-century salons of the era of the house's founder. In this creative reconstruction of the past, the show was staged without music in a space that had been renovated and artificially aged to reinforce the immersive sensation in the history of haute couture. For these shows, flashback, irony,

Jacquemus, *L'Amour*, prêt-à-porter Spring/Summer 2021 show, Parc naturel régional du Vexin français, July 2020. Courtesy Jacquemus.

and pastiche are blended together in a postmodern way in a form of exhibition that oscillates between a place of memory and a reproducible set, in which the real and the fake are purposefully confused in the name of the spectacle.

Reappropriating spaces
In all these examples, the choice of location and set design have become almost indispensable elements in the fashion show narrative in order to attract the attention of the press and social media. The catwalk space is given symbolic meaning through its staging of the theatrical event and its visualization of narrative; it can also raise questions and highlight issues that go beyond the commercial dimension of the industry. When Martin Margiela chose to show his Spring/Summer 1990 collection in a wasteland in a working-class district of Paris, he was looking for a way to attract the attention of the press in an alternative way and with little financial means to do so. But he was also addressing issues linked to the deconstruction of the very idea of fashion, where it should exist and how it should be articulated. With the heterotopic manner in which his designs were visualized, by appropriating other spaces that are not utopian but more a kind of physical localization of utopia, the brand created concrete spaces that house the imagination, as Michel Foucault put it.[2] This technique is also reminiscent of the work of Katharine Hamnett, who presented a collection in 1984 in a West London car park, or that of Issey Miyake, who took over a Paris metro station in 1989 in the form of adaptive reuse of space.

In their wake, a number of contemporary designers have reappropriated spaces thereby establishing a dialogue between the narratives of space and the construction of fashion,

2   Michel Foucault, "Les hétérotopies," in *Le corps utopique, suivi de Les hétérotopies* (Fécamp: Lignes, 2009).

between artistic performance and fashion communications. Regardless of their market positioning, most brands now re-appropriate space for their shows: from Demna Gvasalia's for Vetements at a McDonald's (Spring/Summer 2020) to Dries Van Noten's in a dilapidated Paris building (Spring/Summer 2024), to Marine Serre's in a cellar on the outskirts of Paris (Fall/Winter 2019–20), or Sabato De Sarno's third show for Gucci in a warehouse that had formerly housed a foundry on the outskirts of Milan (Fall/Winter 2024–25); all of these shows stage the symbolic meanings and values of fashion brands through their interpretation and manipulation of space.

Fashion is a practice and an industry in which shaping the style and allure of tomorrow is often a mix of looking to the future and drawing inspiration from the past, as a "tiger's

Jacquemus, *Le Coup de Soleil*, prêt-à-porter Spring/Summer 2020 show, Valensole, France, June 2019. Courtesy Jacquemus.

leap into the past," based on constant recycling and reinterpreting aesthetic influences, as Walter Benjamin put it.[3] Like Saint Laurent in 1971 with his *Libération* collection, in which he drew inspiration from Nazi-occupied Paris of the 1940s, which met with a largely hostile reaction but had the merit of calling into question the canons of good taste and the way in which the past can be aesthetically resignified. The same phenomenon of recycling and drawing inspiration from the past is present in the practice of the fashion show, notably through the techniques of reappropriating space. In their own way, today's brands and designers follow the footsteps of the avant-garde artists of the second half of the twentieth century, who took over disused buildings, warehouses, and other unusual places, including Allan Kaprow or Claes Oldenburg, who took advantage of the "margin of freedom that these places offered to invent forms of performance with different configurations and temporalities."[4] While for Kaprow and Oldenburg these happenings and performances often attempted to penetrate the audience's own sense of reality, in the case of fashion shows, the desire to get closer to reality is not the main objective. Through their choice of setting and staging, or even through spaces created entirely from scratch, some brands seek to create the illusion of and the felling of perfection, in what might also be perceived of as a type of heterotopia.

One of the most striking examples is that of Louis Vuitton, a brand accustomed to using the courtyard of the Louvre Museum in Paris for its shows, which, for its Fall/Winter 2019–20 collection, decided to reproduce the façade of the Centre Pompidou within the same space. In this exercise in *mise en abyme* — of a museum within a museum — Vuitton staged a heterotopia as much through the illusory dimension of the image as through the perfection of the construction. In this sense, the presentations in spaces that have been reappropriated, reconfigured, or built from scratch have impact through a dimension that is sometimes intended to be radically disjunctive but which in reality often has its roots in the artistic practices of the past that are commercially reconfigured for the purposes of marketing and communications.

Through these commercial projects, which consist of fashion brands creating their own "world" for the duration of a show, brands adopt an artistic posture. By building worlds around the catwalk for a show, whether by reappropriating or constructing a space from scratch, the brands therefore elevate the mere product, transforming the garment from a simple good into an alluring image through the considerable investment in theatrical display and artistic performance.

At the same time, by creating or reinforcing their own legitimacy fashion designers are thereby "transformed" into artists with the catwalk as the ideal space for a hybrid artistic practice that mixes creative disciplines. Rick Owens, for example, shook up the codes of the runway by bringing a troupe of American step dancers on stage for his Spring/Summer 2014 show; Dior transformed the works of visual artist Joana Vasconcelos into the backdrop for the presentation of a collection (ready-to-wear Fall/Winter 2023–24); and Jacquemus had its models walk around a display of works by Giacometti (ready-to-wear Spring/Summer 2024) at the Maeght Foundation in Saint-Paul de Vence, in a process of *artification* of the catwalk that drew on other artistic practices to create its own commodified form of art.

3   Walter Benjamin, "Theses on the Philosophy of History," in *Illuminations: Essays and Reflections* (New York: Schocken, 1969), 261.

4   Marie-Noëlle Semet-Haviaras, *Les plasticiens au défi de la scène (2000–2015)* (Paris: L'Harmattan, 2017), 211.

In spatial terms, the catwalk could therefore be defined as a site-specific practice that articulates through its codified nature and repeated display mode the inherent performativity of the fashion industry. Here, I am referring less to J. L. Austin's famous definition of performativity applied to the philosophy of language[5] but more to Richard Schechner's spectacular understanding of the term, according to which the inherent performance is visualized.[6] Because if fashion is said to perform at the same time as it makes legible the very act of performing—to put things in more explicitly Butlerian terms[7]—, at the moment of the catwalk presentation (at least the more artistically elaborate shows) the clothes at times perform as works of art. This iteration of artistic performance enables the fashion brands to perform their role as cultural brokers by disguising their function to make us forget, albeit momentarily, their commercial activity.

Creating Atmosphere
Despite their multifarious differences in setting, scale, and tone, what most contemporary fashion shows have in common is the desire to create an *atmosphere*, a nebulous concept that is difficult to define and goes far beyond the

5   J. L. Austin, *How to Do Things with Words*, 2nd ed. (Oxford: Clarendon Press, 1975).

6   Richard Schechner, *Performance Theory*, new ed. (New York: Routledge, 2003).

7   Judith Butler, "Performative Agency," in "Performativity, Economics and Politics," special issue, *Journal of Cultural Economy* 3, no. 2 (2010): 147–61, https://doi.org/10.1080/17530 350.2010.494117.

8   Gernot Böhme, "Les atmosphères comme objet de l'architecture," in "Atmosphères: Philosophie, esthétique, architecture," ed. Mildred Galland-Szymkowiak and Mickaël Labbé, special issue, *Les cahiers philosophiques de Strasbourg*, no. 46 (2019): 169–94, https://doi.org/10.4000/cps.3435.

9   Gernot Böhme, "L'atmosphère, fondement d'une nouvelle esthétique?," in "Exercices d'ambiances," ed. Maxime Le Calvé and Olivier Gaudin, special issue, *Communications* 102, no. 1 (2018): 26, https://doi.org/10.3917/ commu.102.0025.

exercise of describing or analyzing the content of a fashion show. An atmosphere is not necessarily physical or tangible even if it is always subject related and linked to a physical presence, as the German philosopher Gernot Böhme put it.[8] The very perception of an atmosphere is entirely subjective because it is above all something that affects us emotionally and not just sensorially, even though being exposed to it also implies a kind of immersion.

In the case of the catwalk, this atmosphere is traditionally experienced only by those who are present and apart from the halt to proceedings during the Covid-19 pandemic when some brands organized catwalks without an audience, the human presence is often one of the components that makes the magic happen. The spatiality of atmosphere as a phenomenon is more potent and easier to produce in the actual physical spaces in which it occurs and according to its capacity to produce a sensory or affective impact. Like few other practices, the fashion show is part of this quest for impact through the use of atmospheric elements that audiences experience.

For the presentation of the Hermès Fall/Winter 2024-25 women's collection, the house produced artificial rain during its show, staged inside the Garde Républicaine barracks in Paris: a scenic effect that was commented on by the press and was clearly set up as an atmospheric element in the tonality of the set design. In fact, when the house presented the show on its website, a text entitled "The Atmosphere" used the rain as a key element in the show's narrative construction: "In the late afternoon light, the rays reflect off the wet ground and trace the trajectory of the silhouettes. Slowly, the senses are awakened by the sound of rain," read the commentary to the show.

Böhme argued that atmospheres fill space with their affective tones, a bit like how fog alters our sensory perception of landscape.[9] From this perspective, few contemporary fashion shows have been able to embody this idea of atmosphere as vividly as John Galliano's memorable show for Maison Margiela's Spring/Summer 2024 couture collection. An atmosphere created by the setting at the elaborate Alexandre III bridge in Paris, by the partial darkness of the room, by the light of the first full moon of the year that illuminated a part of the presentation, by the inspiration drawn from Brassaï's work, and by the models' sometimes hesitant gait and exaggerated poses, choreographed by former model-turned-movement director Pat Boguslawski. These were all elements that "revealed the invisible," as the house described it, creating an impact at once visual and sensorial for those present (in situ and online). There was also a use of images filmed before the show, which added to the impact of the staging, images that were edited and broadcast by the brand's communication channels as well as by the guests, in a mediated multiplication of image so typical of our digital age.

The main challenge of the fashion show as a contemporary practice consists precisely in juggling between these two expectations: creating atmospheres that "fill the space like a fog,"[10] but whose media and viral potential also makes this "fog" attractive on a mobile phone screen.

As Böhme commented, by experiencing an atmosphere, the self dissolves, escapes, and itself becomes indeterminate.[11] Through the use of atmospheric elements, while the self that constitutes the audience member of a fashion show might not dissolve exactly, its role has certainly changed because it is no longer present in the room simply as a client attending the presentation or an industry professional analyzing a collection, but rather as an expectant spectator attending a show that is immediately spreadable online but also more importantly potentially memorable.

10   Böhme, "L'atmosphère," 26.
11   Gernot Böhme, *Aisthétique. Pour une esthétique de l'expérience sensible* (Dijon: Les presses du réel, 2020).

Turtles and Flying Dragons

I get to New York in the middle of the night and I have to wait in the lobby. My host, all the way up on the twenty-ninth floor, is asleep. The woman at the desk is unable to wake him in order to confirm that I am, in fact, his guest. She tries him again and again on the intercom, which hums like an empty stomach between the long sighs of relief exhaled by sleepless elevators. Lost in this labyrinth of intersecting expectations, leaning on the telescopic handle of my carry-on bag, I pull my phone out of the soft pajama pants that I wear when I travel. Shall I call him myself? Shall I text? Shall I just wait? In any event, the inconvenience that I have already caused embarrasses me. Unable to make up my mind, I open Instagram. The first image that pops on my timeline—as it often happens when I don't get much sleep and everything feels like an omen—suddenly turns the screen into a looking glass. Gazing at me from the other side of that mirror is a man with very short hair, slouching, his shoulders slumped as if he were as tired and pensive as I am right now. I say that he is gazing at me, but he's really looking at something behind me, and perhaps he's not even looking at that: his eyes are just resting somewhere, like my forearm on the handle of the trolley. This man is fully wrapped in a magnificent, majestic, monochrome coat. Indeed, on close examination, the subject of the image is undoubtedly the coat itself: it is the coat that actively wraps the man, who in turn wraps himself in a hug.

At last, the intercom comes to life and, sleepy Narcissus that I am, I don't have time to realize that what I have been staring at is Sabato De Sarno's latest post.[1] Only a week from now, when I will set out to write these lines, I will track down

and clutch at nothing, and embrace the world.
One imprisons me, who neither frees nor jails me
Petrarch, *Rerum vulgarium fragmenta*, 134

Coating Men: Hugs and Prisons
Alessandro Giammei

that post, and I will find out that it expands to a little gallery: images of hugs between men, skin to skin, alternating with images of men crossing their arms while wrapped in the coats that De Sarno designed for them—"for me," is what I will actually think, but I'm going to need a few pages to explain why. The caption says: "It wrapped me tight, it felt like home. / Gucci Men, first chapter." I don't know if the Instagram post of a creative director can be considered an advertising campaign. However, to me, this one looks like a manifesto, a theory even. Encountered by chance in the lobby of a 1960s skyscraper in the Greenwich Village, the image of the coat (hugging the man, who hugs himself) triggers synapses in my own personal memory and in the broad-

er, deeper memory, collective and subconscious, that I have been investigating all my life as an Italianist and a bookworm. It says something about me, a millennial man from Roma Sud, and about the idea of man that textual and iconographic codes have composed, for centuries, in the mind of anyone who inhabits Western culture. It reminds me of a man (the man that I have been, and still am) and of "Man" tout court. That is why I place it here, at the beginning of this brief spelunking in the memory cave (my memory and our memory) of which it has revealed to me the depths.

In the following pages I would like to articulate the theory of masculine attire that Sabato De Sarno's wrapping coats suggested to me by animating a wave of transhistorical echoes. The image that I am starting from is one of the earliest consequences of the staggering change of paradigm that Gucci has recently imparted to its brand of menswear—from the strapped, pinstriped pants of Alessandro Michele's late poetics, flaunted in the Baroque maximalism of an archeologically euphoric Rome, to the fully wrapped, sulking young men of Milanese charm that embody the brand's new direction,

Post

sabatods ✔
Milan, Italy

♡ 6,753   💬 189   ✈

🔖

Liked by **avannetti** and **others**
sabatods It wrapped me tight, it felt like home. Gucci Men, first chapter. ❤️

View all comments

June 11

Sabato De Sarno, gallery posted on Instagram (@sabatods) on June 11, 2024. Gucci Fall/Winter 2024-25 men's advertising campaign (creative direction Sabato De Sarno, artistic direction Riccardo Zanola, photography David Sims, styling Alastair McKimm).

Post

sabatods ✔
Milan, Italy

7/8

all squeezed into the most elementary of structures: that of their own shoulders. Rather than a theory of clothing, it is a theory of covering, of coating: of the patina, the peel, the bark, the armor that fashion places, as a more or less permeable boundary, between a man and the world.

Debunked in biology and outdated in grammar, finally challenged in the structures of economy and society, the difference between "masculine" and "feminine" remains meaningful perhaps only in fashion (menswear vs womens-wear) — just like the difference between seasons (Spring/Summer, Fall/Winter) that, in the actual climate, bleed into one another or are even inverted. If any essential feature of masculinity is going to survive, it will be not *in*, but *on* bodies: in the things that we devise so that bodies can say something about themselves, can allude to a history. Whoever puts on the clothes in it, the masculine wardrobe (so easy to pene-trate for any gender, unlike the more exposed and treacher-ous, even exclusive, feminine wardrobe) alludes to a cultural history that is, I believe, founded on one imperative: to cover, to wrap, to coat. To protect, as De Sarno's caption suggests. But also to imprison, since any protective hug may eventually get dangerously claustrophobic — think of Daphne, renounc-ing her humanity as she fled from Apollo, think of the Tin Man of the *Wizard of Oz*, who aspires to a fallible biological heart while keeping an oil can close at hand.

Here is a summary, then, of the modest theory that I am going to articulate: coating/fashioning masculinity requires a constant negotiation between the two poles of maternal and paternal approaches to men: the hug[2] and the prison.[3] Clothing men is an ambition analogous to the one that, over

2   In the first pages of her crucial book on mascu-linity, bell hooks explains that the main test of manhood that the Patriarchy induces men to internalize is the willingness to accept, from puberty onward, a loss of what they see as "that feeling of being loved, of being embraced." This last keyword (although it is a hapax in the book) is the only physical metaphor that takes the place, in hooks's book, of the more general *love* of the title. bell hooks, *The Will to Change: Men, Masculinity, and Love* (New York: Atria Books, 2004), 15.

3   I take the liberty here, under Foucault's aegis, of stretching language by speaking of prison as gesture. In making use of this second key-word, *prison*, I am thinking in particular of a short but crucial essay on Gide by James Baldwin, written in 1954 and included in 1961 in his *Nobody Knows My Name*: James Baldwin, "The Male Prison," now in Baldwin, *Collected Essays* (New York: Library of America, 1998), 232–36. For a more recent interdisciplinary examination of the relationship between mas-culinity and the carceral system (and of mascu-linity as a prison in itself), see Don Sabo, Terry A. Kupers, and Willie London, eds., *Prison Masculinities* (Philadelphia: Temple University Press, 2001).

KACHUGA TERRAPIN, EMYS KACHUGA
From Dr Buchanan Hamiltons Drawings.
India.

4   See Ben Morgan and Steve Parker, *The Skeleton Book* (New York: DK, 2016), 47. I would like to thank Professor Daniel T. Grimes for his suggestion of this Darwinian parallel.

5   Alberto Savinio, "Bago," in *Great Italian Stories: Ten Parallel Texts* (London: Penguin, 2024), 10–23.

DRACO QUINQUE FASCIATA   FIVE BANDED DRAGON LIZARD

millions of years, the mindless intelligence of nature has cultivated by shaping the ribs of reptiles.[4] Extended beyond the limits of the torso along the genetic branches of the evolution of species, the ribs of our coldblooded cousins have provided their Darwinian artisan — evolution I mean, through the obtuse, incredibly slow creativity of natural selection — with a range of options. At one extreme, complete and perfect, we find the bony fortress of the carapace of turtles and tortoises: the peak of protection but also of dead weight, a constriction that extends the protective coating of what we call a "rib cage" to the whole of the body. At the other extreme there is the membranous hug of the webbed ribs of flying dragons: reptiles able to take hold of those coat tails, called patagia, and spread them out as if they were a pair of wings. And to take flight.

Is De Sarno's man, who enchanted and disquieted me in New York in the early summer of 2024, a turtle or a flying dragon?

Traps and Armors

In a wonderful short story by Alberto Savinio, "Bago," the young protagonist Ismene falls in love with her armoire.[5] The armoire, or wardrobe (which she calls Bago and speaks of with masculine pronouns), frees her from an undesirable but necessary marriage, and protects her from the world. This inanimate father and lover, favored over the human ones (one dead, the other elderly) who force Ismene to play the constrictive role of "mistress of the house," is a closet of which it's better not to come out. It (he?) is an archive, an arsenal of clothes of course, but also a fortress that Ismene can inhab-

John Edward Gray, red-crowned roofed turtle (Kachuga Terrapin; *Emys Kachuga*) and flying dragon (Five Banded Dragon Lizard; *Draco quinque-fasciata*), plates from Gray's book *Illustrations of Indian Zoology*, published in London in two volumes in 1830–35 (New York Public Library).

it. Bago is smaller than the house that contains it, but paradoxically less claustrophobic. It holds feminine clothes, sure, but it is not a feminine wardrobe: at a certain point, Ismene's elderly husband proposes to get "new furniture" that would be "more suitable for the bedroom of a young bride."[6] Ismene, of course, rejects such a feminization of her furniture and, in particular, of her beloved armor/armoire. Savinio tells us that, at the end of the surreal domestic quarrel, Ismene resolves to stop eating until she dies "on the armchair next to Bago's half-closed doors," leaving a note with her last wish: "I want to be locked inside the dark and good body of Bago too." Respecting this wish, the widower has Ismene placed inside the armoire, and the armoire lowered into the grave: "a tomb with double doors that was too big for such a small body. Like a father folding a daughter against his chest."[7]

The prison of a masculine wardrobe, like any jail, can disturbingly become a space of comfort: a bubble that keeps the grip of the space that contains it at a distance. But, like any embrace, such comfort can be final, impossible to escape, grave-like. Is it out of love, then, that anxious fathers shut their sons in closets—and that, therefore, the Patriarchy clasps men in a mortal embrace?[8] Ruggiero, a protagonist of chivalric romance (and an orphan, like Ismene), was raised, according to legend, by a particularly anxious foster father: the sorcerer Atlante. In the *Orlando innamorato* (II, XVI), Atlante conjures a magnificent garden on the top of Mount Carena—a peak in the Atlas Mountains, the mountain range of Mediterranean Africa after which the sorcerer is named. He lures the young hero to this garden in order to distract him from the war between Christians and Saracens in which he wants to fight. He encircles that garden, which in turn encircles Ruggiero, in an impenetrable transparent barrier: an enchanted glass coating that imprisons the young man under a dome, preventing him from fulfilling his destiny as a knight—and thus, at the same time, from dying in battle. In the *Orlando furioso* (XII) Atlante resorts to more sophisticated tricks, since the outer world, in the form of a tournament, has reached his secret garden, and his spell is broken. So he decides to build a castle, less hidden and more accessible, enchanting it with a spell of absolute enter-/de-tainment: anyone entering the building will find whatever they desire most in the universe, but that object of desire will forever flee from their pursuit. The magic works very well: Ruggiero, coming across the castle, remains voluntarily imprisoned in it, ceaselessly chasing the image of the woman he loves through its corridors. It works so well that the trick ends up interrupting all the tangled plots of the poem, as other protagonists find, and are caught in, the castle, deserting war and adventures in order to aimlessly pursue the unattainable objects of their desire. If it were not for a woman, Angelica, and her magic ring able to break the spell, Atlante's castle would have swallowed up all the armies and stories of the most gigantic chivalric poem of the Renaissance, safely confining them in an endless, lifeless loop.

One could object now that, as Ariosto himself often does, I am straying from the topic; that I am talking about furniture, gardening, and architecture instead of fashion. But the paternal snares that I have evoked so far help define the ambiguous patriarchal affect that, by detaining and entertaining the users of its wardrobe, informs the concept of men's fashion that I glimpsed in the image of the coat from which I started out: a fashion that responds to the same affect but makes

Parade armor of King Erik XIV of Sweden, 1564. Photo Helena Bonnevier and Jens Mohr, The Royal Armoury/SHM (CC BY).

it mobile, portable—indeed, wearable. If fathers lock their sons inside their dark and good bosoms, trapping them in a surrogate world that distracts them from the real world, it is mothers who desire for them a closer, but paradoxically less constrictive, hug. Aphrodite and Thetis are just as protective as Atlante, or even more so, but, instead of burying their sons in a closet-tomb-uterus, they pay a visit to the blacksmith. And so Aeneas and Achilles receive prêt-à-porter traps, articles of clothing that coat their invulnerable masculine bodies: suits of armor. In this way they escape both a violent death and a meaningless life, clasped in the embrace of the metal suits tailored to them on the order of their mothers.

I believe that those who dress men should constantly think of metallurgy. Deleuze and Guattari, in *A Thousand Plateaus*, insist on the vitality of the inorganic matter of which Achilles' shield is made. That shield, after all, represents the intuition (indeed, the invention) of an energy and activeness extraneous to biology.[9] Metal can be melted, cast, manipulated like a liquid or epoxy, and then beaten and tempered until it becomes inflexible. The skintight armor that Tony Stark bequeaths to Spider-Man is made of a very thin layer of metal wired with circuits of artificial intelligence, allowing for a kind of limberness (and sensuality) that was impossible for Stark's bulky alter ego, Iron Man, who had no superpowers besides those given him by technology. Tony, however, is, like Atlante, an anxious foster

6   Savinio, 17.
7   Savinio, 23.
8   What I said in note 2 was not entirely true. Although hapax as a past participle (and in a physical sense), the word *embrace* is used again by hooks later in the book. The second time it appears, it is in fact the Patriarchy itself that does the embracing: "Many men caught in patriarchy's embrace are living in a wilderness of spirit where they are utterly and always alone." hooks, *Will to Change*, 73.
9   Gilles Deleuze and Félix Guattari, *A Thousand Plateaus: Capitalism and Schizophrenia* (Minneapolis: University of Minnesota Press, 1987), 454.

Luigi Russolo, Carlo Carrà, Filippo Tommaso Marinetti, Umberto Boccioni, and Gino Severini in front of *Le Figaro*, Paris, February 9, 1912.

father, and is unable to put his trust entirely in the portable hug of the armor. So he stuffs it with firewalls, barriers, and redundant levels of security that do everything they can to keep Spider-Man out of danger—and in doing so get him, inadvertently, into hot water. Divine mothers, in contrast, like the she-goat that nursed Zeus, are willing to make compromises with paranoia, and so they came up with the aegis.

The suit of armor, the "second skin of the modern gentleman,"[10] is the archetype of masculine attire. It is a trap with a view, a mobile prison, a jointed hug. On it, and on the accessories that go with it, are displayed symbols and visions that are more vital than what is offered by the mere life available outside of metal. In fortifying the frailty of their wearer, armors also discipline his abnormalities. An armor is a garden, a castle like Atlante's but on the scale of a man's body, and therefore also the yardstick against which that body is measured. The aging kings of fantasy novels, from Théoden of Rohan to Robert Baratheon, realize that they are no longer able to perform their role when they try to fit into the armors they used to wear, nostalgic for the maternal embrace they once found in them. Meaningfully, like Ismene with her armo(i)r(e), kings, heroes, Carolingian knights and Knights of the Zodiac want to be buried in their armor, and that is how we find them in medieval sarcophagi, still in one piece and legible by way of the metal that coats their remains.

Lil Nas X, a wunderkind hard to pigeonhole into any particular musical genre, turned up for the Met Gala of 2021 wearing a suit of armor. It was a golden suit, forged by Versace, glittering and finely wrought. And it was interposed, as he laboriously showed to the flashes of photographers, between two other coatings: a skintight brown bodysuit, embroidered with gold nuggets, and an ample cape, also gilded, with velvet shoulders and a high collar worthy of a papal outfit. The armor became a second body, a hugged hug ideally linking two sartorial extremes—the bodysuit, which faithfully exhibited every line of the body it contained, and the cape, which did away with that body entirely. A too tight embrace and a too loose one, separated by a rigid metal boundary.

My Coat and Balzac's
My mother did not ask Hephaistos to forge a suit of armor for me. Instead, she bought me a coat. It is undoubtedly the most memorable of my clothing acquisitions, by now the stuff of legend in my family. I was thirteen, I'd just started high school and had discovered that my generically urban attire (one part childish, one part boorish, very "boy from the outskirts of Rome" style) was no good. At the *liceo scientifico* in the EUR (though in the annex on the new avenue down in the Torrino district) those outfits no longer coincided with my teenage identity, suddenly refined by the new options offered by the conformist elegance of the so-called *pariolini*.[11] Magnum shoes, Pit Stop pants, Pickwick T-shirts from the outlet and secondhand Quicksilver sweatshirts no longer protected me, as they had in middle school, from the suspicion that I wasn't like everybody else. So I began to invest Christmas and birthday presents, my allowance, little rewards, and the small sums I got paid for private lessons and the like in the systematic purchase of items that would renew my masculine closet. The coat, the top layer of these strata of coverings, always exhibited when outdoors, was clearly a fundamental item, a keystone.

10   Amedeo Quondam, *Cavallo e cavaliere: L'armatura come seconda pelle del gentiluomo moderno* (Rome: Donzelli, 2003).

11   The word literally means "inhabitants of the Parioli district of Rome," but it has come to be used for people with a bourgeois lifestyle and right-of-center politics. On the subject, see the song "I pariolini di diciott'anni" by I Cani, in *Il sorprendente album d'esordio de i Cani*, recorded in Rome and released by 42Records in 2011.

It was also a prohibitive item though, for coats are expensive. So, to persuade my mother, I instinctively adopted the strategy suggested by what I have written thus far. I didn't make it a question of style or image, I didn't let her know that my intention was to imitate what I saw others wearing. I told my mother, instead, that I needed a rain- and windproof coat. I said to her that, in just a few months, I'd be starting to ride a Vespa, that my legs and neck would get cold, and that therefore I needed a long coat, one with a collar. I told her that, without a good-quality coat, I would be too exposed to bad weather. That I would be in danger. And so, going along with her own desire to keep me in her protective hug even when not at home, to arm and love me, to entertain and detain me without preventing me from leaving safe castles or gardens, she drove me to Manzetti Sport, in front of the abandoned velodrome, to watch me try on a new model of RefrigiWear—a brand that, for some reason, was among those prescribed by the official fashion of my school.[12] It was a perfect suit of armor: sleeves hermetically sealed at the wrist, side openings to reach the pockets of one's pants without having to undo the buttons, a soft and scratch-resistant black layer of protection scored by large and very tight seams. This was in 2001. The price was five hundred thousand lira, more than an entire year of my monthly allowance.

My mom didn't sleep for two days after buying the coat, tormented by the idea that she might have irresponsibly indulged a caprice. Instead, it turned out to be a remarkable (in)vestment: I'm still wearing that coat today, twenty-three years later. I wore it in Canada, in tundra weather, the January that I flew there for my first job interview—for a teaching post that I didn't get. It has been my blanket on countless transatlantic flights, my salvation in the pervasive humidity of Pisa, the repository, in its very large pockets, of my exam books during college. I have been photographed in it at various public events, I've gone skiing in it, I've camped out in it below freezing temp. After all, that coat was designed for butchers working long hours inside refrigerators—even though it remains an elegant garment, as is sometimes the case with certain useful things that perform a precise function, like a suit of armor for instance. It has adapted to all the identities that have reshaped my wardrobe over the last two decades: it has covered and sealed them all in the same, transitive, hug.

A coat (and now we come to the point) is the most direct heir of the armors of mythology and poetry. There is a tricky curve among the lines of pine trees that separate my neighborhood, Mostacciano, from the nearby area of Spinaceto. I've almost always managed to avoid it on my Vespa. Once, however, I absentmindedly took that road on my way back

12 Professor Luca Zipoli of Bryn Mawr College tells me that RefrigiWear is run by a Roman friend of his, and that, according to this friend, it's just a local brand from Rome. However, RefrigiWear's website confirms the story that the sales clerk at Manzetti rattled off to me and my mother: the brand was born in 1950s America as a manufacturer of garments for people who had to work in the cold, setting an efficient and technologically advanced style. What is certain is that, for some reason, that style has inserted itself into the aspirations of twenty-first-century teenagers in Rome, and remains widespread in today's high schools.

from the Pasolini library, with books in the two big pockets of the RefrigiWear coat. I think I must have been sixteen. It was the first time I fell off the Vespa. We drifted apart, me and the Vespa, almost at once: the Vespa kept on sliding, noisily, for just a few seconds, quickly coming to a halt thanks to the friction against the asphalt. I, on the other hand, went on sliding for quite a while longer, to my great surprise. I remember very clearly what I thought when, at last, I came to a stop: "There it is, now the shock will pass and I'll realize that I've broken

Alessandro Giammei wearing his RefrigiWear coat, purchased in 2001, at the Rizzoli Galleria bookstore in Milan in March 2023. Photo Ivano Pierantozzi.

every bone in my body." I got to my feet instead, steady on my legs, and realized with even greater surprise that I hadn't hurt myself at all. If I slid so smoothly on the road it was because my coat, strong and almost scaly in its waterproof plastic fabric, did not oppose the friction, withstanding the impact and the chafing in lieu of my body. On close examination that coat still bears the scars of the fall instead of me, confirming to my mother the wisdom of the purchase.

Having grown up inside that coat makes me think of the most famous picture of the futurists, the one taken in 1912 with Marinetti in the middle and Russolo, Carrà, Boccioni, and Severini at his flanks. When I show it to my students, and ask them if those dour men match the idea they have of an avant-garde artist, they tell me that they look, instead, like respectable people. If I ask why, they point to their coats. My professor of art history at the Scuola Normale, Flavio Fergonzi, once told me that the only one wearing his own coat was probably Marinetti: the others had borrowed good ones for the photograph — and it is true that Marinetti's coat fits him well, while those of his standard bearers look slightly the wrong size. When Mario Schifano turned that iconic photograph into a work of pop art by making a stencil out of it and spraying paint on top in his *Futurismo rivisitato* series, the five futurists became five uninhabited coats, with hats.

A few decades earlier than the futurists, Auguste Rodin was asked to conceive a monument to Honoré de Balzac. Famous for his lean and muscular men reminiscent of Michelangelo's statues, inspired by athletic and somewhat feral models picked up in Southern Italy, Rodin quickly renounced the idea of sculpting the puffy, overweight body of Balzac in the nude. He didn't want to misrepresent the reality of his features, but neither did he wish to put a potbelly on the pedestal. So he decided to cover him up: to wrap him in a bark that would protect him from the gaze of the public without abstracting or idealizing his figure. He put a coat on him. In his workshop, we can still find the sculptural experiments with which he developed the final solution, publicly exhibited in Paris since 1939. For that definitive version, Rodin dipped an entire bathrobe, or perhaps a dressing gown, in a tub filled with plaster, which then solidified into a sculptural coat, as empty as those of Schifano's revisited futurists, or the armor of Calvino's Agilulf in *The Nonexistent Knight*. Looking at Balzac's statue, one has the impression that the French author was poured like a liquid into his rigid coat: a vertical suit of armor that gives him his shape and holds him upright. It is a coat that prevents him from melting like a snowman in the sun, and forces him into the shape of a monument. From its folds we can see that, in the hug of that bronze robe, Balzac is hugging himself: he is holding himself together.

The English word *coat* also means "covering," "shell," "membrane" — a coat of paint, a clear coat, an enamel coat. So a "coat" can be both the Gucci one from which I started out (or the RefrigiWear at which I arrived) and the silver paint in which Lil Nas X covered his body two Met Galas after his famous armor outfit: a coat of color applied directly on his skin, conceived by Dior Men with Pat McGrath and inspired by Karl Lagerfeld. Several commentators said that he looked like he was naked. To me, he looked "coated": en-

Aegidius Sadeler, device of Giovanni Caracciolo, prince of Melfi, in Anselmus de Boodt et al., *Symbola divina et humana pontificum, imperatorum, regum*, published in three volumes in Prague in 1601–3, vol. 1, p. 154, detail (Library of the University of Illinois Urbana-Champaign).
Auguste Rodin, *Final Study for the Monument to Balzac*, 1897 (cast by Georges Rudier in 1972), bronze, 106 × 44.5 × 41.9 cm, Metropolitan Museum of Art, New York (gift of Iris and B. Gerald Cantor Foundation, 1984).

Alessandro Giammei

gulfed in the hug of the most tight-fitting of the coats that protect and imprison heroic masculine fragility.

(A Dragon's Tail) End

Sherlock's coat, in the popular BBC series that launched Benedict Cumberbatch's career, flutters through the streets of a postmodern London while he, turning its collar up, dashes with Watson towards a new adventure. That coat is obviously the immediate ancestor of the magic cloak that hugs the same actor, as he plays almost the same part, in *Doctor Strange*: a coat that evolves into a cloak, an armor that becomes a wingspan. Inspector Gadget's coat also inflates to make him levitate, and agile Jedi knights favor airy robes over the heavy armor of their Arthurian counterparts — robes that resemble, I reckon, Balzac's coat. Howl, Miyazaki's wizard, turns his cloak into a pair of feathered wings, gliding from his castle that, unlike Atlante's, follows him through the air like a furnished suit of armor, animated by a fire spirit.

I still haven't decided, it seems, whether De Sarno's coated man (the image that triggered these pages) is a turtle or a flying dragon. Perhaps, on the basis of the hybrid examples I trotted out in the last paragraph, it would be best to say that he is both, leapfrogging the requirements of proper evolutionary biology in exchange for the speculations of a fantastic and symbolic one.

The word *coat* is also used in the expression *coat of arms*. The coat of arms of Cosimo I de' Medici, visible in the frescoes by Lorenzo Sabbatini and Marco Marchetti in Palazzo Vecchio and described by Vasari in his *Ragionamenti*, is a turtle rigged with a sail. A further evolution of this symbol of temperance is Alfonso Cambi's more daring emblem, conceived with Annibal Caro, in which the turtle is equipped with proper wings, and flies, with the motto "Amor Addidit."[13] Winged by love, the reptile remains protected in its coat of ribs, able to withstand clashes of civilizations and falls from a Vespa. At the same time, it is capable of flying like a dragon. The aspiration to coat men is rooted in fear, in apprehension, in disciplining instincts: all feelings that can be joyfully counterbalanced by love. After all, my coat was born as a normative shield and turned into an idiosyncratic traveling companion, while those of the futurists turned into signs of petty bourgeoisie. Balzac's coat transfigured into the cloak of a Jedi, and Lil Nas X's armor shrunk to the thinnest enamel skin.

Apparently, feathers evolved over the skin of dinosaurs as a way of keeping their bodies warm. Only by chance did that useful innovation, which developed into stunning lavishly colored outfits, prove even more useful to the descendants of those prehistoric creatures when they flapped their coats of feathers while running, and found out they could fly. As anybody can immediately tell by looking at a peacock in midair, flying is, when one is well dressed, just an alternation of protective contractions and liberating relaxations: an oscillation between opening and closing. It's a bit like hugging yourself, rhythmically, again and again.

I would like to thank Maria Luisa Frisa for making me realize that, when I talk about a certain set of (masculine) things, I'm really talking about fashion — and for her patience. I must also thank Ara H. Merjian for having put me up at his apartment house on the nights when I started to write this essay.

13   "Love Added." See Giovanni Ferro, *Teatro d'imprese* (Venice: Giacomo Sarzina, 1623), part 2, p. 689.

Of course, it was during the very years that Michael [Powell] was struggling and sinking into obscurity that people like me and Francis Coppola were discovering his work on the other side of the Atlantic. And our great fortune was that we were watching the Powell Pressburger films without any cultural baggage. We had no prejudices based on when they were made or how they were received. We just saw them as enjoyable films, and sometimes wonderful works of art.[1]

This is how the director Martin Scorsese described his approach to the films of Michael Powell and Emeric Pressburger, the British duo who made such classics as *The Red Shoes* and *Black Narcissus*. And in fact what is most moving and beautiful in the documentary *Made in England: The Films of Powell & Pressburger* is Scorsese's narration. He analyzes the extraordinary work of the two filmmakers, but he does so above all through the lens of his own story, that of a lover of cinema who as a child used to watch their movies on TV, in what was for him a formative experience. For every image filled him with wonder.

This is what exhibitions of fashion, especially in Italy, need: a public that will approach them without prejudices or preconceptions, and without cultural hang-ups. Paradoxically, in order for us to finally accept fashion as a complex cultural phenomenon able to speak to us of our past, our present, and our possible futures, situations are needed in which it is tackled as something to be preserved and studied. This would make it possible to get away from the trivializing dimension of an exclusively commercial perspective, or from the superficiality that associates it with a phenomenon of frivolity, with the red carpet. I believe that in order for this

With No Memory
Gabriele Monti

to happen there is a fundamental need for institutions able to embrace and promote fashion, in its material and immaterial forms and expressions, and to do so through exhibitions.

The situation in Italy has remained broadly unchanged since the 1980s, with some exceptional and extremely precise premises[2] that have never been truly and effectively maintained: we have not succeeded in setting up a cultural institution able to collect, analyze, and promote fashion, and in particular Italian fashion, so hard to decipher given the way it interweaves forms of high craftsmanship and industrial expertise. Making exhibitions on fashion means recalling the past, keeping the memory of it alive: it signifies stringing together reflections that are layered in time, that give rise to new reflections and that foster the design of pieces and their imagery. To make fashion exhibitions is to render this discipline and its culture memorable. And spaces are needed where actions of this kind can break out of the limitations of the amateurish undertaking, so as to become places of wonder and debate.

Memorabile: Ipermoda brings me back to the MAXXI exactly ten years after the exhibition *Bellissima: Italy and High Fashion 1945-1968*.[3] Even though this institution is not primarily devoted to fashion, it is willing to take it on. The exhibitions on fashion at the MAXXI allow us to reflect on the way in which the question of staging fashion exhibitions has been much more clearly defined in recent years. The evolution in curatorial practices and exhibition making underlines more or less directly the importance of the part that fashion plays in our daily lives, in our shared imagination, and in helping us to understand the complexity of our culture. This essay is not the place to list the most visited or most spectacular exhibitions on fashion of the last twenty years. Rather it is an opportunity to look at how they have evolved, reflecting the role of the discipline in our cultural horizons.

There can be no doubt that the first couple of decades of the twenty-first century saw the Costume Institute of the Metropolitan Museum of Art in New York offer us exhibitions that have redefined the mode of their staging, attracting large numbers of visitors in the process. *Alexander McQueen: Savage Beauty*, organized at the Costume Institute by Andrew Bolton with the support of Harold Koda in 2011,[4] was seen by over 650,000 people. It proved one of the most popular exhibitions in the history of the museum. In an image that appeared in the Spring-Summer 2012 issue of the magazine *LOVE* we see Andrew Bolton literally "in flames," in a photo digitally retouched by the fashion photographer Sølve Sundsbø. The picture accompanied an interview with Bolton, celebrated as the curator responsible for the phenomenon of the blockbuster fashion exhibition, a true superstar capable of attracting and seducing the public. These experiences, connected with events like the Met Gala, which is to all intents and purposes the most important contemporary occasion on which the red carpet is rolled out, have progressively main-

1   Martin Scorsese in *Made in England: The Films of Powell and Pressburger*, directed by David Hinton (Ten Thousand 86; Ice Cream Films, 2024).

2   See Gabriele Monti, "An Exhibition to Define a Museum: *1922-1943: Vent'anni di moda italiana* at Poldi Pezzoli," in *Memos: On Fashion in This Millennium*, ed. Maria Luisa Frisa, catalogue of the exhibition at the Museo Poldi Pezzoli, Milan, February 21-September 28, 2020 (Venice: Marsilio, 2020), 36-57; and Monti, "1980-2020: Fashion Curating and Cultural Policy in Italy," in *Fashion Heritage: Narrative and Knowledge Creation*, ed. Isabel Cantista and Damien Delille (Cham: Palgrave Macmillan, 2022), 55-80.

3   See Maria Luisa Frisa, Anna Mattirolo, and Stefano Tonchi, eds., *Bellissima: Italy and High Fashion 1945-1968*, catalogue of the exhibition at the MAXXI, Rome, December 2, 2014-May 3, 2015 (Milan: Electa; Rome: MAXXI, 2014).

4   See Andrew Bolton, ed., *Alexander McQueen: Savage Beauty*, catalogue of the exhibition at the Metropolitan Museum of Art, New York, May 4-August 7, 2011 (New York: Metropolitan Museum of Art, 2011).

streamed solutions aimed at updating more traditional modes of staging, in particular the ones developed in the wake of the exhibitions on fashion curated over the course of the 1970s and 1980s by Diana Vreeland at that same Costume Institute.[5] Curators like Bolton work on a spectacularization of the display and on the search for innovative solutions, culminating in the recent actions that have introduced artificial intelligence and digital displays to offer visitors an engrossing experience: the latest fashion exhibition that opened at the Met this year, *Sleeping Beauties: Reawakening Fashion*, presents multiple sensory experiences of an immersive nature, including video animations, soundscapes, and olfactory experiences.[6]

As far back as 2014, however, the exhibition *Charles James: Beyond Fashion*—curated at the Met by Harold Koda and Jan Glier Reeder and devoted to the work of the legendary Anglo-American couturier—had already introduced into this museum specializing in blockbuster exhibitions the idea of superseding the more usual modes of display in order to promote a more multifaceted approach to interpreting the objects of fashion, by putting on show the technical work required to realize the complex structures of clothing for which James was famous.[7] The involvement of an external studio in addition to the museum staff—in this case Diller Scofidio + Renfro—was fundamental to the display and digital design of the exhibition, through the integration of a system of digital supports and optical devices with which to analyze the clothes and draw attention to their details. A series of digital animations described and illustrated the unique structure of each garment. The system of digital display and the animations utilized dynamic computerized models construct-

Italiana: Italy through the Lens of Fashion 1971–2001, exhibition views, Palazzo Reale, Milan, 2018. Photos and courtesy Francesco de Luca.

ed from three-dimensional scans, microscopic images, and original technical research conducted with the assistance of the Costume Institute's team of curators. In conjunction with each animation, robotic arms equipped with video cameras and digital projectors interacted slowly with the clothing, revealing microdetails not visible to the naked eye and permitting the visitor to observe closely the technical properties of the object on display without losing sight of its curatorial interpretation.

The operations that go on around fashion curating obviously pose problems when the staging of an exhibition becomes an opportunity to introduce into the project a reflection on the making of fashion, on its design and production processes, and not merely on the finished articles. Tackling fashion from this perspective means raising questions not only with regard to its disciplinary status, but also about what should be acquired, archived, preserved, and put on show by a museum that intends to include fashion and clothing in its purview and thus in its collections. Not just the end product, but also the traces that can offer an insight into the practices and describe the complex process that leads from conception to design and to realization and consumption. It is a very interesting curatorial approach and one that, in recent years, has characterized in particular the activity of the MoMu (ModeMuseum) in Antwerp. Since it opened in 2002, the museum's exhibition programming has added to the traditional models (the retrospective devoted to one

5   See Judith Clark and Maria Luisa Frisa, eds., *Diana Vreeland after Diana Vreeland* (Venice: Marsilio, 2012).

6   See Andrew Bolton, ed., *Sleeping Beauties: Reawakening Fashion*, catalogue of the exhibition at the Metropolitan Museum of Art, New York, May 10–September 2, 2024 (New York: Metropolitan Museum of Art; New Haven: Yale University Press, 2024).

7   See Harold Koda and Jan Glier Reeder, eds., *Charles James: Beyond Fashion*, catalogue of the exhibition at the Metropolitan Museum of Art, New York, May 8–August 10, 2014 (New York: Metropolitan Museum of Art, 2014).

creator, the thematic exhibition, the one on a historical period) projects able to interrogate the language of fashion and thus its definition as a discipline.

If the first show at the MoMu in 2002 was devoted to the museum's archive, to its backstage,[8] the ambition of the exhibition *Patronen/Patterns* in 2003 was to shift attention onto the paper pattern and the processes of construction of clothing, from the sartorial to the industrial.[9] A reflection on the DNA of clothing and fashion that in the exhibition turned into a reexamination of the morphology of the garment, for the exploded patterns became landscapes capable of suggesting new approaches to the interpretation of dress and its forms. As the catalogue points out, patternmaking and the pattern are usually seen as technical matters, which tend to be overlooked in a museum's policies of acquisition or display. And yet they are the key to the relationship between clothing and the body, with its proportions and its movement. They also make it possible to visualize and interpret the relations between body, design of the garment, and fabric. Choosing to make these elements the focus of an exhibition and turn them into things that a fashion museum cannot ignore signifies broadening and deepening the definition of fashion, including in it practices and processes and not limiting the discipline to its finished products. In this way exhibiting fashion becomes an extremely complex and multifaceted undertaking.

The Victoria and Albert Museum in London, an institution that has established an absolutely central role in the exhibition of

8   Kaat Debo, the current director of the MoMu, wrote in the catalogue that "a museum can never keep up with fashion; it is bound to be a step behind the times. What a museum of fashion can offer, however, is a context in which to place fashion, a place for reflection and analysis where we can distance ourselves from our subject, which means not merely lingering on the final product—the piece of clothing—but paying as much attention to the artistic process." Kaat Debo, "The Fashion Museum Backstage," in *Het ModeMuseum / The Fashion Museum: Backstage*, catalogue of the exhibition *Selection I: Backstage* at the MoMu, Antwerp, September 21, 2002–February 16, 2003 (Ghent: Ludion, 2002), 11.

9   See Bob Verhelst and Kaat Debo, eds., *Patronen/Patterns*, catalogue of the exhibition at the MoMu, Antwerp, April 24–August 10, 2003 (Ghent: Ludion, 2003).

Italiana: Italy through the Lens of Fashion 1971–2001, exhibition view, Palazzo Reale, Milan, 2018. Photo and courtesy Francesco de Luca.

contemporary fashion through the blockbuster events it has staged,[10] has to some extent taken up this suggestion and recently stressed the importance of looking at the discipline's processes of design. The exhibition *Balenciaga: Shaping Fashion*, curated by Cassie Davies-Strodder (May 27, 2017–February 18, 2018) set out to "stage" a collaboration between school and museum in a very interesting way: the museum invited students of the MA Pattern and Garment Technology course at the London College of Fashion to analyze Balenciaga's processes of construction. The students traced the patterns of the original dresses and then digitized and refined them to the point where they could be used to make muslins, displayed in the exhibition alongside Balenciaga's pieces. It was a way of drawing attention to the couturier's extraordinary technical skill and revealing the language of design proper to fashion.

Going back for a moment to the first exhibition at the MoMu, *Selection I: Backstage*, in the catalogue produced for the event the choice was precisely to look at what a museum dedicated to fashion should be and do, through a series of statements made by curators. Not just figures connected with museums, but also independent curators like Judith Clark, who in that very publication proposed an interpretation of the act of curating and making exhibitions as the possibility of putting together unexpected narrations by creating completely new connections between pieces.[11] A curator who acts not as a conservator, someone who studies and restores the garment and in doing so also finds the best ways to put it on display and thus bring it back to life; rather as a figure who moves with more freedom, utilizing the design of the exhibition to develop an argument, often irrespective of the material nature of the pieces that will be put on show. In the titles of her projects Clark uses words that reflect the choices made with regard to the display and at the same time indicate a methodology of inquiry, one that utilizes the exhibition to raise questions rather than offer the visitor simple answers or a didactic narration. "Allusions" and "conversations" are terms that are often used in the considerations of the exhibition maker, but it is above all in her curatorial work that Clark puts these words into three-dimensional effect: the display involves a materialization of

Memos: On Fashion in This Millennium, exhibition views, Museo Poldi Pezzoli, Milan, 2020. Photos and courtesy Francesco de Luca.

10   As evidence for the crucial part played by the V&A in the history of fashion exhibitions it suffices to recall *Fashion: An Anthology by Cecil Beaton*, the celebrated show it staged in 1971. On this see Judith Clark and Amy de la Haye, *Exhibiting Fashion: Before and after 1971* (New Haven: Yale University Press, 2014).
11   Judith Clark, "Statement I," in *Het ModeMuseum*, 146–51.

terms that we are more used to encountering in reflections couched in the written or spoken word.

The reflection on the role of the museum that Clark associates with her curating has made it possible over the last few years to highlight the relations between the approach to design typical of fashion and the one to the design of exhibitions. Creative directors assume the attitude of the curator when they explore the archives, whether in order to produce collections or to design or participate in the design of exhibitions that set out to celebrate the brands for which they are working (it suffices to think of outstanding examples like Dior and Gucci). And this relationship between design and exhibition making suggests a discourse on method, a reflection on the modes of interpretation and realization of the various products of the fashion industry: not just the clothes, but also the images and the words. Design as analysis and self-analysis, and not only as the start of a mechanism of production. In 2017 the exhibition *Disobedient Bodies: JW Anderson Curates The Hepworth Wakefield* saw one of the best-known contemporary designers and creative directors take on the impressive collection of modern and contemporary art at the

Hepworth Wakefield gallery, in West Yorkshire. Out of this emerged an exhibition that explored the way in which the human form has been reimagined by artists and designers in the twentieth and twenty-first centuries. *Disobedient Bodies* brought together over a hundred objects, from the worlds of art, fashion, ceramics, and design, selected by Anderson and presented in unexpected conversations. Works by artists like Louise Bourgeois, Naum Gabo, Alberto Giacometti, Barbara Hepworth, Henry Moore, and Dorothea Tanning were placed in direct dialogue with pieces designed by Christian Dior, Jean Paul Gaultier, Comme des Garçons, Helmut Lang, and Rick Owens. For the exhibition Anderson also created an installation composed of a forest of elongated and oversized sweaters that visitors could walk through. So vision and touch were equally important for Anderson, who had conceived the exhibition as a way of revealing and analyzing his creative processes. He also saw it as an opportunity to look at how we consume images today, by designing—in open dialogue with the gallery's extraordinary art collection—a space in which visitors could explore the ideas of body and gender, which lie at the heart of his creative process and his poetics.

Memos: On Fashion in This Millennium, exhibition view, Museo Poldi Pezzoli, Milan, 2020. Photo and courtesy Francesco de Luca.

And if the entry of a figure from outside the museum—such as a designer or creative director—makes it possible to show how certain creative processes are initiated and how the objects in the museum can assume unexpected significance when inserted into nontraditional narrations (in contrast to those arranged on the basis of author or chronology), the need to come up with alternative ways of presenting the collections can also emerge from within. In 2012 Olivier Saillard, at the time director of the Palais Galliera, curated a performance with Tilda Swinton (the first in a now legend-

12   See Tilda Swinton and Olivier Saillard, *Impossible Wardrobes* (New York: Rizzoli International, 2015), [vol. 1], *The Impossible Wardrobe*.

ary series) entitled *The Impossible Wardrobe*, staged at the Palais de Tokyo between September 29 and October 1 as part of Paris's Festival d'Automne.[12] An actor and a muse of fashion, Swinton was the protagonist of a poetic performance on the catwalk. Dressed in a white robe and wearing cotton gloves of the same color, she played the role of the museum conservator. The clothes and other items from the Galliera's archives, which could not be worn or used for obvious reasons of conservation, were brought back to "life" through an interaction between the two. The action was performed on the catwalk, where a tall mirror had been placed: Saillard delicately passed the clothes to the actor, who took

Bellissima: Italy and High Fashion 1945–1968, exhibition view, MAXXI, Rome, 2014–15. Photo Musacchio&Ianniello. Courtesy Fondazione MAXXI.

them with the solemn and almost religious gestures of the conservator and invented others, suggested by the garments. The show sought new curatorial modes of displaying clothing, which all too often, in a museum setting, are associated with a sense of dusty immobility. The almost everlasting quest for movement and change in a fashion exhibition, traditionally peopled by lifeless mannequins, seems to have found an answer in this experiment, which set out to tell the story of costume and fashion in the language of performance and the atmosphere of a contemporary fashion show. Thus the component of performance has become part of curatorial language and movement an element that an exhibition showcasing fashion can no longer escape, just as the body can no longer be evoked simply by a dummy.

The *Memorabile: Ipermoda* project, like others before it (I'm thinking of *Bellissima*, *Italiana*, and *Memos*[13]), arose out of impulsive and at the same time extremely precise intuitions on the part of Maria Luisa Frisa, who with this exhibition intends to look at the mechanisms and modalities that recent fashion has devised in order to make itself an indelible part of our imagination. But this project is also intended as a reflection on the capacity of exhibitions on fashion to offer an experience that is at once thought provoking and spectacular, in other words *memorable*, an opportunity to keep memory alive. To do this two levels of awareness and action are required: on the one hand it is necessary to see the act of

13   See Frisa, Mattirolo, and Tonchi, *Bellissima*; Frisa, Monti, and Tonchi, eds., *Italiana: Italy through the Lens of Fashion 1971–2001*, catalogue of the exhibition at Palazzo Reale, Milan, February 22–May 6, 2018 (Venice: Marsilio, 2018); and Frisa, *Memos*.

Bellissima: Italy and High Fashion 1945–1968, exhibition view, MAXXI, Rome, 2014–15. Photo Musacchio&Ianniello. Courtesy Fondazione MAXXI.

curating as something to be interpreted in a different way on each occasion, in order to identify and invent new solutions for display able not only to illustrate but also to problematize fashion (but without ignoring the constant relationship with the commercial dimension of display); on the other spaces and institutions need to be found that, by putting fashion on show, can keep the memory of it alive, that is to say maintain a record of the expository and curatorial work carried out around the cultures of fashion. Only in this way can we avoid having every exhibition start again from scratch, in a sort of dystopian cultural amnesia. *Memorabile* is intended to be this too: an opportunity to try to imagine, especially in Italy, a space able to initiate a fully conscious approach to culture of fashion.

Let's go back to our starting point. In the constant oscillation and dialogue between institutional actions and areas of independence, *Memorabile: Ipermoda* does not speak to us solely of what has left an indelible mark on our imagination over the last few decades. It also speaks to us of the importance of keeping memory alive, in order to be able to put on and at the same time experience an exhibition on fashion with that willingness to let ourselves be fascinated that Scorsese evoked with regard to the cinema. So as not to be left with an irremediable loss of memory.

Fashion and Sustainability: A Difficult Relationship

More than five hundred years ago, Thomas More entirely excluded fashion and adornment from his vision of a perfect and desirable world. In the island of Utopia, described by the traveler Raphael Hythloday, the inhabitants are content with a modest and purely functional wardrobe. All clothes are of a single style and color that never change; the end of their life as products is determined only by physical deterioration. By eliminating fashion, Utopia achieves significant labor and material savings,[1] a result we would today consider sustainable.

Do we, therefore, have to give up the aesthetic, symbolic, and identity components that are the favorite themes of fashion in exchange for sustainability? Or can we protect the environment, ensure workers' rights, and promote well-being while continuing "to dress attractively and according to trends,"[2] so as to express our identity, or multiple identities?

For much of the five hundred years since More's book, fashion has been associated with values totally at odds with those of sustainability. Montaigne (*Essays*, first edition published in 1580) considers that fashion and adornment generate futile values; Veblen (*The Theory of the Leisure Class*, 1899) deems it unnecessary and wasteful; Virginia Woolf (*To the Lighthouse*, 1927) sees it as harmful because it distracts from virtue and life's more essential purposes; Marcuse (*One-Dimensional Man*, 1964) believes it contributes to creating false needs.

Fashion's bad reputation is not entirely undeserved. Its inherent value is the continuous creative pursuit of the new, but this entails waste and overproduction. This condition is worsened by the rapid obsolescence of products that clutter

The Sustainable Future of Fashion
Marco Ricchetti

the market as soon as they have to make way for new collections. Overproduction had a negligible impact as long as fashion was an attribute of the leisure class and the elites. The development of prêt-à-porter in the 1970s made it accessible to a broader segment of the population, turning it into a global phenomenon and increasing its impact; fast fashion in the first decade of the twenty-first century made fashion trends accessible to all, but accelerated obsolescence cycles and reduced the number of times a garment is worn. Thus, integrating sustainability principles into fashion is a challenge within a challenge.

The poor working conditions that have marked the history of the textile industry have not helped mitigate the contradiction. Consider the March 1911 fire at the Triangle Shirtwaist factory in New York, which killed 146 textile workers, mostly young immigrant women. The fire broke out just days after the first International Women's Day, tragically highlighting the importance of the fight for women's labor rights (a few years later, the Day was moved to March 8, when it is still celebrated today).[3] In our times, remember the tragedy of the 2013 collapse near Dhaka in Bangladesh of the Rana Plaza building, which housed five garment factories. The collapse caused over 1,100 deaths and 2,500 injuries among workers.

Paradigm Shift: Fashion Reconciled with Sustainability
Today, a new activism for greater sustainability in fashion is evident, a change both inevitable and necessary. Inevitable because fashion cannot help but reflect the deep movements of contemporary society and the spirit of the times, today driven by fears for the planet's future, rejection of social injustices, and demands for greater social and cultural inclusion. Necessary because fashion has a significant economic impact on a global scale. Besides being a primary

component of the consumer goods market, it involves many other sectors, from agriculture to industry, to the international logistics and distribution system. It is a network of activities generating employment for millions of people worldwide. This position gives fashion a prominent role and responsibility in the global sustainability challenge. From being part of the problem, it can become a crucial part of the solution.

It took until the early 2010s for this new activism to become evident in the mainstream. An abrupt acceleration occurred in 2011 following Greenpeace's Detox My Fashion campaign, which involved major international brands in eliminating hazardous chemicals from their products and supply chains. The 2013 Rana Plaza tragedy restored to the forefront respect for workers' rights and safety in subcontracting companies. The term *circular fashion* entered the fashion lexicon in 2014 during an event in Stockholm, though it remained an "elusive" concept until recent years, as described by Rachel Cernansky in *Vogue Business*.[4] Its full integration was confirmed in 2022 by the title of a European Commission's industrial strategy document, which reads: EU Strategy for Sustainable and Circular Textiles.[5]

Between 2009 and 2019, almost all the profit and nonprofit organizations that today populate the fashion sustainability landscape were founded. In 2009, the Sustainable

1 See Mila Burcikova, "Introduction: Fashion in Utopia, Utopia in Fashion," in "Utopia and Fashion," special issue, *Utopian Studies* 28, no. 3 (November 2017): 381–97, https://doi.org/10.5325/utopianstudies.28.3.0381.

2 Alberto Pecci, "Foreword," in *The Beautiful and the Good: Reasons for Sustainable Fashion*, ed. Maria Luisa Frisa and Marco Ricchetti (Florence: Centro di Firenze per la Moda Italiana; Venice: Marsilio, 2012), 8.

3 See Kat Eschner, "The American Garment Workers Who Helped Inspire International Women's Day," *Smithsonian Magazine*, March 8, 2017, https://www.smithsonianmag.com/smart-news/american-garment-workers-who-helped-inspire-international-womens-day-180962364/.

4 Rachel Cernansky, "Sustainable Fashion: Where the Industry Is Heading in 2022," *Vogue Business*, January 5, 2022, https://www.voguebusiness.com/sustainability/sustainability-where-fashion-is-heading-in-2022.

5 European Commission, Communication from the Commission to the European Parliament, the Council, the European Economic and Social Committee and the Committee of the Regions: EU Strategy for Sustainable and Circular Textiles (March 30, 2022), https://eur-lex.europa.eu/legal-content/EN/TXT/PDF/?uri=CELEX:52022DC0141.

Apparel Coalition was formed (recently rebranded as Cascale), and the first Copenhagen Fashion Summit (later renamed Global Fashion Summit) took place; in 2011, the ZDHC (Zero Discharge of Hazardous Chemicals) organization was established; 2012 saw the publication of the "Manifesto for the Sustainability in Italian Fashion" by the Camera Nazionale della Moda Italiana; Fashion Revolution was founded in 2013 in response to the Rana Plaza tragedy; the Global Fashion Agenda platform started in 2016; Fashion for Good in 2017; also in 2017, the first Green Carpet Fashion Awards took place in Milan, renamed CNMI Sustainable Fashion Awards in 2022, and the report *A New Textiles Economy: Redesigning Fashion's Future* was published by the Ellen MacArthur Foundation; the United Nations Alliance for Sustainable Fashion was born in 2019. In the same year, thirty-two major groups representing over 160 brands and claiming to account for a third of the global fashion turnover signed the Fashion Pact, committing to defending biodiversity, combating climate change, and protecting oceans from plastic pollution.

Much remains to be done, but the steps taken in the last fifteen years are promising. Measuring how much of the journey is behind us and how much is still ahead is difficult (read impossible) due to a massive information gap, which will be discussed in the final paragraph of this essay. However, limited progress can be seen in some specific fields.

The number of fashion companies actively engaged in fighting climate change has increased. By the end of 2022, there were 125, five times more than in 2019, including all major global groups. Most of these companies have set reduction targets for greenhouse gas emissions, not only for activities under their direct control but also for the entire supply chain, meaning that thousands of supplier companies are indirectly involved.

Progress has been made in eliminating hazardous chemicals. In just over a decade, the use of chemicals in textiles has radically changed. Brands have committed to safer and greener chemistry: legal but hazardous substances considered indispensable for the quality of fabrics and yarns fifteen years ago are now abandoned in favor of green alternatives.

The share of materials with better sustainability performance than conventional ones has grown. For example, in cotton this share reached 27% of the total material produced, compared to 7% ten years ago, in 2014. Synthetic fibers made not from fossil materials but from biomass, hence renewable and with lower greenhouse gas emissions, have also entered the market.

Other areas, such as biodiversity protection, the adoption of regenerative agriculture techniques, traceability, or design for recyclability, are still, so to speak, at the starting line.

Sustainability between Reason, Management, and Ethics
Having noted the new activism, we must reflect on the direction to take: what is the destination? And by what means will we travel?

The path is not straightforward, and not just for textiles and fashion; the directions may be divergent. Two in partic-

Michelangelo Pistoletto, *Venus of the Rags — CNMI Sustainable Fashion Awards*, 2023, 3D print from recycled nylon thread, 26.5 × 24.5 × 19 cm. Photo and courtesy Archivio Pistoletto.

ular divide the scene: the first rational, the second conservationist, guided more by ethical considerations that require radical changes to social and economic organization.

The rational vision of sustainability is inspired by the 1987 report *Our Common Future* by the World Commission on Environment and Development of the United Nations, which formulated a classic definition of sustainable development: "Development that meets the needs of the present without compromising the ability of future generations to meet their own needs." The definition has an intergenerational utilitarian basis well summarized by a simple slogan in a work by Maria João Calisto, a young Portuguese artist, alumna of the Unidee artistic residency program by Michelangelo Pistoletto and Cittadellarte in Biella, who, in 2002, created a collection of cups for the illy Art Collection titled *no water no coffee*. In other words, we will not enjoy good coffee in the future unless we take care of water resources today.

This vision emphasizes the role of innovation and technology, finds solutions in recycling and the circular economy, and pushes companies to commit to ambitious but achievable goals. The same vision is present in what was proba-

6   See Fabio Guenza, "Sustainable Business: Edward Freeman Discusses Managing for Stakeholders," in Frisa and Ricchetti, *The Beautiful and the Good*.

7   Grant McConnell, "The Environmental Movement: Ambiguities and Meanings," *Natural Resources Journal* 11, no. 3 (Summer 1971): 427–35 (also available at the URL https://digitalrepository.unm.edu/cgi/viewcontent.cgi?article=3169&context=nrj).

bly the first use of the term *sustainability*. In 1713, Hans Carl von Carlowitz, a German mining administrator, used the term *Nachhaltigkeit*, "sustainability," in a book on sound forest management methods to ensure a perpetual supply of wood, avoiding the risk of interrupting production in the Saxon metallurgical and mining industry, which used wood massively in furnaces and quarries, so destroying forests: "No Forest No Steel," we might say.

This line of thought includes authors who deal with management, such as John Elkington, inventor of the triple bottom line model (people, planet, profit), or Ed Freeman, founder of the management for stakeholders theory, which considers sustainability as a reflection of the balance between the interests of all stakeholders.[6]

The conservationist vision, on the other hand, is based on a value system centered on nature as opposed to an anthropocentric one, leading to an ethical choice according to which human activities cannot override nature, but must be limited by it. This vision inspired the creation of large American parks—Yellowstone, established in 1872, is the oldest national park in the world—spaces to defend the integrity of nature from human expansion.

Conservationism also has deep roots. In 1864, in his book *Man and Nature*, George Perkins Marsh warned of "the dangers of recklessness." He emphasized "the need to act with caution" whenever humans "intervene in nature's spontaneous arrangements." A few decades later, in 1890, John Muir, the father of the American national park system, wrote about the need to protect nature from degradation and exploitation for its intrinsic value beyond its utility as "a mere warehouse of resources for human consumption." Nature carries an aesthetic and spiritual dimension, for whose preservation humanity must be willing to limit material well-being. More generally, conservationism "rejects the supremacy of economic materialism."[7]

Today, the degrowth movement draws on this vision. Sustainability is achieved by limiting or reducing economies,

Michelangelo Pistoletto's Third Paradise for the "Manifesto for Sustainability in Italian Fashion," Piazza del Duomo, Milan, September 2012. For the opening of Milano Fashion Week the symbol of the Third Paradise was brought to life by a thousand students. Event curated by the Camera Nazionale della Moda Italiana. Photo Studio Biasion. Courtesy Camera Nazionale della Moda Italiana.

using less energy and resources, and prioritizing spiritual well-being over profit. Actions proposed by this movement include reducing consumption, self-producing food, and ending land consumption.

Arguments consistent with the conservationist perspective are also developed by scholars from the London College of Fashion and the King's College as critiques of sustainability practices, such as using recycled materials in fashion or developing technologies to reduce environmental impact. According to these authors, these practices are insufficient and suffer from a "flawed logic" because they "do not acknowledge the problem of the underlying social relations of capitalism, principally the relentless profit logic."[8]

The divergence between the conservationist and rational visions is evident. For the former, it is impossible to pursue sustainability goals without a radical change in society, production and consumption behaviours and without abandoning the logic of profit. For the latter, sustainability is an achievable path within the current economic and social system, progressing through incremental improvements. Ed Freeman illustrates the point well: "A lot of people seem to think they have something at stake in saying that companies really should be engaged in green business for the sake of the environment: why not say they are doing it because they are making money? To figure out if it's business or it's ethics is an idea flawed by what I call 'the separation fallacy.' Most of the time, the two drivers are joint. Separating out the 'ethics part' is a meaningless exercise for those seeking to identify a purely altruistic model or a purely selfish model. This is a false dilemma that results from a way of thinking that is outdated."[9]

The Future of Sustainability in Fashion
On the path to sustainability, there are many areas where much remains to be done. Even a superficial treatment of "what to do" goes well beyond the scope of this text. However, two prerequisites for the successful transition of the fashion system to sustainability, which have not yet been achieved, need to be briefly addressed. Both concern information.

The first is related to impact measurement: what and how big is fashion's impact on the environment? What is the actual state of social justice, workers' rights, and human rights in the sector? The truth is that despite a commendable effort of analysis and studies, we are still immersed in a dense fog where "zombie data" (i.e., old and invalid data),[10] fake news, and storytelling with little foundation prosper. The data repeated uncritically in conferences and even in official institutional documents are often zombie data. How many times, for example, have we read that "the fashion

8   Andrew Brooks et al., "Fashion, Sustainability, and the Anthropocene," in "Utopia and Fashion": 498, https://doi.org/10.5325/utopianstudies.28.3.0482.

9   Edward Freeman, in Guenza, "Sustainable Business," 19.

10   Zombie data are false, unverifiable, or lacking in credibility, but they are continuously repeated until they become almost commonplace. These include everything from fake news to greenwashing. They are often accompanied by references to publications or websites that are no longer available, or that do not actually contain the cited information, or where the information pertains to a different context.

11   See Vanessa Friedman, "The Biggest Fake News in Fashion," *New York Times*, December 18, 2018, https://www.nytimes.com/2018/12/18/fashion/fashion-second-biggest-polluter-fake-news.html. For other examples of zombie data on the sustainability of fashion, see also Alden Wicker, "Fashion Has a Misinformation Problem: That's Bad for the Environment," *Vox*, January 31, 2020, https://www.vox.com/the-goods/2020/1/27/21080107/fashion-environment-facts-statistics-impact; and "Zombie Data: Fashionably Fake Facts," Planet Tracker, February 1, 2022, https://planet-tracker.org/zombie-data-fashionably-fake-facts/.

industry is the second most polluting in the world"? As recent debunking analyses have widely demonstrated, this is a false claim, not based on any evidence or measurement.[11] Zombie data pollute the discussion, making it challenging to define a baseline for formulating credible goals and measuring progress, as well as for identifying real priorities.

The other side of this coin is greenwashing, or the use of misleading or false claims in corporate or institutional communication to suggest that more is being done to protect the environment than is actually happening.

Fashion to Reconnect, an exhibition curated by the Fondazione Pistoletto Cittadellarte at the Fashion Hub of Milano Fashion Week, February 2024. *Fashion to Reconnect* was inspired by the new dynamic equilibrium of Michelangelo Pistoletto's Third Paradise: fashion becomes a work of art and is viewed as a means of bringing about responsible social change. The pieces on display were selected by Cittadellarte Fashion B.E.S.T., with the support of the Camera Nazionale della Moda Italiana. Photo Valerie Khoury.
Fashion for Planet Open Parliament—Act III, Sala Parlamentino, Palazzo Giureconsulti, Milan, February 2024. Milano Fashion Week, organized by the Camera Nazionale della Moda Italiana, set up in collaboration with the Fondazione Pistoletto Cittadellarte Fashion B.E.S.T. an "open parliament," a space to share stories and ideas and begin a dialogue with the planet. Photo Valerie Khoury.

Many studies show that the lack of trust in sustainability claims and their lack of clarity are among the main obstacles for consumers to translate their feelings of concern for the planet's future and rejection of social injustices into purchasing choices, sentiments that especially animate the younger generations today. It is crucial to regulate the flow of information and prevent greenwashing, a textbook case of market failure in self-regulation, and to allow consumers to have clarity about what they are buying and certainty about not being misled by bad marketing. A significant step forward is the new package of European Union directives to combat greenwashing.[12]

12   The directive against greenwashing, already approved in 2024 by the European Parliament and the Council of the European Union (the so-called ECGT Directive, Empowering Consumers for the Green Transition), and the directive that sets the rules for substantiating environmental claims (known as the Green Claims Directive), which is still in the process of approval.

Ipermoda: Visions

The visual essay in this book is the product of a reflection on the images that illustrate and "make" contemporary fashion, on their circulation and their consumption. On the accessibility of the shows, which, especially since the pandemic, has become immediate and global through the use of digital platforms and devices. Thus we have chosen to present the work of fashion brands, creative directors, and fashion designers through screenshots of shows transmitted online and stills from some fashion films. Events and productions that are the fruit of ever more elaborate approaches to direction, set design, and choreography, aimed at generating images that circulate obsessively on the social networks. The montage we are proposing alludes to the scrolling that is the vehicle for our—often compulsive—consumption of this variegated visual universe.

The sequence is the result of a complex effort, but one that has not allowed us to obtain permission to publish all the images we would have liked to include, given the intricate set of rules that have to be followed even when, as in this case, the use to be made of them is not commercial but one of study. Nevertheless, we believe that the form of this visual atlas of contemporary fashion is one that is capable of prompting a series of questions and reflections not only on how we look at images today, but also on the part they play in our idea of reality.

Maria Luisa Frisa

Viktor&Rolf, *Cutting Edge Couture*, Spring/Summer 2010 haute couture show, Espace Éphémère des Tuileries, Paris, October 2009. Video Team Peter Stigter. Courtesy Viktor&Rolf.

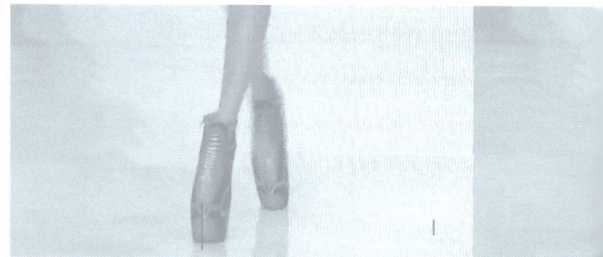

Alexander McQueen, *Plato's Atlantis*, Spring/Summer 2010 ready-to-wear show, Palais Omnisports de Paris-Bercy, Paris, October 2009. Video SHOWstudio. Courtesy Alexander McQueen.

Christian Dior, creative direction Raf Simons, Fall/Winter 2012–13 haute couture show, Paris, July 2012. Model Lara Mullen. Courtesy Christian Dior.

Iris van Herpen, *Wilderness Embodied*, Fall/Winter 2013-14 haute couture show, Palais de la Découverte, Paris, July 2013. Model Othilia Simon. Documented by Fabrice Davillé / Studio Premices.

Prada, creative direction Miuccia Prada, *In the Heart of the Multitude*, Spring/Summer 2014 women's ready-to-wear show, Milan, September 2013. Set design OMA/AMO. Model Katlin Aas. Courtesy Prada.

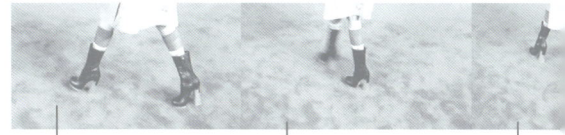

Prada, creative direction Miuccia Prada, Spring/Summer 2015 women's ready-to-wear show, Milan, September 2014. Set design OMA/AMO. Courtesy Prada.

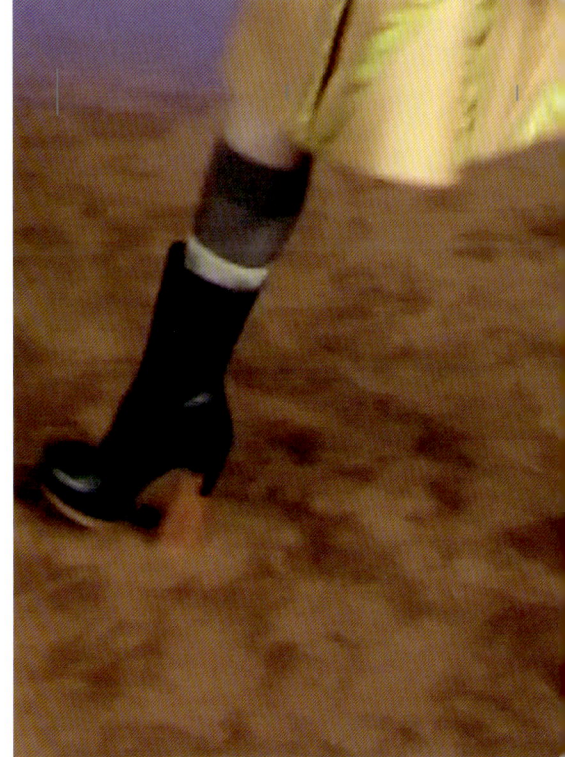

Rick Owens, *Cyclops*, Spring/Summer 2016 women's ready-to-wear show, Palais de Tokyo, Paris, October 2015. Courtesy Owenscorp.

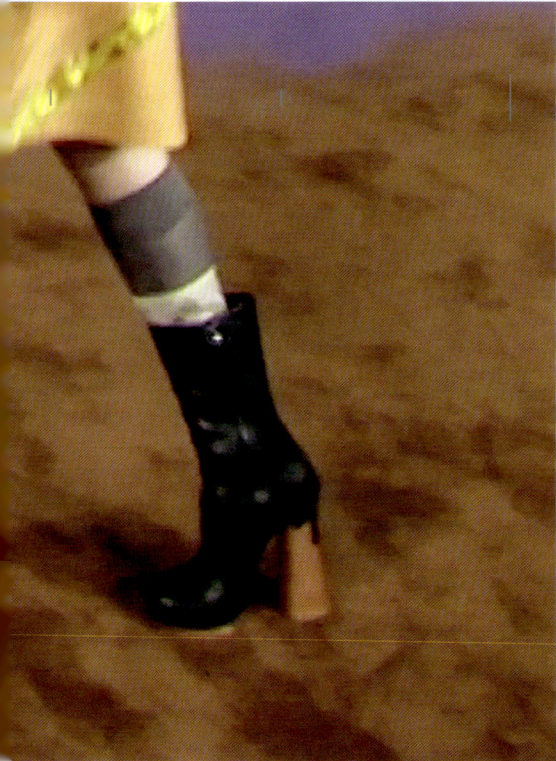

Dolce&Gabbana, *Tropico Italiano*, Spring/Summer 2017 women's ready-to-wear show, Milan, September 2016. Model Vanessa Moody. Video production Sergio Salerni / Urban Production / Videogang. Courtesy Dolce&Gabbana.

Rick Owens, Fall/Winter 2017–18 women's ready-to-wear show, Palais de Tokyo, Paris, January 2017. Courtesy Owenscorp.

Craig Green, Spring/Summer 2018 ready-to-wear show, The Arches, London, June 2017. Video #INDIGITAL.TV. Courtesy Craig Green.

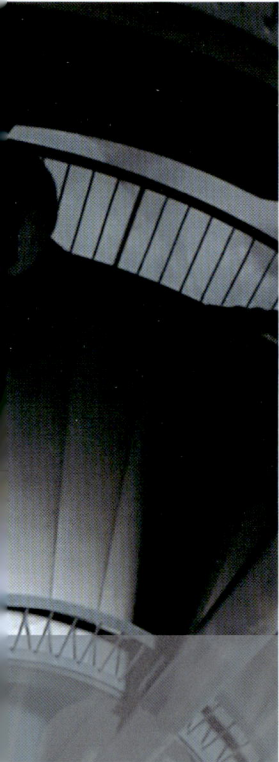

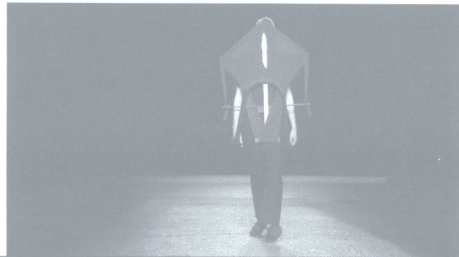

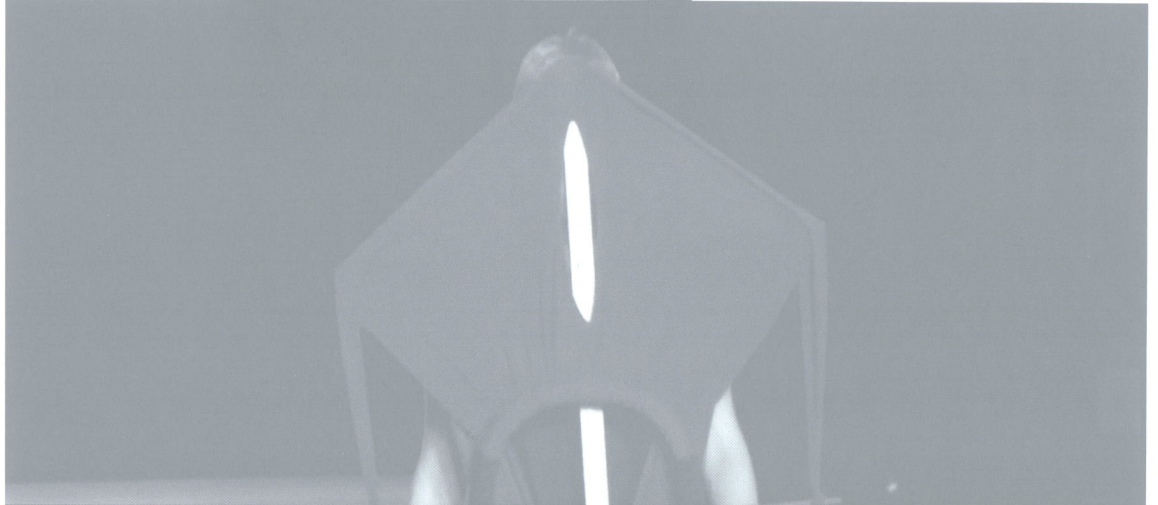

Prada, creative direction Miuccia Prada, Spring/Summer 2018 women's ready-to-wear show, Milan, September 2017. Artists Brigid Elva, Joëlle Jones, Stellar Leuna, Giuliana Maldini, Natsume Ono, Emma Ríos, Trina Robbins, and Fiona Staples. Concept and design 2×4, New York. Courtesy Prada.

Versace, creative direction Donatella Versace, *Tribute Collection*, Spring/Summer 2018 women's ready-to-wear show, Triennale di Milano, Milan, September 2017. Video production Sergio Salerni / Urban Production / Videogang. Courtesy Versace.

Jacquemus, *La Bomba*, Spring/Summer 2018 women's ready-to-wear show, Paris, September 2017. Model Amilna Estevao. Video production and direction Fabrice Davillé / Studio Premices. Courtesy Jacquemus.

Christian Dior, creative direction Maria Grazia Chiuri, Spring/Summer 2019 haute couture show, Musée Rodin, Paris, January 2018. Courtesy Christian Dior.

Christian Dior, creative direction Maria Grazia Chiuri, Fall/Winter 2019–20 women's ready-to-wear show, Musée Rodin, Paris, February 2019. Installations Tomaso Binga. Courtesy Christian Dior.

Jacquemus, *Le Coup de Soleil*, Spring/Summer 2020 ready-to-wear show, Valensole, France, June 2019. Video production and creative direction Bureau Future. Courtesy Jacquemus.

Christian Dior, creative direction Maria Grazia Chiuri, Fall/Winter 2019–20 haute couture show, 30 Avenue Montaigne, Paris, July 2019. Installations Penny Slinger. Model Mona Tougaard. Courtesy Christian Dior.

Giorgio Armani Privé, *Armani Code*, Fall/Winter 2019–20
haute couture show, Petit Palais, Paris, July 2019.
Model Débora Vanoverberghe. Courtesy Giorgio Armani.

Fendi, creative direction Silvia Venturini Fendi, Fall/Winter 2019–20 haute couture show,
Palatine Hill, Rome, July 2019. Video production Sergio Salerni / Urban Production /
Videogang. Courtesy Fendi.

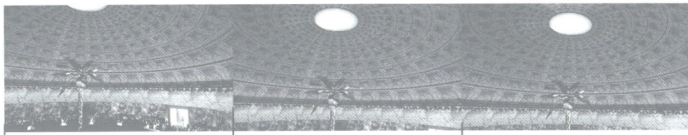

Versace, creative direction Donatella Versace, Spring/Summer 2020 women's ready-to-wear show, Milan, September 2019. Video production Sergio Salerni / Urban Production / Videogang. Courtesy Versace.

Maison Margiela, creative direction John Galliano, *Co-Ed*, Spring/Summer 2020 ready-to-wear show, Salon d'Honneur, Grand Palais, Paris, September 2019. Model Leon Dame. Video Random Studio. Courtesy Maison Margiela.

Balenciaga, creative direction Demna Gvasalia, *Summer 20*, Spring/Summer 2020 ready-to-wear show, Studio 5, La Cité du Cinéma, Paris, September 2019. Model Eliza Douglas. Courtesy Balenciaga.

Prada, creative direction Miuccia Prada, Fall/Winter 2020–21 men's ready-to-wear show, Fondazione Prada, Milan, January 2020. Set design OMA/AMO. Courtesy Prada.

Louis Vuitton, creative direction Virgil Abloh, Fall/Winter 2020–21 men's ready-to-wear show, Jardin des Tuileries, Paris, January 2020. Set design PlayLab Inc. Models Senne Pluym and Jakob Zimny.

memorabile ipermoda

Moncler Genius 2020, *One House, Different Voices*, *8 Moncler Richard Quinn* collection, Milan, February 2020. Direction Tommaso Ottomano, creative production April. Courtesy Moncler.

Christian Dior, creative direction Maria Grazia Chiuri, Fall/Winter 2020–21 women's ready-to-wear show, Jardin des Tuileries, Paris, February 2020. Installations Claire Fontaine. Models Anyelina Rosa and Seolhee Kim. Courtesy Christian Dior.

Jacquemus, *L'Amour*, Spring/Summer 2021 ready-to-wear show, Parc naturel régional du Vexin français, July 2020. Video production and creative direction Bureau Future. Courtesy Jacquemus.

Christian Dior, creative direction Maria Grazia Chiuri, cruise 2021 women's ready-to-wear show, Lecce, July 2020. Installations Marinella Senatore. Model Sophie Koella. Courtesy Christian Dior.

Louis Vuitton, creative direction Virgil Abloh, *Rubber Man*, presentation video of the Spring/Summer 2021 men's ready-to-wear collection and show, Tokyo, August 2020. Show set design PlayLab Inc.

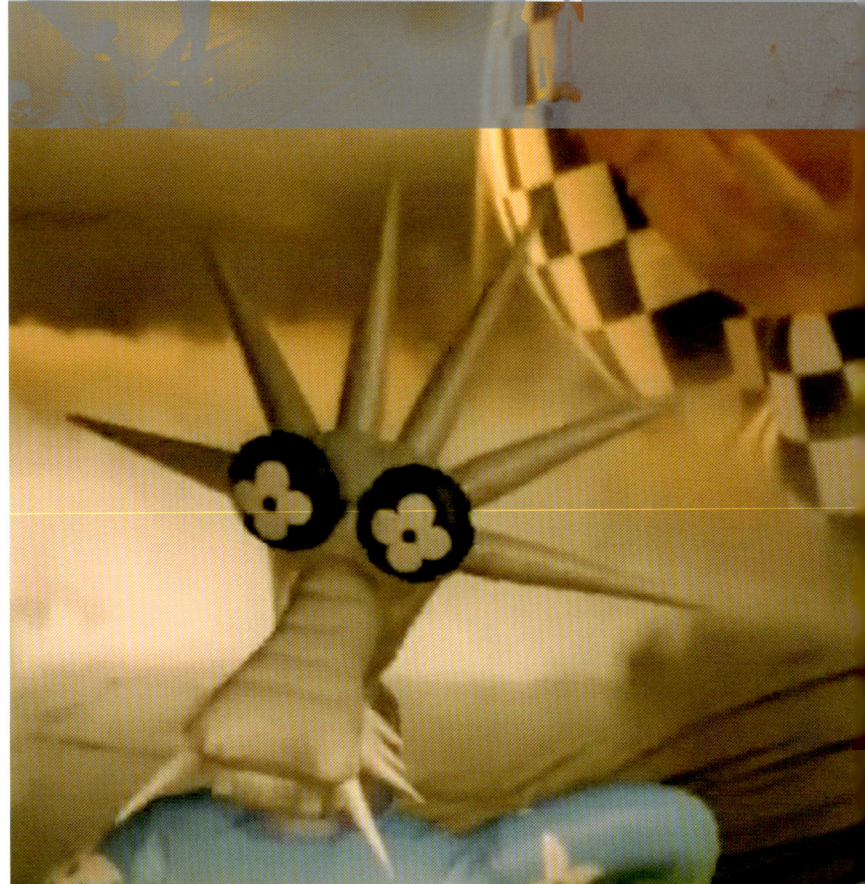

Saint Laurent, creative direction Anthony Vaccarello, *No Matter How Long the Night Is*, presentation video of the Spring/Summer 2021 men's ready-to-wear collection, September 2020. Courtesy Saint Laurent.

Prada, creative direction Miuccia Prada and Raf Simons, *Dialogues*, Spring/Summer 2021 women's ready-to-wear show, Fondazione Prada, Milan, September 2020. Set design OMA/AMO. Courtesy Prada.

Marco Rambaldi, *Auguri per sempre*, Spring/Summer 2021 women's ready-to-wear show, Milan, September 2020. AIRONDRONE videographer Carlo Ferro, XENTEK videographer Maurizio Iovine. Courtesy Rambaldi Group S.r.l.

Louis Vuitton, creative direction Virgil Abloh, *Peculiar Contrast, Perfect Light*, presentation video of the *Ebonics / Snake Oil / The Black Box / Mirror, Mirror* Fall/Winter 2021–22 men's ready-to-wear collection, January 2021. Set design PlayLab Inc., video Kitten Production.

Prada, creative direction Miuccia Prada and Raf Simons, *Possible Feelings II: Transmute*, Fall/Winter 2021–22 women's ready-to-wear show, February 2021. Set design Rem Koolhaas and OMA/AMO. Courtesy Prada.

Balenciaga, creative direction Demna Gvasalia, *Clones: Spring 22*, Spring 2022 ready-to-wear show, Paris, June 2021. Model Eliza Douglas. Courtesy Balenciaga.

Schiaparelli, creative direction Daniel Roseberry, Fall/Winter 2021-22 haute couture show, Place Vendôme, Paris, July 2021. Courtesy © Schiaparelli.

Balenciaga, creative direction Demna Gvasalia, *Couture 50th*, Fall/Winter 2021-22 haute couture show, Avenue George V, Paris, July 2021. Model Lisa Williamson. Courtesy Balenciaga.

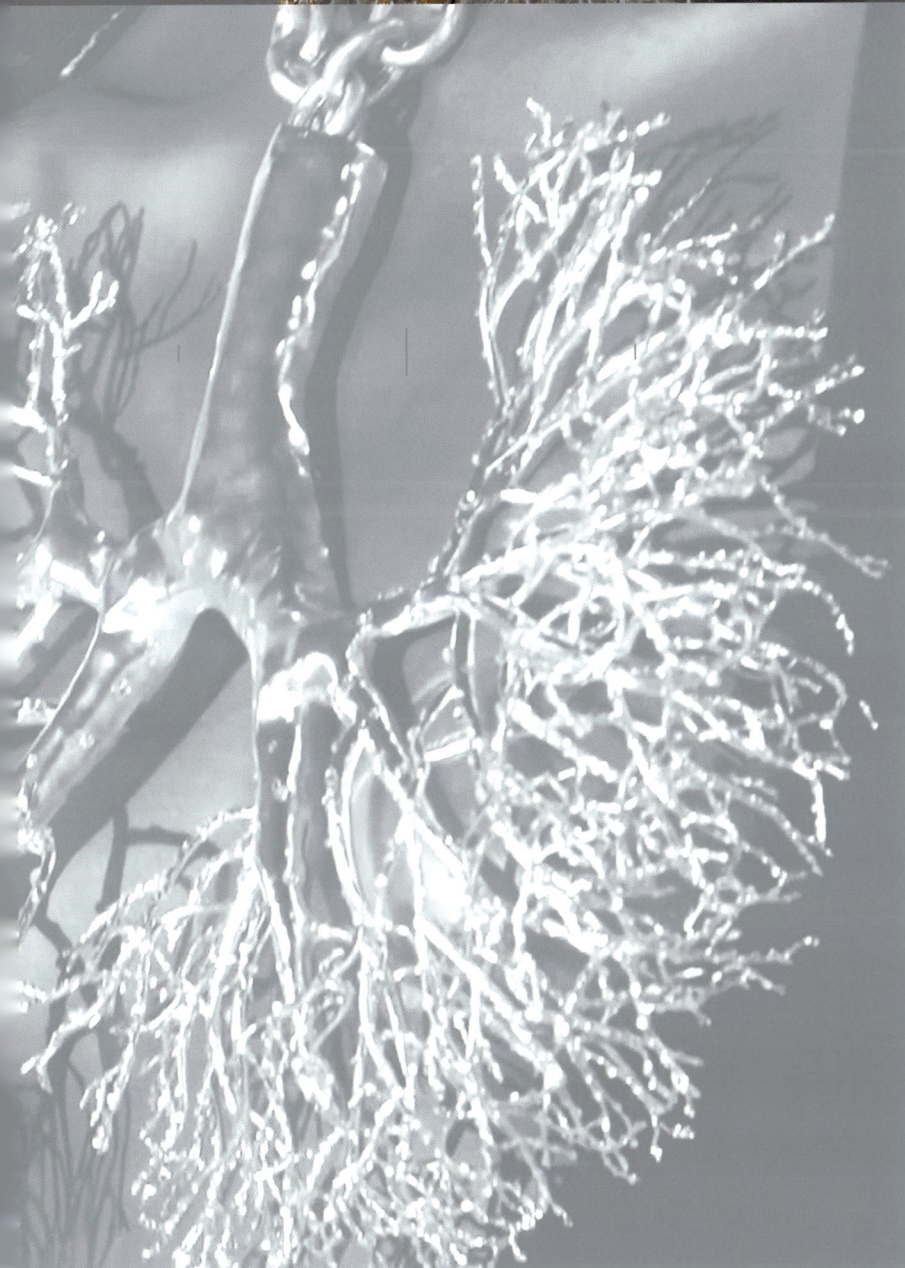

Fendi, creative direction Kim Jones, presentation video of the Fall/Winter 2021–22 haute couture collection, July 2021. Direction Luca Guadagnino. Model Lara Mullen. Courtesy Fendi.

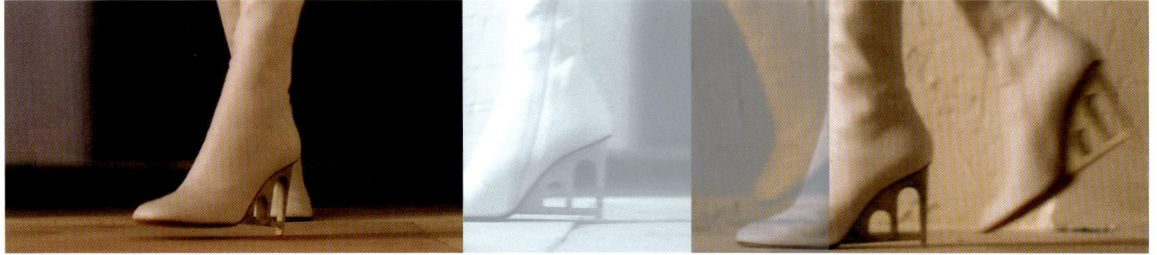

Prada, creative direction Miuccia Prada and Raf Simons, Spring/Summer 2022 women's ready-to-wear show, Fondazione Prada, Milan, and Bund 1, Shanghai, September 2021. Set design OMA/AMO. Models Vira Boshkova and Shao Di. Courtesy Prada.

Fendace, creative direction Donatella Versace and Kim Jones, *Fendi by Versace, Versace by Fendi*, Pre-Fall 2022 ready-to-wear show, Milan, September 2021. Model Mariacarla Boscono. Video production Sergio Salerni / Urban Production / Videogang. Courtesy Versace.

memorabile ipermoda

Loewe, creative direction Jonathan Anderson, Spring/Summer 2022 women's ready-to-wear show, Garde Républicaine, Paris, October 2021. Model Emi Stankovic. Courtesy Loewe.

Miu Miu, Spring/Summer 2022 ready-to-wear show, Palais d'Iéna, Paris, October 2021.
Model Rianne Van Rompaey. Courtesy Miu Miu.

JW Anderson, Fall/Winter 2022–23 men's ready-to-wear show, Milan, January 2022. Courtesy JW Anderson.

Louis Vuitton, creative direction Virgil Abloh, presentation video of *The ∞th Field* Fall/Winter 2022-23 men's ready-to-wear collection and show, Carreau du Temple, Paris, January 2022. Show set design PlayLab Inc. Video Kitten Production. Model Alec Pollentier.

Diesel, creative direction Glenn Martens, Fall/Winter 2022–23 ready-to-wear show, Milan, February 2022. Concept and set design Niklas Bildstein. Courtesy Diesel.

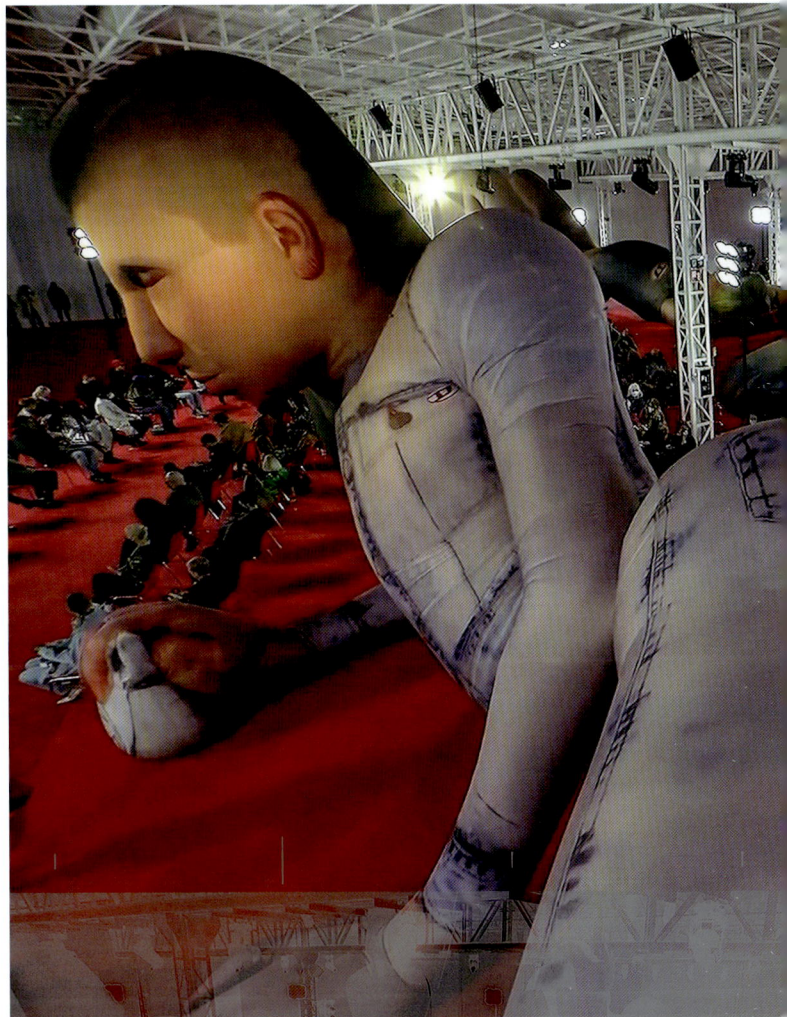

Prada, creative direction Miuccia Prada and Raf Simons, *An Ideology of Prada*, Fall/Winter 2022–23 women's ready-to-wear show, Fondazione Prada, Milan, February 2022. Set design OMA/AMO. Model Sherry Shi. Courtesy Prada.

SUNNEI, Fall/Winter 2022–23 ready-to-wear show, Milan, February 2022. Courtesy SUNNEI.

Balenciaga, creative direction Demna Gvasalia, *360° Show: Winter 22*, Fall/Winter 2022-23 ready-to-wear show, Parc des Expositions, Paris, March 2022. Models Minttu Vesala and Eliza Douglas. Courtesy Balenciaga.

PHOTOSENSITIVE WARNING: TRIGGER SEIZURE

Gucci, creative direction Alessandro Michele, *Cosmogonie*, resort 2023 ready-to-wear show, Castel del Monte, Andria, May 2022. Courtesy Gucci.

Balenciaga, creative direction Demna Gvasalia, *Couture 51st*, Fall/Winter 2022-23 haute couture show, Avenue George V, Paris, July 2022. Model Yuri. Courtesy Balenciaga.

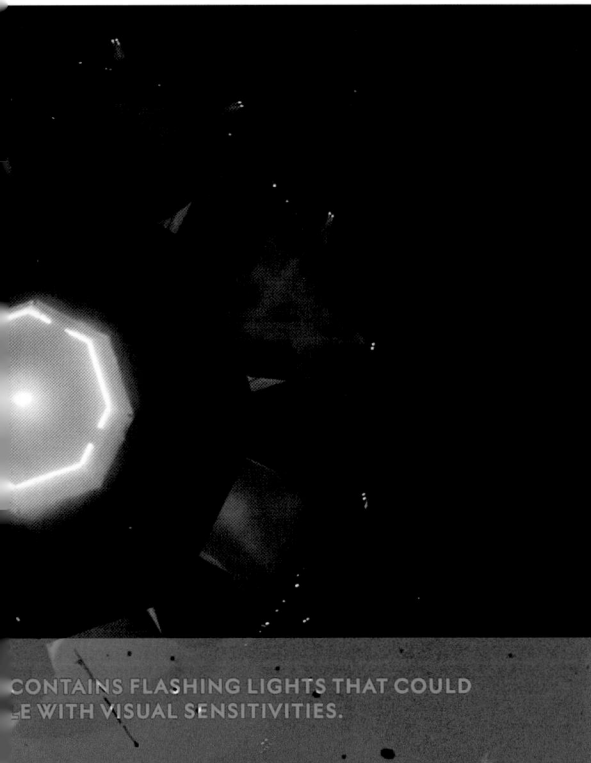

CONTAINS FLASHING LIGHTS THAT COULD
⊥E WITH VISUAL SENSITIVITIES.

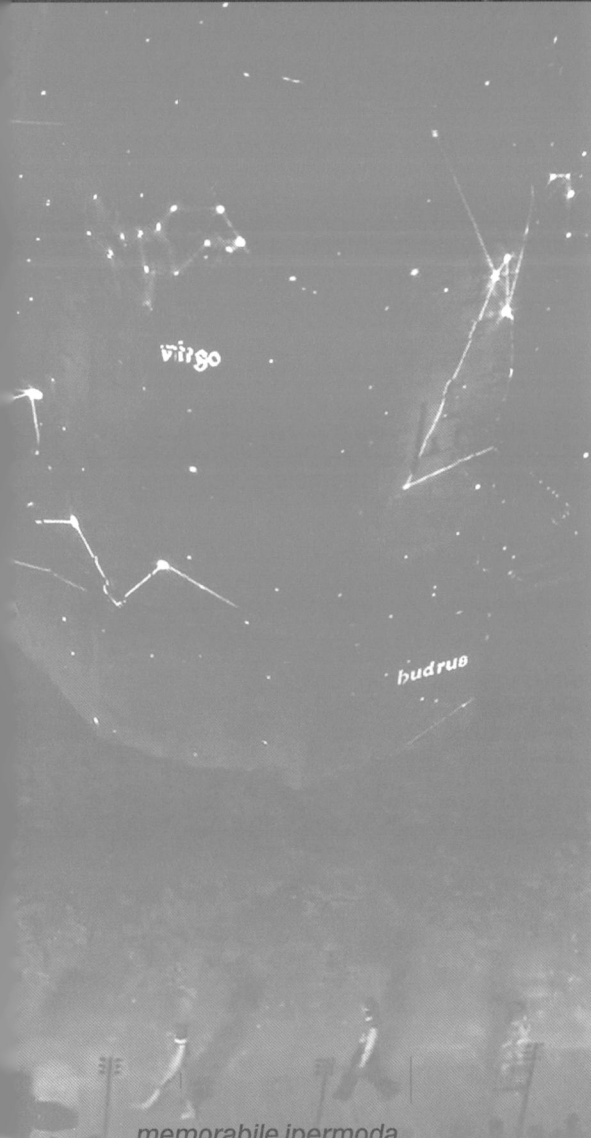

memorabile ipermoda

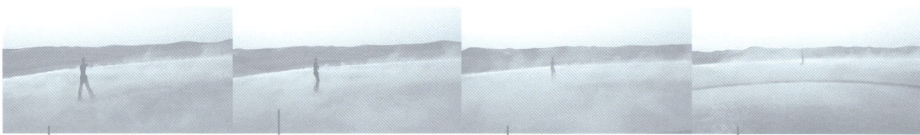

Saint Laurent, artistic direction Anthony Vaccarello, Spring/Summer 2023 men's ready-to-wear show, Agafay Desert, Morocco, July 2022. Courtesy Saint Laurent.

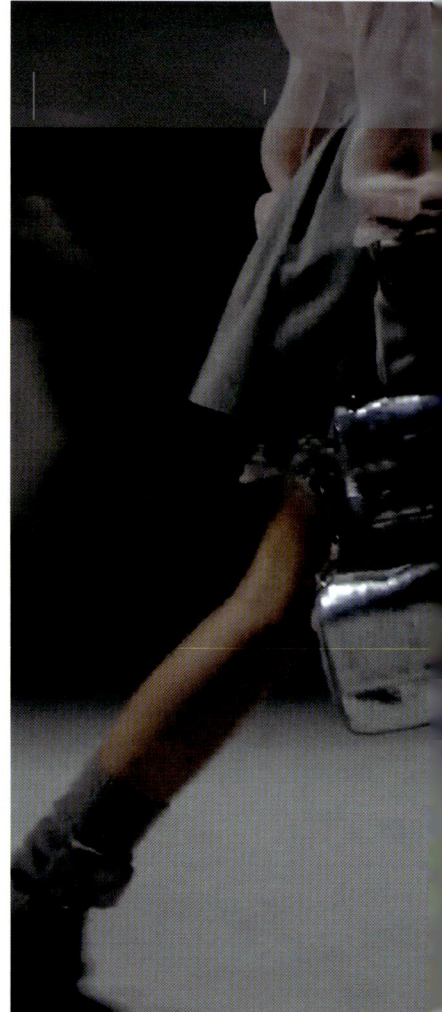

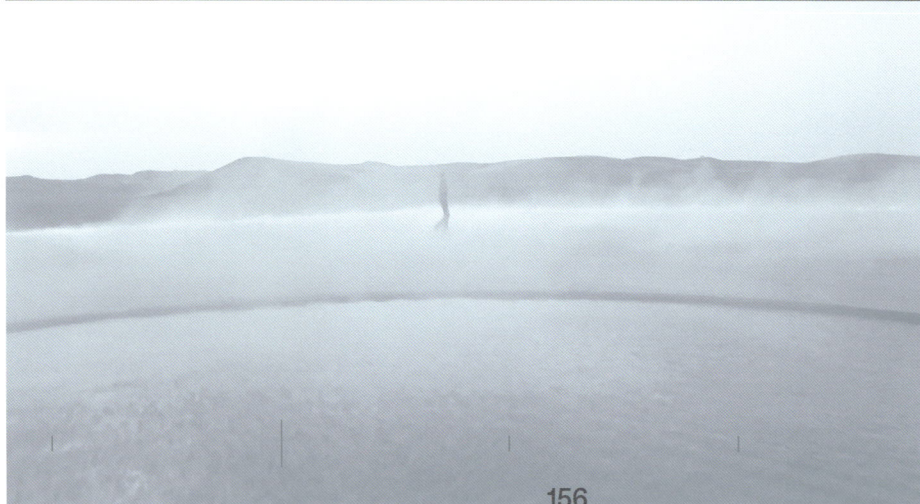

Fendi, *Baguette 25th Anniversary Collections*, resort 2023 ready-to-wear show, Hammerstein Ballroom, New York, September 2022. Video production Walter Films. Courtesy Fendi.

Diesel, creative direction Glenn Martens, Spring/Summer 2023 ready-to-wear show, Milan, September 2022. Concept design Studio Dennis Vanderbroeck. Courtesy Diesel.

Bottega Veneta, creative direction Matthieu Blazy, Spring/Summer 2023 ready-to-wear show, Milan, September 2022. Installation Gaetano Pesce. Models Valentin Aumont, Mariacarla Boscono, Sun Mizrahi, and Liv Walters. Video production Atlantis Film&Video S.r.l. / Nicolas Salet. Courtesy Bottega Veneta.

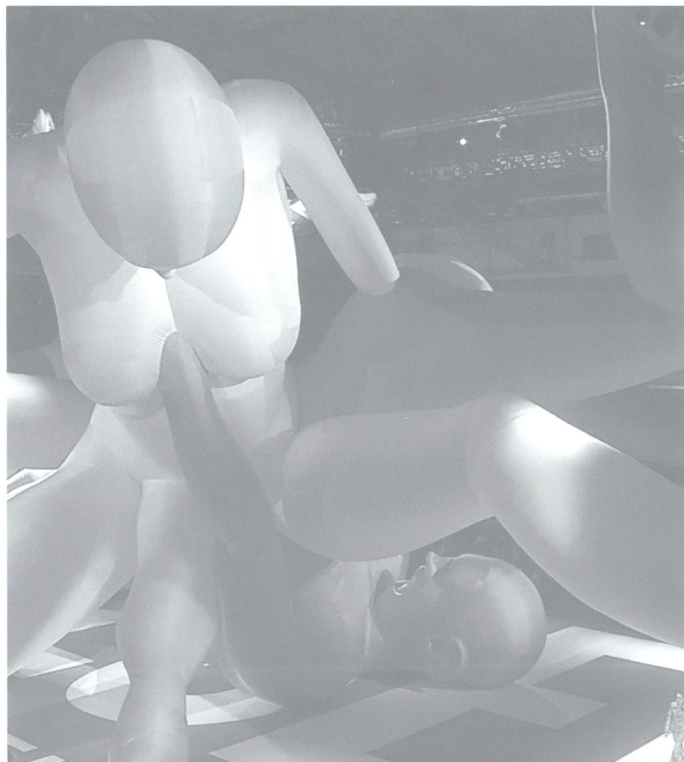

Moncler, *Moncler 70th Anniversary: Extraordinary Forever*, Piazza del Duomo, Milan, September 2022. Creative direction of show and film Etienne Russo. Creative direction and production of video Villa Eugénie, Paris. Courtesy Moncler.

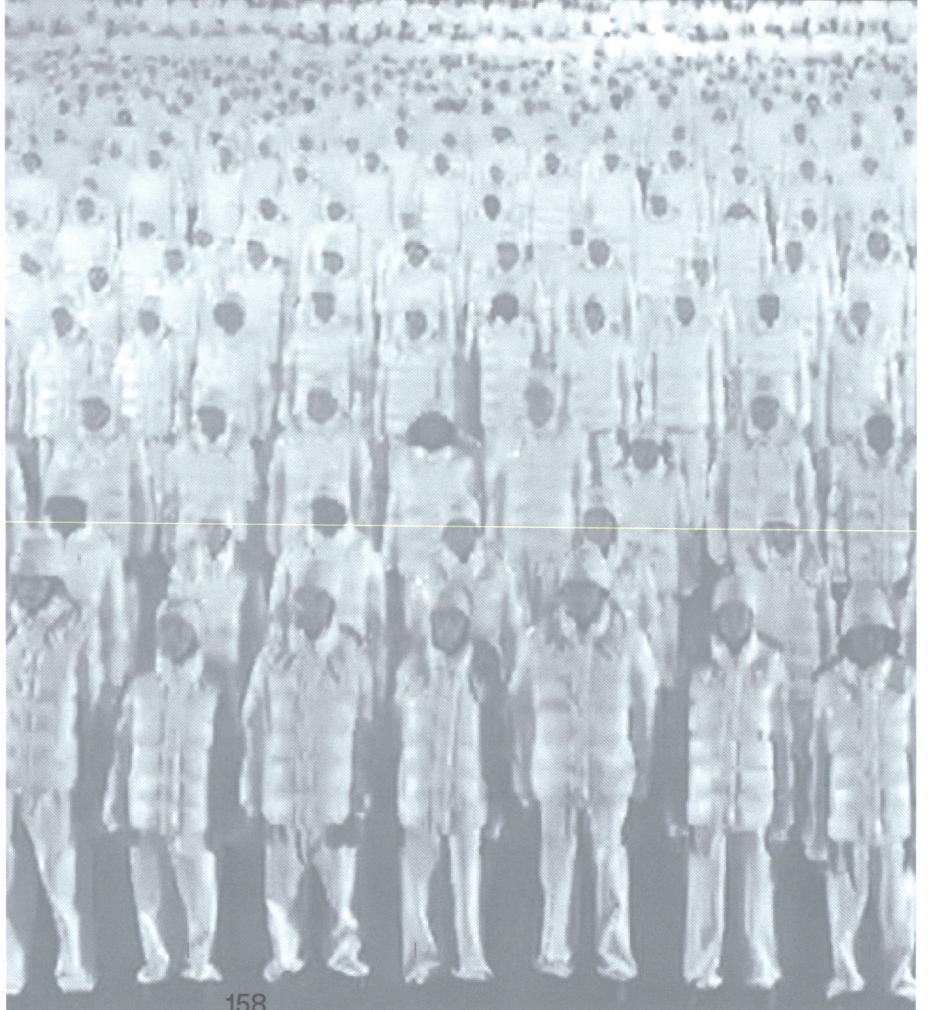

Dolce&Gabbana, *KIM DOLCE&GABBANA*, Spring/Summer 2023 women's ready-to-wear show, Milan, September 2022.
Model Puck Schrover. Video production Atlantis Film&Video S.r.l. Courtesy Dolce&Gabbana.

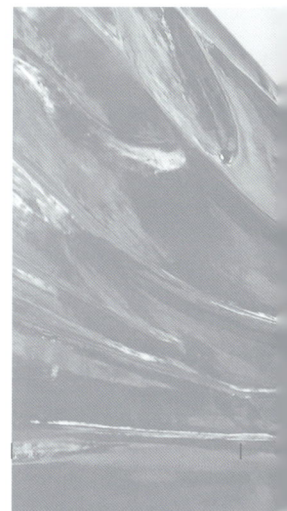

Loewe, creative direction Jonathan Anderson, Spring/Summer 2023
women's ready-to-wear show, Garde Républicaine, Paris, September 2022.
Courtesy Loewe.

Etro, creative direction Marco De Vincenzo, *Matters*, Fall/Winter 2023–24 men's ready-to-wear show, Fabbrica Orobia, Milan, January 2023. Video direction Paolo Pucci @indigitalimages, production Fabio Ceruti @indigitalimages. Courtesy Etro.

Louis Vuitton, Fall/Winter 2023-24 men's ready-to-wear show, Cour Carrée du Louvre, Paris, January 2023. Video Kitten Production.

Viktor&Rolf, *Late Stage Capitalism Waltz*, Spring/Summer 2023 haute couture show, InterContinental Paris le Grand Hotel, Paris, January 2023. Model Hannah Elyse. Video Team Peter Stigter. Courtesy Viktor&Rolf.

Dilara Findikoglu, *Not a Men's Territory*, Fall/Winter 2023–24 ready-to-wear show, The Heritage & Arts Centre, London, February 2023. Courtesy Dilara Findikoglu.

Diesel, creative direction Glenn Martens, Fall/Winter 2023–24 ready-to-wear show, Milan, September 2023. Concept and set design Krzysztof J. Lukasik. Courtesy Diesel.

Etro, creative direction Marco
De Vincenzo, *Radical*, Fall/Winter
2023-24 women's ready-to-wear
show, Palazzo del Senato, Milan,
February 2023. Video direction
Paolo Pucci @indigitalimages,
production Fabio Ceruti
@indigitalimages. Courtesy Etro.

Max Mara, *The Camelocracy*, Fall/Winter 2023-24 women's ready-to-wear show, Rotonda della Besana, Milan,
February 2023. Model Karolina Spakowski. Video direction Paolo Pucci @indigitalimages, production Fabio Ceruti
@indigitalimages. Courtesy Max Mara.

Christian Dior, creative direction Maria Grazia Chiuri, Fall/Winter 2023-24 women's ready-to-wear show, Jardin des Tuileries, Paris, February 2023. Installations Joana Vasconcelos. Model Aline Gaudin. Courtesy Christian Dior.

Miu Miu, Fall/Winter 2023-24 women's ready-to-wear show, Palais d'Iéna, Paris, March 2023. Courtesy Miu Miu.

Balenciaga, creative direction Demna Gvasalia, *Capital B: Spring 2024*, Spring 2024 ready-to-wear show, Avenue George V, Paris, May 2023. Models Eliza Douglas and Kaplan Hani. Courtesy Balenciaga.

Christian Dior, creative direction Maria Grazia Chiuri, Fall/Winter 2023-24 haute couture show, Musée Rodin, Paris, July 2023. Installations Marta Roberti. Courtesy Christian Dior.

Thom Browne, Fall/Winter 2023–24 men's haute couture show, Palais Garnier, Paris, July 2023.
Courtesy Thom Browne.

Etro, creative direction Marco De Vincenzo, *Nowhere: Out of Time, in Another Space*, Spring/Summer 2024 women's ready-to-wear show, The Mall, Milan, September 2023. Video direction Paolo Pucci @indigitalimages, production Fabio Ceruti @indigitalimages. Courtesy Etro.

ACT Nº1, Spring/Summer 2024 women's ready-to-wear show, Milan, September 2023. Model Bu Shan. Video Mario Tirelli, MT Communication. Courtesy © ACT Studio S.r.l.

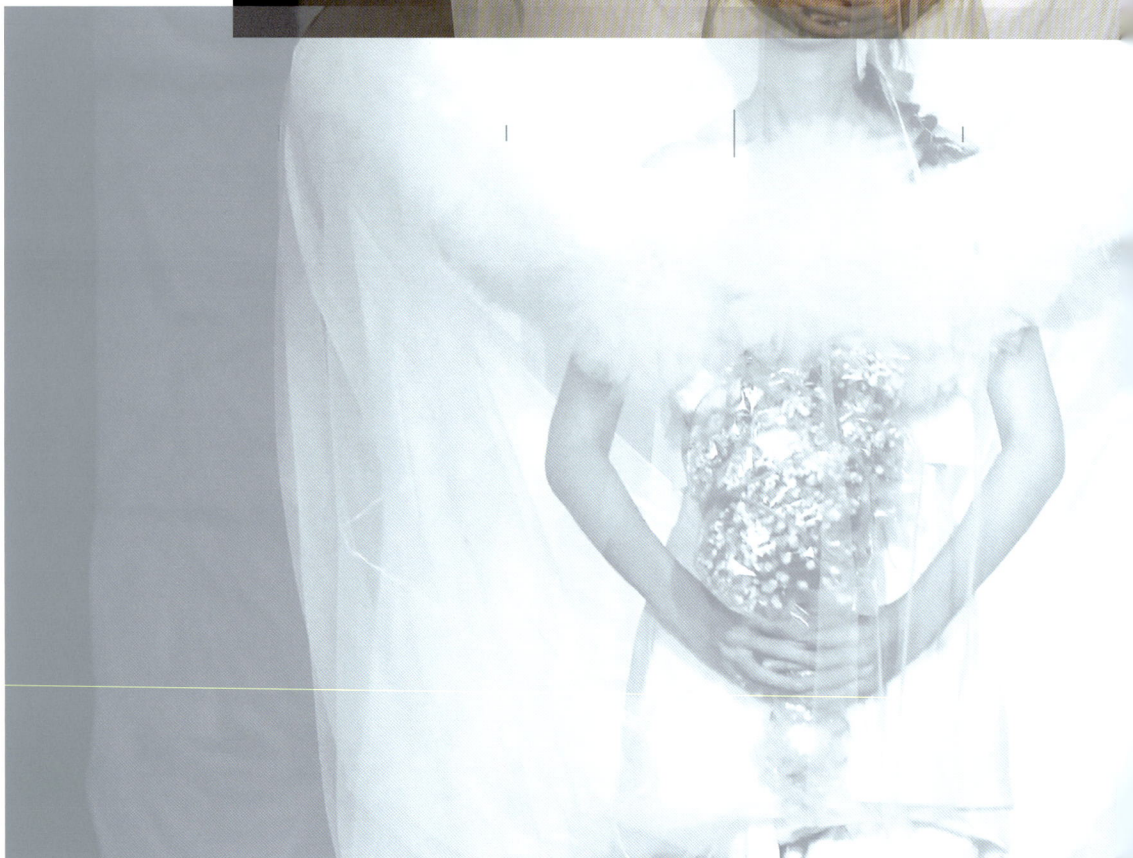

Prada, creative direction Miuccia Prada and Raf Simons, Spring/Summer 2024 women's ready-to-wear show, Fondazione Prada, Milan, September 2023. Set design OMA/AMO. Model Farah Nieuwburg. Courtesy Prada.

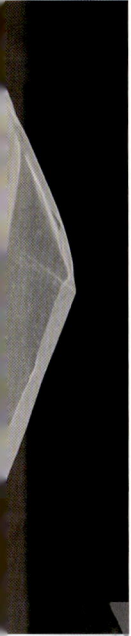

SUNNEI, Spring/Summer 2024 ready-to-wear show, Milan, September 2024. Courtesy SUNNEI.

Balenciaga, creative direction Demna Gvasalia, *Summer 24*, Summer 2024 ready-to-wear show, Paris, October 2023. Model Linda Loppa. Courtesy Balenciaga.

Louis Vuitton, artistic direction Pharrell Williams, Spring/Summer 2024 men's ready-to-wear show, Pont Neuf, Paris, June 2023. Model Teo Cordier. Video Kitten Production.

Christian Dior, creative direction Kim Jones, Spring/Summer 2024 men's ready-to-wear show, École Militaire, Paris, June 2023. Courtesy Christian Dior.

Gucci, creative direction Sabato De Sarno, *Gucci Ancora Notte*, LACMA (Los Angeles County Museum of Art), November 2023. Model Kirsty Hume. Courtesy Gucci.

Marc Jacobs, Spring/Summer 2024 women's ready-to-wear show, Park Avenue Armory, New York, February 2024.
Courtesy Marc Jacobs International.

MSGM, Fall/Winter 2024–25 men's ready-to-wear show, Porta Venezia metro station, Milan, January 2024. Model Axel Hermann.

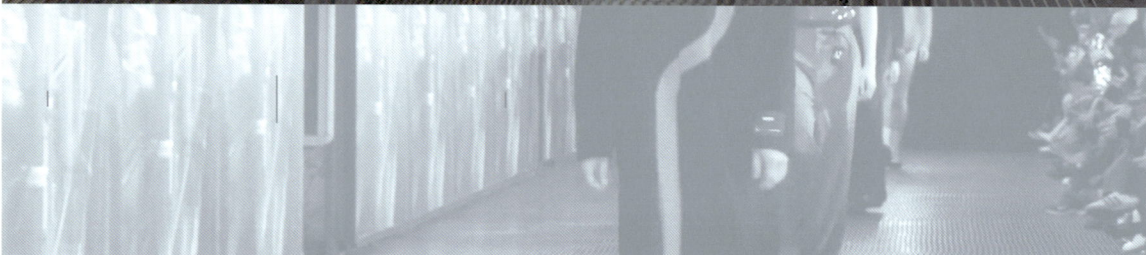

Maison Margiela, creative direction John Galliano, *Artisanal Collection 2024*, Spring/ Summer 2024 haute couture show, Pont Alexandre III, Paris, January 2024. Model Leon Dame. Creative direction and video production Bureau Future. Courtesy Maison Margiela.

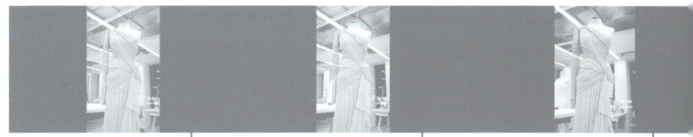

Versace, "Atelier Versace for Tyla and Victoria at #GRAMMYs," TikTok, February 5, 2024.

Etro, creative direction Marco De Vincenzo, *Act*, Fall/Winter 2024–25
women's ready-to-wear show, The Mall, Milan, February 2024. Video direction
Paolo Pucci @indigitalimages, production Fabio Ceruti @indigitalimages.
Courtesy Etro.

Moschino, creative direction Adrian Appiolaza, Fall/Winter 2024–25
ready-to-wear show, Palazzo della Permanente, Milan, February 2024.
Courtesy Moschino.

Ann Demeulemeester, creative direction Stefano Gallici, Fall/Winter 2024–25 women's ready-to-wear show, Espace des Blancs Manteaux, Paris, March 2024. Composer Neuf Voix. Video production Sergio Salerni / Urban Production / Videogang. Courtesy © Ann Demeulemeester.

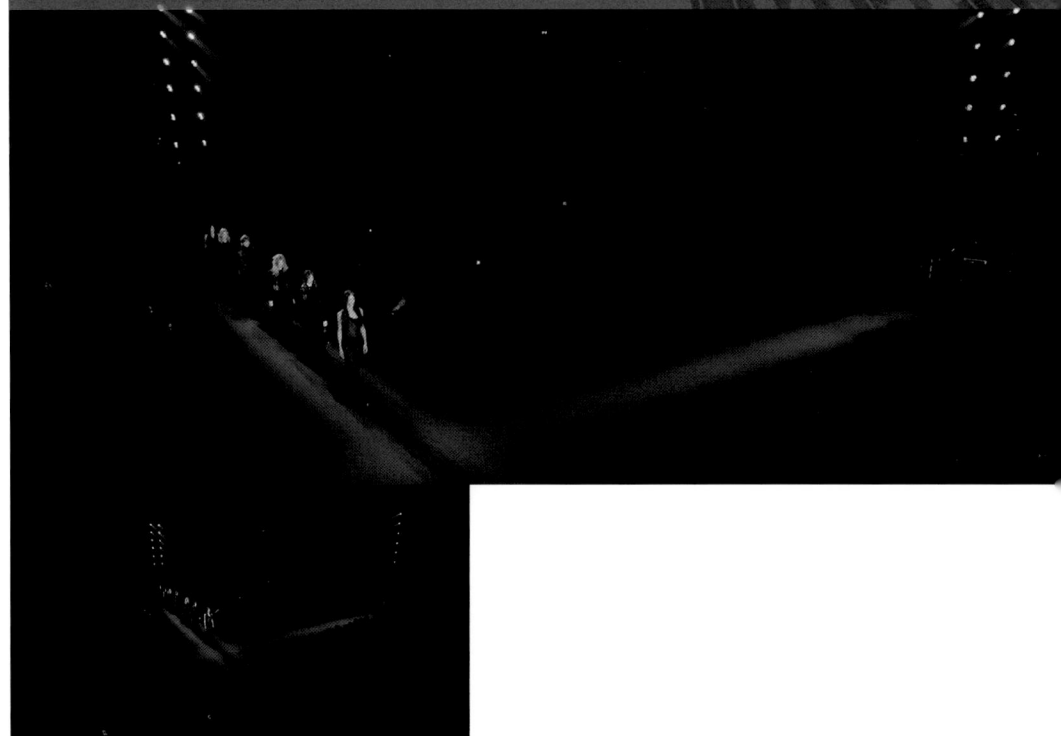

cameramoda, "On the red carpet at #MetGala2024 with some of the looks from Italian Designers," TikTok, May 7, 2024.

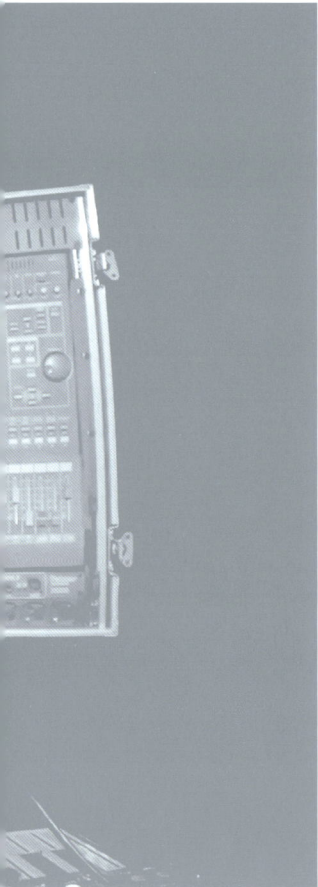

Gucci, creative direction Sabato De Sarno, resort 2025 women's ready-to-wear show, Tate Modern, London, May 2024. Courtesy Gucci.

Gucci, "Fringe that slows #GucciSS25 #MFW," TikTok, June 20, 2024.

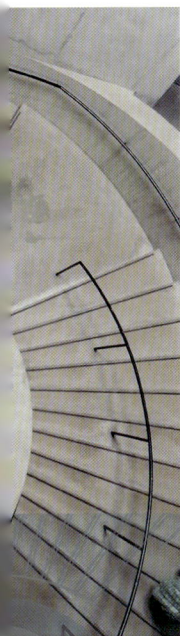

Giorgio Armani Privé, *Pearls*, Fall/Winter 2024–25 haute couture show, Palais de Tokyo, Paris, June 2024. Models Anna Bicanova and Maryana Hordiytsyak. Courtesy Giorgio Armani.

Giorgio Armani Privé, *Pearls*, Fall/Winter 2024–25 haute couture show, Palais de Tokyo, Paris, June 2024. Models Anna Bicanova and Maryana Hordiytsyak. Courtesy Giorgio Armani.

Valentino, creative direction Alessandro Michele, *Pavillon des Folies*, Spring/Summer 2025 women's ready-to-wear show, Paris, September 2024. Installation Alfredo Pirri. Courtesy Valentino S.p.a.

Ipermoda: Voices

In dialectical relationship with the visual atlas created for this book, we have chosen to present some of the forms that paper-based publishing, especially of independent magazines, has assumed in recent years, becoming a space for reflection on the practices, processes, and imagery of contemporary fashion. A selection of the periodical publications that have given space to the voices of the protagonists of fashion makes up an account of the work of design based on the form of the interview. The pages of the magazines have been reproduced with the original graphic layout and format of these publications, which, at a time when the digital seems to have gained the upper hand, represent ever more precisely a space set aside for reflection, one inwhich to assume a critical and questioning position with regard to the fashion system of today.

Maria Luisa Frisa

'There's something wrong about big brands.'

The inimitable Miuccia Prada.

Few, if any, designers match the mind and mindset of Miuccia Prada.

At a time when fashion houses seem increasingly judged on their financial form – like some kind of results-based sporting contest – we can sometimes lose sight of just how unique a voice she is. Intimate yet operating at scale, never afraid to contradict or backtrack, and offering a female presence that's defined only by its wonderfully unpredictable nature – formidable one moment, frivolous the next – there has always been more than one Miuccia Prada.

Which is why we drafted in a few friends to help us explore her world and her work, and listen to the designer in her own words.

In June, we invited Raf Simons to Milan to chat with her about what it means to be a fashion designer today (back then, Raf only had eyes for his own label, but his subsequent appointment as creative director at US giant Calvin Klein now adds an interesting perspective to their conversation). Then super-stylist Katie Grand interviewed Mrs. Prada about their shared favourite subject – Prada clothes – and shot her own enviable Prada and Miu Miu archives with photographer Norbert Schoerner. Next up, 20-year-old writer, actress and Prada-phile, Tavi Gevinson, quizzed Mrs. Prada about what she means to women (of all ages) and what women mean to her. And finally, we sent photographer Juergen Teller down the Carsten Höller slide in Mrs. Prada's office in Milan (and he came back with some pictures of her, too).

What comes to the fore over the following pages is simply confirmation of a long-held belief. Beyond seasonal trends or Q4's financial results, everybody loves Miuccia.

71

'Us designers rarely get the chance to be together.'

Miuccia Prada and Raf Simons in conversation.

By Jonathan Wingfield

96

Raf Simons

'I'm never jealous of the good ones.'

Raf Simons and Miuccia Prada in conversation.

memorabile ipermoda

Miuccia Prada

Let's start the interview by discussing interviews. Love them? Loathe them? Necessary evil?

Miuccia Prada: I generally have a problem with doing interviews because the only way I can talk is if I say what I really think, otherwise it's impossible. But sometimes what I think – and therefore what I say in interviews – is not always deemed politically correct.

Raf Simons: That's one of the things I think we should talk about today; I think that designers should be freer to say what we really think. These days, we are no longer able to; we're supposed to always self-censor ourselves. People express such extreme opinions online about our collections, yet if we dare say one thing that is not politically acceptable…

Miuccia Prada: …we are killed!

That doesn't bode very well for this interview!

Miuccia Prada: [Laughs] No, no, it is not the journalist's questions; it is what gets picked up *after* the interview. If in a context like this, I want to touch on a delicate subject, or express who I am, then I can articulate and discuss that and you will understand, but when a single sentence is taken out of this context – removing any irony or anything else – then it becomes another thing altogether.

Raf Simons: The more visible your position, the more you have to be careful. Having my own brand is different from when I was at Dior; people are not so focused on it. But at that time, I felt like there was all this pressure on how to behave and how not to behave, or how to speak. Not that I was given a list of

course, is fine. Personally, I don't care if somebody hates my work; I have no problem with it.

Do you feel it is important for designers to communicate through words – written or spoken?

Miuccia Prada: I think it is my job to speak through the clothes.

Raf Simons: As designers, we choose to work through clothes and fashion shows and photography and everything. But I think we also have something to say. These days, there are so many people judging the fashion world who I don't even know – beyond the people we know and respect, like Suzy Menkes or Tim Blanks – and they often have such extreme things to say that I feel they sometimes position themselves *above* people who have long-term experi-

'People express such extreme opinions online about our collections, yet if we dare say one thing that is not politically acceptable, we are totally destroyed!'

Raf Simons: And I find that very problematic.

Miuccia Prada: Me, too. I sense this so much, and I always find myself self-censoring because anything interesting that I want to express no longer seems possible. [As a designer] you don't always have the time to explain what it is you want to say; you might be thinking about a complex conceptual idea but you want to be lighter, what you say might come out like a *boutade*,[1] but that *boutade* becomes the headline – one word becomes your mantra. So you feel you don't have any control over your thoughts, and very often – sometimes in a good way, sometimes bad – there is less possibility to answer. You can't say this, you can't say that, so it is better not to talk. The last interview I did, I took out 80 percent.

rules; it just automatically happens like that. I found it very complicated, and [because of that] I started to read less and less about fashion, even though I'm usually really interested in what other people have to say.

Do you feel this is the case across the industry?

Raf Simons: I feel that everybody has become very careful – especially designers, and it is the actual designer's point of view that I like to read the most. I am far more interested in what designers have to say than people might think. I can be a big fan of other designers, though I can also really hate the work of other designers, even though I am not supposed to say that. Hate is the wrong word, of course, but there are things you just don't like, which of

ence. I am somebody who is very into young opinions, young voices, young creativity, but I don't really know who all these people are.

Miuccia Prada: It depends on who you listen to: sometimes there are very good comments on the Internet, and then there can be something stupid. When you just have these naked anonymous comments you should be able to say to yourself, 'Who cares?' The tendency should be *not* to read these anymore, but I can't resist being curious.

Raf Simons: Me neither.

Miuccia Prada: It's our job, we have to know what is happening, but it goes beyond that. I think the complexity we are facing is almost worse than for politicians; up until the 1980s and even the 1990s, there was an audience group in fashion that you basically knew. But

98

now you have to work with *everybody*, for better or worse.

Do you like the fact that you're now talking to a wider audience?

Miuccia Prada: I like the idea of sharing my ideas with more people; that's the interesting part, to work outside the small elite that I know. You are obliged to face the truth of different countries, of different people, but at the same time, the sheer quantity of comments – clever or stupid – that comes with a bigger audience is something that doesn't work. The whole world is talking, but there is nothing coming out.

Raf Simons: While I have no problem with negative responses towards me, I do have a problem that I cannot be negative myself.

Miuccia Prada: I completely agree.

or bloggers? Why do we have to be the only ones under inquisition? I once said to a journalist, 'Listen, you judge us, and although we never say it, we judge you, too'. [Laughs]

Raf Simons: I know that if Miuccia and I were speaking in a closed environment, we would speak in more extreme ways, and about other brands, too, because I know that they are speaking about us. It is not about being good or bad, it is about having an opinion, and I have a very specific opinion about other brands. I mean, right now I could throw two words out onto the table – two brand names – and we could have a discussion about them and if you published it, a bomb will go off! [Laughs]

Do you feel you are able to articulate your opinion about what is happening

Because without that freedom to talk, the mind does not progress; if you cannot say bad things – or things that might be considered politically incorrect – how can you even hold a discussion? Being politically correct doesn't allow you to be objective.

I presume it's the dissemination of information now that's at the root of these issues? I mean, you might have said something 20 years ago and it would have been contained in a magazine or a radio interview. But now you'll say something and 20 minutes later, it is all over the world.

Miuccia Prada: I don't know if it is just the fact it is so spread out. We probably have to be so politically correct because our business has become bigger; if you are small you can say what you like –

'I could throw two words onto the table – two brand names – and we could have a discussion about them, and if you published it, a bomb would go off!'

Who's telling you not to be negative?

Raf Simons: No one is telling us, but you get punished for it. By the public.

Miuccia Prada: It is so true that through our job we cannot talk, and yet we are the minds behind all this big industry success. Maybe we don't take our job into our own hands enough, and we should do.

Raf Simons: I have said things in the past that got me really punished. Publicly. I felt really upset afterwards and I thought, 'God, man, why do I have to be punished by some anonymous person who writes the ugliest thing about my show? And why am I not allowed to react?' I guess, because when you are a public person you have to just shut up.

Miuccia Prada: As designers I feel that we are always very strongly accused. Why does no one accuse journalists

in fashion through the collections and what it is you do as a brand?

Raf Simons: I think with my and Miuccia's shows they are clearly a reaction to specific things that we see. What I saw onstage yesterday [at Prada's Autumn/ Winter 2016/17 menswear show] was a very clear reaction.

Does the self-censorship you've both mentioned impact the way you design?

Miuccia Prada: No, not at all. I feel that in my job as a designer I have complete freedom.

Raf Simons: Yes, me too. I feel free with the collections. More and more. You just let it all out there, in the collection…

Miuccia Prada: On the subject of self-censorship, I feel like we should create a small group in which we can be free to talk, because I cannot stand it anymore.

whether that's something super smart or avant-garde or just stupid – and nothing will happen. But if you are a big brand or part of a big group, it automatically becomes more moralistic. And in general, people are becoming increasingly conservative; and so the more superficial and the more generic that you come across as, the less you are criticized. This censorship has a negative effect and is a very serious thing.

Raf Simons: I think Miuccia's suggestion of discussing these things in a kind of closed group is very interesting. It is important to know that there are other people who are of the same mindset as me, and share the same opinions; to know that I could talk to them about these things is very satisfying. The simple fact that I know Miuccia and a few others are out there is almost enough.

99

Miuccia Prada: I would love to create that group of people – the ones who respect each other – where we can say what we want. And the group should make a designers' declaration; that would be so fun and so interesting and so honest! But the difficult part would be how to share those ideas and thoughts with others afterwards.

Raf Simons: Just doing that would already make us appear pretentious.

Miuccia Prada: Can you imagine? [Laughs] It would be impossible!

Raf, you've mentioned your interest in other designers, interacting with them, exchanging thoughts, and so on. Why did you want to do this conversation with Mrs. Prada?

Raf Simons: Beyond the small group of people around me – my assistants, my

something that you can do with everyone; you need to have mutual respect.

How do you regard the sense of competition among designers?

Raf Simons: There is obviously competition, but there is also respect. I think we are all competitive, and that is a good thing. I mean, I feel competitive towards Miuccia, and she with me…

Miuccia Prada: Of course.

Raf Simons: But that is a healthy competition, which I think we should always maintain, but then I am also really curious to share experiences, emotions…

Miuccia Prada: Yes, if you have mutual respect. I'm always saying, 'I'm never jealous of the good ones'. What drives me crazy is when people are successful and I don't respect them. Or when they are tricky and pretend not to be.

I really want Prada to stay in a context that I like. Because we grow, grow, grow and suddenly you start to lose control, and there's something wrong with that, now I think we stopped that.

Is there a moment in fashion when you think structurally a big house becomes too big?

Raf Simons: I think the problem right now is that there is all this freedom in the actual garments and the performance on stage and whatever, but there is no more freedom in the structure [of a house]. Most of us Belgians have remained small and independent, but for many, structure has evolved into this kind of massive octopus where there is no more freedom; the structure itself has becomes too dominant and too defining.

'Prada is my own company, so it's my own fault that it's the size it is. But I don't have to care if we don't grow enough for the market. Whatever, who cares.'

friends, my family – I really feel a lack of dialogue with people I have something seriously in common with. I mean, I don't think I can relate to absolutely *everybody*, but I was starting to feel very isolated in this world. When he had this LVMH Prize[2] about two years ago, everybody came to Paris the night before it started, so Marc, Phoebe and I had dinner together at Marc's house, which was such an eye-opener for me. And for them as well, I think.

Miuccia Prada: Because you were free to talk?

Raf Simons: Yes. It really set my mind in a different way. The three of us reflecting on things 20 years ago, 10 years ago, and how we feel about the future; it wasn't the kind of conversation I was expecting to have, but everyone felt free. That is, of course, not

Raf Simons: There's lots of them.

Miuccia Prada: Many.

I get the feeling you're both wary of the fact that this industry has become just that – an industry. And with that comes so many more brands, more consumers, more magazines, more opinions, and a greater scale of operations…

Miuccia Prada: I think there's something slightly wrong about this idea of big brands. Raf did the biggest thing by leaving [Dior] – *chapeau*, respect – because he probably didn't feel comfortable anymore. Of course, Prada is my own company, so it's my own fault that it is the size it is, but now I'm at a moment where I really want to focus on what I like, what I care about. I don't have to care if we don't grow enough for the market. Whatever, who cares,

Can you give me an example of how that manifests itself?

Raf Simons: Part of it is this idea of keeping the audience happy, with the events and the dinners and the presents and the advertising systems. Sometimes I think I would like to make it simpler, but more exciting…

Miuccia Prada: …and also more fun. I totally agree with him. One thing that I would really love to do is to work with Raf, and maybe with other people – it would be so much fun. If I could do a show with him, imagine how much fun we would have.

What is stopping you?

Miuccia Prada: Nothing, I think it is an experiment that could really be done.

Raf Simons: Maybe structure might be stopping that. Even my own Raf Simons brand – compared to a big power brand like Dior – is still structured. That gives possibilities, but it also gives a lot of non-possibilities. For me, I would be excited if Miuccia would do the Raf Simons brand for a season, and then I would do a season for Marc Jacobs in New York, and Marc would do Prada; I think the audience would be totally excited by that.

Miuccia Prada: Ah, completely!

Raf Simons: Maybe fashion should operate more like a museum, where you have a museum curator, but you have *guest* curators come in, too. I think that the fashion business has recently stopped exploring its own possibilities; it should become much more liberated once again.

Miuccia Prada: I totally agree. I really think that's true.

know, typically within the creative structure there is the creative director, then the right-hand, and the other internal designers. Other structures might not be compatible. A couple of years ago I did a collection together with the American artist Sterling Ruby[3] – he is a close friend who I trust very much, which is why I said, 'Let's do a collection together, but let's do it all the way'. His voice was as present as mine, which is not usually the case. When you are in your own structure – even if you have a right hand – my voice or Miuccia's voice remains the biggest. But when I invited Sterling, our voices were equal, the label had the two names on it, and it was a real eye opener, because I had to step back.

Miuccia Prada: Did that make you feel uncomfortable?

Raf Simons: For a moment, but not per-

too strange, and sometimes I think to myself, 'Is this the right thing to do?' – because there is that fine line between pure art and fashion. I've always wanted to make clothes that people wear, otherwise I'd change my job and become an artist. I am a fashion designer and I do a commercial job, but at the same time we want to be creative and we always want to push limits. Also there is this entertainment aspect: people just want to be excited. For instance, if Raf did the next Prada show instead of me, the whole world would be going 'Wow!' But maybe that's *all* they would talk about. So you have to be careful that the choices you make are not influenced by this increasing need for entertainment.

Do you feel that fearlessness becomes harder to exercise the bigger you get?

'Could you imagine if, one season, Miuccia did the Raf Simons brand, then I'd go do Marc Jacobs, and Marc would come and do Prada? It'd be so exciting!'

Raf Simons: But it is up to the big voices to make that kind of decision themselves, because fashion is not a system that sits around wanting that. If Miuccia or Marc Jacobs say, 'I am going to let this person do my brand for a season, and then I am going there for a season', *then* others will follow. But it won't happen until then.

Miuccia Prada: Yes, and I am thinking more and more about exactly this kind of idea, because it feels like it is *needed* – not just to get the world talking, but to broaden the horizons of what fashion can be, and also to have fun. What I mainly think is that you have fun when you really do good stuff, and that fun comes with other people.

Raf Simons: But the structure itself within today's fashion business doesn't always allow for that kind of idea. You

sonally, because I love him and collaborating together was easy. But in terms of what Sterling brought, it was something that I would not have come up with alone. I kept thinking the collection had to be more special and he kept saying, 'No, it has to be a normal shirt, and a normal pair of jeans, nothing more, not a special cut or design'. And at the end, when it all came together, I was like, 'Man, you were right'. Sometimes you just need this different eye and different mindset to break out from your own systematic behaviour.

Do you think that fashion is losing its sense of fearlessness?

Miuccia Prada: No, I think that still exists in our work, because many designers are quite risky in what they do now. Perhaps we do things that are

Miuccia Prada: I decided to become bigger, and I like the idea of sharing my ideas with more people, but at some point you lose control of what happens after your show. It's a very interesting moment right now in fashion, because Raf is right, maybe we should have more courage. He certainly did.

Raf Simons: It does feel like that to me. The whole thing about leaving Dior was not that easy, but I found there was a difference between being a creative director and having your own brand. I am one of the few people who has done both. You have people who are creative directors – they are born creative directors, like Ghesquière, Slimane – who do not know what it is to have their own brand. And then there are the others who only have their own brands, and then there are people who do both.

101

And it is really day and night, I think. The responsibility, the emotion...

Miuccia Prada: Do you have any preference between the two?

Raf Simons: No, I like both. When you have your own brand it is something that you build, it is like your own baby. And when you are a creative director, you also treat it like a baby, but it is not *your* baby.

Ironically, it was Mrs. Prada and Mr. Bertelli who first gave you that opportunity to work for another brand, Jil Sander.[4]

Raf Simons: Yes, that was a big thing for me; I hadn't even done womenswear at that point, so I was scared. I was also thinking it would be a long-term thing – in the end it was seven years. Dior was short in comparison, only three-and-

because we can be very demanding, I think, regarding what we want and how we see things in terms of our creative input – but I didn't want to force my thing onto Dior either. I just came to the conclusion that this is where I stand, and this is what I will have to deal with if I sign up for the long term; and it is not how I want it, it's not how I see things. I have my thoughts about what I think Dior could become over time, and they have their ideas of what it *will* become. I wish them the best with it, but it just wasn't my thing in the long run.

Mrs. Prada, what was your feeling when you first heard that Raf was going to leave?

Miuccia Prada: I thought he did something very honest and brave. But I agree, I am sure he sees it as something

in the days when everything was quite calm. When I started my brand it took years before people took any serious notice.

Miuccia Prada: Now everything is so public, everything becomes a big deal, and that is wrong and not necessary.

Raf Simons: It creates unnecessary pressure.

Since leaving Dior, do you feel now that you have regained a sense of ownership because the work you're currently doing has your name on it? And is that ownership and responsibility important to you?

Raf Simons: It *is* important to me, absolutely. But my own brand structure has always been pretty small, and I think that's why subconsciously I also took on these big structure jobs – to kind of

'People like Ghesquière and Slimane are born creative directors, but they don't know what it is to have their own brand. It is day and night, I think.'

a-half years. Going in to these brands, I realized you cannot possibly know what it is like until you are there, being creative director – you just don't know. And as much as there was incredible beauty in that house [Dior], and incredible people and ateliers and everything, I just felt like, 'This isn't for me, I am not the right person for them'. That was very, very complicated.

Miuccia Prada: Do you feel stronger now than you did a year ago?

Raf Simons: No, not necessarily; just the same. It is not something that I see as such a big thing, this whole idea of leaving Dior. I know lots of people were like, 'Oh my God, you left Dior', but I don't see it like that. There was no fight, there was no conflict; it was just a conclusion that I made quite quickly. I don't know if it is because I am Belgian –

much less dramatic than how it was viewed from the outside.

Raf Simons: The whole of the fashion world sees these things as like [feigning shock], 'You cannot leave LVMH; you cannot leave Dior'. But when it comes to things like that I feel that you have to put each other on the same team, on the same level, and I am sure it wasn't easy for them. Sometimes I hate the whole spectacle that surrounds the fashion world.

Miuccia Prada: Yes, too much attention.

You mean the hysteria?

Raf Simons: Yes, when people go into a new position or leave a position there is so much spectacle; the system pumps it up, and very often the brand pumps it up, too. I've always thought, 'Just give me a little bit of time'. I started back

feel that distinction in scale. Now, after two decades, I've started to realize that I am not so unhappy with my own thing being small in scale. Of course, there is very little economic possibility, but with very little you can still do things that are crucial to a certain number of people, and those people react in ways that is really satisfying.

Miuccia Prada: It is absolutely time to rethink these systems and structures that have come to define us.

Raf Simons: Yes, I do think that there is something that we have to rethink. You know, there are a lot of people in charge right now who are not creative, and that is new.

Prada seems to remain an exception. Can I ask you Raf, what is it you admire about Prada?

102

Miuccia Prada: No, no, no, I don't want to hear this. I am sure we respect each other, *punto*!

Raf Simons: That is easy for me to explain: on all levels, I can sense Miuccia's very clear vision, her mindset, her view of the world, her view of art, her political opinions. And as one person she is able to construct and share that on such a huge scale. I find that mind-blowing.

How important is that when it comes to appreciating fashion design– actual garments?

Raf Simons: The reason I wear Prada is not just because I like the clothes; it's also because Miuccia has a mindset that I can relate to. You know, there are all these brands in the world today making so many beautiful things – because

there was this idea of the Margiela woman, or the Dries Van Noten woman, or the Yohji Yamamoto woman or the Helmut Lang woman, or the Prada woman, or Prada man. It was based on mindset and culture. And because I think that the mindset that Prada has is extreme, I am very impressed that it could be scaled up to become this kind of institution. I am a big mess of course, because I have a similarly extreme mindset and yet I am still sitting here with a small brand!

Miuccia Prada: It doesn't matter. You can have a small brand or a big brand, but the influence you have can be huge, in either case.

Do you recognize what Raf is saying about the clothes needing a mindset?

Miuccia Prada: Yes, I agree. You look

it. Memory in fashion doesn't even last six months.

Why do you think that is?

Miuccia Prada: People get too much information, too much of everything.

Raf Simons: When you are a more-established fashion brand, you are not supposed to say things about new people coming through, because then you are thought to be complaining. But I think it is clear enough to everyone what is new and what is not new, what is a copy; what makes sense and what doesn't make sense.

How hard is it to continue finding original ideas? Is originality absolutely fundamental to what you do?

Miuccia Prada: I like the idea of doing something that is new, that is for sure.

'I think that Prada's mindset is quite extreme,
so I am very impressed that it could be scaled up
to become this kind of institution.'

everybody knows how to make clothes and design patterns and make things look beautiful – but I don't want all that shit if the mindset is not what I can relate to. So even if a brand has a beautiful coat, if the person who designed it is not the kind of person I can relate to in terms of vision or opinion or culture, then I just don't want to wear it. And I think that is different from lots of people.

You think for most people garments eclipse meaning?

Raf Simons: I think lots of people just *grab* whatever they can, simply because it is beautiful. And I think that is where fashion became a very different thing in the last decade. You take a bag from this brand, shoes from that one, a coat from another. When I was growing up, I always liked the fact that in fashion

at something and think it is a beautiful, but who cares about clothes if the mindset doesn't correspond to you. Also, without sounding pretentious, I think that while people like us are very demanding, or sophisticated, or whatever you want to say, I think this sense of criticism is quite rare. Most people tend to have such a superficial opinion of things.

Raf Simons: The other outstanding thing about Miuccia is that she is a true pioneer, and there are very few pioneers in the fashion world. There are a *lot* of followers in fashion, as there always has been. In the 1950s and 1960s it was the same. Now I sometimes think that fashion no longer has a memory.

Miuccia Prada: Oh, yes, yes, completely! These days, the last person to have done something, is the one who owns

At least I tend towards that. But it sometimes feels like everything has been done, so today it is sometimes more about context and how you choose to put things together. For instance, you can work on something that is pop, and why women like bows, hearts, pink, and so on, and so the collection plays on that sense of obviousness.

Do you like the idea that you are sometimes referencing yourself in your own archives?

Miuccia Prada: I prefer not to, although I sometimes decide to do it. And anyway I have to say one thing about Raf: sometimes I think I've had a fantastic idea, and Olivier,[5] who works with me and Fabio[6] on shows and knows Raf's work so well, says to me, 'Miuccia, Raf already did that before'. [Laughs]

103

Miuccia Prada

Raf, earlier you made reference to your Belgian-ness, and I was interested to know how relevant or important you think your respective origins are in the context of fashion design?

Raf Simons: Belgians have no real history when it comes to clothing or designing or manufacturing, so in that sense I think it was quite weird that suddenly there was Belgian fashion, with Martin Margiela, Dries Van Noten, Ann Demeulemeester...[7] And I think it was important not to compare Belgian fashion to Paris or Italy – with no production possibilities, no factories in its history.

Miuccia Prada: Maybe that is why it is interesting.

Raf Simons: I think so, yes. And since there was no history, everybody was feeling the desire to do their thing,

from. And I think that a designer like Martin Margiela had a problem thinking about structure during his whole career. He was not structured, he was a creative person, and had he not had his business partner, Jenny Meirens,[8] maybe we would never have even heard about him. I think that's the case for quite a few of us.

Mrs. Prada, as time goes by, do you feel you have a greater ambivalence or a greater fondness for your Italian-ness?

Miuccia Prada: The way I was brought up was never really Italian. I mean, I'm deeply rooted in Italy, but that was never at the top of my thinking. I just wanted to be in the world, so I never felt this Italian-ness, even though I maybe am so Italian. But last year I kind of decided to be more patriotic....

Raf Simons: I think the opposite.

Miuccia Prada: Me, too. More and more. I have to say, when I was starting this job, in the late 1960s and early 1970s, it felt like it was the worst possible moment to be a fashion designer. This was the feminist revolution and I was leftist,[9] working for the [Communist] Party, yet I loved fashion and that prevailed. But there was a real sense of shame for me to be working in fashion because it felt too superficial. And then, maybe 10 years ago, I noticed so much appreciation from intellectuals, artists, architects and so on. They really respect fashion now, they enjoy my position, and seeing what I can do for them with my Fondazione. I think it is curious how what I learned through fashion has had so much influence on the Fondazione, because fashion is very free – at least in

'Sometimes, I'll think I've had a fantastic idea, but Olivier Rizzo, who works with me and knows Raf's work, says, 'Miuccia, Raf's already done that.''

but were shy about the exposure they might get. We feel small because we are a small country, but then deep inside a lot can happen when you feel small. That is a psychological thing, so I could feel from that generation that there was so much they wanted to let out, but they were shy and reluctant. I find that in fashion the people who scream the loudest very often have the least to say. Anyway, I think that my generation, which is the following generation, definitely carried the same weight of not really being supported by the country, because there is no system.

Miuccia Prada: It was very relevant for fashion, that different approach, fashion changed after that.

Raf Simons: With the other countries, Italy, America, France, there was a ground and a fashion structure to build

Raf Simons: Could you see yourself working in another country?

Miuccia Prada: No, I live here. I am very happy and proud of the fact that I live in the home where I was born, and the place where I started to become political is right next door – all my history is here. That grounds me and gives me strength, as do my friends.

Raf Simons: But do you think that your work would look different if you were to design it on a completely different continent?

Miuccia Prada: I have no idea... I don't think so. But who knows?

Another question for you both: an auctioneer in Paris recently told me, 'Fashion no longer has prestige'. It was a comment that's really stuck with me. I wanted to get your thoughts on this.

our minds – and I think that one of my challenges now is to demonstrate how my job as a fashion designer can help improve my work in the Fondazione. So I totally disagree that fashion has lost its prestige.

Raf Simons: I agree completely with Miuccia; I think it is extremely prestigious. In my opinion, the only problem with fashion is that it's become pop.

Miuccia Prada: Completely, like music.

Raf Simons: I didn't study fashion,[10] but for the kids from my generation who studied fashion in the 1980s, there was a slight feeling of shame about it. Parents would say, 'Oh God, our kid's into fashion, why can't he be a painter or something?' Whereas these days, I get the impression that all parents want their kids to be in fashion! Because it's become very popular and mainstream

104

and there is big prestige and there are big-money jobs, and everybody wants to be in that world. So I think it is very wrong what he says. It is not elitist anymore, maybe, but that is something different. I've said this before: I don't think we should feel ashamed that fashion was once elitist, and not for everyone. I don't think it was wrong. But I also don't think it is wrong that now it *is* supposed to be for everybody.

We are clearly in a period of huge democratization in fashion and many other fields. Do you think that elitism has value within that?
Miuccia Prada: It is a difficult question to answer. Elitism is already by definition not such a great word. Elitism is like the word luxury; they are really bad words. But if elitism means study-

Raf Simons: There is definitely a fashion hierarchy and that is connected to the idea of elite. Everybody can buy a ticket to go to a rock concert, but in fashion it is still the fashion people – the designers, the houses – who decide who can and cannot come and see their show. If it is right or wrong, I don't really know, but I would like to explore how it could function in a different way. I mean, I did my last show without *any* seating; people just stood and watched.
Miuccia Prada: Yes, everybody wants to be first row. I say, 'Listen, the world is not democratic! Designers are judged every single season – that one's the best, that's the worst, that's second best, third, fourth – so don't pretend this is a democracy'. To do a show, like Raf has, without seating seems like a much better idea.

Prada fashion and how you are able to bring that into your art foundation. But I was wondering, what are the other metrics of success for you? How do you equate success personally?
Miuccia Prada: Let's just say I am happy that a collection is successful when I feel it from the audience, or when I read comments. But after that I am very sad sometimes because I really don't enjoy the idea of success, I never have done. I am happy if it is not a disaster, but the idea of success has never really given me happiness. I don't know what would happen if my career was a disaster...

Is the day after the show – like we are today – a big comedown, a kind of hangover?
Miuccia Prada: I don't have the time to think about that. Today I have this

'Everybody wants to be on the front row, but listen, designers are judged every season – he's best, she's worst – so don't pretend this is a democracy.'

ing, searching, reading, discussing, then it is a good word.

Are the words elitism and luxury bad because you find them inherently contentious?
Miuccia Prada: When people ask me about the word luxury, I refuse to answer them because I hate that word and anyone who talks about it, whether it's a person saying luxury is a big diamond or someone else saying luxury is walking in the countryside. Personally, I think any answer is wrong when you're talking about luxury. Elite is an equally bad word if it just represents somebody who thinks they are better than another person. Then, it is obviously wrong. But if it represents something of actual worth, then it can be something good. So I don't know how to answer.

Raf Simons: Although I was scared that people would complain, 'Ah, we have to stand so long'. Because, you know, people are often complaining.
Miuccia Prada: With yesterday's show, the first row actually had the worst view; the view from the higher up rows was better! But try explaining that the fourth row is better than the first row; of course, they would prefer to sit in the front row and see less. But you see how every little thing that you say could offend somebody.
Raf Simons: We keep on coming back to what we dare and don't dare say! I mean, I think that I am quite a daring person but...
Miuccia Prada: ...not suicidal!

Mrs. Prada, you mentioned before the importance of the work you do for

interview, and then over the next 10 days, I have to work on the new Miu Miu collection, to invent a whole new world! Maybe we'll get Raf to do it!

Does that pressure to invent new worlds motivate you or make you anxious?
Miuccia Prada: Well, right now, we're in a very anxious and intense moment in general about what is happening around us, with Brexit and the Trump vote coming up. It is a very difficult and daring moment and so I am always thinking, thinking, thinking about everything in relation to my job. In that sense, it is good. But that doesn't leave a lot of time for relaxation.

It is rare that writers or musicians or architects exist within systems that

105

require them to create something entirely new every six months, or less.

Raf Simons: They have their own systems. And, as fashion designers, we still have a choice. Miuccia could say tomorrow, 'I will do one collection a year and show it whenever I want', and *everyone* would be there. But while that might please Miuccia, does that please the turnover of her company? It is as simple as that. With my personal brand I am doing two shows a year, but I could also decide to only do a single show every three years. To please myself I could do that, but I also know what that would mean economically. In the art world, though, there are people who actually do that: Robert Gober[11] doesn't really produce much work; when he is ready he'll just call [his gallerist] Matthew Marks.[12] But there are now a lot of

is just a normal working day, in-house.

Miuccia Prada: That is the moment I enjoy the most, too: when I can finally work without distraction, because there is almost always something that is involving other people. But the day when there is nothing to do except just work is like, 'Ahhhhh'. It's so relaxing.

How often is that?

Miuccia Prada: Not so often, but the pleasure of working without other distractions, those are beautiful days for me.

When and where are you able to be most creative and productive?

Miuccia Prada: I've discovered that when I am in bed – in the early morning when I am still a little bit asleep – is when I can concentrate on what really matters for me. And that helps, because

because they often finish so late. I feel *coupable* because I shouldn't take such advantage of their skills, but the quality of the people and the production is amazing.

Does this quality of production allow you the freedom to spend more time experimenting on the designs?

Miuccia Prada: Yes, and that is my fault. When I start working on a collection, I will say, 'Ah, this is nice, that is nice, this is nice', I like everything. But once the models come to the fittings, I'm more like, 'This is shit, this is shit, this is shit', and so it is only at the last moment that I really know what I want. Sometimes, I just find myself pretending to like something…

Raf Simons: We are very different, I think. Once I have the idea, usually

'Miuccia could say tomorrow, 'I'm only going to do one collection a year and show it whenever I want.' But does that please the turnover of her company?'

young artists following a system: they produce work for every art fair, every event, and there is an agenda for each show. But by doing that, then everything becomes too similar. The weird thing is that as a designer or an artist, you are always confronted with your own sense of will; it is about what *you* want and what you *don't* want, whether you allow yourself or not to do these things. And that is the most difficult thing, I think. When Miuccia speaks about her dissatisfaction, that is something I recognize very much. While sometimes I might pretend to be very satisfied, in a way, I always feel restless.

Creatively speaking, when are you happiest?

Raf Simons: In the creative environment I think I am most at peace when it

I'll arrive at work with a clearer idea. I should say that with my small group of people here, we work *really* last minute, increasingly so. And I accept that it is my fault.

Really, why?

Miuccia Prada: I don't know. There is so much to do: collections, campaigns, there is never a quiet moment. This last men's show we did in less than 15 days.

Raf Simons: You see that everywhere now, within the big structures. For my own brand, we start the collection three months before the show; otherwise it wouldn't be possible, because our structure is too small. Even at Dior, with the couture, we had to start on time.

Miuccia Prada: We have the most fantastic people here, who work miracles and are very generous with their time,

three months before the show, it won't change: the way I see it then stays exactly the same until the end. Nothing changes. I think this is because I am always used to working by myself. I don't work in the evolved fashion system, with consultants and stylists and all those people together on the creative side, except for my own creative right-hand, who is in the company permanently with me. Sometimes I think maybe I should work with more people because putting the whole show together by myself is really stressful.

Is that stress useful though, required even?

Raf Simons: Well, going back to what Miuccia said about dissatisfaction, these days I've started to hate the actual day of the show – no, not actually *hate*,

106

I should avoid using that word [laughs] – but I no longer find it in any way pleasant. I don't know why, but I see myself becoming an idiot that day. I see mistakes and then I am not gentle enough about expressing them to people. Then there is all the press afterwards, and everyone wants the same thing at the same time. I just feel very helpless and I sometimes wish we could skip the show day entirely, but, you know, it's *the* moment that many people have been waiting for. The following day can be very difficult for me, too. This season, I slept until five o'clock in the afternoon. **Miuccia Prada:** You know when I am happy? When, in my head, I know that I've got a clear concept of the show. After that, I can leave it to others, because for me that is when it is done and I am finished. The reality, of course,

maybe use those another time'. Working in a hurry you have to produce more, but there have also been some shows where the refining of the idea was so precise that at the end you have more or less what you need. I know people who do, for instance, 2,000 pieces; they mount earlier and then they select, do the styling, and so on. I don't work like that, I work out of precision and reducing, reducing, reducing.

Do you prefer chaos or calm? Or do you need a little bit of both? Because Raf, you said that the chaos stresses you out…
Raf Simons: I am not a chaotic person. I just can't do that. I can be a mess, but you know what I mean, I am not that kind of person. I am organized, which I think is very Belgian.

smiling, laughing. Until then, if I am not smiling it means I haven't done anything good.

Do you think the people who work closely with you sense that, too?
Miuccia Prada: I think so. It is a communal work, and we all know when there is something good going on.
Raf Simons: I demand from the people around me that they tell me if it is good or bad. I'd hate to be with people who say it is good all the time.
Miuccia Prada: That is one of the reasons why I like to work with Fabio so much, because most of the time he tells me what is wrong, and that is so necessary.

You've talked today about self-censorship of your words. How acute is your

'I am deeply human, even if sometimes I'm nasty with the people around me. You have to be nasty at some point in order to achieve things for everybody.'

is that I work after that moment, and I also realize that the translation of this idea into reality – from a concept into producing garments – is what is difficult, and where you learn a lot about your actual working process. Even if I might pretend that the production part is less necessary, it is of course very necessary, in order to improve my overall thinking.

Are you articulating the concept in your mind right up to the last minute?
Miuccia Prada: Yes, and I don't know if that is because I like to work under stress or because I become more difficult the nearer we get to the show. So I'll typically start with maybe four or five ideas and then one will prevail; we don't always have the time to make the other ideas into toiles, so you think, 'OK, we'll

Is organization one of your attributes, Mrs. Prada?
Miuccia Prada: I don't know. I really don't know! The result is what counts.
Raf Simons: I am only interested if what you make is sublime. If that comes out of chaos or organization, who cares? I was fascinated by the question you asked Miuccia about when you're at your most creative. For me, this comes late at night, when I should be falling asleep, when I don't really want it to, when I don't have a notebook or anything to draw with. Like you say, Miuccia, it comes like an automatism, and you immediately react. I definitely couldn't just sit down at a desk each day for three weeks and start thinking about it.
Miuccia Prada: I know when we are getting good ideas because I find myself

own sense of self-editing, of quality control in your designs or ideas?
Miuccia Prada: Ideas can be so pure when you do the fashion show, but my job forces me to see the bad things – 'This doesn't work; this isn't selling'. It forces you to see the reality, and to understand what people like, even when that isn't always what you like yourself. That is the most relevant point in my work: always to face reality. When it is good that is fine – it doesn't make my life better – but I only care about what doesn't work. Because you have so much to do that you don't have time to enjoy what is working. You have to take care of what doesn't.

Are you able in your own mind to think, 'I'm sure this is what I should be doing?' And then are you confident

107

that the people you are working with will absolutely see that?

Raf Simons: Yes. And I think if I didn't feel that coming naturally anymore then I would step out [of fashion] in a split second.

Miuccia Prada: I agree.

Raf Simons: I could not live with the self-realization of experiencing that. I am too proud for that. I see what is happening in fashion, and you have to be honest with yourself, it is a matter of your own decisions. You see people who used to be *the* most relevant, but who are no longer relevant, and they still go on…

Miuccia Prada: It depends how you see it. Maybe the actual working is more relevant than the being on top. Armani, he likes to work – it is his company, his job – so why should he stop? As a wom-

Do you find escapism in the work?

Miuccia Prada: A bit, yes. The fact that you have to go to work is distracting.

Do you see it as going to work?

Raf Simons: Even if it is demanding, it is a nest that you have created for yourself, a very safe environment. You can always go there and be with people you have a nice time with, and that you like…

Miuccia Prada: …and that those people like you.

What are your feelings about the tension between isolation and unity? Do you feel it is important, as the industry grows ever bigger, that you don't retreat into isolation?

Raf Simons: Yes, definitely. I had been in the game for about a decade

a good relationship, with nearly everyone, and it is very nice. And we don't have the occasion to be so near, because in the art world they go to the same openings, maybe they do group shows; they are forced to be together because they have the occasions. Us designers don't really have the occasion to be together…

Raf Simons: The need to have this dialogue has increased over the past couple of years, as our system has become more fucked up, and I see everybody in a situation where they seem to be more isolated.

In what ways do you feel the system has become fucked up?

Raf Simons: I might get punished for saying this, but when you are creative director in a big group I feel you get

'Sometimes my husband comes home and says, 'Let's not speak about work.' But friends, family, love, work, problems, traumas, death – it's all one.'

an I want to work until late in life. But who knows? Maybe one day I will get fed up, I'll step down, and then it will stop. I don't know exactly. But for sure I like to work.

What percentage of your life would you say you give to fashion?

Miuccia Prada: A lot.

Raf Simons: Personally, I could step out from this now.

Miuccia Prada: Because you are a man, maybe. Being a woman, perhaps if you don't work you start thinking about aging and all that stuff. Maybe you become a mother and are happy to stop, I don't know. But between the job and the Fondazione, it is such a big deal for me; I think that sometimes they are a relief from life, because sometimes life can be so tough.

or so when I realized that designers do not talk with each other. Maybe it is because I come from such a small-scale design environment. Antwerp is like a village, so you would bump into Ann Demeulemeester or Dries or Walter [Van Beirendonck] at the bakery or in a nightclub, and you would just have a dialogue.

Miuccia Prada: You know what, maybe artists and architects are forced to stay away more from one another, because they are always taking part in the same competitions or shows. I am sure they are jealous of each other.

Raf Simons: Every field has its own rules of competition.

Miuccia Prada: But any time I am with other designers – mainly the ones that I respect, but also others to whom I am maybe indifferent – I always have

pampered to the extent of becoming isolated. We've talked a bit about hierarchy today. Sure, there should be structure, but not hierarchy, and definitely not a human hierarchy. There were people at Dior who didn't dare talk to me! That is not normal. That is something I find unhealthy. It is like the king-on-the-throne kind of situation.

It feels, Mrs. Prada, that although the scale of your company has grown, there remains a distinct feeling of humanity. I think that is what defines it.

Miuccia Prada: This is really what I care about most, about human feeling and existence. I am more and more interested in people's lives: moments, fears, passions. Someone once told me, 'I don't want to make interesting things, I want my life to be interesting', and I've

108

kept that in mind, as it was a very clever person who told me.

That's quite post-materialistic.
Miuccia Prada: It's really what I'm interested in and clothes are at the service of your life. Ultimately, it's your life, and the lives of others, that counts. Even if people don't know it, I am deeply human, even if sometimes I'm nasty to people around me. You have to become nasty at some point because you have to achieve things for everybody, but really I'm not nasty at all. If I could spend my days being more generous with people, listening to their problems and so on, I would love that much more. But at some point you have to lead, you know.

It's that corporate world cliché where it's lonely at the top, and you can't share your time with that many people.
Miuccia Prada: The thing that I would love most would be to be seated in a bar with friends, from morning to night! That is what I love: to be with people. It probably doesn't look like that, but even last night I was with my friends and the people who were working at the bar and so on, having finally finished the show. It was a moment with people. I was like that when I was young and in politics. That is what I liked; I like to be with people and to talk.

Raf has spoken before about compartmentalizing his life – there's the work, and then there's the life and the family, and love – is that something that you do too, or do you think that the two merge?
Miuccia Prada: [Pauses] I think that at the end they merge… they merge. When I started to work with artists and the Fondazione, I didn't want people thinking I was taking advantage of art, so I kept them separate, even if in my mind it is not separate at all. As much as you might want to keep separation, your life and your thoughts are one. Sometimes my husband comes home and says, 'Let's not speak about work, OK?' But your life is one: friends, family, love, work, problems, traumas, death, it is all one. And that is life, basically.

Thank you both very much for your time.
Miuccia Prada: I am tired; this was really intense. Thank you, Raf, for coming.
Raf Simons: No, I thank you.
Miuccia Prada: OK, now I need to go to the bar!

1. Originally a French word meaning to 'burst forth', boutade is defined by the Merriam-Webster dictionary as 'an outbreak or burst especially of temper' and 'an 18th century French dance of impromptu character'. The *Nouveau Dictionnaire François* [sic], written by Pierre Richelet in 1710, is more expansive: 'It is a figurative dance, that was invented by the famous Bocan, master dancer, under the reign of Louis XIII, which was called boutade, because it begins in a manner that has something of the brusque, gay and alert.'

2. In 2015, Simons was a jury member of the annual LVMH Prize for young designers. The winners were Marques'Almeida. Other jury members were J.W. Anderson, Nicolas Ghesquière, Marc Jacobs, Karl Lagerfeld, Humberto Leon and Carol Lim, Phoebe Philo, Riccardo Tisci, Delphine Arnault, Jean-Paul Claverie, and Pierre-Yves Roussel.

3. Raf Simons invited Sterling Ruby to work together on his Autumn/Winter 2014 menswear collection.

4. Raf Simons was creative director at Jil Sander from 2005 to 2012. Prada bought a 75-percent stake in the German brand in 1999 before selling it to private-equity firm Change Capital Partners in 2006.

5. Olivier Rizzo is a renowned Belgian stylist. He studied at Antwerp's Royal Academy of Fine Arts, alongside his frequent collaborator, photographer Willy Vanderperre.

6. Fabio Zambernardi first started working with Prada in 1981, and has been design director for Prada and Miu Miu since November 2002.

7. After graduating from Antwerp's Royal Academy of Fine Arts in 1980, Marina Yee, Dries Van Noten, Ann Demeulemeester, Dirk Bikkembergs, Walter Van Beirendonck and Dirk Van Saene — or the Antwerp Six — put their designs in a van and drove to London. As the *New York Times* wrote in 2013, the trip 'ended up putting Belgian fashion on the international map'. Martin Margiela is often mistakenly included in the group, but had actually graduated from the Academy the previous year.

8. When Jenny Meirens co-founded Maison Martin Margiela with the designer in 1988 she was running a designer-clothing shop in Brussels, decorated with furniture found in Paris.

9. 'I was a Communist but being left wing was fashionable then. I was no different from thousands of middle-class kids,' Miuccia Prada told the *Independent* in February 2004.

10. Raf Simons studied industrial and furniture design in Genk, the city that, incidentally, is the birthplace of Martin Margiela.

11. Robert Gober is an American sculptor. Best known for his room-size installations often featuring realistic wax body parts, his work has been shown at the Fondazione Prada.

12. Matthew Marks opened his first gallery in 1989 on Madison Avenue, New York. He later became one of the first art dealers to move to Chelsea. He represents artists including Gober, Nan Goldin and Jasper Johns.

109

Making it big with Martine Rose

When Martine Rose, 37, started her company in 2007, menswear was a sea of preppy suits with dandyish pocket squares. Fast-forward a decade and she's coaxed the fashion world into her marvellously voluminous trousers, the hit of her joyfully utilitarian collections. Taking the best from 1980s and '90s subcultures with a dash of Uncool Dad mixed in, Martine is setting new standards through her own-name brand and the Balenciaga men's line for which she consults. And with the introduction of female models on her catwalk this season, women's fashion can look forward to equally broad horizons.

Photography by Andrea Spotorno, styling by Tamara Rothstein
Text by Susie Rushton

236

Martine Rose in *The Gentlewoman*, no. 16
(Fall–Winter 2017–18).

"This jacket is huge!" Martine says approvingly of her leather cover-up from Autumn/Winter 2015–16, a collaboration with BEEN TRILL. She's always liked capacious clothing. Her degree collection was "very sculptural, oversized. Nothing body-conscious." Underneath, she wears vintage ADIDAS track pants and a BALENCIAGA men's Spring/Summer 2018 T-shirt with the slogan "Think Big!" "Very apt," she says, eight and a half months into her second pregnancy. The trainers are by NIKE.

237

The soft, slightly slumping tailored jacket is from Martine's S/S '18 collection, which was shown at the Stronghold Climbing Centre in Tottenham Hale, London. As usual, the soundtrack was of paramount importance. "I told my friend Sasha [Crnobrnja] of In Flagranti, who did the music, that I wanted synthy, dad music. I wanted it to feel slightly Phil Collins-y." Martine's badge, from A/W '17, is in imitation of the kind that might be given out at a conference, she says. The black cotton T-shirt is from MARTINE ROSE A/W '16.

Hair: Mari Ohashi at LGA Management. Make-up: Gemma Smith Edhouse at LGA Management. Photographic assistance: Nicholas Riley-Bentham. Styling assistance: Camille Marchand.

238

Martine Rose in *The Gentlewoman*, no. 16
(Fall–Winter 2017-18).

Martine Rose

"There are a few reasons I got into fashion, but Michelle was one of them," says Martine Rose of her much older sister, with whom she grew up in south London. "She took me everywhere when she was a teenager and I was a baby. It was like having a younger, cooler mum." This was the 1980s and Michelle Rose, a fan of reggae and lovers rock, wore Hamnett, Gaultier and "amazing Pam Hogg dresses in really bright colours with funny puffed sleeves". Martine also idolised her cousin Darren, whose uniform was Boy London. "He was into acid house, the whole '89 rave scene. I just wanted access to that world. But it wasn't until much later that I identified it." By "it", Martine means the instantly recognisable dress codes of a style tribe.

Over the past decade, as Martine Rose has become the toast of the London fashion industry, those same tribes — plus punk DIY, ravers and '90s bike couriers — have influenced her designs. But she doesn't simply cut and paste references. The extreme silhouettes of Martine's signature pieces, like the supersized trousers and her hunchbacked tailored jackets, come from an interest in proportion play that began when she did her foundation year at Camberwell College of Arts. Then there's her fascination with commonplace characters and the real-life dressing she sees on the street. Martine's repetitive use of logos, sporty outerwear and tweaked tailoring is drawn from her preoccupation with Everyman types, who might be City bankers but lately are more often "dad-y" types, as she puts it. On proud display in her studio in Tottenham, north London, are news photos of Jeff Goldblum and Jeremy Corbyn in cargo shorts and pulled-up sports socks. An image of the latter plus bicycle made it onto her Spring/Summer 2018 show invitation.

"Jeremy's a human being," she says. "I do think he'll be prime minister, though I don't for one second think he'll get it all right."

The non-specific type of menswear these "dads" inspire is so appealing that, for many seasons, women have been buying and wearing it too. Leaning against a rail of clothes from the S/S 2018 collection, dressed in a vintage T-shirt and Adidas track pants, curly hair piled on top of her head, Martine herself is like the cheerful sister anyone would wish to have — relaxed, dry-witted and calm, despite her mounting responsibilities. She's pregnant and due any moment (her first child, a daughter, is two); she's in the middle of applying for two major fashion prizes, awarded by Andam and LVMH; and most pressingly, she has orders to produce from the latest, roundly admired autumn collection, "which we've been scrabbling to meet," she admits.

As if that weren't enough, Martine is also acting as a consulting designer for the Balenciaga menswear collections at the invitation of the brand's creative director, Demna Gvasalia. The pair met in Paris for the first time more than a year ago. "I'm a very informal person," Martine says, as we find a table in the cafe of Tottenham's Bernie Grant Arts Centre. Demna asked Martine if she would be part of his plan to reinvigorate Balenciaga's menswear. She agreed, she says, because the two designers "got on really well. For me, it was the fact that I really, really liked him. Also, I'm Georgian Orthodox, too. I had to convert when I was asked to be godmother to the daughter of a Georgian friend. I went there on holiday last summer. Anyway, Demna found that whole thing insane."

Balenciaga is her first proper job, she says, and it's been a long, almost entirely self-funded journey here from art school and then fashion college at Middlesex University. In between,

there was a small T-shirt brand, LMNOP, run with Tamara Rothstein — now her stylist — followed by shows supported by Fashion East and NewGen, and then

solo presentations in London. In the early days, Martine also worked shifts at Blacks members' club in Soho. "Ten years is a long time to keep chipping away at something before it becomes commercial, but that wasn't really what interested me about fashion. I've never been a businessperson, thinking of what people are going to buy."

Despite her dedication to work, Martine's personal life hasn't suffered. She describes big, frequent gatherings of family and friends, "always with billions of kids", held across south London or at her home in Bethnal Green, east London. Her parents — her mother, Sonia, is a former nurse and her father, Clifford, an accountant, and at one time a Black Panther — have always supported her unquestioningly, as has her partner, a plasterer, whom she met, in a true coup de foudre, outside the LMNOP studio 13 years ago. "The building had scaffolding on it, and he shouted down at me. Something really irritating. I was in a stinking mood that day, and I remember thinking, Ugh, fuck off. Then I looked up and saw that he was quite fit. I was trying to get a big roll of pattern paper into the car, and he swung down from the scaffolding to help me. I was a little bit impressed by that." He's audacious, then — enough to wear her clothes?

Martine thinks for a second. "Not the wild pieces," she says. "Not the triple-waistband trousers. But the tamer pieces, yes."

38 Martine Rose logo
39 Boy London
40 Jeff Goldblum
41 Spring/Summer 2018 collection
    See Glossary on pages 344—346.

239

'On the days we wore uniform, everyone was equal.'

Mixing function and folklore, ritual and gender, Craig Green is redefining menswear.

Interview by Hans Ulrich Obrist
Photographs by Lena C. Emery
Styling by Camille Bidault-Waddington

114

115

Craig Green's story reads like a route map for young British designers to follow. First, complete the MA in fashion design at Central Saint Martins. Then, using the momentum of your graduate show land a spot with Lulu Kennedy's support platform Fashion East or the British Fashion Council's NEWGEN. After three seasons, having solidified your position as an emerging designer in the press and winning the trust of buyers, go solo. If you'd like, then you could always apply for the LVMH Prize or the ANDAM, and in the process gain more recognition and advice from industry professionals.

None of this will happen, however, without the sort of raw design talent and clear vision that Craig Green has shown since his first collection in January 2013. The London-born design-

created sculptures for almost all his collections, transforming basic and found materials (plywood, tennis balls) into portable, wearable structures that complement and play off the clothes. While this has occasionally created some background noise – the face masks in his first collection, made from broken garden fencing, provoked a wave of sneering vitriol from Britain's most conservative tabloid newspaper – his approach has been hailed by both buyers and critics who have praised its deep emotional resonance. Indeed, Green's vision collects new converts with each passing season.

Artistic director of London's Serpentine Gallery, Hans Ulrich Obrist, sat down with Green to discuss how the designer discovered the work of artist Rachel Whiteread, how he studied

a household of just making things. I've always liked to draw and originally I thought I wanted to be a portrait painter, because at school it was one of the things I seemed to be good at. But at that point I didn't even know what Central Saint Martins was; I'd never read a fashion magazine. I was going to study art because I wanted to be a painter or sculptor.

Did you grow up here in London?
Yes, north-west London, just on the outskirts, Hendon. It's a bit like a village-y community.

So, the countryside?
Almost. It's on the edge of London where it has loads of green fields. People don't really think of it as London; it is on the motorway that leads you up to

'My dad is a plumber and my mum is a nurse; no one from my family is in a creative field. But our house was always filled with building materials.'

er started small, first working out of his parents' house in 2012, then at the Sarabande Foundation – set up in memory of Alexander McQueen – where he had a studio until late 2017, always helped by close collaborators, who are often also friends and family. While his business has grown, his vision – built on the foundation of his MA graduate collection, created under the nurturing eye of the late Louise Wilson – has remained constant. His ongoing investigation into ideas of function and protection, ritual and folklore, has produced menswear that is complicated in its simplicity and speaks across gender and geography: beautifully cut "uniforms" with carefully judged detail. He has also made each of his catwalk shows a celebration of artistic freedom. Originally at Central Saint Martins to study art, he has

in Walter Van Beirendonck's library, and how he creates clothing inspired by nuns and knights.

Hans Ulrich Obrist: Let's talk beginnings. Was it an epiphany during your childhood or adolescence that led you to fashion or was it a gradual awakening?
Craig Green: I come from a home that was really unrelated to art and fashion. My dad is a plumber and my mum is a nurse, so no one from my family is in a creative field at all. But our house was always filled with building materials, like big immersion boilers, and so was our garden, which was always really overgrown. I always had these things surrounding me, as well as people who made things. My mum was a Brownies leader,[1] so she was always doing arts and crafts, and I guess we came from

the north. It's one of those places where everyone knew each other in the pub, everyone knew each other's business. I went to the same school that my mum and my grandfather went to. It is like a village within London. In terms of an 'epiphany', it was more of a gradual process. I applied to Saint Martins because a friend of mine's dad was a prop maker for the BBC, and he said it was the best art school to go to, so I went to the open day with them. Then, when I was on the foundation course, there was something about the people I met on the fashion course: everyone was there all the time, and everyone would go out together and work really hard. I was really drawn to that community feeling. I applied to the fashion-print course, because I thought that if I am bad at making clothes, then at least I can maybe paint or draw. It was

134

very haphazard actually. I feel like you can't really make mistakes any more in how you choose your education because the fees are so high. When I was there, I was lucky enough to have a scholarship.

It's very different when your education is free. You can experiment more.
Yes. I thought I could maybe go on the fashion course for one year, then change at the end of that year and go back on to the art course. I was lucky to have that freedom to pick and choose as it went, which I imagine is very different to now.

You were testing things. The future is often made of fragments from the past, so did you have any role models? Who were or became your heroes and heroines?
I was drawn to Rachel Whiteread.[2] I

What I loved about Rachel was the idea of space, and that it was also a physical form like a house. Maybe there's something about that: our house was always full of people; the door was always open; my mum would make friends with everyone; she was very social. She was also a childminder, so after school there would be like 10 children every night. We had animals and it was all about our *house*. So maybe there was something in that.

So you had artists who inspired you, but you also had a mentor at Central Saint Martins, the late Louise Wilson.[5] This interview could be an opportunity to pay tribute to her great influence. She was someone who helped so many people. How did you meet her, and what was you experience with her

she very fearlessly encouraged you to do what you wanted to, not to worry about things, but just to enjoy the moment and what you were doing at college. On the bachelor's course, it never really clicked for me. I was never making work that I really liked, and I wasn't at the top of the class. But I had a much better time on the master's course with Louise, and I felt like we understood each other. When you respect someone like that you strive to make them proud. It is a motivation because you want to do well by her. Also, she was one of those people who would come in the morning and say: 'I woke up last night and I was thinking about those trousers you're making, and I really think you should do this.' The fact that she cared so much it almost took over her life, that was inspiring to me and probably everyone there.

'What I loved about Louise Wilson was that you always knew where you stood; she'd tell you if you looked fat or if she didn't like what you were wearing.'

loved the pure and simple but really ingenious idea of what her work was about. Fischli & Weiss[3] was one of the first things I saw at the Tate around 2007; they had that full room where they'd remade things in other materials. But from the very beginning, it was the painters Lucien Freud and Jenny Saville[4] who I found inspirational. I was obsessed with realism and trying to paint something exactly as it was. I didn't really know anything about art. I just liked to paint and draw at the beginning, but then when I discovered other artists, I guess my mind was a bit more open to that.

It's interesting about Rachel Whiteread and Fischli & Weiss. From the beginning, it seems you had very sculptural inspirations.

like? I never really spent time with her, so she has always been this mystery to me, this amazing person who was at the beginning of everybody's career. What was the secret of Louise Wilson?
Just to backtrack, I had two very important teachers. The first was my A-level teacher at college and the second was Louise Wilson. When I finished my bachelor's degree, I didn't know what I was going to do – whether I wanted a job or if I was going to do a master's. Then I met Louise and she offered me a place with a scholarship on the Saint Martins MA fashion course. What I loved about her was that you always knew exactly where you stood; she would tell you if you looked fat or if she didn't like what you were wearing. There was no beating about the bush with Louise. And what was amazing about her was that

So, her life was all about these other people she cared about.
Yes, I think so, and it showed in the work and the people who came from that course. She had amazing opinions on fashion and understood it on so many different levels. To be able to understand the work of 10 such different students, and to encourage them down their different paths, is a huge skill. But what made her so inspiring was having someone who cared that much and who made you care about what you were doing.

There's something magical when someone inspires so many people. How did she help you?
She made you realize that nothing is ever finished and nothing is ever complete. Even up to the last minute,

135

everything is open to change. Just because something took you ages doesn't mean it's great, and because you did something quickly doesn't make it no good. You can rip it up and start all over again. She would make you question your work as well, and that was important. She was strong and strict and, above all, honest, which I think that is very rare in a lot of industries now. So many other voices can tell you things, but they might have an ulterior motive. Louise had a pure voice; you trusted her and you wanted her to trust you. When we were on the course, between students we were all telling stories about Louise. We would go to the pub and someone would say: 'Oh I heard from another student that she did this to them or this.' It all worked to make everyone really care and be there

intern for him when I was on my placement year. He is quite community-ish as well, which is something that comes up a lot with me. It was a very small studio, with only one other intern, and when Walter was at the Antwerp Academy he would let us use the studio, as well as at weekends and the evenings. He had the most incredible library and I spent so long educating myself while I was there. I remember when I discovered his work about halfway through my fashion course. At the time in British fashion, it was all very floral, and that idea of dark feminine sexuality, but I never really fitted in with what everyone else was doing. I remember finding his work and that was when I shifted into menswear because he made me realize that fashion could be about anything and come from anywhere. I love

and pulling the staples out of things. At weekends, I would help them do up houses and things like that.

You've mentioned that Walter Van Beirendonck never compromises – that leads us nicely to your first collection.[6] A lack of compromise is like you and your approach to fashion. Is that first collection the beginning of your visual resume or is there earlier work that you still consider valid?

There are some house sculptures that I made for my MA collection that I still think are good. I guess that's where it kind of started. The first collection was based around the relationship between workwear and religious wear: one was for a physical function and the other for a spiritual function. It was about the similarities in the utilitarian functions

'My first collection was based around the rapport between workwear and religious wear: one for a physical function, the other for a spiritual function.'

all the time. It was teaching us: 'If you don't care, then why should I?'

And who was your second influence?
He was called Andy Barby and he was why I ended up going into further education in art. He was a teacher at Hendon School and passed away a year after I left, just after I had started at Saint Martins. I remember he taught me one really important thing, which I guess is something you don't realize when you are younger: that it's usually 1% inspiration and 99% perspiration. Just because you have the ability doesn't mean it's going to happen. He instilled in me that hard work is the most important thing.

Do you have fashion heroes or heroines?
My one hero is Walter Van Beirendonck, because I was lucky enough to

Walter because he never compromises – and that is an incredible and rare thing in fashion.

The idea that fashion could be anything is interesting.
It didn't need to have a tradition or what my rather naive idea of fashion was at the time. It didn't have to be that. It could be about anything; it could be about you, even if you don't have the most interesting background or childhood, or you weren't drawing dresses from a young age. That was when I started working with wood and sculpture, because my upbringing was all about building stuff. Besides my dad being a plumber, my uncle was a carpenter, and my other uncle was an upholsterer; it was all very physical. My after-school job was dismantling sofas

of them both, and the idea of one size fits all. It was my first catwalk collection and the clothes were kind of sexless and almost genderless in some way.

Tell me more about the first collection. It was not only very sculptural, but you erased the face. Where did that come from? It became a cause célèbre in a similar way to certain art shows in the 1990s. How did you deal with the ensuing criticism and the instant fame?
The show was in January 2013. It was a very strange, double-edged time. We had just got a studio and everyone working on the collection was either a friend or family; we did it with almost no money. The fabric was calico, which we washed and painted. The wooden sculptures were just fence panels from B&Q.[7] The whole idea came from an

136

image I found of an old collection I'd done and I'd scribbled over this person, scratched them out completely. I'd drawn on a photograph, and I just thought, 'Oh wouldn't it be amazing if we could make it look like the person had been scribbled out?' So we literally just smashed up the wooden fences and put them in piles and then joined them together. We then made a replica version of that instant and chaotic energy by painstakingly snapping wood to make it the same as the original version. So, it was almost the idea of replicating something that was not replicable. Then in terms of covering the face or shielding people, our brand is built around the idea of workwear and communal ways of dressing, and there was that idea of protection that runs through everything. That show was really about eve-

happened in fashion are more shocking than that. I just thought the sculptures were beautiful objects to see walking, more than anything else. Maybe it was because it was the first ever men's London Fashion Week,[8] and there was so much more media there, so it got picked up in a different way. But people later helped me see the opinions that really mattered, fashion people who had liked it. Looking back, it was a good thing to split opinion and to make people react, even if they hated it. That's still better than no reaction at all.

Like Walter Van Beirendonck, you did not compromise. So, the next collection…

…was all about chaos and control.[9] It all started with a tie-dye technique that is both controlled and so chaotic that you

The Spring/Summer 2015 show coincided with the aftermath of Louise Wilson's death. It was a very emotionally charged moment for you and many people in the fashion world. It was like a shockwave.

It was a very difficult time for everyone.

You seemed to capture that moment; there's a sense of mourning in that collection. How did you channel that? Was the collection an homage to your tutor?

I think it probably was an homage. With that show we went from the really painterly, really overworked collection to making everything out of cotton and bare feet. It was all about a minimalism, which I guess is something Louise always stood for. It was a very weird emotional time. I think she passed away

'I remember thinking: 'Maybe this isn't for me. It's a joke; my work is a joke. Maybe I should do something else.' There was definite doubt.'

ryone who helped. It was very much a group effort. I really can't believe we got that collection together, you know. To begin with, I was doing it in my bedroom at my mum's house, and we got a studio halfway through. Then when we showed it and the reactions! When you are young and doing your first collection… I remember thinking: 'Maybe this isn't for me. It's a joke; my work is a joke. Maybe I should do something else.' There was definite doubt.

How do you pick yourself up after that? How do you get to the next collection?

All the media things were going on over the first collection and people were making it into a joke or being offended by it, and I was kind of shocked that it would get that reaction, especially because so many other things that have

can never really control the outcome. Everything was hand-dyed. There was this idea of making someone look as if they had been crushed or squashed into a ball. We made the pieces in 3D and then painted the tie-dye onto it, so it looked like a 2D visual from the front, but like a 3D smashed visual from the side. We didn't give in, we just made something more extreme again. This one was more painterly.

That was 2014?

The end of 2013. After that, we didn't do sculpture in the collections. We made these hand-painted rugs on a table with four bags of paint. We were painting them and folding and opening, over and over again. That was kind of obsessive, like things being overly ornate and that romantic idea.

a month and a half before, so we were about halfway preparing the collection. I remember the morning of the show, when we got to the venue and John Vial, who does the hair for the shows and was a very close and very old friend of Louise's, mentioned something about her. It was just a weird and emotional day; everyone was upset and started reminiscing. But yes, maybe indirectly, it was an homage to her.

That was our first solo show;[10] the three before that had been group shows with Fashion East. The sculptures in it were very instant; they were just pieces of muslin and we knocked them up like two days before the show. We were walking up and down the street with pieces of muslin and I just loved the way it moved. We were trying to think of the most simplistic way of joining or

137

adjusting a garment, and that is where all the strings and ties came from. We kind of cinched garments in. They could be tied together in different ways.

It was very architectural and minimalist.
The clothes had an environment around them, in some way. When we were making them, we liked the idea of it being a protest, but a protest about nothing, a silent protest. That was the main idea. Our press releases sometimes sound as if we start from the beginning with these concepts, but it is really about reacting in the studio: 'Oh, that feels nice'; 'I like this piece of fabric'; 'What about this?' And usually there will be 10 failed attempts at things that don't even relate in the end. We just allow it to happen. I guess that comes from Louise Wilson as well. Just because it was

Wearable wooden sculptures and the idea of obscuring the face were back in the most recent collection,[11] but this time with fabrics attached…
That collection, now I look back at it, felt like it was all about time. We were joking around with the idea of past, future, and present, which maybe sounds like an *X-Men* movie.

There was a red and yellow sculpture and a monochrome brown one, which had a very strange sculpture in the middle.
I loved that they looked like doors – or a portal to somewhere – but also that they looked like confession booths. And I like that the fabric in the middle makes it look like if the model layed down he would be like a human seat, but also like a prayer cushion. And there are ropes like they use to swing the incense

is negative. The clothes were about that idea of seeing, like maybe seeing a photograph of something and not knowing what it was made of and then trying to recreate it, but in all the wrong materials. It was as if every time we thought of something futuristic it ended up medieval. So at the end of the collection, for example, we had these futuristic shapes that were put onto things, but in fact the shapes were taken from Celtic flags joined together. It was that idea of when you're trying to be futuristic, you end up coming full circle and being medieval.

So there is a medieval connection…
Yes. With the last collection, the line-up of 30 looks was almost the most traditional thing we could think of, but it was also the most futuristic thing we could think of. It kind of came full circle.

'Every time we thought of something futuristic it ended up medieval. We made futuristic shapes that were in fact taken from Celtic flags joined together.'

the first idea, and you spent ages on it, doesn't make it the right idea.

There is often something of the procession in your collections, an idea of medieval rituals that appeal to all the senses. In some of your collections, there is something almost monastic, with armour and protective shields. I was wondering if there is a connection to the Middle Ages?
I think there is, even in my MA collection. I've always loved clothing that has a purpose and I love religious wear; there is something so beautiful and simplistic about it. So that balance between the two is always like a constant conversation. Sometimes it goes deep into protection and armour, and then even if it starts as workwear, it often ends up feeling spiritual, maybe.

that swung when they walked. I loved the idea that they looked like scales or some weird balancing thing. I also like the way they look like an ugly clock, a cuckoo clock when they have those hanging pendulums underneath. If you think about it in terms of past, present, future, they would be the past.

And then the future and the present?
The present was a sculpture that looked like you'd photographed a jet-ski from above and then there was the seat and the protective parts of the jet ski. I like that they flapped, like a flying machine or a bird, when the models walked. It looked like they were trying to fly or like a kite. There was an idea of movement and the futuristic idea that they can fly. There was also a sense of naivety, the idea that sometimes knowing too much

So, the past present and future come together.
Yes, like with the idea of movement, of futurism.

And when you say we, who is we?
My team: seven full-time and two part-time.

So when someone is not wearing one of these structures, it becomes a sculpture. I was wondering about this double sense because you started out doing art, then moved into fashion. It's as if you are still doing sculpture.
Yes, I guess so, but what I think is fun about fashion is that there's always a person involved and they have to walk. It's really like problem solving for the body: what it's like being next to it, and how that changes.

138

Obscuring the face was in your first collection and it keeps coming back, like an eternal return in the Nietzschean sense. Where does that come from? Is it connected to giving your models a sense of anonymity or gender neutrality? From early on you've always emphasized the unisex character of your collections.

The core of everything is always based around the idea of communal ways of dress or a group of people who wear the same uniform. Which I guess relates to cults or a work force or a school uniform. I remember when I was a kid and we used to think that a school uniform was really oppressive and we really wanted to express ourselves, but then whenever it came to the no-school-uniform day – when we could wear our own clothing – all the richer kids would

was, and still is in certain communities, deemed to be men's dress; it's not about a man in a modern women's dress. There is always an idea of masculinity running through everything. It is also about functionality.

There is a lot of debate in the architecture world at the moment about communal living; there is a bigger emphasis on communal space. You talk a lot about communal dressing and that seems to put your work in sync with that movement. It's something democratic because it crosses genders and people...

I've always felt that there is something very romantic about that vision of a group of people all wearing the same kind of dress, because you don't see it very often. People don't even wear

That maybe takes us to Spring/Summer 2016, one collection of sculptures that we've skipped. I've always been obsessed with the symbol of a circle. I love horror films, and they draw that protective circle around themselves to stop the bad things coming in. Then there are circles of people. I always look up the meanings of circles. It's the sun and the moon, and I like that it's an equal distance from the centre all the way around. The sculptures in that show were called 'walking operating tables' by someone, because they look like the sheet they put over someone during an operation. There was also the idea of emphasizing the most vulnerable part of the body – like in cartoons, when people die and their souls leave their bodies and fly away. That's what those were about.

'I've always felt that there is something romantic about a group of people all wearing the same kind of dress, because you don't see it much any more.'

show off all their amazing clothing and their fancy trainers, and the poorer kids wouldn't be able to. It was like people were being compared to each other for what they had and judged, when usually, on the days we wore uniform, everyone was equal. That idea of a work force or a group of people goes back to the idea of community. I have an obsession with that and the idea of protection and the idea of how it's not about the individual, but about the group as a whole. That might also be related to obscuring the face in some way.

Did you conceive of the collections as gender neutral from the beginning or did this gradually develop over time?

Whenever we have done things like robes – you might call them skirts for men – there is always that idea that this

suits and ties to the office anymore; you don't see groups of nurses walking down the street. It is something that has been lost. Sub-cultures are different to before; now everything is much more globalized and mixed. It isn't a negative thing; it's just a different era. But I just love that idea of community and a communal way of dressing. I think that goes back to where I grew up, and my crazy mum's house filled with people.

Does your mum come to the shows?

Oh yes, she always comes. She was wearing one of the paradise jackets[12] last time; she loved it. My parents have been very supportive since the beginning.

A uniform can feel very ritualistic. Can we talk some more about rituals?

That idea of the ritual has always been there. At the very beginning of my MA course in 2011, I won a competition to do a shoe collaboration with Bally of Switzerland and the whole collection was based around the original *Wicker Man* film. I've always loved that film and I always look at folkloric ideas of tradition.

Did they produce the shoes?

Yes, once. We hacked up shoes and then put them back together, with cork and leather. Like worker boots mixed up with sandals; those kinds of ideas. We wanted to use natural crepe and rubber.

Have you designed shoes since then?

We did a collaboration this season with Grenson.[13] We wanted to make a shoe that would look like a toy soldier's shoe,

139

so we had all the ridges down the back and the front, like it had been made in plastic. That goes back to the Rachel Whiteread idea of taking something out of a mould.

The first fashion designer I met as a student in the 1980s was Helmut Lang, he told me at the time that he didn't want to open his own shops but infiltrate the existing system. What are the practical and business realities of being a fashion designer? Can you tell me about the economics, the idea of your brand and how you have remained independent?
I remember when we had to write our first business plan. Up until then it was about solving each problem as it came up, and enjoying that things were still happening. Then we had to write what the brand was about and where we

stay and who can't terrifies me. I want to decide which decisions I should make; the idea of having to justify my decisions to someone else scares me.

It's your business, but you do work on collaborations. How did the one with Moncler come about? How do these collaborations with bigger commercial brands operate?
When we were first approached by Moncler, I couldn't initially see the similarities between us. I wasn't sure about what we would do. Then I began looking into their history, and it's all about functionality and protection – which is something that we also investigate, but in a different way. When I think of Moncler I always think of that specific shape and about things being solid but as light as air. That's Moncler. We have done

working with Moncler is that they have the ability and the factories to do anything. As a young brand, you are working within the constraints of the factories or the suppliers you have around you. Also, Moncler is very open to what I think might be good. They are very open to strange ideas, which is rare.

And then there is the cinema. I am particularly fascinated by your costumes for *Alien: Covenant* and that Ridley Scott noticed your work. How do you go from the catwalk to big screen?
Janty Yates, the costume designer who has worked with Ridley Scott on a lot of his films,[16] tried calling the studio and couldn't get through. So she turned up in her car, knocked on the door and told us: 'I am Janty Yates, here is my card. I'm working on the new *Alien* film and

'I like the idea that one person can look at something and see innocence within it, while another person sees that same thing as sexual or dark.'

wanted it to go, but fashion is so haphazard and things happen and change so quickly that it is very hard to have a plan. You can have a loose plan, for the next six months or so, but it is forever changing. I think maybe that is why people within fashion are so obsessed with change. Fashion is never allowed to rest; it is a never-stop kind of thing. What I love is that I've managed to keep the brand independent, and that allows me to make decisions I feel are right. A lot of the people who work at the brand have been here since the very beginning or have stayed a long time, and it is like an extended family. We spend more time together than we do with our friends and actual family; we work really long hours, every weekend, travelling together. The idea of having someone come in and tell me who can

two seasons of capsule collections with them now.[14] In the first, we played with ideas of form and ideas of protection and functionality again, and we looked at down fetishists who dress in multiple layers of feather down and sleeping bags. The collection's shapes ended up looking very Bauhaus in terms of structure; they had solid 'roundedness' about them. Moncler thought it was like a spaceman, someone else called it a poodle man, and then someone had a more sexual reference: they called it anal-bead man. I like that idea that one person can look at something and see something innocent, and someone else sees something sexual or dark, even though it's the same thing.

We recently did a presentation of the project and Skepta[15] came along and wore the pieces. What is exciting about

saw some of your pieces. I sent pictures to Ridley Scott, and he is into maybe borrowing some samples to see them in real life, and then maybe we can go from there.' And her dog was barking in the car and she had to run out, and it was all very chaotic. And then I realised that it was Janty Yates who is the Oscar-winning costume designer for *Gladiator*. Later I found out that she had gone to Selfridges to have a look around and had seen our Autumn/Winter 2015 collection. She said that it related to exactly what she had spoken to Ridley about and his ideas for the new *Alien* film, which was kind of a mix between medieval and futuristic. It was the collection where we had the jumper with the hole. Weirdly, when we were doing that collection, we joked about how it looks like the scene when the alien jumps out

140

of the chest in *Alien*, and then a few months later, we met Janty Yates. So I don't know if there was a weird universe thing going on there. It's funny because I remember watching all the *Alien* films at my best friend's house when we were in primary school, but never did I think that I would even get to meet someone in that world, let alone be a part of the *Alien* legacy. It was such a surreal and exciting thing to do.

We haven't talked about that Autumn/Winter 2015 collection, in which faces aren't obscured, but there are repeated holes.
For that collection, we did T-shirts that looked like scars, and sewing them onto the body to adjust them. We had red looks in the middle of the show and black and white dotted throughout,

we also had the paradise ponchos. We began by looking at paradise in an innocent way, until a friend of mine said: 'Oh, but paradise is an aesthetic. It is not a thing – it is a negative idea.' I had never thought about paradise like that before, and we ended up with this idea of darkness and playing with different ideas of paradise.

A dark paradise! It's like an oxymoron.
Yes, a sinister dark paradise. The sculptures for that collection came about from trying to make a weird exercise machine. That idea of going to the gym and the aspiration of making your own ideal body relates to paradise. Some of the sculptures also look a bit like a parrot, a bird of paradise or an animal being dissected. Like a dissected frog when you pull the skin back. And some-

around, how would you describe the overall story of your label?
I always think that each collection is very different, but other people always say they're the same, but twisted. Someone said each one is the story of what it is to be a man. Maybe that is just because even if we try to be very different every time, and find something else, we always come back to one idea.

Like a leitmotif...
Sometimes it is spirituality, sometimes it is about protection, more militaristic, and falling in line. There's always that exploration of the different ways it is to be a man, maybe. Talking about the collections like this makes our process sound really conceptual, but we never start with a concept. We are about reacting and then, as we are building

'People say symmetrical faces are the most beautiful, so I liked the idea of breaking it up, dissecting the body and measuring to test if it's perfect.'

so if you saw the collection lined up, it looked like a striped flag. Janty had seen it and wanted the twisted jersey bodysuit for all the sleepwear in the film.

That was your first cinema experience?
Yes, and it was amazing how many pieces we had to make for the film. Each actor needed 12 of every single one. They were all hand-sewn, so it was a nightmare because you have to put them onto a person to sew them. I think we made like 150 full suits in jersey that had the twists all the way.

We've discussed all the collections...
There is one collection left! The one before last, the multicoloured one based around the idea of paradise, with stretched stripes.[17] The clothes were made out of sportswear jersey, and

one said the ropes on them looked like a girl's pigtails as well, which was sinister. The lines started off as pretend talismans. I like the idea of a talisman that is believed to have power, because that's again the idea of striving for paradise. And then there were the ponchos at the end with big patchwork scenes of parrots. I liked the idea that wearing it, you could stand behind someone, and become the backdrop, like when you take a photo in paradise. Also, I liked that the sculptures looked like they were measuring the body. People often say the most symmetrical face is the most beautiful, so I liked the idea of breaking it up, and dissecting the body and measuring to test if it's perfect.

Now we've discussed all your collections, even if we've slightly jumped

the idea, things are all over the place, but then it all weirdly comes together in the end. I like the fact everything is open to interpretation as we build the collection; we're not strict or directive. That's why our show notes are always just a piece of paper with two paragraphs that don't really describe anything, but just set the scene. Because I think it's really interesting to see what other people see in a collection.

Do you ever collaborate with visual artists?
I collaborate on the sculptures with a friend of mine, David Curtis-Ring;[18] we've been friends for a long time. We build sets in the studio together. In terms of visual artists, it's mainly photographers like Dan Tobin Smith;[19] he shot the last campaign. He is an

141

amazingly technical photographer and is great to work with because nothing is ever impossible. We are working on a campaign that we are shooting next week, where we are burning these huge versions of the Spring/Summer 2018 sculpture. We are making these huge burning effigies outside, all with coloured flames, but we just found out it's going to be minus 10 that day.

How do you typically start a collection? Do you sketch and draw?
I am always drawing things.

You have notebooks?
No, just weird bits of paper that I then fold up and put inside my bag.

And always by hand?
Yes, I do computer drawings because

There should be a monographic book of everything that you have done.
We often laugh and say we should do a book of all the terrible things we've made that no one's seen. A book of our failed attempts. We have photos of all of them. Because one day we are like, 'Wow, this is amazing'; then the next, 'This is terrible!' It would be a fun book.

In just a few years, you have created an amazing body of work. You must now have a younger generation of fashion designers looking up to you for advice. What would you say to a Central Saint Martins student now reading this?
I think that inspiring someone is probably the whole reason I went into fashion in the first place. I remember being at Saint Martins and one of my main aims was to be in a book in the library,

by what he wants to do and never compromises. He is completely self-taught and if you ever go to his studio, you'll see that he just makes things through the night and all day. There are lots of half-finished, weird and incredible hat inventions. He is a real genius, I think. Then, Raf Simons is a huge inspiration to everybody. He has a story within his work, which I think is very important, especially with menswear. He paved the way for everyone in menswear. I really like what Simone Rocha does, too.

I had lunch with her recently. She's extraordinary.
She is doing Moncler, too.[21] She is doing the women's and I'm doing the men's. I feel that she creates such incredible work, which has a really clear story as well; it's just amazing. The other

'Some of my favourite times are spent just making something in the studio, even if that's really rare these days. Fashion is sometimes so overwhelming.'

you have to for the factories, but I always think there is something nicer about a handmade drawing. That's where those smashed fences came from.

What about any unrealized projects? Architects publish books about their unrealized projects, but there are rarely books about artists and fashion designers'. Do you have dreams or unrealized projects within or outside fashion?
I've always wanted to do something in architecture. I've always loved ceramics, too; they are so tactile and functional. I love the materials, and the fact that they last forever. I've always wanted to make furniture, too. I think I just love making things. Some of my favourite days are spent just making something in the studio, even if that's really rare now. Fashion is sometimes so overwhelming.

and for a student to open it and make it part of their research. I think that is such an important thing to do. And for a long time, I wanted to be a teacher. In terms of advice, though: work very, very, very hard and never ask someone to do something that you wouldn't do yourself or are not prepared to do. That is what I have learned and what I have done. You have to dedicate your whole life to it, but if you love it, it doesn't matter, because life is work. It's about devotion.

Which designers of your own generation do you feel a kinship with? A proximity, maybe even a friendship?
One would be Nasir Mazhar; he is an incredible maker, a hat maker and, I think, a sculptor.[20] He's based in London and he's a real creator. He stands

people I like in London are all people I feel strongly about, and from what I understand they are all very nice people. That's important to me: working in a way that is respectful and about being kind. Kindness is key for everything – I think it comes across in the work of people who are good.

I think the keys to the 21st century are kindness and also generosity.
Yes. I went to help Nasir for a few months, just before I started on the MA and ever since then he has been very generous with his help, with materials or by teaching me how to make things. Kindness and generosity are so important.

That's a perfect conclusion. Thank you.
Thank you, that was nice.

142

1. Brownies is the section of the Girl Guides movement for girls aged 7-10 and was originally called Rosebuds. Each Brownies troop is run by an adult referred to as Brown Owl.

2. Rachel Whiteread is a British artist best known for creating artworks by casting the negative space of objects – from stairwells to tables – with concrete, plaster or resin. She was the first female artist to win the prestigious Turner Prize, awarded in 1993 for work including *House*, the cast of the interior of an entire 19th-century house in east London. Completed on October 25, 1993, the monumental sculpture was demolished on January 11, 1994. The leader of the local council, Eric Flounders, which owned the land on which it stood and ordered its destruction, called the sculpture 'utter rubbish'.

3. Swiss artists Peter Fischli and David Weiss (who died in 2012) are best known for their filmed sculptures, such as *The Way Things Go*, in which ordinary objects bump into each to create a falling-domino-style chain reaction. Their work has been much copied in advertising. The exhibition seen by Craig Green was the major retrospective of the duo's work, *Flowers & Questions*, held at London's Tate Modern from October 11, 2006, to January 14, 2007.

4. Lucian Freud (1922-2011) was, alongside Francis Bacon, the leader of the post-war London School of figurative artists. One of the 20th century's great portraitists, he was born in Berlin, the grandson of Sigmund Freud, and fled to the UK with his family in 1933. Around 2002, he was introduced to Kate Moss, and went on to paint her portrait (which later sold for £3.9 million) and tattoo two swallows at the base of her spine. Jenny Saville is a painter who first came to prominence with the group known as the Young British Artists, whose work was bought and promoted by Charles Saatchi in the 1990s. Her paintings and drawings, mainly aggressively fleshy nude portraits, do not attempt to hide their debt to Freud.

5. Louise Wilson was course director of the Fashion Design MA at Central Saint Martins from 1992 to her death, aged 52, in 2014. During her tenure, graduates from the course included Green, Alexander McQueen, Phoebe Philo, Kim Jones and Jonathan Saunders.

6. Green's first collection was Autumn/Winter 2013. The runway show featured models' faces covered by pieces of painted wood and was included in a January 2013 *Daily Mail* article under the headline: 'Is There a Prize for the Stupidest Outfit at London Fashion Week…?' Not content with this first story, the newspaper then sent a reporter around London wearing a replica of the collection's face sculptures. Under the headline, 'You Can't Wear That in Here, You Plank!', the reporter was photographed wearing it while getting on a bus and trying to drink a pint of beer.

7. B&Q is one of the UK's leading chains of home-improvement stores, with 300 branches across the country. It was founded in 1969 and for many years had one of the country's most recognizable advertising slogans: 'Don't just do it, B&Q it.'

8. The men's section of London Fashion Week was created in 2013; the most recent event attracted 46 different designers.

9. Spring/Summer 2014.

10. Tim Blanks began his Vogue Runway review of the show: 'You hear about this thing called a fashion moment – a storm of emotion leaving the audience *verklemmt* and the designer overwhelmed – but the genuine article is rare enough to be an urban myth. Until it actually happens. Which it did today during Craig Green's show.'

11. Green's Autumn/Winter 2018 runway show featured wooden frames holding swathes of fabric with tennis balls in drape latex dangling from them, which were worn in front of the body and part of the face like shields.

12. The 'paradise jackets' are straight-cut, quilted cotton jackets with brightly coloured all-over block patterns of sunsets and palm trees. They have a zip fastening.

13. Grenson was founded by William Green in Rushden, Northamptonshire, UK, in 1866. The shoes are still manufactured in the town, which is 120 kilometres north-west of London.

14. The collaboration is called Moncler C. The first capsule collection was released in September 2017 and featured glossy, black, down jackets and ski suits with adjustable straps across the body; the second, featuring lighter wear for Spring/Summer 2018, went on sale in February 2018.

15. Skepta is a British grime artist, rapper, music producer and activist. He was born Joseph Junior Adenuga in 1982 in Tottenham, north London, to Nigerian parents.

16. Janty Yates has worked on 12 films with Ridley Scott, beginning with *Gladiator* in 2000. IMDb lists her first feature-film credit as a wardrobe assistant on Jean-Jacques Annaud's prehistoric (and largely naked) epic *Quest for Fire* in 1981.

17. Spring/Summer 2018.

18. David Curtis-Ring is a London-based artist, art director and production designer who works in fashion, film and performance. He has collaborated with the Arctic Monkeys and the late Stephen Hawking.

19. Dan Tobin Smith specializes in installation and still-life photography.

20. Nasir Mazhar also designs clothing. His most recent collection was Spring/Summer 2017 menswear, and was described by Vogue Runway as no less than 'an extension of his ongoing development of an almost ceremonially stylized, extravagant sub-variety of sports-technical wear with overtones of bondage and recreational self-constraint'.

21. The collaboration is called Simone Rocha 4 Moncler. The latest collection was unveiled at Milan Fashion Week in February 2018.

Special thanks:
The Atopos CVC collection
Bath Fashion Museum
All sculptures made in collaboration with David Curtis-Ring

143

'The personal and the undeniable.'

For Francesco Risso, Marni is a platform to explore the outer limits of consciousness.

By Tim Blanks
Photographs by Ethan James Green
Styling by Tom Guinness

344

Francesco Risso was born on the deck of a boat during a winter storm at sea, and raised in the bosom of an extended, eccentric family of tailors and aesthetes in Genoa. He was not destined for ordinariness, and his stewardship of the Italian label Marni, itself a repository of the unpredictable and the arcane in its 25-year existence, has provided Risso with a platform to explore the outer limits of his consciousness *and* his creativity. It made perfect sense that I found him in the middle of the Balinese jungle, where he was on a silent qigong retreat for two weeks. I hated to break the silence with a phone call, but *System*'s needs must. He reassured me: 'I am out of my silence – I'm ready to talk.'

Tim Blanks: Is qigong a particularly esoteric discipline?

collection, I started to work with the Miao community in southern China? I kind of had this lateral experience with them and it was very, very illuminating. Somehow, it made me wonder a lot about time, and taking more of it. You know when designers used to go on long holidays and come back radiant and inspired? Through that experience with the Miao, I started asking myself all these questions and that is why I am here.

This sounds like a personal quest.
Actually, it is more about finding other ways to gather inspiration. I have always been quite obsessive about my fashion and literature and movies, almost as if I've been driving the collections through my familiarity with certain literary phenomena , while also

with *psychedelissima*, you can have a very good trip but, obviously, you can also have a very bad one.
Absolutely.

Same thing with the notion of child's play in your work. Children are innocent, but they can also be cruel. There's always that dichotomy in what you do.
There are a lot of truths in children, in how they relate to the world. It is quite spontaneous. I guess I am quite into spontaneity of thought.

Do you have to work at that or does it just come naturally?
It's more like a process of evolution. One idea gathers the other and so on, inspiration after inspiration. There is a path between the ideas. But many times, it comes from other people. The

'When I was young, I was obsessed by horror movies and really dark shit. I was fascinated by extreme romanticism that can somehow turn into tragedy.'

Francesco Risso: It comes from Chinese medicine and was born out of Taoism and the moment when people were actually trying to go a bit against the government, years and years ago, and then it became a sort of practice. I just discovered that it is used a lot as therapies in the hospitals in China. It's very much about how the body and mind are related, and it is quite amazing. I have been here for 12 days in the jungle and I haven't seen anything of Bali at all. I am just surrounded by nature and it is really beautiful.

That's a curious coincidence. That is really where the last collection was: an interplay between flesh and spirit in the jungle.
You know that between the men's collection in June and the women's

building up the stories and personalities through that process. I never believed I could stop thinking like, I don't know, Saint Laurent going to Marrakech for a month and then coming back with this amazing collection. But the Miao project was like experiencing and learning other types of processes and coming up with something else.

It's easy to see this as a search for enlightenment. You've never used fashion terminology to talk about your work. You seem as interested in expanding your mind as you are in expanding your métier – and you push the limits of your métier by pushing the limits of your mind. Like when you talked about *psychedelissima* at the last show. I think you are touching on something unusual in fashion because

last collection, the *Psychedelissima* collection, came from the people that I met in Brazil, and my interaction with them. Usually I dive a lot into books or movies, but movies are becoming a bit exclusive. It's almost like you think of people watching a movie at home rather than sharing an experience. So, lately I have been diving more into music. Particularly, the Tropicália movement in Brazil, a mix of artists who were passionate and full of so much love and creativity, as well as so motivated by politics.

You could see the people you spent time with in Brazil have been struggling for years against regimes that represent the death of nature, creativity and the imagination. I think it was Lawrence [Steele, Risso's partner in life and at Marni] who brought up the

368

idea of 'beauty as protest' after your show. That idea kind of worked its way through the whole season. But obviously you need some force behind it.

There are many versions of beauty. I see beauty when I see somebody turn their head in a particular way; that is my personal interpretation of beauty. It is very subjective. But there is also absolute beauty in nature and beauty in the body — that is undeniable. So it's about playing between the two: the personal and the undeniable. I love that.

You had a past connection with Alexander McQueen and the dichotomy that fuelled him was beauty and horror; yours is innocence and corruption. In your last show notes, you mentioned 'the fine line between beautiful vertigo and what the fuck is happening'.

You are. You get the violence. For me what you do is like Dada much of the time. The only way you get people to look at things differently is by destroying the things they are looking at. How important is the dark side to you?

It's as important as the light side, I guess. There's a lot of romanticism in the dark side. When I was young, I was obsessed by horror movies and really dark shit; people were a bit concerned. But actually, I was very fascinated by the extreme romanticism, that extreme love and beauty that somehow turns into a tragedy. I was not into torture porn or anything like that – I was passionate about *Nosferatu*, *Dracula*, the Gothicism behind those dark stories.

You call yourself @asliceofbambi on Instagram. *Bambi* is a horror movie

those gestures of pulling up the fabric and moulding it onto the body and also making it quite spontaneous and not too finished. It was underlining the process of the studio and exalting each hand somehow.

That's very against the whole mechanical aspect of fashion. We have entered an era where fashion is like a machine, but there is a spirit of defiance in what you do, even in the way you talk about your collections, very deliberately in quite abstract or surreal terms. Are you deliberately defiant of the orthodox way of doing things?

There is something interesting in diving into processes that can possibly lead how you make things, as well as resonate in the pieces that you find in stores. For instance, there was noth-

'When I wake up and have to put clothes on, I never like the way they are and sometimes I rip them off. It's not just taking away, it's *detaching*.'

It's not even something that you can define so much, but a few days ago, I was thinking that I like to destroy things and to rip them apart. That made me dig deep, and I thought, 'What is this? Am I a destructive person?' So when I dig into it, there is something about detaching from the things you are creating, detaching from the creative act itself, where you are not just this thing you have learned, you can go beyond it to find the pure essence of it. It's almost like you play with those beauty references, but then you have to destroy them so you can see the essence better. It is a part of my daily processes, a bit like a mantra. Even when I wake up and I have to put on some clothes, I never like the way they are and sometimes I rip them off. It's not just taking away, it's *detaching*. Am I explaining it well?

for little kids.

Oh, totally. But such a beauty as well.

Yes, it's like whenever human beings try to work nature out, they always get drawn into its rawness. That is what I feel in your work, in the Matisse jungle of the last collection and the one that came after you saw the Francis Bacon and Lucian Freud paintings in the *All Too Human* exhibition at the Tate in London. The way you used colour in that collection, putting it on by hand so that the paint was almost like flesh, that was so incredibly primal.

That was a beautiful process for that collection, and I really treasured those moments, working with the team and everyone in the studio. At a certain point we all sat down and said, 'We have to make this with our hands.' All

ing haute couture in that collection. It was more about how to drape with your hands to make these pleats and how to stitch them quickly and how to exalt that gesture. Everything was coded, so that it could be shown in that way, but also go into the shops and not just be like falling-apart pieces of clothing. I'm fascinated by exploring the mechanical *and* unmechanical processes of what we do. It is something that I found so interesting with the Miao people, because it is totally against the core of fast fashion and the speed of our world. It is really like diving into I-don't-know-how-many-years ago and I find it a fascinating challenge to somehow preserve those values rather than speed. I am a son of speed, but it's so beautiful to find a different reality to preserve as well.

369

Do you think it is possible?

Totally, absolutely. I mean with the trends and the power and money that goes around in fashion nowadays, why not? It would be crazy if we weren't aware of those things. I mean, are we just becoming monsters digesting everything like obsessed vacuum cleaners? I don't think so. Most people I know understand time and speed, but also appreciate the value of things and the objects they can treasure in their wardrobes. It's all possible in that sense.

Instead of 'why?', you ask 'why not?' — and to me that is the critical question in fashion. Rei Kawakubo asks it a lot. It's interesting because the sense of human possibility is becoming more and more acute as the sense of automated possibilities gets stronger with AI and so on.

I'm not sure. Maybe it's not. I want to reach them; I don't pretend they want to reach me. I'm so fucking curious. If you are outside looking in, they are so inspiring. You look at the young people in the streets protesting and they are so cool, so individual, so beautiful.

What is so powerful is the sense that they have nothing to lose because they have everything to lose. You say that maybe what you do can't be relevant to them, but what you do, more than most people in the industry, is work to create something communal, something handmade. Everything about that last show, from the clothes and the set to the models with the mud in their hair, felt like a ritual, a pagan celebration.

It is funny because the beautiful side of that ritual is that it was multiple hands

Being born on a boat during a storm, in air and water, made you some kind of fabulous fairy child. Did you feel special or different when you were young?

No. I grew up in a family with many brothers and sisters and, like any family I know, my siblings were good at making me feel not special. I was the last one, so they were like, 'Oh, he is the luckiest.' I grew up with this judgemental vibe and was silent until I was 16 when I was like, 'Bye, I'm off to have my own experience!' Maybe that is where being born on a boat came back to me, because I was able to leave. But no, I don't relate my childhood to feeling special.

How could your quest to find the relevance in irrelevance apply to fashion?

It's a really interesting question. I had a look around fashion this season and

'Are we becoming monsters digesting everything like vacuum cleaners? I don't think so. Most people appreciate the value of things they can treasure.'

It's all a bit scary, but I believe there is a renewed, *positive* emphasis on what humans are capable of.

Look at these young children marching on the streets; it gives me goosebumps. My God, it is so inspiring. Maybe we're on the edge of extinction, but on the other hand, there is this incredible force of young people. It's probably never happened before that we know. And now we have these incredible minds out on the street doing incredible things. They care about the environment, they are really pushing. And this is the 'why not?' There is the testimony of something happening out there that is the opposite of just straight consumption.

How do you make your world relevant to them?

merging in one process, in that show, in those clothes. It was all the people that I work with, a dance of multiple hands circulating around one idea.

We were talking about beauty and horror, but that is the world we live in: the hand creates and the hand destroys. It becomes this perfect metaphor for humanity. There is a huge amount of philosophy in what you do. Do you believe in destiny?

I do. There is destiny and synchronizing, I guess. Thank God I don't remember being born on a boat on a cold day in December. I do remember moments afterwards with my dad and adventurous times when I was surrounded by characters. I think that experience sets a certain DNA that synchronizes with the other experiences in my life.

more than ever it felt like everything was the opposite of everything else. What is relevant? What is irrelevant? Do you know?

Relevance to me has everything to do with engagement, urgency, accountability, compassion.

For me, it's connections. When everything in the world seems designed to divide us, anything that brings us back together is powerful. This is what Greta Thunberg and these young kids are doing now.

Looking at all that is going on in your work makes me wonder if fashion is enough for you to communicate everything you have inside you...

Maybe not. But really, is fashion enough for anybody at the moment?

370

OUT-OF-

ALESSANDRO MICHELE
Gucci mastermind unwinds outside Rome

■It's a story as old as time itself: fabulous Roman finds peace and good times in rural surroundings. Back in the days of the ancient empire it was called *otium* – a term denoting blissful moments that statesmen would take outside the urban centre for leisurely pursuits that were at turns tranquil and scholarly and sometimes debauched. ■Carrying on this fabulous tradition is GUCCI's creative director, ALESSANDRO MICHELE, a Roman boy who just likes to get away from it all from time to time. ■In an undisclosed location somewhere in the rolling hills of Umbria, ALESSANDRO has plans to turn his villa into an inspiring space for others to use while doggedly protecting his surrounding countryside from development by spa resorts, geothermal plants and chocolate-spread manufacturers. Beautiful!

Story by GERT JONKERS
Portraits by ALASDAIR McLELLAN

Alessandro Michele in *Fantastic Man*, no. 31
(Spring–Summer 2020).

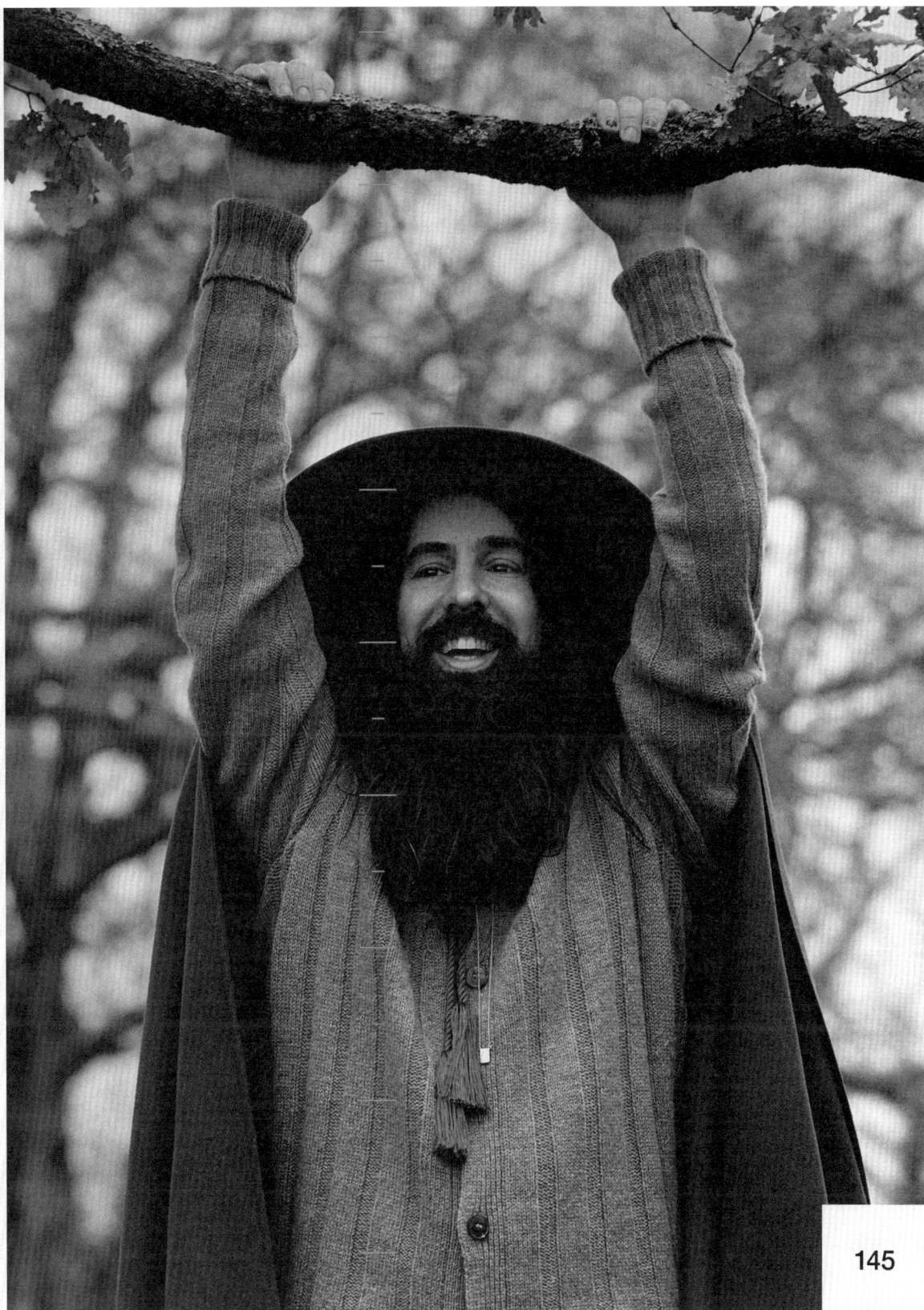

TOWN

As ALESSANDRO MICHELE's house looms up through the trees, I spot a group of five or six people standing on the lawn. They're quite far away but one figure stands out in particular. I see him from the back, moving slowly, face turned away, wrapped in a huge blue cape with long, jet-black hair cascading from a big red hat. There's an aura of magic around him. That's ALESSANDRO.

By the time I reach the house, the group has disappeared inside. We convene in a cosy room that looks like a kitchen, dining room and living room all at once. What an amazing place, I say. "Isn't it beautiful?" says ALESSANDRO. "I love beautiful things, of course." The designer has just returned from Miami, where GUCCI, together with SNAPCHAT, hosted a beach party in honour of HARMONY KORINE's new film. ALESSANDRO had never been to Miami before. "What a crazy place!" he says. "It's really an invention." He rolls his eyes. From his hotel room he had the most amazing view onto the ocean, he says.

The party coincided with Art Basel Miami Beach, so ALESSANDRO attended the fair. Did he see any art that he'd like to get for himself? "Oh, no. It's not really me. But I thought it was fun to be able to see so many galleries in one go. It's like travelling from LA to Tokyo, Berlin, London, Rome and San Francisco to see the latest art, all in one day. That's amazing."

"But," he continues, "the contemporary art market! My God, the people you see there! Crazy! They interested me more than the art, to be honest. The artists, the new rich. It's like a fruit salad of crazy people. Creepy and fabulous. So... really something for me!" He laughs. "It made me wonder if I could ever live in Miami."

Why not? I say. His fellow Italian GIANNI VERSACE famously lived there.

"You still see a lot of VERSACE in Miami," he says. "They're as obsessed with him as they were in the '90s. The one thing I found very odd was when I was walking around, looking for a place to get a coffee, and I passed by Casa Casuarina, VERSACE's house, and they've opened a restaurant in it called Gianni's. Strange, no? I use the word *strange*. It's *more* than strange! Can you imagine, creating a restaurant right there where he was killed on the stairs, and calling it Gianni's? Wow!" ALESSANDRO has a way of talking that's seeped with puzzlement and excitement. "The world is *such* a crazy place! That's why I don't want to die!"

Two years ago DONATELLA VERSACE gave ALESSANDRO a tour of GIANNI's old apartment in Milan. "GIANNI was obsessed with the past. There wasn't one thing in the house that didn't belong to the past. But I adore him for how, out of his obsession for the past, he invented something so psychedelic, so pop, so unbelievably modern. I think he's one of the most influential designers of our times. He invented what is now considered completely normal: this mix of fashion and rock 'n' roll. GIANNI, and maybe also TOM," he says, referring to his old boss, TOM FORD, who hired ALESSANDRO as senior leather-goods designer at GUCCI in 2002. "They invented a whole new way to be a fashion designer, somewhere between a movie star and a kind of fashion god. Since GIANNI and TOM, fashion design is not about how to design a skirt, but how to create a world."

A bit like you, too, I suggest, hinting at his unparalleled overhaul of GUCCI, making ALESSANDRO easily the world's most influential designer in the last half decade.

"I don't know," he says. "I'm just a country boy from Rome who's looking for something beautiful and who is trying to understand life."

If that sounds like a fabulous simplification of what could well be a terribly complex job, well, maybe that's exactly how ALESSANDRO operates his creative directorship of one of the world's biggest brands: with gut feeling and a slight sense of the philosophical. "I see my work as an investigation and I hope it'll bring me a little bit closer to understanding why we are here," he says. But, he also just loves nice clothes. I remember a great quote from ALESSANDRO, when he said that he likes the idea of dressing up and looking happy and alive so that "death doesn't recognise you."

"Yes, exactly," he says today. "When you feel bad and you put on something crazy, maybe it can carry you away and make you feel that the end is still far."

■ WALK-IN

ALESSANDRO spent two days in Miami, and when he landed back in Rome he went straight to his country house, a good two-hour drive north, which is where we meet today, on a Monday morning in December. "*Allora*," he says. "I love it here. It's like a village. I'd love to live here permanently one day."

ALESSANDRO currently lives in Rome. If I'm counting right, he has five houses: his humble old apartment in Rome, and a super swanky new apartment that he and his boyfriend, GIOVANNI ATTILI (known to everyone as VANNI), recently moved into and where, allegedly, ALESSANDRO's walk-in closet is bigger than the entirety of their previous flat. They already have a country place in Civita di Bagnoregio, which they've had for years, and they bought a second house in the same town, for visiting friends. "These two little houses," ALESSANDRO calls them. Their original house in Civita has often been described in the press, as has the way ALESSANDRO, after landing the GUCCI job exactly five years ago, holed up there alone to drum up the outline of his first women's collection. Perched on a hilltop and surrounded by steep ravines, Civita di Bagnoregio is incredibly picturesque and now so touristic that in 2013 the municipality started charging tourists

Alessandro Michele in *Fantastic Man*, no. 31
(Spring-Summer 2020).

226

146

ALESSANDRO, who is 47 years old, says he'll likely retire from fashion one day, but he'll never retire from life; it's just too much fun, he thinks.

Just to the right of his enormous front door, ALESSANDRO is wearing his favourite country cape, a cardigan, jeans, and the red hat he designed for himself to wear to the LACMA gala in LA, 2019. Sewn inside the hat are two labels: one says GUCCI and the other LALLO, his nickname.
Photographic assistance by Lex Kembery and Simon Mackinlay.

Alessandro Michele in *Fantastic Man*, no. 31 (Spring–Summer 2020).

(currently €5) to enter. "They must be making millions," ALESSANDRO says, and since it made him feel a little bit like a tourist attraction himself, ALESSANDRO and VANNI started looking for a new house in the countryside.

The term "house" doesn't really do justice to where we are today. ALESSANDRO has kindly asked me to not go into details about where it is that he spends his time off. Maybe it's because, still, after five years at GUCCI's creative helm and a hundred public appearances alongside ELTON JOHN or JARED LETO, he's slightly uncomfortable with being at the centre of attention. But also, who wants fans knocking on your door on a free weekend away? But let's just say the venue is pretty remote and amazingly gorgeous. It has 360° views over the sprawling hills around it, and yes, given that the complex comprises several buildings, there's something village-like to it. Some of the structures are in ruins and need substantial work, which ALESSANDRO and VANNI, a professor in urban planning at the Sapienza University of Rome, have embraced with a certain patience. They bought the place almost three years ago, and part of the house, following some renovation, is perfectly liveable. We're sat in the kitchen/living room, where an assistant serves espresso in jaunty coffee cups that close with a lid. (They could well be from GUCCI, or from RICHARD GINORI, the Kering-owned tableware brand where ALESSANDRO served as a creative director, part time, when he was assisting GUCCI's previous creative director, FRIDA GIANNINI. They gave him the job at the chic ceramics brand to keep him motivated.)

There's incense burning and CHET BAKER is singing. It's a wonderfully cosy place. Friends are walking in and out, and one of them brought a pit bull that plays with ALESSANDRO's two Boston terriers, BOSCO and ORSO. VANNI, carrying a laptop, walks by and says hello. He's a towering man with bright blue eyes and a ravishing beard, who wears a long, tweed coat with a bear embroidered on the back.

How did they find this amazing location? "I was looking for something…," says ALESSANDRO. "No, I wasn't *looking*, I was *dreaming* of an empty place with a lot of land, and then this place found *me*. Mutual attraction. This old lady was living here – it was her family's estate. The place was collapsing. She was looking to sell and she was about to sign with a real estate developer who wanted to turn this into a spa hotel! Can you imagine?" There's an expression of horror on his face. "So I told her that I wanted to live here, and she started to cry. 'I don't know who you are, but you just saved my life,' she said."

It's an exemplary tale of the demise of Italian aristocracy, says ALESSANDRO; the old rich can't afford this kind of country fabulosity any more. Aren't you the *new* Italian aristocracy, I suggest, and isn't that why this place lives on with your loving help? "Interesting," he says. "I'm definitely trying to buy more land around here. We were just discussing that last night when we were standing outside and we saw these deer playing like kids. It was so beautiful… There's the constant danger of investors trying to develop the land around here." Big conglomerates are wanting to buy tracts of land to grow hazelnuts for their chocolate spread, in order to keep their "Made in Italy" label. "They'll cultivate the land intensively," says ALESSANDRO. (A few weeks after our meeting, ALESSANDRO is mentioned in a story in 'The New York Times' that hints not only at the threat of nut harvesting in the area but also – even worse – a geothermal plant being built near his estate. "Hasn't beauty a value?" the paper quotes him as saying, and "I ask myself, in 2020, do we really need to still destroy everything?")

■ GUCCY

The very first time I saw ALESSANDRO was the moment a lot of people saw ALESSANDRO for the first time: on Monday, 19 January 2015, at 1.20pm, on a stage in Milan. A shy man with half-long hair and a bushy beard, wearing a cream Aran jumper and grey, baggy jeans, took a bow after the first GUCCI show he was in charge of. He had spent a frantic few days with the design team whipping up a brand-new and completely radical collection of gender-challenging dress-up fun. It felt quite retro, as if he'd plundered someone's attic full of fabulous silk blouses, oddly proportioned suits with the creases from years of storage still clearly visible, vintage granny glasses and fur-lined house slippers. It was different from everything else being shown at the time. Where did this come from? From a thrift-shopping fan, clearly, and someone who loves a bit of history. He was officially appointed as creative director two days after the show – much to everyone's surprise, including his own.

ALESSANDRO's touch demanded a huge overhaul of the company, from somewhat glitzy and cold to fun and warm. It proved a runaway success for GUCCI, with the house's total revenue growing from €3.9 billion when he started (sales rose 13 per cent in the quarter after that first menswear show), to €9.6 billion in 2019. That's a lot of expansion in five years.

What's extra startling, though, is how ALESSANDRO's vision seems quite singular yet can embrace seemingly opposite styles so naturally in a total hodgepodge of yesteryear influences. I'm old enough (as is ALESSANDRO) to remember how certain style movements would clash, sometimes aggressively so, in the 1970s and '80s. Hippies hated punks and vice versa, and punks looked down on disco and its happy glitziness. Skinheads hated everyone who wasn't a skinhead, and everyone hated skinheads, even if their bleached, rolled-up jeans worn with

Dr. MARTENS were a hot look. Then one day in June 2016 I saw a GUCCI show in the hallowed halls of Westminster Abbey in London where punk T-shirts and disco shoes and hippie bags and skinhead jeans all merged in happy unity, and it still made sense. And even when you think you know what you'll find in a GUCCI store, it can be a surprise to see what's on offer. Is that a house painter's uniform next to a chic blazer covered in Gs and a sweatshirt with "Guccy" scribbled on it with a sharpie? It has the exciting what-am-I-going-to-find-here-today? factor of a dream flea market. ALESSANDRO's is an eccentric signature that looks unmistakably GUCCI yet can encompass almost everything. What a brilliant concept!

His inspirations are clearly more historical than futuristic, but ALESSANDRO doesn't like the notion of nostalgia. "Unlike the Renaissance or Classicism, which were about revamping something that's interesting for the present, I think it's only in our current era that we treat the past as something that needs to be preserved. And to preserve something that is dead feels wrong to me. You risk ending up with a postcard, something without life. So I want to preserve this place by pushing it into the now," he says of his house in the countryside. "I'd like to preserve the atmosphere of this place. But it's important to start a conversation between the past and the present. I'm not really a nostalgic person. I mean, I love the past, but only when the past is really alive in the present. Otherwise you're just sitting in a ruin." And anyway, who knows exactly what happened here in the past? "Maybe they held raves here in the Middle Ages," says ALESSANDRO.

■ JOLLY HEDONISM

ALESSANDRO and VANNI are here a few days per month, and for longer stretches of time around Christmas and in the summer. It's huge for just the two of them and their cute dogs, but ALESSANDRO's idea is to breathe life into the place. "We want to give young, beautiful people the chance to work here, study here. They should have the opportunity to live in beauty." They're planning a theatre, classrooms for VANNI's students, and studios for residencies. "Maybe the GUCCI studio can set up here," he says. But he might be joking. The place is a perfect example of *otium* – that ancient Roman tradition where the empire's high society would spend their time off in the countryside, for contemplation, meditation and maybe some jolly hedonism. Although he clearly appreciates the rest and relaxation and tranquillity that are to be had from his country retreat, when I mention the concept he doesn't seem so keen on the idea of compartmentalising one's life. "Does that strict divide of city and country still really apply? You don't have to stand in the middle of Trafalgar Square to get a sense of the city.   151

"*I'm not really a nostalgic person. I mean, I love the past, but only when the past is really alive in the present.*"

You can be in the middle of nowhere and still be in the middle of everything happening." Yesterday, here, in countryside bliss, ALESSANDRO was working on some red-carpet dresses. "I don't mind. I open my laptop or iPad, work a bit, and close it again, and I'm done. I'm not a slave, you see? That's the magic of technology: you can switch it off."

■ STOIC

The first time I met ALESSANDRO properly was on a Monday in Rome, 15 February 2016, at 3pm. That morning, on landing at Fiumicino Airport, I'd got a hint of ALESSANDRO's universe. Instead of the ubiquitous chauffeur in a black suit, ALESSANDRO's PR man was awaiting me in a super jolly see-through knitted jumper with a big butterfly embroidered on the chest.

ALESSANDRO occupied a chapel in GUCCI's headquarters, in a palazzo designed by RAPHAEL, the Renaissance painter and architect. MICHELANGELO used to live on the other side of the street. ALESSANDRO was in a baggy T-shirt, brown corduroy trousers and turquoise slip-on shoes with bees embroidered on them in gold thread. "I'm sorry, they're a bit outrageous," he said. On a shelf behind his desk sat a stuffed bird and a collection of wooden hands on sticks like you'd see in the window of an antique glove shop. On ALESSANDRO's wrist, a gold ROLEX. We chatted for 15 minutes. His assistant served an extremely strong espresso. WIM MERTENS's modern minimalism played in the background. At the time, ALESSANDRO was just over one year into his tenure at GUCCI. The whole world was banging on his door, but he didn't seem too fussed about the pressure. "To be honest, I expected to be fired immediately after that first show," he said, so all this felt like a bonus, which is a very stoic way of looking at stress.

And that's still the vibe I get from ALESSANDRO today, in and around his country residence. There must be massive pressure to deliver, to keep GUCCI's perpendicular growth figures going, even when fashion's eternal cycle will one day turn back from maximalism to simplicity. But if that's on ALESSANDRO's mind, he's good at hiding it. He's busy preparing his first stand-alone men's show in years, after he pushed for showing menswear and womenswear simultaneously. He's not reverting for financial or visibility reasons. "I just feel like it," he says. Just like he feels the urge to support young, new fashion designers in Milan (but he'll do it behind the scenes, he says). He also wants to restore the old, overgrown oak-lined drive to the house. He points to a building that's boarded up. "We think that could be classrooms," he says. I don't see a pool, or an orchard, or even a terrace for a breakfast in the sun. "Oh, but I hate the sun on my skin," says ALESSANDRO, hence the wide-brimmed red hat he keeps on hand all the time.

ALESSANDRO grew up in Rome with an airline-engineer father, who was also an accomplished sculptor, and a mother working in the film industry. Their city apartment had a huge garden with lots of birds in cages, and dogs, cats and turtles roaming around. "I'd love to get a third dog," he says, as ORSO and BOSCO snore loudly through our conversation. "Or, even better, I'd like to *find* another dog, or to have another dog find *me*. The countryside is such a delight for dogs. When I see ORSO and BOSCO running around here, being happy and free, that's beautiful."

Beautiful is, naturally, ALESSANDRO's favourite word. "Isn't it beautiful here? I love beautiful things, of course," was the first thing I heard him say today. And beautiful applies to almost anything:
– The view on the nearby lake is beautiful.
– The Renaissance villas that old aristocrat families built in the area are beautiful.
– Montefiascone is a beautiful town, as is Civita di Bagnoregio.
– The upper floor of his house is still in ruins: that's beautiful.
– The beautiful people that he puts in his GUCCI shows and campaigns may not be the supermodel type of beautiful, but "my kind of beautiful, nerdy Milanese students with beautiful ugly faces."
– If ALESSANDRO ever retires from fashion, he might open a beautiful flower shop.
– INSTAGRAM was beautiful when it started, but ALESSANDRO is bored with it now. These days his 685,000 followers get only the occasional glimpse of his life.
– Ugly fashion from the '90s can be beautiful.
– My chipping nail polish is beautiful.
– He recommends a visit to Orvieto Cathedral's Cappella Nuova to see the Renaissance frescoes – showing mass gatherings of medieval people, naked, in paradise, or being received in hell. "They're crazy and look like a contemporary movie," says ALESSANDRO. "So beautiful. I sometimes go there for inspiration."

ALESSANDRO's favourite realm of inspiration and contemplation is his storage space in Rome, stuffed with artefacts. "I used to have three warehouses full of stuff," he says, with a hint of embarrassment. He would probably qualify as a hoarder. "Yes, I buy at CHRISTIE'S, DOROTHEUM. 1stDIBS not so much; it isn't very good any more, I find. My favourites are little English auction houses away from the city – you find the most beautiful Tudor and Stuart Age portrait paintings. I won't say they go for nothing, but they're still really cheap. I shouldn't say this, of course; I'm ruining my own market."

The charm of a good old physical, Sunday-morning flea market is already long gone, he finds, although as a dedicated collector he can't stop trying. His finds often inform his work at GUCCI. "Old books, weird children's dresses, odd objects... Things that aren't really fashionable. Relics, I call them. I don't care about

a vintage PACO RABANNE or SAINT LAURENT dress, you see?" Today, after lunch, ALESSANDRO and his friends are heading to an antique building-materials outlet nearby. "You can find the most amazing things there: fireplaces, stairways, fences. It's not always clear where they got it, and you wonder if they got it the regular way. In other words, very Italian!" He bursts out laughing.

Tomorrow he's heading back to Rome. ALESSANDRO is known to thrive on the interaction he has with his team and is said to ask people's opinion constantly. "I want to know how people perceive things. What's the response? I don't want to make things that are just fancy or nice. If someone from my team says, 'Oh, that's cute, that's nice' – I hate that! It makes me want to scream! I want to make things that are *unbelievably fabulous* or *terrible*! I can be happy with *terrible*. I hate *cute*."

■ CAPE

We're standing on the porch of ALESSANDRO's premises. The designer is wearing sturdy hiking boots (not GUCCI), a pair of jeans, an old white T-shirt, a generous camel cardigan, his big red hat and a big, ornate cape. "So practical; it's like a blanket," he says. "And it's fun. It makes me happy." He may have saved the property from the claws of a 5-star-spa-hotel developer, but he's turned it into his own haven of mindfulness. While we're talking, the GUCCI press machine is busy sending out news of a capsule collection featuring MICKEY MOUSE, a range of beauty products, new sneakers, a GUCCI-sponsored art show in Seoul, South Korea, and the launch of a photography book in Milan. But ALESSANDRO MICHELE is perfectly in the now, relaxed, enjoying a leisurely start to the week, his mind uncluttered with regrets of things past or future worries. "I bought a new camera," he says. "I love taking still pictures. I don't pretend to be a photographer; I just love to play with it. Nothing serious."

Alessandro Michele in *Fantastic Man*, no. 31 (Spring-Summer 2020).

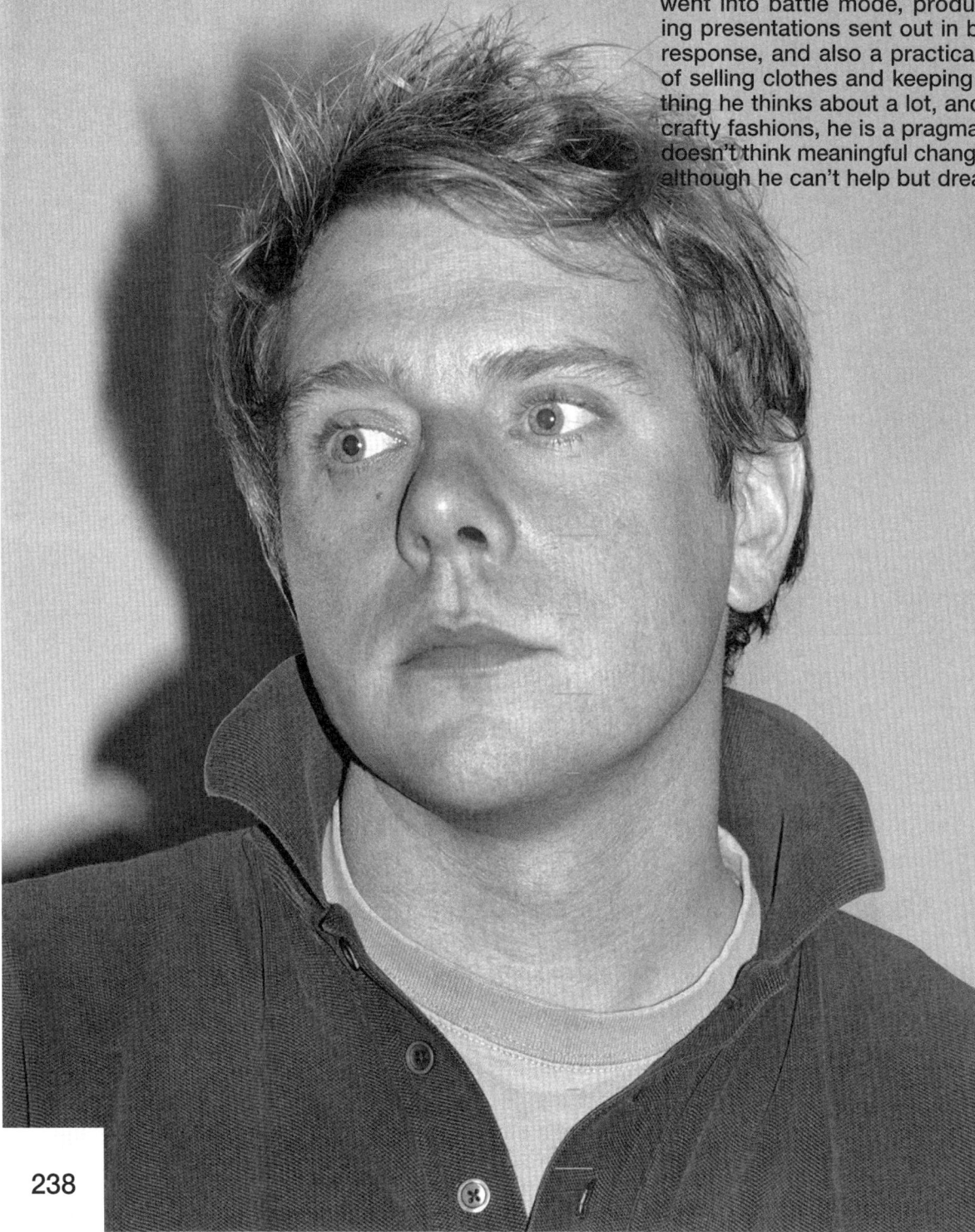

JONATHAN ANDERSON
of LOEWE

■ Designer JONATHAN ANDERSON runs two exciting labels: Parisian-based LOEWE and the eponymous JW ANDERSON. When the world went into lockdown, he went into battle mode, producing two thought-provoking presentations sent out in boxes. ■ It was a creative response, and also a practical solution, to the problem of selling clothes and keeping people in jobs. It's something he thinks about a lot, and beneath his fantastically crafty fashions, he is a pragmatic business leader. ■ He doesn't think meaningful change is coming any time soon, although he can't help but dream.

238

Jonathan Anderson in *Fantastic Man*, no. 32
(Fall–Winter 2020–21).

Interview by GERT JONKERS
Portrait by RETO SCHMID

GERT: Congratulations on your recent projects and on actually making two collections in lockdown. How did you manage?

JONATHAN: In the first couple of weeks I was, kind of like, "How the hell is this going to work?" I had no idea what we were going to do, or how. I was in one country, most of my team was in another, someone else in yet another. Fashion is a tactile process, and from one day to the next it became a non-tactile process. We were literally dropping our tools. But then things started to fall in place, and within a week or two, I was, like, "Oh well, in a way this is actually better. I can sit at home and still talk to everybody, and, you know, I can also hang up!"

G: Discovering the benefits of Zoom!

J: That's the great part of it. Anyway, all my days this year have been doing meetings back to back, but in my own kind of comfort. It was kind of interesting. And I weirdly think that I've actually become better through this process. I feel fashion, including me, was on cruise control in this weird fashion orgy. You went to Fashion Week and you would do your show. You were putting all this work in, and you were forgotten three hours later. It was just eating itself. Don't get me wrong: I'm a full advocate of the fashion show because I feel it's important. A show draws a line in the sand, and when you finish it, you can creatively move on. That's why I had to make that box for LOEWE, because I needed something I could close and just be, like, "Okay, that's it. Gone!" Of course, at the beginning I felt completely ridiculous. I was talking to my parents and to my boyfriend and to BENJAMIN BRUNO, saying, "What can I do? I can't engage, I can't say anything about the situation, I'm a hypocrite if I do…" And my dad was, like, "Your job right now is to keep other people's jobs. That's the good thing you can do." And it's true. Every job that you can save makes it worth doing what you're doing. And that's also why we made that box as an alternative to the fashion show – you're giving work to the printer and all the people involved. It may not save them, but they have something to do. You can only do your little bit.

G: Can you describe the clothes you've made with LOEWE for Spring and Summer 2021?

J: I think the collection is fragmented. It's more about pieces. I told the teams sitting at home to make whatever they wanted to work on. If it's a shearling jacket, let's get that right. And if we're experimenting with volume, let's go for it. All this might never make it to the store anyway. In a weird way I find this collection very domestic, because it was made in the domestic space. Each piece is an odd character. It's kind of like a family party with your aunt and your uncle and everybody arguing.

G: Do you think the current situation will have a huge effect on the fashion world?

J: I found it really funny at the beginning that everyone, every fashion designer, was suddenly a philosopher, and everyone was, like, "Fashion is going to change tomorrow," and, "We need to break this entire system apart," and "I'm putting the knife in the ground and we're going to decide that this or that is going to happen." Everyone acted like there was some existential crisis, but it just looked like panic to me. Unfortunately, it doesn't really work that way. Revolutions do not happen overnight. So, my thing is to live in real time, and I feel quite excited about it. It's about cutting out all the noise. I feel like I'm working as a shop assistant and I have to talk to customers and work out their problems: "How can I help you?" And I kind of enjoy that. As much as fashion sometimes needs to be about fantasy, in this moment there's only so much fantasy people can take. Fashion needs to be a bit of a mirror, and there's so much obsolete fashion. We do this project called EYE LOEWE NATURE, and I've actually had more enjoyment doing that than anything else, because it's just about normality.

G: But we're not going back to normal?

J: Eh, well, I always see myself as a very positive person. But at the same time I'm a realist, and I don't want to be some Debby Downer about it, but still: THIS IS JUST THE BEGINNING. Something in my gut tells me that what we're in is a marathon, not a sprint. And that this weird situation we're in will last for years.

G: Isn't that terribly depressing?

J: Or I could be completely wrong: they're going to find a vaccine by the end of the year and it's going to be all great. But I really doubt it.

G: One theory I've always found interesting is that it could take around 20 years for the 21st century to really start. And indeed, if you look at style and fashion, the past two decades were a lot about looking back, retro, nostalgia. Do you think we needed the current huge crisis to finally launch the 21st century?

J: I don't know. Look at Italy, where so many people's grandparents were dying of Covid. I remember when my grandparents died, you'd go to their house and go through their belongings and you got nostalgic about things. So I'm wondering, will we get a few years of nostalgia for a generation that's being wiped out? I think that nostalgia will come through making things. People who may never have thought they were creative have started making things, baking bread. Even tidying your house has become a creative act, reorganising everything by colour… I like that idea. There's a lot of things that we've done in LOEWE that, when we started them, didn't really make that much sense, but that now I think make total sense. I was doing them because I wanted to. But now,

in this crisis, I think there's a real purpose and need for them, such as our basket project or the craft projects we did. I'm so glad we started them five years ago and that they can now really come into fruition without it feeling like we're jumping on some sort of bandwagon.

G: Do you think the fashion show as we know it will become obsolete?

J: I can't imagine. I remember that when I started at London Fashion Week, people were all saying, "The fashion show is over." And in the middle of the pandemic we're reading the same articles again. "Fashion shows are over, no one ever wants to go to a show again, it's all going to be digital." Sure. I remember STEFANO PILATI doing these beautiful videos for YSL; they were fantastic. But there's something about a fashion show that people want. The fact that it has its imperfections. Things can and will go wrong. Models might fall. Make-up can look bad. People in the audience might be sat beside people they don't like. And that's the thing I miss. In fact, I think it's the audience that actually makes the show. Sometimes you need that person in the background wearing a fluo T-shirt that makes you think, "Thank you, you destroyed the entire collection." But that's why you actually remember that moment. Because there's someone sitting there in a fluo shirt, and it's in every runway picture of that show. Now it's that sort of tactility that I miss, because it's like a performance, really.

G: But you won't be doing any shows this year, I gather?

J: That's correct. And I feel like it's better to accept it. This is what 2020 is like: take your time to find new ways of working. Either restructure your team, or find new talent, or find inspiration in new ways of working. And let's get rid of the stuff we don't need. I feel there could be quite a harsh moment of cutting out.

G: What would you like to see cut?

J: Maybe it's just me trying to slay myself, but while we've heard about there being too many shows and the speed of fashion being too fast, isn't the real big question whether there are too many brands? And how bad would it be if some brands collapsed? HALSTON didn't always exist; it stopped at some point. ANNE MARIE BERETTA was an amazing designer, but that brand no longer exists. That doesn't mean it wasn't good or successful. It was good in its moment. So I think those harsher questions will need to be asked in the next 15, 16 months: "Is this business going to be viable?" In a weird way, I like that pragmatic approach to it. I'm dealing with two businesses, LOEWE and JW ANDERSON, and my job right now is to fight to save employment. That's my biggest priority. We're in the rag trade, selling shoes and bags, so every day I look at the figures and if I think we can sell ten bags somewhere, I'll do it. There are so many people in the business complain-

ing about the system right now, but they weren't complaining when the system was working for them.

G: Surely it's time for a lot of things to change. That's inevitable after Covid, the death of GEORGE FLOYD, the crash of the economy, the climate crisis.

J: Well, yes. I think we're all starting to become more empathetic. I keep thinking of the housing crisis in Northern Ireland, which was horrific. People lost everything. Ireland had to go through a rebuild and there was no longer any point in having sectarian violence. It just felt stupid. Fashion has gone through this huge growth in the last three years, and then suddenly there's this big bang. I think there might be a softening, where we're thinking, "Do we need this? Can we do this better? Can we focus more? Maybe we don't need this many stores. Maybe we can make a better product."

G: What do you think will change for LOEWE?

J: Well, no brand is going to make what they made last year, let's be honest. We missed six months of business. It's impossible. The key for me now is to break even. That's what I'm hoping for. If you can break even, it's a miracle. We're seeing a good recovery in China, in Asia. But it's a long road. You can cut back on stock and you can cut back on overhead, but the key is not to fuck with the talent. I want want to keep all the talent we have. That's what 2021 is about for me.

G: Are you excited about next year?

J: I am. Things can only get better. Well, no, it'll probably get a little worse first, but then it can only get better. I think 2021 will be a transition year and it's going to be a bit of a rollercoaster. It's not going to be perfect, but we'll have to get through it, and then 2022 will be great.

G: That's the spirit!

J: Yes, and I think creativity will soar. Sometimes you realise the best things are made in hard times. At JW ANDERSON we did our early collections for, like, £19,000, and some of these collections were awful. But every single time that someone wants to borrow something for a museum show, it's always from that one collection with the ruffled shorts and the bustier. We made that when we were nearly bankrupt. I remember computers being carried out the door because we couldn't pay the electricity bills. And in retrospect, that's fine. It was worth doing it. ∎

239

■ GRACE WALES BONNER

■ Forensic and surprising forms of research are the basis of GRACE WALES BONNER's mesmerising collections. Everything is fully connected and continuous. So what happens when the world turns upside down and everyone is clamouring for change, newness, ripping it all up and starting again? ■ GRACE just keeps on going with her naturally curious and gentle methods of working. Stay calm, stay smart, stay true to who you are. That's where the future lies.

254

Grace Wales Bonner in *Fantastic Man*, no. 32 (Fall-Winter 2020-21).

Interview by MAHFUZ SULTAN
Portrait by ANDREAS LARSSON

MAHFUZ: Right now, everyone is describing this moment as a great reset for the fashion industry. Several designers have decided to forgo seasonal presentations and traditional runway shows altogether. Is the runway show something you plan on continuing?

GRACE: I do think creating experiences is something that's important. Whether that's a sound meditation or a fashion show or creating clothing. I love to bring in sensory experience, sound, texture and environment. Inviting someone into your world and into your physical environment has a lot of potential to change someone's perspective or mood. I'm also interested in the idea of communicating outside of the fashion show. Working on exhibitions has opened me up to other ways of communicating, to communicating for time periods longer than ten minutes. I think it's interesting for the audience to have more of a deep dive and a sustained engagement with subjects. Especially since some of the collections I work on have a whole world of research behind them, which in itself has potential to be its own thing for people who are interested in engaging with that.

M: Do you foresee a convergence between your fashion presentations and exhibitions in the future?
G: You know, sometimes I do feel that the characters from my shows can exist within an exhibition space, but I do see them as quite separate practices in my mind, and very different approaches. I need to think more about how well the two can interact.

M: Are you considering working more with film or other media that might live online? I loved the film you did a few years ago with HARLEY WEIR and DEV HYNES, 'Practice'.
G: I really like film as a way of communicating a universe. It's a medium I've been working with over the past five years or so and it's definitely something that I will continue to explore in my own way. Even separately from fashion.

M: Have you been asked a lot recently about how "this moment" for Black people shifts things for you? Like yours, my work has always been grounded in Black history and aesthetics, so I find that question odd and a bit ahistorical. I was really moved by something RUJEKO HOCKLEY, a curator at the Whitney Museum in New York City, said last year when someone asked her about the "moment" for Black art. She said something like, and I'm paraphrasing here, "It's not a moment for me – it's my life. It's the work that I do, the people I care about, my family. It's everything. I can't think about myself and my interests as momentary – they're not; they're foundational. And whether or not the larger art world or popular culture is seeing that at the time is irrelevant to me because it's always there; it's always been there."
G: I'm really grateful you shared that. It's really beautiful. I think a lot about the expansiveness of time, being connected to an intellectual or spiritual lineage – there are so many different forces and elements that are present with us. There's a reaction in this moment, and there are lots of different roles people can play. Some of those roles are very physical, very grounded, in terms of marching, protesting, using one's physicality and connection to the earth. There are so many different levels at which things are operating and influencing change. I'm quite comforted by spirituality and ancestral connections, the different ways to express your divinity and to express your contribution to your people. I think that should be really valued and appreciated: the richness and the variety in what people can offer the world.

M: Yeah, if the quote-unquote moment has changed anything for me, it's that I've found myself thinking a lot about care. I'm reminded of how WALES BONNER has always explored these aspects of our history, which makes the brand quite different from other brands.
G: Yes, it's reinforced the mission of the brand and affirmed the importance of what I've been building with WALES BONNER and what I've dedicated my professional life to creating. I've always been connected to this. I don't feel the need to react differently now, because I hope that my intentions have been evident in what I've been creating.

M: You've always been doing this work.
G: And what you're saying about care and gentleness as well... I remember you've mentioned that to me before, and it really stuck with me.

M: What have you been reading lately?
G: I've been reading quite a lot of spiritual texts. I'm really interested in the poetry and rhythmic aesthetics of PETERO KALULÉ, a Ugandan poet I've been speaking to recently. I've been thinking a lot about coming back to myself and the starting point of my interest in aesthetics, in rhythmicality, and how you can express that visually even though it's something that's quite intangible. And I'm also interested in INAYAT KHAN, a Sufi writer who has written incredible things about sound and music and meditations on nature.

M: My family is Sufi; we're Ethiopian. It's an extremely musical culture.
G: Exactly. I think I've been interested in reading things that are quite pure, that get to the heart of experience. I've been appreciating texts that are abstract. I have phases where I like to read very theoretical texts or quite dense literature. I've been having these experiences where I'm reading, and it's almost like you're observing nature and something unravels, and that's been beautiful.

M: In your reading, when do you realise that you're at the beginning of something that could result in a concrete body of work, such as a runway show or an exhibition?
G: I think about time in a very expansive way, about things always being present, or things from the past becoming relevant again. The way I engage with reading and research in general is always without a specific intention. Just going through it instinctively, and then there's a process of it becoming something beyond itself. I allow myself space within that and don't expect to make connections.

M: When do you decide to start translating all that research into something that is visual?
G: It starts with recollections of literature or a memory – recalling fragments of a mood, or a character, or an environment. I build out a visual world through my research; then that makes me think about textures in terms of fabrics, and of characters in terms of silhouettes. That's then the foundation for being able to create. The 'Mumbo Jumbo' [AW19] collection came together with me thinking about the Black intellectual, which is a constant fascination of mine. I also had this idea of the Black artist-slash-spiritualist, an artist who has a shamanic relationship with creation. I created a world around those two characters.

M: Yes, there is that duality to certain Black figures – the artist or intellectual and the shaman, particularly ones you examine in your work, such as STUART HALL and TERRY ADKINS. What was the moment in your life when you became aware of postcolonial studies or the Black radical tradition?
G: Growing up, I remember reading this book about Black women's lives in Britain, a collection of firsthand experiences, of different women's stories. There were women responding to the Black Power movement, for example, or talking about the experience of their children being educated in London. The multiplicity of voices and real experiences that framed important movements really interested me. It was at Central Saint Martins, reading people like HOMI K. BHABHA and STUART HALL, that I first came to find a language and a set of frameworks to make sense of a lot of the real people, real stories, even documentary photography that intrigued me. Frameworks for thinking about mixed identities, how identities can be created in the between-space, liminality.

M: Do you feel that fashion is a form of knowledge, that the garments carry some truth about a time or people and that one can read the stories you're crafting through the garments?
G: Yes, I definitely think there's a lot you can read from clothing and the way things are worn. There is a lot of emotion stored in clothing. I think that style is a form of communication. Though it can be quite subtle, through creating imagery and clothing, you can communicate quite immediately with people. That's what drew me to fashion: the idea that you can communicate something quite specific and nuanced in a way that people can immediately understand. I often look at things that have existed historically, through imagery and recollection, just getting a sense of style or spirit, a way of wearing, or an attitude around clothing.

M: When you start collaborating on a collection, how do you bring your collaborators into your world? I'm imagining that you do go very deep into your subjects...
G: I have quite specific research for every collection. I share this with anyone I collaborate with so they can read and understand from their own perspective. It's mainly visual research, but it could be literature or sound, and sharing that is always the starting point for a conversation with anyone I collaborate with. The research creates a world or a focal point, but then within that, how can you look at this and bring another perspective to it? People I collaborate with expand the world and the potential of it by looking at it through another lens.

M: Did Covid-19, isolation, etcetera change any of that process for you, that moment of transition from your private practice and what you do alone, in terms of how you collaborate with other people?
G: Not really, because even my research process is quite collaborative. I work with researchers, compiling things, putting things together, and there's a dialogue and conversation. I think the lockdown has forced me to be more essential and refined and specific about everything I'm doing, to have even more of a framework than I would tend to. To just to be, like, "What am I trying to say? How does this translate?"

M: Do you feel any obligation to be contemporary or respond to the times?
G: It comes back to the way I communicate. It will always be quite gentle. I know what my mode of communication is, and I don't feel obliged to communicate through other mediums. I'm a fashion designer or a researcher or an artist. That's how I express myself best and how I can best contribute. ∎

255

'Am I guilty sometimes of romanticizing doom and gloom? Maybe.'

The heart and darkness of Rick Owens.

Interview by Tim Blanks
Photographs by Juergen Teller; creative partner Dovile Drizyte
Styling by Jodie Barnes

54

Few fashion designers have so successfully created a world as fiercely idiosyncratic as Rick Owens'. Serving up dark, riotous glamour and challenging orthodoxy are his line of business – and he's been doing it majestically for almost 30 years. Today, OWENSCORP, the incongruously corporate-sounding business he and his longtime partner Michèle Lamy have built, generates annual revenue in the hundreds of millions.

Along the way, he's attracted the kind of devoted (read: obsessive) global following more commonly reserved for scaled-up cultish pop stars. To his fans, Owens's domestic arrangements, cultural tastes, and lifestyle choices (psychedelics, enthusiastic clubbing, committed body transformation) offer a kind of portal into an all-encompassing world. Buying his clothes, it seems, is the entry-level ticket to exploring it.

Now aged 60, Rick Owens shows no signs of slowing down. *Au contraire.* His recent shows and collections – both during and since the pandemic – have arguably been his most masterful, most emotionally charged, and, at times, most conventionally (and deliberately) beautiful.

With all this swirling in our minds, *System* was keen to have a closer look inside the Rick Owens story, and take stock of the sometimes turbulent rise, enduring aesthetic, and endearing honesty that are part of his otherwise guru-like presence. Who better than confessional conversationalist Tim Blanks to spend the day in Paris in Rick's intoxicating company? They discussed life and death, friendships and family, kinks and conquests, mothers and muses.

The following day, Owens jetted out to the Concordia base of OWENSCORP to be photographed by Juergen Teller, before Teller and stylist Jodie Barnes captured an ensemble cast of Owensian beauties who showcase the designer's recent-era collection archives.

Finally, we invited a dozen of Owens's most fervent followers to swap stories and ask him their questions. 'Rick's like a chameleon in pursuit of beauty,' says superfan Matt Campo. 'He imbues his clothes with undeniable ego and brashness, but also genuine sincerity and warmth.' Reflecting on his own trajectory and success, Rick is humble, grateful, godlike: 'I sent out a message and people responded. That is the best you can ask for in life.'

62

Rick Owens is worried we will have nothing to talk about. 'My story is pretty simple and straightforward. It is not overly complex and I have tried to be direct about it, and I don't overanalyse things, so everything I say will be a repeat of something I have already said to you.' It's not true, of course. Aside from the fact that droll self-deprecation is something of a default position for Owens, it's a simple truth that the man's life and work are no open book, whatever he says. They unfold like a lotus, sometimes mystifying, always fascinating. He wonders what *he* would want to read about himself, then, in a flash, answers his own question: 'I would want to read *gossip.*' And Rick has given fashion tattletales something to twitter about over the past couple of years.

He and his partner of more than

in its passage. As Owens approached the milestone of 60, he found a young male muse, whose Viking visage will be familiar to anyone who saw the designer's presentations during lockdown. In his perfect physical embodiment of the Owens ethos, he opened a Pandora's box for Rick of what once was, what might have been, and what now seemed possible all over again. A defiant antidote to *tempus fugit*, in other words. Even for someone whose sensibility comfortably embraces antiquity and the future in equal degree, that possibility was still a profound shock to the system.

It has taken a difficult while, but Owens insists he has managed to process the inner turmoil, balance his emotional allegiances, maybe even reconcile his past, present and future. In March, he returned to live shows in

Owens geography alone: birthed in Porterville, California, transmogrified on Hollywood Boulevard, transplanted to Paris, working in Concordia sulla Secchia in the Emilia-Romagna, living on the Lido in Venice... but let's start with the truly wild card. Egypt!

Rick Owens: A while ago, Paris and Italy were a little uncomfortable for me personally. I felt like I was running from one to the other. But when Michèle and I went to Egypt, there was something about going so far out of my personal zone that just put everything back into perspective, and I got all my comfort back. I've been twice in the last year. It is just the legend of it I love. I was talking to one of my team members who went to Egypt last month and was so disturbed by the contrast between the haves and

'People talk about legacy, and I guess that is what I am doing. I'm thinking about what impression I want to leave. I turned 60 in November.'

three decades, the formidable Michèle Lamy, have built their business OWENSCORP on one of the industry's most defiantly uncompromising aesthetics, a thrilling combination of eldritch glamour and barbaric futurism. They've taken it to the bank and back to the tune of cash registers ringing up hundreds of millions of dollars in sales of clothing, accessories, and the Lamy-supervised collection of brutalist furniture that extends the Owens ethos into the world of interiors. The couple have led a charmed life, uniquely bonded in their challenge to orthodox thought and deed. But there are other challenges greater by far. Take the pandemic, for instance, and the way it has unhinged social stability and, to a depressing degree, simple human reason. Then there's time, brutal and unforgiving

Paris with what was, quite possibly, the show of his career. Of course, that's a hard call with a designer who has regularly provoked and stunned over the years. For all the step dancers, death-metal acrobats, penises in full effect, and pyres of raging flame so flagrant in those past presentations, there was something even more powerful about the discreet grace of Owens's models parading through a Venetian-like fog in their goddess dresses to the strains of Mahler's Fifth Symphony in the same week that Tsar Vladimir invaded Ukraine. The worship of beauty felt like an act of defiance in the face of fascist ugliness. Ultimately futile, maybe, but breathtakingly poignant in the moment.

What crucible shaped such visions? I'll never stop wondering, and we'll never *not* have plenty to talk about. The

the have-nots that he didn't enjoy it. My perspective was that there is discomfort all over the world, and Egypt to me is more about proportion and space. There is so much. I go to this very old and shabby hotel and there is this emptiness. The Valley of the Gods and these massive monuments that are *soooooo* ancient, and then desert and scrubland, and a pool. There was something about the simplicity of all that was working for me. It was what I needed right then. And probably it was about mortality, too. I mean, these are monuments built for people who are dead, and this is how they wanted to be remembered. And deciding to be remembered is quite interesting. People talk about legacy a lot, and I guess that is what I am doing. I'm thinking about what impression I want to leave. I turned 60 in November.

63

And there is nothing I love more than reading biographies of weird eccentrics from the past. Michèle is always telling me that I only love dead artists and I'm like, 'Yeah, because I want to see how it all worked out! I want to see if they were able to sustain the momentum and maintain their conditions to the very end.' I don't want to invest in someone who is going to change or turn into a different person.

Tim Blanks: Didn't you say once that you are always fundamentally who you are? There is no escape.
Yeah, I mean that is why I commit to things. It's as simple as what I wear. I have a uniform that I wear all the time and I have decided who I want to be. Here, let me show you the *Vogue* video we did.

however, of his Egyptian sarcophagus. He waited for a long time for the right one. He calls her Liza, after Liza Minnelli. Rick would have made a wonderful reclusive rock star, à la Mick Jagger in Performance.

You are very, very serious in that video. I don't think of you as being so serious. Do you think it comes across that way? If you know me, then I guess it is a bit deadpan. But anyway, when they suggested it to me, this is what I'd wanted to get, something sedate and calm, not too pop and too lively, kind of a non-flashy alternative designer kind of thing. And it came out great.

Those kids who follow you on Discord are going to go crazy. This will be like Moses coming down from the moun-

I must have been in my 20s. I'm sure it was at the Vista Theatre, a big decrepit barn of a building, with Egyptian gold motifs.[2] I went with my roommate Linda. We were both goths living in a goth house. She went on to be a nursery-school teacher in Seattle. So we go with her bag full of wine and get shit-faced during the movie, and that was the first time I saw *Death in Venice*.

Does that come back to you when you're in your apartment on the Lido? Living right next door to the Grand Hôtel des Bains.[3]
That is why I moved there. I never read the book, but my first attraction to the Lido was that movie, that era. The exoticism of Venice, how it really is one of the most glamorous places in the particular world that I'm interested in.

'My dad would oil and polish all his guns and then leave them out on the dining-room table, with all the oily mess everywhere. Like a gutted animal.'

We pause to watch Rick's edition of Vogue's 'Objects of Affection', for which he took viewers on a video tour of his apartment in Concordia sulla Secchia, near Modena. It's a two-hour drive south-west of the Lido in Venice, where he has another apartment, the location for his digital presentations during the industry's Covid shutdown. In Concordia, he lives across the street from his factory in an apartment as stark as you might expect. The space is partially carpeted and upholstered with army blankets, as all his apartments have been since he lived on Hollywood Boulevard in the 1980s. ('Inspired by Joseph Beuys, who was my first art hero when I went to art school.') As he says in the video, he is not very acquisitive and doesn't like living with a lot of things. Rick is particularly proud,

tain with the Ten Commandments.
There is a lot there that's ripe for parody, like when I say I have 20 pairs of shorts.

When Jonathan [Wingfield, *System*'s editor] and I were thinking about this conversation at the beginning, we came up with 'A Tale of Three Cities: Hollywood, Paris and Venice'. But I'm more inclined to two, Hollywood and Venice, because everything that you made yourself into in Hollywood is consummated by you living in that Visconti environment in Venice.
It is, it is. The full arc.

What does Venice mean? It does feel like an arc completed. How old were you when you first saw *Death in Venice*?[1]

How relevant do you think growing up in Porterville is to the fact that you now live in Venice?[4]
I was propelled, wasn't I? I mean, if I had had a perfectly well-adjusted sedate childhood, where would I be now? You need something to push you.

Where *would* you be now?
I'd be something my dad would have wanted me to be.

Have you seen *The Most Beautiful Boy in the World*?[5]
Yes. It is irresistible to compose something with youth and beauty and threat and decline. It's always been one of the most compelling stories. Glorious beauty, threatened. Of course there is sadness because there is decline at the end. But that is how the world works; there is

64

always going to be a sad ending.

The Most Beautiful Boy in the World *documents the blighted life of Björn Andrésen, subsequent to his appearance as Tadzio, the golden youth in Visconti's* Death in Venice. *Owens drolly acknowledges that the film adds an irresistibly emblematic edge to his own male-muse situation, but, as he so accurately notes, that story is hardly his story. And, after all, doom – manifested in the gorgeous dying fall of transient beauty – has been a regular Owens go-to over the years. As this issue of* System *appears, he is presenting his latest men's collection, in which a blazing globe representing the sun is raised high by a forklift, before crashing to the ground.*

Is the collapsing sun your comment on

can you live with those vibes?', and I am like, 'How can you *not* live with those vibes?' Life is about death and threat, and civilizations have got all sorts of ways of dealing with it. Why are there are crosses all over everyone's houses? It's to remind us all that Christ suffered more than anyone ever will, and in times of stress and pain, you are being reminded that someone suffered longer or more intensely than you. Suffering is something that you have to get used to, and that is why there are all those depictions of a dying man on a cross. I mean, besides the morality and the spirituality of it, it serves a very practical purpose: to get us not to be afraid of suffering – or at least not to be surprised by it.

We talk about Rick's background. An only child, he was raised in a staunchly

When you have that many people depending on you, do you feel like the shaman of the tribe?
More like the village idiot. I feel like we are all lucky, I'm basically the goose that lays the golden egg, and we all have to figure out what to do with it.

It seems really gutsy of your mom to move.
I have a really nice house for her near the factory, with nice high ceilings and a huge garden. Mom is scared of leaving the house she is so attached to in Porterville. It was her sanctuary, the house I built for her across town so she could escape from Dad at a point when he was getting very dark as he got older. He was bitter and angry, and he wasn't speaking to me for years before he died. She had that house for three years, and

'I always thought I looked soft and vulnerable. A little Liza Minnelli-ish. Big, cow-like eyes. An innocent gerbil in the big city, trying to look tough.'

the climate crisis?
It's just doom, and frustration with world issues. The sun, goodness over evil, crashing to the ground, destroyed…

Evil triumphs?
Well, the repetition implies that it doesn't triumph, it's just repeating.

You say 'doom' with such a dry chuckle, but I know you mean it.
I console myself with the fact that the good has somehow always managed to triumph over evil. That is always my message. Am I guilty sometimes of romanticizing gloom and doom? Maybe. But glamorizing it is also a way of processing it because it's something that is omnipresent. There was another article where I had this sarcophagus and this skull, and the writer was like, 'How

Catholic environment. His father, John, died in 2015; his mother Connie, now 88, has had serious health issues. He is moving her from Porterville to Concordia. I think that's incredibly brave on everyone's part.

If you're moving your mom to Concordia, you're planning on being there a lot?
As soon as we were able to travel after Covid, I thought of Concordia as the basis of all our survival. We all need Concordia to work for all of us, so I kind of hunkered down there, because there was a bit of restabilizing to do. I always said Italy is where I go to create and Paris is where I go to be judged. Paris is not the most welcoming place, but in Concordia I have a whole army – maybe 200 people – working, so it ends up being a cosier place.

every day she would go furniture shopping and buy stuff for it. He thought she was out with friends, so he never knew. She could decorate it how she wanted it without him leaving all his stuff all over the place. He would oil and polish all his guns and then leave them out on the dining-room table, with all the oily mess everywhere. Like a gutted animal. It was a sort of display in a way, like a puzzle for him, and a symbol of manhood and of accomplishment.

Did he use them?
We would go out target practising. Recently I've been to the target-practice place in Venice; it's like a concrete bunker and it's where they train the police force, and these guys were like, 'You should join the police force; you are good'. Apparently I am good

65

enough for the Lido police force. So anyway, I understand Mom's connection with that house. She is afraid, she is like, 'You are not going to put me into a hospital are you?' I'm like, 'I swear I will never do that.' But all her friends are dying, and I have to pull her out of there. I told her this isn't a definitive plan: 'You have your house there, you have your house in Concordia, you have your family in Mexico, you can circulate. You can do anything you want, and you know I am getting you a ticket with a return flight, so you don't feel trapped in Italy.' But it is time to come and see how it feels. She has no choice.

Is it literally that bad in Porterville?
All her friends are dying. She was a teacher's aide for migrant farm workers. She would interpret for them, so she has

Why am I happy here now? I am still not sure.

So it wasn't like Ingrid Bergman and *The Visit*?[6] You remember that film? She returned to the town where she was raised, where Anthony Quinn's character had raped her when she was young. She had left town under a cloud, gone off and married the richest man in the world. She inherits his wealth, and then comes back to town, where Quinn is now the mayor, and sets about destroying him by slowly corrupting the whole place and turning everyone against him.
Why didn't I do that?

I thought that is what you were going to say.
I can't wait to see this movie!

I perceived as his bigotry, and that he couldn't forgive. Because I would not debate with him, and he wanted to have a debate to prove empirically that he was not bigoted. I was, like, this is just my interpretation. I mean, who am I? But I had a louder megaphone than he did; I had been able to say that in front of everyone, and he couldn't retaliate with a bigger microphone. That was what broke us. It wasn't the fact we disagreed; it was the fact that I was louder.

Surely everything about you – the way you were living, the way you transformed yourself – he would have seen as a total rejection of what he was.
It was, and I have to hand it to him, he was a good sport. He showed up to the shows and he sat next to the drag queens, and he shook hands with the

'I stopped drinking because my alcoholism was so bad. They had to give me downers so that I wouldn't hyperventilate because I had the shakes so bad.'

a following of all these kids who grew up with her as their maternal figure. They visit with their grandkids and they are very attentive, but they're not *her* family. I'm the only one, and I can't be over there that much.

Were you going more often?
I went for the first time recently in like 20 years, when she started struggling. I have always resisted because I thought I didn't want to return to a place where I had been weak or struggling or frustrated. I mean, why would I want to remember that? But it was great. I totally underestimated how great it feels to go back at full power. It felt very reassuring and comforting, and very familiar. I was like, why am I in such a good mood here? I was never happy here; this was where I was frustrated and threatened.

So you went back and felt comfortable there?
I felt great comfort and serenity there, hanging out with mom in her garden. Yeah, it was lovely.

Did you ever resolve things with your dad?
There was nothing to resolve really. It was a war that we had together. My dad was such a big lesson because we had always been very frank about everything, like hard-ass blunt. So I didn't think anything was off the table with him. I had described our relationship as tense because he was very right-wing. In one article I described him as an adorable Nazi, and he was fine with that; he did have a sense of humour. He thought that was funny. But then in another article, I said I had a hard time with what

homosexuals, which was amazing. I mean, he bit his lip, but he showed up. So that is impressive.

And he was proud?
Yeah, he wasn't gushy, but he definitely said, 'It is amazing what you have done.' I mean, he hated it, but he was definitely impressed. But anyway that was the last thing where my voice was louder. That was a lesson because – and this has happened with Michèle, too – sometimes I've said something that, out of context, didn't sound comfortable to her, and while it never became a huge problem, I've learned that anything I say in this context is going to change and be amplified once it is printed – and I can't do that to people I love any more, even though I am dying to talk about them all the time. I would love

66

to, but it is just like a power that is too unwieldly in a way.

After a conversation Rick and I had in March, I was painfully conscious of that amplification. He was trying to clarify his feelings about the presence in his life of someone who was much younger, carefree, vibrant. It was almost as though he was thinking aloud, thinking through a difficult situation.

I was also getting so vulnerable. I have gotten to the other side of it now. When I spoke to you then, there was a lot of desperation, but I have found myself again and found my specialness and my powers.

Thank God for that. You were doubting yourself and I was like, please, no!

co-founder] Tommy Gear and I didn't know if that was for real or not.[7]
That I fucked Tommy Gear?

Well, that you were *with* him [pause for TB's attack of the vapours]. I fell in love with the Screamers in 1978 and that seems a little… *early* for this story.
I graduated in 1979 and my wild years in LA were through to 1985 and then I was with Michèle.

So tell me about those wild years.
I graduated in 1979 from high school in Porterville, then I worked as a pharmacy delivery boy for a while. They had a truck, and I would deliver pills until… they had a prescription for diet pills that nobody picked up for a long time and I think that was probably a trap for delivery boys. So I took them and then I got

Like an innocent gerbil in the big city, trying to look tough.

And your hair?
There were so many variations. I mean, after I met [extreme performance artist] Ron Athey, I started doing the spikes like Ron.[10] I had spikes in the front and at the back.

As an innocent gerbil in the big city, how on earth did you meet Ron Athey?
I got a job as an extras scout, so I was supposed to go out and put together a punk club scene. I saw Ron Athey on the street and I got his number and asked if he wanted a job. He needed a ride, so I ended up driving him to the set. He didn't have all the tattoos yet. He had a very soft face, too, but he had these eyes that were really evil and then a teardrop

'Art was too hard. I didn't understand it enough. It was too cerebral and intimidating for me, and I just thought I can't be an artist, I don't get all that.'

I never doubted what I do; I was just destabilized. There is like this regret when you see this shining example of vitality and you see your reflection in that. It's kind of, wow, I don't think I ever was that. There is no way I am ever going to be that in my entire life – and that is a kind of death. There is a mourning and a shock. You know, this is my drama, this doesn't happen to every single 60-year-old man. It was circumstantial I think.

It's really hard for me to even conceptualize what sort of vitality you imagine you could have never had. That's why I'm fascinated by your early life in LA. We've never really talked about it. I remember telling you how much I loved the Screamers, and you made a throwaway comment about [the band's

fired, but they never said that was why. So I am never really sure if that was it.

Were those the Quaalude years?
No, it was always speed. We never had good Quaaludes in Porterville.[8] I was mainly drinking, and I think mom could see that I was just going down the drain. I think my school counsellor suggested Otis [College of Art and Design], so mom organized a trip to go see it with me.[9] She helped me get an apartment and she kind of set me up there. I think her friend had a daughter who was living in Los Angeles.

What did you look like at that point?
I always thought I looked really soft and vulnerable. I was always a bit embarrassed. I looked a little Liza Minnelli-ish… big, open cow-like eyes, innocent.

here [Rick indicates the corner of his eye], and these hair spikes. He was the most beautiful thing I had ever seen in my life. Anyway, I totally pursued him, though he never really responded. I was going out with Michael, this guy from a band – I forget its name – and he lived with his lover, Spider, who worked at Basic Plumbing, a sex club on La Brea Avenue. They had been together for a long time, so it was fine for me to be Michael's boyfriend, and we all went to a party in downtown LA on the tracks. Ron Athey was there, and I snuck off with Ron and we had sex on the railroad tracks. I actually already told this story to this cute little punk rock magazine called *Insurrection*.

I think the Screamers were in a punk movie. *Population: 1*. Was it that?

67

In the words of...

It wasn't even a punk movie; it was a John Candy movie that never even came out. It was a comedy, and he blunders into a punk club at one point. It was really stupid. So anyway, I've been in contact with Ron over the years. Michèle and I would go to his performances years after I met him. He was my age, so we would have been 30 by then, and he had become *the* performance artist, and we would go see him at Club Fuck! in Silverlake, the thing where he would cut himself, then put the paper towels across his back and string them across the audience.[11] He was spectacular.

I'm grasping at chronology here. You moved to LA in 1980?
It was a year after I graduated from high school. I was still drinking in Porterville

art-school stuff, very much in that area, downtown LA, but not the downtown that is fabulous, just art-student-poor-people downtown. I mean, I must have had drive and ambition, but I think the lazy side of me was drinking too much out of frustration and bitterness. My drinking was always very dark.

What would you drink?
Vodka. Get me there fast; I didn't have time for beer.

Even at Otis, you were plagued by bitter drinking?
No, everything there was new; there was probably potential because I was going to school. I was creating stuff; I was going somewhere; I was moving forward. So I wasn't as self-loathing or frustrated that I couldn't break

living above Swingers, this coffee shop that Sean MacPherson[12] was running. He had the Bar Marmont, and all the cool restaurants in Los Angeles. It was a coffee shop that was also a really funny motel. I had my studio, and Michèle was building her restaurant, Café des Artistes[13], across the street on Hollywood Boulevard. We were really broke, and that was when my alcoholism reached a peak. I think Michèle and I got together when I was 27, so I was drinking from 25 to 35.

It didn't all change when you connected with her?
It wasn't a huge life change, but it was definitely an alliance. It was very much a soulful connection, like this is my other half. Or like, that we belonged together.

'I loved going to sex clubs every night. It was just being in an extreme, exotic environment, where everybody was going as far as they could go.'

and my mom pushed me to LA. And I went to Otis, the art school. For the two years I was there, I didn't really explore that much. I was very devoted to art school and that area, downtown LA. I didn't even go to that many punk clubs.

Did you go to the Veil?
I might have. Someone said they saw me once, but I don't think so. I went to Power Tools. It was kind of after goth. There was Plastic Passion. There was the Bitter End. Paul Fortune had something… wait, *he* was the one running the Veil. And in his book he said he remembers a young Rick Owens hanging out by the back door or something. I don't think I was there. [Laughs] For the two years of college where I didn't really circulate that much, I had a very small circle of friends. I was kind of quiet, doing

through. Then I stopped going, because I just couldn't afford it any more. I took out student loans and then I got scared of taking out more, so financially it wasn't working. Then I went to trade school, and there was just nothing for a while.

Were you out at this point?
Oh, yeah.

Were you ever scared for yourself?
Oh, yeah, that is why I stopped drinking because my alcoholism was so bad. They had to give me downers so that I wouldn't hyperventilate because I had the shakes so bad. That was what scared me the most.

Did Michèle try and stop you?
She would call the doctors. We were

That whole thing about your drinking blows out of the water my notion about you being always in control.
When I wasn't drinking, I was always very driven and very organized, and I got a lot of stuff done. But then I would have these three-day binges where I would just pass out, wake up and then just pass out again as quickly as I could to sort of escape. It was very self-destructive.

Riven with self-loathing?
I don't think I hated myself, I think there was a sort of gay shame somewhere from my dad, my family and Porterville. Also all that energy and ambition that was not coming to fruition… I think that was what it was. I was shy, so I needed courage to demand the attention or the validation that I craved.

68

And you thought that drinking brought out the attention?

No, no, it gave me the courage to go out and be somebody. Then when that wasn't fulfilling, it just comforted me. The other thing I have learned is that when you are expressing yourself creatively, the people who do so successfully are successful because they have a higher sensitivity. In the worst of circumstances, that can translate into being a drama queen. I get to be poetic, that is my job, to try and create poetry and to try and make compositions of things that feel emotionally compelling. The bad side to that, though, is that in your personal life, you can be overly romantic and over-idealistic, overly emotional or sensitive. So there is a drama-queen side to it. And that is what happened to me. I wasn't drinking for attention but

So you were doing all that while you were drinking yourself to death.

Yeah, I was getting a lot done. That was who I was. I was a big drinker; Michèle was, too. We drank a lot together, so it made sense. We were a perfect match.

When did your physical transformation begin?

Very soon after we got together. I was an office boy at this architectural administration firm. They were very charming, very bohemian, very sophisticated. They would do these hand-drawn architectural illustrations for potential buildings, like handmade renderings. The owner was the main illustrator, and we were in this really charming sort of Spanish building downtown. It was very *World of Interiors*. These people had a very clear line about what was

Did she interview you for the job?

She did. I had a nose ring, and I wore a long durag in this very beautiful brown silk jersey that I found in a hat-trim place in downtown Los Angeles. I must have worn make-up. I don't know what I was trying to do.

And your hair?

It was always black, and very wavy.

So you must have looked kind of cholo, very masculine.

I think I did, but I was super, super white. For some reason, I had very pale skin. Michèle had all the jewellery and the bracelets. She was more kittenish then, very languorous. We didn't hook up for two years because we didn't do that much in the factory right next to each other. She just passed by. She

'I had soft nipples, and softness in the thighs and belly. Then I took steroids and worked out with a trainer, and it bulked me up and I got really thick.'

trying to get attention for the work I was doing. The drinking was to give me the courage to go out and pursue it, that was the attention I wanted. I wanted to be validated. I didn't perform; I wasn't a performer. I stopped because I really thought I was going to die. So it was fear. It wasn't anything noble, just dumb fear.

When you stopped, could you look at where you had been and understand why you had been there?

Yeah, I was frustrated. I thought I was a failure.

And when did you stop?

I did my first runway show in 1994; I stopped drinking maybe a year before. But I was doing clothes for maybe five years before the show. I sold to Charles Gallay,[14] Bendel's, Joyce, Charivari…[15]

ostentatious or tacky. They would have office parties and invite people to look at slides of their latest Italian tour. It was a great environment. At the same time, I started going to fashion school to be a pattern-maker. Art was too hard. I didn't understand it enough; it was too cerebral for me. There were these art-theory classes that were so abstract and intimidating and I just thought I can't be an artist, I don't get all that. They scared me out of pursuing being an artist, so I thought: 'Well, I am smart enough to be a designer, so I'll do that.' So I went to design school and then I got a job as a pattern maker in the garment industry downtown. I was doing patterns and kind of fast-fashion patterns and then somebody told me there was a job at Michèle's label. I went there and the rest is history.

would sometimes have a party at her house and I would go, or we would run into each other at clubs. Stuff like that for two years because I didn't really know her.

And what was the trigger to connect?

I mean, she was so adorable and cute, and had such great body language and style. We were just drunk one night, and I made a move.

And you had been gay up until then?

Yeah, I mean I had a girlfriend way before, so I wasn't completely innocent, but she was just so cute. She was married, but it was all very casual and bohemian. I don't remember any confrontations. I just remember one night at the club, Michèle and I were there, and I had my arm around her and then

69

Richard [Newton, Lamy's first husband[16]] showed up, and he had a drink with us, but it was like nothing. Like we knew it was a moment where decisions could be made and things were being revealed and an understanding was being met, but no one really said anything.

One thing I was curious about in LA was the way that AIDS decimated things.
I was going to bring that up. Death was everywhere. Friends of mine were always going to funerals. I wasn't though; I went to, like, two. That period was my sex period, but I loved the sex clubs, that was where we would go every night. That was my clubhouse. And it was just being in an extreme, exotic environment, where everybody was going as far as they could go.

mean, it's not like anyone did anything to me, but my sexual tension and that environment with all of these guys, all that masculinity. Like the games when you had to pick the teams? Finally in the end, they would just let me sit down and read. That masculinity was so threatening to me. All that nudity and sexual tension was a nightmare to me. So when I came into my power, I took over that space. I had power suddenly. I could recreate that situation with me winning.

That's why I mentioned Ingrid Bergman going back to that town. You restructured.
Well, a lot of what I put on the runway is vengeful. Showing exposed dicks on the runway, showing dicks indifferently… it was after Dad passed, but having

Now, looking back on it, that was a great idea and worked out pretty well.

Listening to Wagner didn't compensate for missing *The Munsters* though.
I hated it! I hated having to sit through all that music.

As an only child who was close to his mom, did you gang up on your dad?
We were both afraid of him, not in an abusive way, but he was very dominating. And mom had grown up in a Mexican Catholic family and was very conscious of her position as a wife and mother, and what was expected of her. I guess we did protest together a bit, yeah. I did mention sex clubs to him as a provocation. I never really considered it, but I think the revenge I looked for was over the past. Here was a guy who grew up in

'For me, having a puritanical father whose machismo was so sacred, to show exposed dicks on the runway while he was alive would have killed him.'

And you were a voyeur?
No, I participated, very gleefully. That sounded a bit boyish.

I once walked past [legendary New York club] Mineshaft and I was kind of sorry I never went in, but it just smelled so bad.
Yes, but that was part of it. You see, I'm a pig, you're not. I had kind of a prissy childhood; my family was a little puritanical but also very prissy about hygiene, so those were forbidden fruits, to be in that environment. By the way, when I was in grade school, I was terrified about having to go to high school and be naked in the showers with other boys. That made me so uncomfortable. Then when it finally happened, obviously I was super uncomfortable and really, well it was just terrible… I

a puritanical father whose machismo was so sacred, for me to do that would have killed him.

Do you think it's that fundamental? That there's this kind of Oedipal challenge through your career, that you're creating with your father on your mind a lot of the time?
Your father is your god when you are young, so everything you do is based around seeking approval from that god or dealing with the rejection. Also, because we were in a small town with no relatives or no cousins, I didn't have a lot of other kids around. I was kind of a lonely child. Our little Catholic family was very insulated.

He also denied you access to all the things your peers had, like television.

a certain time in a certain way. I always thought that mom and I felt really bad for him; we felt that he had problems, like he was emotionally stunted, so we protected him. We knew that all of this came from fear and self-doubt and insecurity and vulnerability. We both felt protective towards him.

What do you see of him in you?
Bigotry, and I see 'judginess'. I also see that I have a set of rules that I think should apply to everybody; I catch myself being narrow sometimes and it is almost like a genetic disease that I am really aware of. I have to be careful not to disapprove. I can also go in the other direction, and not make up my mind, and always play devil's advocate. I have this moral superiority and then I feel that I overcompensate to make up for it.

70

Does that sort itself out with time? Do you feel you are mellowing?

I feel very mellow in relationships. I feel you need to let a person be who they want to be; you need to be happy with what they can give you and not expect more. You can't expect one person to satisfy all of your needs. I have been telling myself these things over the past five years. I think that has evolved. On the other hand, with the clothes I am making and what I am trying to do with the company, I feel more ferocious than ever. And on the other hand, I feel frustrated with this world's moralism.

For years, you shied away from any political connotations in what you do, and now you are embracing them.

Everything is political. I always think of the human condition, for sure. I

done before Putin invaded Ukraine, but you were able to recontextualize the show by using the Mahler symphony rather than what would have been one of your more typically aggressive soundtracks. At that moment you chose to exalt beauty as a defiant gesture, and it was stunning. Where do you feel you are now?

It was all so sad; there was a definite melancholy to it all.

Melancholy in the light of the context you were showing it in?

I hadn't really thought about that.

There is a rich seam of melancholia in much that Owens makes. The sense of lost worlds is strong. He can convincingly equate Babylon in 2000 BC and Hollywood in 1920 AD. The com-

to Hollywood Boulevard. Maybe the fact that it was buried under the house. It was always shadowy. Those books didn't belong on the real bookshelves in the house; they were in the basement. It's not like they were dirty books. I mean, we had the Marquis de Sade upstairs; I was free to read that.

The sense of Old Hollywood is one of the most poignant things in your work, the way you ravishingly recreate the atmosphere, the shadowy, bias-cut languor, the beauty of those dresses.

Black-and-white movies in the basement. It was the imagery and the environments, too. Theda Bara's boudoir![17] That kind of life, that kind of scale. All those Cecil B. DeMille movies, the scale was so huge. Living in these monumental sets, the dresses dragging on

'I went back to Porterville for the first time recently in 20 years. It felt very reassuring. I was like, why am I in such a good mood here? I am still not sure.'

don't like to address specific things that are happening in the world. I never feel like I have the authority to make great political statements; that is something that my father would do. I don't feel like I studied enough to have that kind of authority. But I do know, and I understand how to protest. I also understand that what I do cannot correct anything. It is only ever a protest, but that can be good.

You've said that you choose politeness over defiance, which I thought was strange, even though you are an incredibly mannerly and gracious person.

There is a lot of defiance in what I do, in a nice way.

What about the last women's collection? Admittedly, the collection was

mon thread is scale. The human form is elongated, exaggerated, swathed to create an illusion of almost superhuman glamour. The illusion is often confrontational, monstrous, even, but there is an extreme beauty in the strange. It was less extreme in the last women's collection, where even Owens acknowledged the classical beauty of his bias-cut gowns. An unwitting synchronicity with world events made those dresses a peculiarly appropriate fashion response to the bottomless ugliness Vladimir Putin was unleashing to the East.

Old Hollywood was a frame of reference for you. How? When? Why?

In my dad's basement library. I remember it always having a sense of dissipation that corresponded

the floor... Oh, is that dress going to get dirty? People weren't asking that back then. It was beyond that.

The whole thing about fashion in LA is that it did exist in a hothouse. It was the most influential fashion in the world in a way, in that people saw it in the movies.

It really was the Hollywood thing – that was the only reference that there was in LA. Nothing contemporary. I had the most beautiful apartment, a block above Hollywood Boulevard, part of the top floor of a house, a bedroom, a living room and a little kitchen. And I had a black T-Top Camaro with a V8 engine.[18] I had such a tight little driveway that I don't know how I got in and out after a long night. Not always successfully, because the car ended up getting kind of scratched

71

up. I remember looking at Southern Crescent Heights and dreaming of living there, because the buildings just looked like something out of Armistead Maupin[19], with an eccentric landlady and someone playing piano in one of the apartments and the fountain tinkling in the courtyard. It just seemed magical. And I was like: 'Wow, I'm going to live here some day.' And *now*… [a single Owens eyebrow flexes at the wonder of it all].

You'd never go back.
Oh God, no! I could see myself living there, but only on an estate with peacocks and maybe a tiger or two. Then it could be great.

What is your favourite representation of Old Hollywood?

is, I can't do fillers. I tried Botox and I couldn't tell the difference. I can't go there, but I did steroids for a time and that really helped. It got everything in place.

What's 'everything'?
Before the steroids, I had softness. I had soft nipples; I had kind of little girl's boobs, and softness in the thighs and belly. When I took the steroids and worked out with a trainer regularly, it bulked me up and I got really thick. I have pictures of me that are kind of shocking. Then when I stopped the steroids and dropped all the weight, all of a sudden this framework of muscles and the nipples got harder. It kind of created a scaffolding inside of me. It was probably 30 years ago when my body transformed.

thing that he was proudest of – from ballet dancer to that massive man mountain!
He was so handsome. There is a Rudolf Nureyev biography on Netflix that I have been watching it with the sound off. It's just so beautiful, the old imagery of him dancing and leaping.

So sad.
Why? I look at his life and I think it was a triumph. It was just glorious. Of course, there is the decline at the end. There always is; there has to be.

Do you see that for you?
I do admit the reason that I am reading biographies is to see how they negotiate and live their entire lives. Yeah, because I am 60, things are changing. I am thinking about the next chapters. I

'I could see myself living back in Hollywood, but only if it was on an estate, with peacocks and maybe a tiger or two. Then it could be great.'

My main one is *Cleopatra*, the Cecil B. DeMille movie with Claudette Colbert, the most improbable Cleopatra ever;[20] you couldn't have picked a worse one. The entire thing is entirely ridiculous.

Theda Bara's real name was Theodosia Goodman. Claudette Colbert's was Lily Chauchoin. Nothing and no one was real in Old Hollywood. It was all self-invention. One of the first conversations we ever had, you listed everything you'd done to yourself, like you were trying to coach me to believe that everything I was looking at was entirely artificial.
Not entirely artificial, but definitely 'manipulated'.

Self-invention.
Yes, self-invention. The funny thing

And that was something you did for yourself?
Michèle got me started. She was going to the trainer, and she was like, 'You should go; you drink too much. It'll be good for your hangovers.' So I did and then it just kind of stuck. And then when I saw things changing, it was just addictive. Also, it just felt like being the best that I could be, like doing everything I possibly could. Probably at that time it was also a satisfying sort of control. More than the results of my career maybe. It's not like things were going badly, but it was just insecure. You don't know if the whole fashion business thing is going to work out. So controlling my body was one way of feeling in control.

A few months before he died, Thierry Mugler told me that his body was the

am really conscious of how people did things.

When you read these biographies that have a beginning, middle and an end, has anything ever stood out for you about how you would like your life to be? Will it end with people loving you for posterity?
I feel like that is going to happen; I'm not worried about that. I have people who care for me, and I feel that unless I do something incredibly stupid, I will leave a body of work that has a sense of purpose and honour. Yes, I feel good about it. Though it was kind of shocking to me that I could be so emotionally vulnerable. Maybe I am reading these biographies to reassure myself that people can be a little bit messy, to reassure myself that I am not doing it all wrong.

72

How is your balance of Apollo and Dionysus sitting after the past few years?

Oh, Apollo, definitely! I tried Dionysus and it wasn't for me. It has to be Apollo.

Do you actually like the fact that life is still capable of surprising you, just when you thought everything was set?

I think a couple of things have happened. In the beginning, I maybe went overboard but this last collection is more stabilizing. Like all my influences, I have balanced them out better and probably filtered them better. Maybe analysing relationships in general fed into that, just living in my emotions more than I used to.

I felt like in that last collection there was so much less ambiguity than there is usually, like you wanted it to just be beauty at its most breathtaking, rather than challenging.

Yeah, I don't know where that came from actually. I know what you are saying about challenging beauty; I do react against the standards of beauty. The laws are so rigid, every advertisement, every Instagram post – there is just such a narrow set of parameters of beauty. I always try to push that a bit because I resent being told what to do. And also because I think there are other people out there who are feeling left out of that whole world, and they want something different. So that is what I am always trying to explore. And it is tricky. I can't go too far because then it is impossible for anyone to relate to it. But this one did get pretty close to classical beauty. Though I always want everyone to be covered. I want the freaks to be covered, too.

You do have a following that is a little more intense than the average. How do you feel about that?

It means it's working; it means that what I put out there has a reason for polluting the world with our dyes and our extra fabrics. We have an excuse; we have a reason to be here. I see the kids in it, and I am like, 'Wow, they wear this stuff so beautifully.'

Could you ever have conceived of success like this?

No, I don't think so. Though I'm not really sure. There is something in me that remembers I would be frustrated about having to balance my check book, and there was nothing really to suggest otherwise. I just somehow knew I would never have to do that. Like, OK, I will do that now, but I will never have to do that in the future.

So you believe in manifest destiny?

Could be. Maybe I was just a spoiled and pretentious kid from Porterville.

Are you happy now?

Yes, I am. I got myself together. I figured shit out and I'm not such a pussy with the whole relationship thing any more.

1. First published in 1913, Thomas Mann's novella *Death in Venice* tells the story of celebrated author, Gustav von Aschenbach, and his growing – and ultimately tragic – obsession with a beautiful 14-year-old Polish boy, Tadzio, based partly on a child Mann saw in 1911. The book's themes of male aging, youthful beauty and regret were magnified in Luchino Visconti's 1971 adaptation of the book, which starred Dirk Bogarde (as a composer, not a writer) and a young Björn Andrésen. The film famously opens and closes with the Adagietto from Gustav Mahler's Fifth Symphony.

2. The Vista Theatre at 4473 Sunset Drive in Los Angeles opened in 1923 with an architecturally curious Spanish colonial-style exterior and Egyptian-style interior. Since then it has hosted vaudeville acts, shown first-run and classic films, and pornography, both gay and straight. In late 2020, director Quentin Tarantino announced that he had bought the cinema.

3. The imposing and luxurious Grand Hôtel des Bains on the Lido in Venice opened at 7pm on 5 July 1900 and closed 16 years later after a fire. Its 172 rooms and 19 suites were reopened in 1919, welcoming guests ranging from Adolf Hitler to Elizabeth Taylor, until it closed again in 1966 after serious storm damage. A second reopening took place in time for Visconti to film *Death in Venice* in the hotel in 1970. The hotel was again shuttered in 2010, as developers planned to convert it into luxury apartments. That work barely started and today, the hotel remains boarded up and poignantly empty.

4. Lying 260 kilometres north of Los Angeles in the San Joaquin Valley, Porterville (population: 60,000) is, according to its website, 'full of history and small town charm [...] and home to a large man-made body of water, Lake Success'. As well as Owens, other Portervilleans include Charlotte Pendragon, the first woman to win Magician of the Year,

and Vernon Grant, the artist who created the Snap!, Crackle! and Pop! characters on every box of Kellogg's Rice Krispies.

5. In Kristina Lindström and Kristian Petri's documentary *The Most Beautiful Boy in the World* (2021), Björn Andrésen has a succinct description of his life after starring in *Death in Venice*: 'It was a living nightmare.'

6. Based upon a hit Broadway play by German writer Friedrich Dürrenmatt, *The Visit* was optioned by 20th Century Fox in February 1960. Ingrid Bergman and Anthony Quinn were cast, celebrated playwright Clifford Odetts hired to write a screenplay, and J. Lee Thompson chosen to direct. The entire project was then cancelled in March 1962 after budget cuts at Fox. The film was finally made, directed by Bernhard Wicki, and released in 1964.

7. Pioneering Los Angeles-electro-punk group the Screamers, founded by Tomata du Plenty and Tommy

Gear, was active from 1975 to 1981. According to Pitchfork, its song catalogue mainly 'deals with sex and sexuality'. One of the band's numbers 'Anything', showcases the band's obsessions: 'I get so sick of the fashion and the fascism / Makes me crazy, wanna try a little smash-ism! / You wanna have fun, you want a reaction / I wanna have you, I want a sex action.'

8. Quaalude was a tradename for methaqualone, a drug first synthesized in India in 1951 and used to treat insomnia and anxiety. The pills became such a popular recreational drug in the late 1970s in the US that, according to the BBC, they were nicknamed 'disco biscuits'. The drug was made illegal in many countries in the early 1980s, although it is widely used as a street drug in South Africa.

9. Established in 1918 as the Otis Art Institute and Los Angeles first professional school of the arts, the Otis College of Art and Design today has

73

In the words of…

1,200 students. Norman Rockwell was the school's artist in residence for much of the 1940s.

10. Self-taught artist Ron Athey, who 'has been working at the vanguard of performance art for 25 years', was an enthusiastic member of the 1980s underground punk scene in Los Angeles, and built an artistic reputation for performances that dealt with subjects including AIDS, body modification, and religious rituals. One of his more notorious works is *Solar Anus* (1999), which Hyperallergic describes as a 're-interpretation of Georges Bataille's 1931 surrealist text in which Athey inserts a stiletto-heel dildo into his anus and dons a golden crown held in place with facial piercings'.

11. 'FUCK! puts it in your face,' wrote Craig Lee in an April 1991 article for *LA Weekly*. 'It's a club celebrating post-AIDS sexuality as body manipulation, set against a non-stop electro-techno danse/trance drone, a mutant version of post-punk S&M.' Held weekly at Basgo's Disco in Silver Lake, Los Angeles, from 1989 to 1992, Club Fuck! was, according to Ron Athey, a place of 'piercing and cutting rituals' and 'a voyeurism/exhibitionism exchange'. For Cliff Diller, one of the night's founders, it was also a place of resistance. 'The way this country is going conservative, you've got to find a way to fight back,' he told Lee. 'So that's why I'll do something like have someone apply 250 clothespins to my body at the club. It releases the endorphins, but it's also a political act.'

12. One Wednesday in August 1993, legendary *Los Angeles Times* restaurant critic Jonathan Gold visited Swingers, four months after restaurateurs Jon Sidel and Sean MacPherson had opened it in the old Beverly Laurel Motor Hotel. After noting that half the male clientele had 'goatees, tribal tattoos, groovy pirate earrings', he declared: 'there is no cooler place in town to scarf a veggie sub, a bowl of gazpacho, a banana-orange smoothie that has been transformed, with amino acids, into something called a thermite bomb.'

13. Café des Artistes was Michèle Lamy's first restaurant venture – 'a romantic, verdant bistro with a … monied boho clientele', according to *Los Angeles* – and the location of the shows for her fashion label. In 1996, she opened Les Deux Cafés, which the magazine described as the 'world's most successful boîte situated in a parking lot' until it closed after, in Lamy's words, 'the front part of the building collapsed, and everything

stop'. It reopened in 1997 and finally closed in 2003. 'The service was abysmal (infamously, and intentionally so),' wrote ex-employee and journalist Chris Wallace in *The Paris Review* in 2012, 'the food was *okay*, but the *scene* … the scene was the thing.'

14. The 'Fred and Ginger of the retail business,' according to a 1988 *Los Angeles Times* article, Charles Gallay and his wife Madeleine ran Charles Gallay, their 'chic and sophisticated' Beverly Hills clothing store from 1971 until 1985. After their divorce, Madeleine had some plastic surgery, lost 10 kilos ('I was a heifer,' she told the *Times*), and in 1988 opened her own eponymous clothing store directly opposite Charles' solo venture. She stocked Galliano and Rifat Ozbek; he sold Alaïa and Romeo Gigli. Both stores are now closed.

15. Luxury department store Henri Bendel opened in 1895 in New York and finally shut its doors 123 years later in January 2019, because its then-owner L Brands wanted 'to improve company profitability and focus on our larger brands'. Charivari opened its first store in April 1967 and for much of the 1970s and 1980s was considered New York's most cutting-edge fashion destination. It introduced many European and Japanese designers to the US, including Yohji Yamamoto and Martin Margiela. Charivari later expanded to six stores across Manhattan, but filed for bankruptcy in 1998.

16. Michèle Lamy's first husband Richard Newton, a visual artist and filmmaker, began working with trash in the early 1970s, 'dumpster diving and recycling … to create environmental works of art'. The couple met in 1979, had a daughter (visual artist Scarlett Rouge), and during the 1980s, built a fashion label – Lamy designing and Newton running the business – which, according to a profile of the couple in the *Los Angeles Times*, was worth $10 million by 1990. 'Maybe it's just our temperaments,' Newton told the newspaper, 'but Michèle and I are good for each other.'

17. Born Theodosia Burr Goodman in Cincinnati, Ohio, in 1885, Theda Bara was a silent-movie star whose nearly 40 films have been almost entirely lost. Discovered by producer William Fox and promoted as the daughter of a mysterious Eastern nabob – her stage name is an anagram of 'Death Arab' – her popularity peaked with her sensual portrayal of the Egyptian queen in *Cleopatra* (1917). After an unsuccessful Broadway debut and a failed Hol-

lywood comeback, she retired in 1926, and died in 1955.

18. The pony car par excellence, the Chevrolet Camaro was introduced in September 1966 as rival to Ford's Mustang. Originally set to be called Panther, its name was changed to Camaro – a made-up word – shortly before its launch.

19. Armistead Maupin's *Tales from the City* chronicled the lives of Mary Ann Singleton, a naive young woman; Michael 'Mouse' Tolliver, her gay friend; and Anna Madrigal, a transgender woman, who all live in an apartment complex, 28 Barbary Lane, in 1970s San Francisco. First published in 1978, the novel was a hit and spawned five sequels that tracked the characters' lives through various vicissitudes, including parenthood, AIDS and cancer.

20. Cecil B. DeMille's big-budget *Cleopatra*, starring Claudette Colbert, opened in 1934. The *New York Times* found her performance in the bigbudget 90-minute extravaganza 'both competent and attractive'.

74

Rick Owens

75

'Everyone processes their rebellion in a different way.'

Daniel Roseberry's own coming-of-age tale is bringing dramatic surrealism back to the house of Schiaparelli.

Interview by **Jerry Stafford**
Photographs by **Nadine Ijewere**
Styling by **Nell Kalonji**
Portrait by **Christophe Coënon**

300

Daniel Roseberry in *System*, no. 19 (2022).

Daniel Roseberry is designing a new desk for his spacious office at Schiaparelli's HQ, which looks out onto the grandiose symmetry of the Place Vendôme in Paris. After three challenging years at the helm of the legendary house, it feels like he is discreetly loosening his stays and slipping into something a little more comfortable. 'It's very much a work in progress,' he says, almost tentatively, 'but this is a signal that I am settling in!'

In the wake of the 2020 pandemic that threw everyone and everything into a maelstrom of confusion and self-doubt, Roseberry confidently burst back onto a newly reopened international stage last year with a series of sensational *coups de théâtre* worthy of the house's illustrious founder, Elsa Schiaparelli.

just a whisper on Mae West's lips!

'The house of Schiaparelli is a singular thing,' says performer Tilda Swinton, who has also worn Roseberry's chimeric creations over the past year. 'The landscape of its legacy – the practical magic of its resonance – is something almost mythical in the wide geography of the fashion universe. Schiaparelli means an intimate and ancient relationship between art and fashion, in particular with the vernacular of a Surrealism dear to the heart of Elsa Schiaparelli herself. In the hands of Daniel Roseberry, this resonance pulses with an energy and freshness that regularly takes the breath away.'

The designer's latest couture collection – a palette-cleansing exercise in monochromatic minimalist maximalism – was his first live presentation since

dramatically charged coming-of-age novel in which the protagonist ultimately achieves self-awareness and self-confidence through art and creativity.

Geography has played an important role in that journey, and those places with which he has fallen in or out of love have influenced both his life choices – or his 'forks in the road', as he calls them – and his sensibility: the claustrophobia of his upbringing in Dallas, Texas; the revelation of the New York years working alongside Thom Browne; and the escapism of the coastline of Maine which, as he explains is, 'the place where I think I first met myself as an adult, and ironically, it's the place I run to when I want to feel like a kid again.'

Hanya Yanigahara, the acclaimed author of bestseller *A Little Life*,

'I like the idea of being able to hide behind the heritage and the weight of something, like Schiaparelli, that existed before me. It's legitimizing.'

In January 2021, at the inauguration of Joe Biden, Lady Gaga serenaded the newly elected President of the United States in a navy jacket by the designer, decorated with an extravagant gilded dove of peace, and a skirt that exploded into volumetric tiers of washed red silk faille. Seven months later, Roseberry's reputation was further sealed with Bella Hadid's other-worldly appearance on the red carpet at the Cannes Film Festival, wearing an exquisite gold bustier masterfully cast and crafted to represent a pair of life-giving lungs. The vision was pure Elsa and recalled her own celebrated collaborations with Salvador Dalí.

After long being starved of such spectacle, the fashion world gasped at the sight of this almost saintly apparition. The house of Schiaparelli was no longer

Covid had sent everyone racing into the metaverse. Monolithic dresses stalked the runway like charismatic megafauna beamed down from outer space into a Kubrickian dreamscape.

Roseberry recently launched his first ready-to-wear collections, sold exclusively through Bergdorf Goodman, which both complement and extend his couture process and creative vision. The iconic Surrealist signifiers and stylistic hybridization of his couture collections have now been integrated into clothes and accessories to accompany the new Schiaparelli woman as she descends from her gilded pedestal and steps into the 'real world'.

As a designer, Roseberry seems to find inspiration in a narrative that has its roots in his childhood. His own sentimental education reads like a

recently dedicated her new dystopian epic *To Paradise* to Roseberry and they share an intimate, intuitive relationship. 'When you're a writer, you write when you feel like it,' Yanigahara explains, 'and (ideally) only when you feel like it. Daniel and his peers don't have that luxury. Some artistic directors turn their gaze outward in response, always looking for something to inspire them, but some – and I believe that, ultimately, Daniel belongs in this category – venture ever-further inward, to an emotional landscape they've created and tend year after year. They're constantly harvesting from this invented world, one accessible only to them. It's a special way to create, but a punishing one as well. For the most imaginative among them, though, the results are unmistakable and undeniable.'

315

In conversation

Jerry Stafford: Let's start by discussing where you grew up, your childhood, and your home life.

Daniel Roseberry: I grew up in Texas, in a middle-class suburb of Dallas. My dad was a preacher in a church that he founded the year I was born, which became a mega-church of sorts. Both of my parents were born-again Christians; they were not brought up religiously but met at the seminary. My mum had two kids from a prior marriage and then they had me and my little sister. I guess my childhood was one of searching, of longing. I went to a private school in Dallas where everyone had tons and tons of money. We basically had none. I was daydreaming all the time of the things we couldn't have.

What are your earliest visual memories?

Who was the actor?

I don't remember… oh, it was the shower scene in that terrible but amazing movie with Kurt Russell called *Captain Ron*.[1]

How did you experience growing up as a young gay man in the southern states of America?

Tortuous is a dramatic word, but it was sort of tortuous. It was a journey of deep self-hatred and thinking that I was a broken and failed heterosexual. That was the message: this is in God's best interest for you; you are a failed version of what you should have been and it's your job to bring yourself back to a general semblance of normality; if not, then celibacy would be the ideal solution.

Did you yearn to leave that environ-

to make. I was a Christian missionary for a year prior to moving to New York – I really did try *every* option.[3]

Were you exposed to art growing up? You were brought up in Texas, so were you aware of the Menil Collection, for example, or the other great art institutions in the state?

I remember when the Nasher opened[4], that was a big deal. I come from a family of artists: my mom and my grandmothers on both sides and two of my uncles were extremely prolific artists. That was the foil to all the religious and spiritual dogma; there was always an appreciation for that world. I remember my grandmother had expensive museum catalogues, which were really inspiring for me, but I always felt really out of my depth talking about current modern art.

'My dad was a preacher in a church that he founded the year I was born. Both of my parents were born-again Christians.'

I remember watching my mum getting dressed for church, putting on her jewellery. I also remember playing with my sister in a pile of fallen leaves near my parents' house. In the fall. A lot of my early memories are related to fall.

What or who were your first sexual or sensual fantasies?

Good question. I remember being in seventh or eighth grade and I was sleeping over at my friend's house. We were lying on the bed and talking about this sex scene in a movie, and for the first time, I confessed to him that I had loved the movie, but that I couldn't stop looking at the boy. He thought that was really weird, and I don't think it was ever the same between us again. That was the first time I remember verbalizing something homoerotic.

ment and if so, to go where and why?

I was so terrified. I remember when I was at school, in my freshman year at college, and I had got into FIT, but rejected the idea of going twice because I was so scared of going to New York and falling into some crazy drugs scene and sex den.

You were scared of actually living the life you desired.

Yes, yes. Everyone processes their rebellion in a different way, and I was so cautious and nervous because I didn't want to disappoint anybody. I remember being a freshman and I was sitting alone reading *W* magazine and there was a story on Tom Ford, with a Steven Klein shoot.[2] I was filled with so much confusion and fear, and also longing. New York was a really difficult decision

Who were your favourite writers back then?

I had a very classic education. I was really into Dickens, Brontë's *Wuthering Heights*. I have this thing with Hanya Yanagihara[5] called EGS, which stands for 'exquisite gay sorrow'. We're always talking about what triggers EGS, like did you have an EGS sort of a day? A lot of the writing I was drawn to that predated this life was very EGS.

Was music an important part of your life at that time?

Music hit me after, like mid-high school and after high school. Before that I was obsessed with the movies, and I wanted to be a Disney animator. So it wasn't until I moved to New York when music completely replaced cinema as my number-one inspiration.

316

Where or what was your first encounter with what could be termed as fashion? The one that made you feel it was an area of interest that could possibly take you somewhere?

I started to draw women and clothes before this moment, but the *real* moment happened when I was 16. Style Network came to Texas, and they did a free bundle, with *Fashion File, Behind the Velvet Ropes*, all those things. There was a special on Michael Kors and I saw in detail the journey of his collection, and at the same time learned that he was from a similar middle-class background. He had gone to FIT and dropped out, and then his collection was on display at Barneys, and someone came and bought it, some crazy story like that. And I was like, 'OK, I could do that.'

What about your own personal style at that time? Did you follow any trends or movements?

I have always been a bit clueless about what to do with my own style and talking to you, it's so obvious, there are some people whose style and physicality are totally embedded with who they are. I just never felt like that. I remember watching the McQueen collections and then he would come out at the end, and the disconnect really resonated with me. I have never successfully been able to dress myself in an identifiable style. That is why Thom Browne was such a relief. Of course, I'd been in uniform since second grade. So through Thom Browne I learned everything.

What do you think was your real motivation behind this interest in design

and fashion?

The answer is not very glamourous, but it was a way for me to justify my own existence; I think that being told that your identity is wrong…

As in your sexual identity?

My sexuality, which felt like my entire being. Design and the ability to wow people and to impress them, and to give them something else to applaud me for because I knew they would never applaud me for the decisions in my personal life – that became a huge motivating factor.

Did you ever have a mentor or someone who actively encouraged you in your studies and then your career?

Mentors have thankfully been a huge part of my life. At every step of the way I have had someone mentoring me; I have never been on my own. The first one was my mom, who taught me how to draw for hours and hours; she would stand over my shoulder as I did artworks for doctors' offices and stuff. Later there was the dean of the seminary who mentored me theologically and who also released me from a lot of this self-hatred. I almost went to seminary, and he told me absolutely not, you have to go to New York to be a designer. And then once in New York it was Thom, so yes, there have been lots of mentors.

Are you an ambitious person or are you more intuitive? Have you been drawn almost inexplicably and unconsciously towards the future and your place in it?

I know this sounds insane, but I always felt that the hand of God has been in my

life from the beginning. I have always felt like this; I didn't really have a say. I felt that fashion chose me in a way, and I have been toiling to get to this place. I have never even considered doing anything else.

Are you still a practising Christian? Do you still believe in a Christian God?

I believe that the Christian God is a mechanism by which I can understand God, but I do not at all prescribe to the narrowness of a Christian faith. I do also believe that Jesus represents one aspect of maybe the way that God or a creator wants to relate to the world, but I don't know if I would call myself a Christian any more.

Jumping forward, how did you navigate the move to Paris from the States

in 2019, and what is your relationship to the city? How do you fit in here?

I had prepared my life in New York so I could abandon it. I had already moved out of my apartment, and I was sleeping on a friend's floor. Everything I owned was already in storage because I really believed this job was mine. When it happened, I literally came here with two suitcases. Everything else I own is still in storage in New York. Looking back on my arrival in Paris, I was so glad that I really had no idea what it meant to be doing my first collection. I had no idea, and the great thing was that no one really had any expectations because the house was so sleepy at the time. My relationship with Paris has been really rough, though. I really feel like a stranger in this city; I have never lived somewhere and felt like this. New

'I got into FIT, but rejected the idea of going twice because I was so scared of going to New York and falling into some crazy drugs scene and sex den.'

317

York was such an amazing life; it was so rich. I had friendships; I had Sunday-night dinners; I was surrounded by people who loved me, and I always entertained at my house. I have never spent more time alone than I have here over the past three years.

How would you sum up that time when you lived and worked in New York, the changes that you experienced in the city, the shifting political framework and creative challenges?

I was 23 when I started at Thom Browne. I came out to my parents a week before I started my internship. I was in the closet throughout college, completely shut down, so I was really born then, this second birth, the second coming out. In those first five or six years at Thom Browne, when we were

Did you always aspire to head up an important historical fashion house? Was all the experience you acquired part of this ambition?

Yes, 100%. All of my years working at Thom were spent pining for my own thing, but I never thought it would be my own brand. I like the idea of being able to hide behind the heritage and the weight of something that existed before me.

Would you say that's connected to your childhood?

Yes, completely. Something that is legitimizing. It was really one of the most uncomfortable things when I left Thom Browne. It was not very long, just six or seven months, but I was so uncomfortable because I had nothing with which to justify myself to the world. You go to a party, and no one knows who you are;

a starting point, the better it makes my work. Her legacy feels like an untold story. The exhibition that is opening in July is the first step I think in maybe telling that story to a wider audience.[6] She was the kind of person, with her voice and her personality and her character, who if I met her at a dinner party, I would be probably the most intimidated to talk to. That's probably why I've refused to read her biographies.

Nonetheless, the house archive is an invaluable source for your work. How do you approach and navigate it and how has this research manifested itself in specific pieces?

What we do every season is go back to the archive. It's mainly imagery because we don't have physical archives here. They have a huge archive at the Met, I

'With Chanel, Dior or Balenciaga, you don't get a true personality or a sense of humour like you do with Elsa Schiaparelli. That is her greatest legacy.'

really building the foundation of that company, it was like the Wild West. It was unsupervised, plus my life in Brooklyn, it was such a dream. I look back at that time with such nostalgia. I had the best friends in Brooklyn. We have all disbanded now, everyone has scattered because of Covid and everything, but there was a summer in 2018 – or 2016, 2017, I can't remember – when we went to Maine. At the end of that trip, something had shifted in my mind, and I thought: 'I never am going to get to where I want to be in my career if I stay in this Brooklyn neverland world, and if I stay at Thom Browne.' That was a turning point for me and within a few months I moved to the West Village in a studio and started over. I walked away from a lot, and I am extremely nostalgic for that.

you are constantly having to justify your existence to people, especially in New York. So I always wanted it.

Now you are here in Paris and installed at Schiaparelli, what importance does the house's history and heritage have for you? You've said that you have never read a biography of Elsa Schiaparelli, why?

When I first started I had no interest in tapping into the heritage because I felt it had already been the focal point of prior years. I really tried to re-establish the voice of the house *and* make it personal. When I felt that we had done that on some level, I was able to return to her work. I have been truly blown away, humbled and proven wrong about the relevance that her work still has. The more I reference her work and use it as

think, and most of the great pieces are at the Philadelphia Museum of Art; it has the lobster dress.[7] We always print out all the imagery of, like, iconic Schiaparelli jackets or accessories – because she did these outrageous accessories, these titbits that went along with the collection – and we have them out as the collection grows. It all becomes the subtext for everything. There are normally one or two pieces that present themselves, like the teacup coat, which just felt right. And some time last year, being sort of literal with the archives suddenly felt fun, like the shoe on the head. Sometimes it is about abstracting it; other times, it is about holding it very tight and being literal. What I enjoy the most here is that with Chanel or Dior or definitely with Balenciaga, you don't get a true personality like you do with

318

Schiaparelli. You get a vision, you get savoir-faire and technique, and you get world-changing silhouettes – but you don't get personality or a sense of humour. That is her greatest legacy, and what gives me permission to imbue that into the work as well.

You can be quite cavalier about it. Has the Surrealist movement, so important in Schiaparelli's lifetime and to her work, been an influence on your own process or design? There are many signifiers, surreal objects, masks, and so on that are integrated into the clothes, but beyond that I feel that the way you have pieced together couture garments from the narratives of other designers is reminiscent of the Surrealist parlour game, the Exquisite Corpse.[8] Was this in your mind during that process?

of accessing the unconscious and opening oneself up to chance – '*le hasard*'! Something that intrigues me is that there are so many utterly compelling narratives around the history of the house, aside from the obvious relationships with Cocteau and Dalí. The poet and patron Edward James for example whom Schiaparelli called the 'true English eccentric'.[9] She remembers James giving Dalí a stuffed polar bear dyed shocking pink! Are any of these eccentrics that surrounded Schiaparelli attractive to you? Does eccentricity in itself inspire you?**

That's a great question. Yes, it does. What's hard for me about eccentricity in other people is that I have a tough time accessing a real connection with it and that can kind of throw me off sometimes. My best friend, for exam-

specific pieces. Do you see these as collaborations, and do you enjoy the collaborative process? Would you work with an artist on a collaboration as so many people do these days in fashion?**
I didn't want to do collaborations at the beginning, because I didn't want the legitimacy of the house or of me to be linked with or indebted to the collaborator. There are two types of collaborations: there is the process collaboration, which you go through with an artisan, which is a chain reaction of creative decisions informed by their skill set. I owe everything to that. Then there is the kind of collaboration that you put out to the world and announce with an artist. In my original project, Sarah Lucas was actually someone who I proposed doing a collaboration with. I even did sketches of what we could do...

'I tried to re-establish the voice of the house *and* make it personal. When I felt that we had done that, I was able to return to Elsa's work.'

You're the only person who has ever really verbalized that for me because it's true the Surrealist movement, as an art movement, is far less inspiring than building a Surrealist *process*. That space where pre-associations can be made is like gymnastics, you know. That idea of collaging together different fetishizations of other designers' work is something I try and be really open about, because it's so obvious sometimes. It's like when Virgil [Abloh] said, 'You only need to change things 10%.' I am definitely not trying to copy, but I love scratching that itch – like, what if we do something that is this designer on top and bottom, but the middle is Lacroix? I love playing that game.

It is a game, and it's a wonderful one, whether visual or textual, as it's a way

ple, is wildly eccentric; she's living a life that is not really in accordance with the way other people live, and I find it endlessly inspiring to have those conversations, and to spend time with her and learn about that. I am very earthbound in the way that I live my life. We had that conversation about Edward James in Mexico, and I always think about that because I love that sensual side to Surrealism, which I think about a lot.

When I see your work I always think of artists like Méret Oppenheim, Louise Bourgeois, and more contemporary figures like David Altmejd or Sarah Lucas. Who were or are, of course, sculptors. Your work has often been called 'sculptural', for want of a better word, and you have collaborated with ceramicist and metallurgist artisans on

Did you approach her?
No, never, but there was definitely a conversation with her in my mind with the original project. I would love to do that. I'd love to collaborate not only with visual artists; doing music together would be almost more interesting, something about visual and non-visual together feels less contrived. There is something more open about the musical process. It is a playground for me where I can create something visual within a space like this. Sometimes I have albums that I remember specifically listening to while creating a collection that are then so inextricably linked. I remember the project I made to be hired for Thom Browne was done in accordance with Björk's *Homogenic*. That would be a dream of mine to collaborate with musicians.

319

Contentious question: do you believe that what you do is art?

I think couture can approach art, but for the most part I would say that it's an applied art.

How do you feel about social media? You have a personal Instagram, but do you fantasize about being able to present a collection where iPhones are banned and the experience remains purely within the moment, held as a memory communicated verbally without an accompanying barrage of imagery? Perhaps even going back to the golden age of illustration?

I do fantasize, if not every day, then every other day, about getting off all social media. I would love it. I remember when Tom Ford came back for his first collection[10] and there were no photographers

a point never to bring my phone out. It's not that it is disrespectful, but it's a major missed opportunity. Lacroix said, 'I want people leaping', but no one is going to leap through their phone, like why watch it? You have to really let go to leap. I have a really contentious relationship with the digital world, but at the same time I know there's no point in fighting it. It's happening no matter what.

Yet you do enjoy the photographic process these days, shooting your own lookbooks for the last couple of seasons. Do you feel you are the person who is most trusted to represent your own work?

I know what goes through the minds of people when a designer says, 'I want to shoot it myself', because every single person I talked to about it literally

so all-consuming that it consumes your whole life? I'm thinking about that first show with you at the centre... Do you have time out from that identity? Can you step aside from your work?

It's everything to me. All of me is wrapped up in it, and using of myself, exposing myself felt really urgent in that show. It's an impulse I have every season that I have to fight a bit because a designer putting himself at the centre can be distracting or just really unwelcome; not many people want to see that. It made sense with that first show because it was an introduction, a coming-out of sorts, but I feel most myself when we are in fittings upstairs at the Place Vendôme.[12] I feel this sort of split personality thing happens when we are creating couture; I literally feel so connected with what I am supposed to be

'I'd gag for the opportunity to present work to an engaged audience, because when I look on the monitor backstage, they're looking at their phones.'

and no phones allowed, and I remember Steven Stipelman[11] was there to do illustrations instead. That was an impossible throwback. I'm 36 and I'm the last generation that remembers what it was like to go through high school without any social media. I would gag for the opportunity to present work to an engaged audience, because when I look on the monitor backstage, no one is even looking at the collection, they are looking at their phone screens. It is unreal to me that we have spent hundreds of thousands of euros and hours creating what we would hope would approach art and then the people who are there physically are just watching it through their screens… It's like going to a movie theatre and watching a movie through your phone screen. It is totally devastating. Whenever I have gone to a show, I make

rolled their eyes and said, 'OK, here's another one.' I've heard the way people talk about other designers' photographs, but I felt like it was a sort of an extension of the creative process. When we came back from Covid, we did this shoot outside because we wanted to do it without masks, and it was so much fun. I just absolutely loved it. It was going to be me and [stylist] Marie Chaix, whom I see as a partner in crime, especially on those shoot days, and to have to go through a photographer's vision for a lookbook didn't seem necessary. For an editorial, yes, it is completely different. Do I think I'm the world's greatest photographer? Well, no! [Laughs]

How much of yourself have you written into the creative process or is it just

doing. The only other place that I truly feel that way is when I am in Maine, and there is always this sort of fork in the road between the hyper-introverted way and then this extroverted performative way. That is what I love about dressing celebs, because it is as close I will probably come to being on that red carpet.

Do you dream, and if yes are they vivid and visual?

I rarely remember my dreams and when I do it's because they are sexual in nature.

I was about to ask you to describe a recent one!

I had an erotic dream two nights ago, but the person was just laying on top of me, like I just could feel the person's

320

weight and I woke up in the middle of the dream and they were whispering in my ear. It was a very intense sensual dream…

Do your dreams in any way motivate your work?
My daydreams are the motivation and that goes back to the Surrealist process. I daydream during walks, on a train or a plane; it's very EGS, looking out of the window, listening to music. That sort of free association, daydream world, which is 95% of the dreamworld.

This is the wonderful Surrealist idea of *disponibilité* or availability. How important is storytelling in your work? Do you start with any kind of meta-narrative, like a figure from a movie or someone you've found really inspi-

sort of chase this – this is what I want people to say about this show – and I write as if I am writing it for *Vogue* in the third person, then I put it away until after the show. It's a meta mantra-setting exercise.

I'm intrigued by the passion you have for Hanya Yanagihara and her extraordinary books. Her most recent novel, *To Paradise*, which I just finished, is dedicated to you. Can you talk a bit about your relationship with her and how and why her work has been so important to you?
My entire youth up until the age of 23 was a conversation between me and shame, which was like the devil on my back the entire time. Right when I came out, I also started taking prescription Adderall, which I took eve-

conversations are debates because for her that book is basically a treatise on the idea that certain people are beyond repair, and that there's a point at which redemption cannot really access you, and – this is the Christian side to me – I fundamentally disagree with that; I have to. That book really triggered a flashback to the co-dependent relationships that I had been in. That's what I said to her, I said that book is bullshit, because the relationship between Jude and Willow is an impossible relationship that you make work – but it's not real. It's a complete facade. I have been in those relationships with straight men who bend to be your partner, and it was just such a sham. Co-dependency was a huge thing for me in my relationships. But I still loved every page of that book – it blew me away.

'My relationship with Paris has been rough. I feel like a stranger in this city. I've never spent more time alone than I have in the past three years.'

rational? Is it something technical or material, or is it more ephemeral, just a feeling?**
It is more about what I want the emotional payoff to be. It's not literal. I think sometimes of the muses and the different inspirations that present themselves, but they are all a consequence of how I want people to feel during and after the show, and where I want the house to be placed in their mind, in the echelon of the different houses. It is a very emotional strategy. Sometimes I will write the review that I want to be written about us, months in advance, as a way of setting a goal. I remember doing this first because I read a Tim Blanks review of a Thom Browne show. I love the way Tim reviews, and his work has always been super-inspiring. It became like a mantra for me to

ry day for eight years. It was the hardest thing to quit, quitting smoking was nothing compared to quitting that, because I couldn't do anything without it. I couldn't work without it. That really marked my twenties; it was a huge burden for me. Just this sort of hyper self-hating conversation I was having as I was trying to remove myself from the shame of being gay in the Christian world and being a broken heterosexual, or whatever the narrative was. When I read *A Little Life*, there were moments where I literally slammed the book closed and would audibly yell at Hanya because she was in my head and putting words and actions to the inner workings of my mind and the past experiences that I'd had, and I was so upset with her for that and also for the way that she ended the book. Many of our

Do you think her third novel is a response to that idea of redemption?
I'm only half-way through *To Paradise*, but I do know that that novel was dedicated to me because it was written during our friendship and during extensive conversations that we were having about each other and the global potential for redemption. So I'm very curious to see how she bends or doesn't bend to that idea.

There is one quote that struck me in *To Paradise,* which reads: 'it's funny because of all the things I was scared of, I was never scared of the dark, I was never scared of the dark, in the dark everyone was helpless, and knowing that I was just like everyone else, no less, everyone made me feel braver.' Are you scared of the darkness? Of the

321

unknown or on the contrary, like David in the book, are you reassured and empowered by the knowledge that we can never know ourselves or anything? I know that I'm being influenced by my Christian upbringing, but I don't believe in that at all. I don't believe that we cannot know ourselves. There is no way we can grasp everything, but I also don't think that God wants to remain unknowable. That's the thing – the point is to try and know and to try and excavate, and I think that inside of that there could be redemption. So, no that is not me.

Does Hanya's dystopian vision of the past and present, and her engagement in this narrative, inform your own way of seeing things in any way? Is potential environmental disaster or a glob-

This is the kind of comment that Hanya would want to kill me for, but I remember watching that movie when I was 13 years old. It's a terrible reference, but it is pre-everything, pre 9/11, pre-Covid; it's just like this blissful innocence, similar to when I watched the Warhol documentary,[14] with its pre-AIDS world... I find myself running to those periods as a point of reference and when we talk about the Exquisite Corpse and the *Frankenstein*-ing of different designer's work, I'm always going towards that sort of time compared to now; those naive periods, where glamour could just be glamour, and there was a freedom to it. I have a hard time knowing how to address the meaninglessness of all of it.

You were talking before about fantasy

even sleep the night before? And then you get dressed, you brush your teeth, you go to the bathroom, you have your coffee before you literally perform for the entire world – live.

Balancing those mundane everyday life actions with a global performance. I imagine there is something extremely destructive about that as well. We have both been around enough famous people, we know that maintaining your humanity and your connection to what is real is a challenge. I have been around many famous people in the last few years, and I often feel that even if they are asking you questions about yourself, they are just going through the motions because they know it's what they should be doing. It's really rare to meet someone who has been able to stay real.

'Sometimes I'll write the review that I want to be written about us, months in advance. I write as if I am writing it for *Vogue*, in the third person.'

al conflict or pandemic factored into your own design fantasy? Could you call your work political, like the Surrealists? Do you have a manifesto? A lot of people ask me what designing clothes for the end of the world looks like, because when I started at Schiaparelli, I said, how do you dress for the end of the world? That was in 2018. I guess you have two options: you can sort of address the reality and embrace it or you can create an imaginary space in which we can all be naive again. The last collection we did was a little sombre, a bit stoic; it was definitely rooted in rigour, which felt comforting, given the times. But the season before that and the season I am working on now are, let's say, much more like the first 10 minutes of *Father of the Bride*[13]; I don't know if you have seen that film.

and celebrities and of course, you and your designs are no stranger to the red carpet, whether it's cinema, music, or a presidential inauguration. What is your perspective on this form of performance or power dressing? I am so inspired and interested by the idea of fame and celebrity, and the way that human beings can create pop culture. What it does to you as a human being has always been super inspiring for me. Michael Jackson, from the very beginning, became a sort of keynote figure for me because he was extraordinarily shy, but he became a more alive version of himself on stage. I'm always thinking about that whenever we are dressing people. When we dressed Gaga for the inauguration, I was thinking about what it must be like to wake up in the morning.[15] I mean, how do you

It has been inspiring how your clothes have been worn by such a diverse and amazing community of artists. What have been some of the most satisfying moments for you, when you have felt there was a perfect osmosis of form and figure, of celebrity and humanity, of appearance and being? I think that 2021 was so unique because although we didn't even realize it until 2022, there were a lot of first moments last year, like the first post-Covid moment. We had Gaga at the inauguration and then Bella [Hadid], who was the first red-carpet moment in Cannes.[16] I was particularly proud of Bella because it felt like a really harmonious marriage between something that was approaching art with someone who was purely representing a pop-culture moment in time. For me, it was all so simple. I think

322

that the idea of the lungs was literally to see just her face and those lungs and that was the entire moment. I am really proud of how pure that moment was, and for me it was *the* moment of last year.

Having worked with the actress Tilda Swinton myself for many years, it is a pleasure to experience a fitting where the star and the designer feel a real frisson of excitement and pleasure at the craftsmanship and vision with which they are engaging. In Tilda's case, she also feels a real connection with the brand and the house's historical past. How do you experience these moments? Is it inspiring?
The first ever movie I saw Tilda in was *The Beach*,[17] and I remember it very well because her role was hyper-sexual, and I was quite unnerved by it. It

Tilda is very specific in her engagement with the world of fashion. She demands an intimacy with her collaborators, which as we know is not always the case. Is Tilda seductive because she wears the clothes in a more 'real' way and navigates a real space, rather than the fantasy of a public-performance arena? Do you prefer your clothes to perform, to project, or do you want them to exist in the present?
The reason why we have had such a diverse clientele on the red carpet is because I think I can do both – and I want to do both. The conversation with Tilda, and the personal connection that we felt when we were dressing her, was indeed the reality of her being and it didn't feel like a superficial celebrity artifice that she was going to project. You know when you dress a pop star

collection over the past few seasons. How have you been exploring that in relation to couture? Are they like *vases communicants* – communicating vessels – to use a particularly Surrealist idea, or do you approach the two collections very differently?**
What really connects them is the colour story. As long as the colour stories echo each other, the connection can be made even if the silhouettes are wildly different. Our couture process is really well defined now, and it's just about fittings, even more fittings with artisans. We had over 20 fittings for the last couture collection. There are things in the couture fittings that we think would be amazing for the ready-to-wear, for which my rule is that these insanely chic people who come for press appointments or private shopping should be able to

'Look at the direction that houses like Chanel and Dior have taken; it is undeniably mainstream. That opens the door for us to do something alternative.'

wasn't until *I Am Love* that she became seared in my mind. Do you remember when she eats the prawns?[18] That scene, I return to that scene, I would say, weekly in my mind. I just love that moment, that hiding in plain sight; it's one of the most key scenes I have seen in a long time. To be with her in a fitting, and to be working on dressing her and seeing these clothes come to life is electrifying. It is hard to know if the aura, the glow, the inspiration is coming because of the moment or because of the build-up to that moment that I have had for years. It is just so gratifying, and in this particular case, it was the first fitting I had had with a human being for almost two years because of Covid. It was the first time a human being who was not one of the house models had come to try things on. It really felt dreamlike in a way.

they are looking to project out and hold everything back inside. With Tilda, you feel there is a generosity, like she's letting you access a true part of herself. That is what makes the magic happen on the red carpet, because she is doing that there as well. That's how it felt. But for someone else, like an iconic global popstar, that is not what the world really wants from them. Like Gaga, there is a necessary boundary between who they truly are and then what they are giving to the world, which I totally understand.

We can endlessly debate the relative importance, value and impact of clothes that exist on the red carpet with their exquisite unobtainable fantasy as opposed to something that is commercial and accessible. You have been developing the ready-to-wear

leave wearing something with their jeans. It needs to be about the ease of something, about the ease of it all. Couture is designed for the most extraordinary and precious moments of your life, whether it's a wedding, a bat mitzvah, an opening of something or an event that you are hosting. And the ready-to-wear should be for everything else, for all of the other moments.

How has your relationship with Diego Della Valle evolved over these last years, and do you share the same vision for the house?
Diego has been in love with Schiaparelli and Elsa Schiaparelli for years and years and years, and he acquired Schiaparelli right about the time he acquired Vivier.[19] Diego and I connect first and foremost about the

323

dream of Schiaparelli – he calls it the 'last great dream in fashion'. It is this sort of untapped or pure uncontaminated house that has not been spoiled in any way and we both really deeply connect on the potential of the house. At the beginning, the relationship was just going through a defining and redefining phase. I think that my aesthetic vision was different to the one he was expecting, and I was not referencing the codes of the house enough. We had to have a come-to-Jesus type meeting about that, and I will never forget it. He kind of explained more explicitly what he needed to see in order to feel good about pouring all this money into the project. I love an assignment and that reckoning was an assignment. Then Covid hit. I had peace and quiet because no one was able to visit for over a year. Diego was not able to come here, even if we could meet up in Italy and we could communicate, but I was largely left to work on my own and I think that what emerged was this vision that's in accordance with what he wants, too. It's something hyper-luxurious, but also – and this is important to me – it is also hyper-alternative. When you look at the direction that Chanel and Dior and all of those houses have taken, it is undeniably mainstream. That opens the door for us to do something that feels almost like alternative music, and that is what I would hope we are establishing.

If there were to be a new perfume, what would be the ideal components? I am not asking in a literal sense, the components could be abstract, an emotion. For the house to re-engage in a conversation with fragrance, we would need to entirely revisit the way in which Elsa approached perfume. As with everything, she had her own unique way of doing fragrance, and the way she marketed it was completely revolutionary. Some of these more iconic old perfumes no longer resonate with today, but their formulas usually hold the key as to how to move forward. What Schiaparelli's answer to fragrance would look like today feels very intriguing.

There is a quote from *A Little Life* **about happiness, where Willow says: 'but what was happiness but an extravagance, an impossible state to maintain. Partly because it was so difficult to articulate.' What is happiness to you? Are you happy in your creative environment?** I would say the past six months have been extremely difficult here in Paris, just because I feel so married to the job and so alone in it as well. It's like a season I guess, and I think that Paris holds something bigger for me to unlock.

I'm sure. Paris is a hard nut to crack on many levels!

324

1. *Captain Ron*, directed by Thomas Eberhardt and released in 1992, starred Ken Russell as the eponymous and drunken sailor hired to skipper a yacht for a family of unhappy yuppies. According to Vincent Canby in the *New York Times*, '"Captain Ron" looks like the pilot film for an unsold sitcom.' The son – remembered by Roseberry – was played by Benjamin Salisbury, who would later star in a hit sitcom: from 1993 to 1999, he played Brighton Sheffield in *The Nanny*.

2. This story was most likely 'Tom Ford: Fordbitten', a Steven Klein series published in *W* in January 2005. The *Gattaca*-style shoot sees Ford dressed in a black suit with robotic-looking models in states of undress. In one image, Ford appears to be using an industrial polisher to buff the naked buttocks of a male model.

3. In January 2021, Roseberry told *L'Officiel*: 'I was a missionary in India, Pakistan, Jordan, and Kashmir when I was 19 years old. It was another life.'

4. The Menil Collection in Houston, Texas, was founded by John de Menil and Dominique de Menil, to house their 17,000 drawings, paintings, photographs, prints, rare books, and sculptures. The museum building, designed by Renzo Piano, opened in 1987, and a Cy Twombly Gallery was added in 1995. The Rothko Chapel, also founded by the Menils, is a neighbour to the Collection. The Nasher Sculpture Center opened in 2003 in a building also designed by Piano and showcases the over-300-piece Raymond and Patsy Nasher Collection, which includes work by Alexander Calder, Willem de Kooning, Alberto Giacometti, Pablo Picasso, Henry Moore, and Barbara Hepworth.

5. Hanya Yanagihara is an American author and journalist. Her second novel, *A Little Life*, was published to wide acclaim and unexpectedly strong sales in 2015 and nominated for the Man Booker Prize. She recently published her third, *To Paradise*. She has been editor-in-chief of *T*, the *New York Times*' style magazine, since 2017.

6. *Shocking! Les Mondes Surréalistes d'Elsa Schiaparelli* will run from 6 July 2022 to 22 January 2023 at the Musée des Arts Décoratifs, Paris. It is the first exhibition dedicated to the designer at the museum since 2004.

7. The Metropolitan Museum of Art's Costume Institute has over 300 Schiaparelli pieces in its archive, from couture dresses and hats to buttons and belts. The Philadelphia Museum of Art's 66 pieces by Schiaparelli were a gift from the designer herself in 1969, and include the celebrated 'lobster dress', first shown in February 1937. Made of printed silk organza and synthetic horsehair and co-designed with Salvador Dalí, it was made famous after Wallis Simpson bought one from Schiaparelli before her scandalous marriage to the Duke of Windsor in 1937. She was photographed wearing it by Cecil Beaton for *Vogue* the same year.

8. Popular in the 1920s and much loved by Surrealists, exquisite corpse or *cadavre exquis* is a game that consists of each participant writing or drawing on a sheet of paper, folding it so as to hide their addition, and then passing it to the next player. The result is a collaborative and often surprising work.

9. Edward James (1907-1984) was a British poet and patron of the arts. Using his inherited wealth, he supported many members of the Surrealist movement including Dalí and René Magritte, who painted his portrait twice. He is now perhaps better remembered for Las Pozas, a collection of his Surrealist concrete sculptures set in 32 hectares of subtropical rainforest in the Sierra Gora mountains in Mexico.

10. Tom Ford's Spring/Summer 2011 collection was unveiled in September 2010 at a discreet show, with the clothes worn by models including Beyoncé, Julianne Moore, Lou Doillon and Rinko Kikuchi. The first images of the collection appeared in an exclusive shoot in the December 2010 issue of French *Vogue*.

11. Steven Stipelman worked as a fashion illustrator for *WWD* from 1965 until 1993 when all the newspaper's illustrators were fired. He has taught at the Fashion Institute of Technology, New York, since 1994.

12. Elsa Schiaparelli moved into the 98-room, 5-storey Hôtel de Fontpertuis at 21 Place Vendômein 1935. It housed an atelier and a ground-floor boutique in an interior decorated by designer Jean-Michel Frank and artist Alberto Giacometti.

13. *Father of the Bride*, directed by Charles Shyer, was released in 1991. Starring Steve Martin, Diane Keaton, and – like *Captain Ron* – Martin Short, the comedy was a remake of Vincente Minnelli's 1950 film of the same name, which starred Spencer Tracy and Elizabeth Taylor. In his *Washington Post* review of Shyer's film, Desson Howe wrote: 'Very often it look as though *Bride* magazine scripted the whole affair. Undoubtedly, there's an audience for it.'

14. *The Andy Warhol Diaries* premiered on Netflix on 9 March 2022. In the documentary series, the artist's own private journals are read by an actor whose voice has been altered using AI to sound more like Warhol himself.

15. In December 2021, Lady Gaga told British *Vogue* that the Roseberry-designed jacket that she wore at the inauguration was actually bulletproof.

16. The Schiaparelli Autumn/Winter 2021 haute-couture dress worn by Bella Hadid on the red carpet at the rescheduled Cannes Film Festival on 11 July 2021 was low-cut black crepe with, across the chest, brass lungs featuring rhinestones on the bronchioles.

17. Tilda Swinton's performance as the intense and unbalanced Sal is a highlight of the otherwise disappointing Danny Boyle-directed 2000 adaptation of Alex Garland's cult novel *The Beach*.

18. In Luca Gaudagnino's 2009 film *I Am Love*, Tilda Swinton's character, Emma, is deeply aroused by eating two shrimps. The crustaceans become the first step in what will become a tragic affair with the young chef who prepared them.

19. Diego Della Valle and his brother Andrea bought Roger Vivier in 2001. In November 2015, they sold it for €415 million to Tod's, a company of which Diego is president and Andrea vice-president. Della Valle bought Schiaparelli in 2007, but the house did not present a collection until 2014.

325

◼ Who exactly is he?

Introducing the new leader of luxury house BOTTEGA VENETA and the youngest addition to the fraternity of fashion's famous Belgians. MATTHIEU BLAZY has previously worked behind the scenes at some of the most revered brands in France, Belgium and America. He loves fashion, but embraces a refreshingly quiet approach to luxury.

Story by SARAH MOWER
Portraits by SOLÈNE ŞAHMARAN GÜN
Fashion shoot by VALENTIN HENNEQUIN
Styling by STUART WILLIAMSON

MATTHIEU BL

Matthieu Blazy in *Fantastic Man*, no. 36
(Fall-Winter 2022-23).

266

AZY

143

MATTHIEU BLAZY is taking time out to talk to me in his studio at BOTTEGA VENETA. He's right in the middle of finishing his sophomore collection for the Milan powerhouse before the Italian factories close down for summer, but no worries! This super talented, multi-experienced design director has been at the eye of so many storms of fashion pressure that he knows how to pace himself. For years, industry insiders have been talking about the boyish-looking, low-key nice guy – and partner of PIETER MULIER (now of ALAÏA) – as a design-room supertalent. Generally, this much was known about him: he's a younger member of the intergenerational Belgian brotherhood of fashion and a hot property with a dazzling 15-year résumé running from RAF SIMONS, to MARGIELA, to CÉLINE with PHOEBE PHILO, to CALVIN KLEIN with RAF again, and thence to BOTTEGA VENETA in 2020…

And yet he's not had a speaking job in all of that time. Not, that is, until 15 November 2021, the day Kering announced that BLAZY had been appointed as BOTTEGA VENETA's creative director. "It was surprising, and it was very stressful," he says. "But somehow, I was calm." Nobody in fashion needs to be reminded that the news broke just under a week after the abrupt exit of DANIEL LEE, who had been BLAZY's boss. Starting with his appointment in 2018 and continuing throughout the height of the pandemic in Italy, LEE had presided over an explosive success. For the first time in its stealth-wealthy history, BOTTEGA VENETA had forged a demographic connection with young people, wielding an influence so vast that copies of its puffy accessories – the Cassette bag and Lido sandals – and of the BOTTEGA "parakeet" green swiftly turned into a parallel fast-fashion pandemic of their own.

■

Speculation roiled over the reasons behind the shockingly swift severance between BOTTEGA VENETA and LEE. As I remember it, though, the attention quickly shifted to an elated discussion of what this much-liked and highly rated designer MATTHIEU BLAZY might bring. The fact was, he was already in the house. "I worked with DAN as design director, working with the team and proposing ideas – the same way I had done with RAF, and with PHOEBE at CÉLINE. So we knew each other. I was spending time with him, but more time with the team, because that's what you do when you're a design director." This is all he's prepared to say, but it's as if Kering suddenly realised they already had a hot property right under their noses. Despite fashion's history of painfully public hirings and firings of designers who've been airlifted into brands from the outside, it's true that the decision to promote "backroom" talent just as often leads to dazzling long-term results.

144

After all, both ALESSANDRO MICHELE and TOM FORD before him were in-house unknowns who went on to revolutionise the fortunes of GUCCI, the powerhouse in Kering's roster of brands.

So this was BLAZY's moment to decide to step into the limelight. Heading a house had always been his eventual plan, he says, but not before he was good and ready and totally certain that he knew all the ropes, from design to merchandising and marketing. "I thought it was better to take a bit of time," he understates. "It's a good way to test

ideas, and to test yourself. So what I can say is that when I took over the job at BOTTEGA, somehow, I was armed. I knew my weapons."

At 38, he calmly displayed his subtle approach to BOTTEGA's men's and womenswear during his frantically anticipated debut show in Milan last February. Somehow, it smartly signalled both a fresh start and continuity. "Excitingly normal" was one incisive comment from a menswear expert in the audience. I put that to BLAZY, wondering how he'd take it. He nods. "That was actually the idea behind

it. I wanted things to look very simple. Not simple…" He paused to consider, "but fake-simple."

It's a blast of fresh air to hear him talk with unjaded enthusiasm about why he lavished so much work on perfecting a series of blue jeans, singlets and white pinstriped shirts. It's the plainest, least complicated statement he could have opened his show with, but there's a punch: they're actually made of incredibly refined nubuck and printed leather. "That first look was really a question of how to take the message of a jeans and T-shirt – an everyday look – and to elevate it to the maximum. We spent three months printing and printing, and fighting against this material: to really get the feeling that when you look at it, you can't tell it's leather. Not until you touch it," BLAZY laughs. "Which I find quite seductive, by the way. Slightly perverse."

It sounds as if there was a bit of a behind-the-scenes battle to get this statement through – not that it was all of the collection, but still: "Boring! Some people told me it's boring. I said, 'Nòn! Look twice!'" When I remark that you literally can't read any of it on the runway pictures, he exclaims, "But that's fine as well! We're very used to this system where everything has to be immediate; everything must be extremely literal. There's this kind of excessive desire to want to reinvent things, and try the new, new, new. I think there's some stuff that simply works, and it should be used as it is – but maybe the silhouette is different."

Still, the huge responsibility was naturally not to chuck the baby out with the bathwater. When a brand becomes as ridiculously trendy as BOTTEGA, it's a multi-edged problem: how to preserve a luxury identity, and sales, while also steering the property towards something excitingly new? BLAZY is clear-eyed about it. "I'm not someone who just throws everything off the table. For me, it was evident that DAN's bestselling bags are part of the history of the company. So is the Cabat [the famous intreccio tote] that was done by TOMAS MAIER. It's part of the company I work for. So you know, if some bags continue to sell, I'm very happy to have them in the store," he smiles. "Which gives me the time to replace rather than erase."

He has a theoretical brand-heritage inspiration to back up his instincts about the way things should evolve. In the beginning, BOTTEGA VENETA, a luxury Italian leather house, never made any ready-to-wear. "When you see the imagery, it's about the accessories – a man in a suit and a girl in jeans. Always styled with clothes which are not BOTTEGA." He cites LAUREN HUTTON in 'American Gigolo' in 1980, clutching a soft intreccio BOTTEGA VENETA pouch under her arm – her anonymously cool wardrobe was by BASILE, the Italian fashion house. Pared-backness, you might call it.

I'm beginning to feel increasingly refreshed by BLAZY's conversation as he

Matthieu Blazy in *Fantastic Man*, no. 36 (Fall-Winter 2022–23).

268

Deceptively simple. SAUL is wearing a white printed-leather pinstriped shirt, blue denim-effect printed-nubuck trousers, black grainy calf-leather shoes and a Kalimero intreccio leather bucket bag. Here and throughout, it's all from BOTTEGA VENETA's Winter 2022 collection.

145

starts to describe what a pair of trousers should be for a man – it's an actual pair of trousers! "Fashion today is very focused on, you know, imagery. On being Instagram-friendly. But then, when you go to the stores, you have this feeling, like, "Where can I buy pants that I'm actually going to wear every day?" I look around me. I look at what my team wear, and what I see on the street in Italy," he reasons. "You know, we can all do very bombastic fashion, but at the same time, I was interested in rooting the collection in something that looked more like style,

loops, and there's a pleat in the pants. So there are those ingredients which are very classic and they are studied in the fabric as well." Then he laughs, "I mean, *obviously*, I don't want to make boring clothes. They have to be balanced: they need to be exciting, but also perfect for everyday use."

Another layer of his research has been studying how Italian men dress in movies. "They never look 'too fashion.' They look extremely stylish. It's style over fashion. That was also something I wanted to work with: an idea of reality,

rather than fashion pieces. I didn't want to get into an exercise of making big statements."

He thought of a man in profile, hurrying along the street, capturing his dynamic forward movement in the curve in the back of a peacoat and in the hem of his pants, with "a strange flare," sliced slightly longer in front to double that effect. "The silhouette is layered. We kind of translated this idea of movement. But when you see the trouser, there the frame is quite classic: you have a waistband, you have belt

148

but very, very alluring, pushed to an extreme in a way that the pieces look very sophisticated. If I see this silhouette in five years, I think it should still work. That was the exercise."

But back to where BLAZY comes from. When you look at how his tastes were formed, and the experiences he's lived through, a complete picture emerges of a cultured man who's also down to earth and psychologically trained by experience to deal with living through fashion's volatile times. Put it this way: for 15 years, BLAZY's been working

in the background at some of the most furnace-hot luxury brands in Paris, Milan and New York – and has seen first hand how things that quickly flare can also just as quickly burn.

■

He was born in Paris in 1984, along with his twin sister, to a Belgian mother and French father. "My dad is an art expert. And my mom, she's an historian, and also fun. She's very, very full of style and sophisticated, in a cool way. When I was a kid, she would sometimes wear SAINT LAURENT or incredible stuff from MUGLER. But then she was also, like, a mom in jeans, doing stuff with us children, and working at the same time," he remembers. "In the family, there was always the idea that you have to *dress*, you know."

It wasn't just being brought up in a cultured Parisian household with a well-dressed mother that set the child MATTHIEU on his path to fashion – it was also the coincidence of its location. "Our neighbour had a model agency. The trash was full of magazines. Rummaging around in there I'd find 'Harper's Bazaar', 'Vogue', 'The Face'," he laughs. "I call it my trash education, literally." This was the second half of the '90s – that moment when grunge was transitioning into a whole new visual culture of minimalism and stealth-wealth fashion in New York. "We were digging in the trash and getting *obsessed* with KATE MOSS. Obsessed with CALVIN KLEIN!" Everyone in fashion knows that it's one's earliest experiences that lay down a reservoir of images and feelings that one can then drawn on for a lifetime. It's not hard to see why BLAZY is so much part of the rising generation that's now celebrating the values and shared references of the '90s.

He chose to study at La Cambre in Brussels; not the Antwerp Academy, Central Saint Martins, or any of the French schools which focused solely on fashion education. That was the first of his life decisions that, looking back, helped determine his destiny: the structure of La Cambre's five-year liberal arts course was the ideal deep prep for the complex role of a modern creative director – a job which now demands fluency in the intellectual and visual communication of fashion through everything from photography to interiors to knowing who to collaborate with in the arts. "You had history of art, history of music, scenography. You'd sketch, do painting classes," he says. "Then in the afternoons, you could do stitching and atelier workshops. So there was something slightly more generous on offer. And I also love Brussels."

He's bringing that holistic mentality to what he's doing today. "I love the idea of bringing BOTTEGA together, almost into a complete landscape. Who are the customers in an ideal world – the people on the runway, where do they live? Is their house designed by CARLO SCARPA? Do

Matthieu Blazy in *Fantastic Man*, no. 36 (Fall-Winter 2022-23).

270

they buy glass from VENINI? What kind of movies do they watch? So obviously I look a lot at Italian design in general. But then I also love pop culture," he smiles. "There's this cartoon, CALIMERO, which is Italian and Japanese. There's this little bird with a huge egg on his head. The way he carries his bag inspired the bag of the opening night."

Enter the incredibly luxurious, tactile Kalimero bag – a chunkily woven bucket in juicy leather strands that honours all the craft of the famed BOTTEGA VENETA intrecciato technique, but updates it for the generation that loves to carry around an accessory which is also a kind of pet. "I always liked when a bag has something almost cartoony, almost like an object in itself – a creature! It needs to have a certain personality," he laughs. " The beauty of those bags is that they cannot be reproduced twice. So you make one, and then you will have a small mistake, which is not a mistake. It's done by hand. It's timeless."

On graduating, BLAZY went to work for RAF SIMONS from 2007 to 2011. His deep training in menswear is now one of the foundation stones of his discipline. Of SIMONS – his supporter ever since – he says: "I was with RAF five years, in the tailoring. It was really a school of precision – the Flemish approach, something quite sharp. Even when RAF would take fantasies, there's always a concept or an idea behind it. It's quite cerebral."

That was also where BLAZY met the love of his life, PIETER MULIER, who was SIMONS's right-hand man. Their lives and careers have been entwined ever since, through all the ups and downs of the Belgian fraternity's adventures in high fashion that took off from that point. Change, creative idealism, high-stakes risk-taking and the collective mutual support of that tight circle of friends all turned into a normal way of life for him.

While MULIER went to JIL SANDER with RAF in Milan, and then on to CHRISTIAN DIOR in Paris in 2012, BLAZY, then aged 27, landed his first big job at MARGIELA, as creative director of the brand's Artisanal collection. When I ask him about that appointment, he sighs. "A few of the people that carry the temple of MARGIELA were basically telling me it was going to be a dead end for me. And I thought it was actually the opposite, because MARTIN was no longer there. I thought I could maybe find my way of interpreting his legacy, but also somehow take distance, and to do my MARGIELA."

Within a couple of seasons, BLAZY was doing a conspicuously fantastic job – palpably the best since MARTIN had left the building. His inspired, wildly bejewelled head coverings – a reinterpretation of MARGIELA's identity-masking devices – were seen by KANYE WEST and later adapted along with a custom wardrobe for his 2013–14 Yeezus tour. Then came

BLAZY's first experience of the unpredictable dramas that beset the workings of a fashion machine. His identity as the in-house designer was always meant to stay "silent" (that being the house policy – a fact he also liked). Then, SUZY MENKES suddenly went rogue and named him in an Instagram photo she took of BLAZY and RAF SIMONS backstage.

"Trust me. It was a very, very strange moment. What anonymity gave me was a certain comfort. And then suddenly, I was outed. My Instagram account exploded. I stopped it. I had a lot of issues with the company." He's forgiven MENKES now. "I kind of cherish that page in my book," he laughs. But being publicly recognised as a rising behind-the-scenes supertalent had an immediate impact. Now, he was headhunted by the next major figure in the firmament of fashion: PHOEBE PHILO at CÉLINE. He worked on the CÉLINE precollections – the part of the business that had women flocking to stores to accumulate the perfectly cut pants, super-long-sleeved oversized men's shirts and Crombie coats that underpinned the cult of the label. "For me, the pre-collection was the bridge I needed. I really, really, really had a lot of pleasure there, whether it was observing PHOEBE, or working with the head of the atelier. This guy was extraordinary. It was almost a school, again. When I talk about excellence, about how to make proper clothes, this is what I mean."

It was at CÉLINE that he first worked alongside DANIEL LEE – which explains why he later joined him at BOTTEGA VENETA. But in between, in a next dramatic chapter, he went to New York and CALVIN KLEIN with RAF SIMONS and MULIER in 2016. It was during those thrilling two years that SIMONS reinvented the collection as CALVIN KLEIN 205W39NYC and staged some of the most spectacular scenario shows that New York Fashion Week had ever witnessed. It all came to a shocking end in 2018, when the corporate owners suddenly pulled the plug. The disillusionment of that moment rocked the the fashion industry. "I had a little break," BLAZY relates. "I went to work with STERLING RUBY on his collection in LA. It was therapeutic, after CALVIN. Because I'd really thought I wanted to stop working in fashion after such an abrupt ending."

Yet having been inadvertently caught up in the high dramas and ruthless debacles of the past decade of luxury fashion has blessed BLAZY with a huge amount of experience and insight – as well as a unique perspective on what matters to him and what it is he loves about the work he does. His recipe for flying high in the firmament of fashion is grounded in the normal-life stuff that he and MULIER share with their dog John John in Antwerp. When not in their respective studios in Milan or Paris, the couple lives

in a Brutalist high-rise apartment with spectacular views over the city. "I cook. I love going to the dog park," he laughs. "And John John gets to see his best friend Luca, RAF's dog."

On the way to and from work in Milan, BLAZY also carves out normal time for himself. "There's nothing more liberating than going to a bar or sitting somewhere to be on your own and decompress after work. Sometimes, you open a book, sometimes you just kind of dream, sometimes you flick through Instagram. But I'm alone with my beer. And it's heaven."

I'll bet he's also enjoying observing real life while he's doing this, too. The words "real life" were repeated over and over as a mantra voiceover on the soundtrack of his debut show. It's not, I think, that BLAZY's turning away from the excitement of the unexpected thrill in fashion. Not at all. In the studio, he likes to run a happy ship, where there's always room for surprises. "When I do a meeting, I have five, six people in the room. Whether it's the intern, or people from the product team, everyone has a word to say, not just the designers. Sometimes, the people from the atelier have a brilliant idea. That way of working for me is the only way I have fun – when I don't know what is going happen. It's like collectivism."

BLAZY's idea about how he'll navigate BOTTEGA into the future seems to be rooted in his subtly radical instinct for not following the runaway bandwagons of fashion trends. What seems avant-garde to him now? Showing BOTTEGA in Milan, during fashion week! (Prior to his debut, the label's last three shows had been held off-schedule in London, Berlin and Detroit.) He wants BOTTEGA to be identified as an Italian house again, showing "in conversation" with the other landmark Milanese houses. "You know, the idea of newness, novelty – doing stuff off calendar: I don't find it modern. I think you can actually be very modern within a framework." It's going to be the same with the clothes. I'd say Kering has on its hands someone who really has the ambition and foresight to do things that others aren't doing, have forgotten about, or simply lack the depth of experience and insight to execute in the way a MATTHIEU BLAZY is capable of pulling off.

It's early to say, but I'm excited to watch where this will go. As we say goodbye, thinking about the promise of BLAZY's words is making me smile: "It's not that I want to collage on a blazer, or to make a pant look weird. You know, I like the idea of a well-made trouser in an amazing fabric. It's enough. If the attention to detail is there, if there's excellent thought behind it and it doesn't scream laziness or boredom – I think, you know, the goal is achieved."

"You know, I like the idea of a well-made trouser in an amazing fabric. It's enough."

→ Giorgio ARMANI

and his super singular fashion universe

Text by
JEREMY LEWIS
and GERT JONKERS
Photography by
ALASDAIR McLELLAN

(Fantastic Man)

(Giorgio)

(192)

Giorgio Armani in *Fantastic Man*, no. 37
(Fall–Winter 2023–24).

→ ECCENTRICITY is a notion that suits Mr. Armani very well, according to the legendary designer himself. He's the founder of a monumental empire that, by fate more than choice, he runs as the sole proprietor, overseeing more than 8,000 employees. Brand Armani provides everything from fashion and underwear to hotel rooms, food, flowers, books, gyms, sofas, lamps, fragrances, chocolate, sports gear — enough for his fans to live 24/7 in a perfect Armani world, should they so wish.

Of course, it takes a true eccentric to pull all this off and keep things so exciting for half a century. "I am eccentric, and I say this with pride, even though the adjective sometimes associated with crazy, might seem light-years away from what I do," Mr. Armani states in 'Per Amore', his autobiography that hit shelves earlier this year. The word should not be confused with flamboyant, theatrical, or excessive, he adds; to him it's "the rigour of absolute purism" that makes him so strange — and so super, super successful. He is the first fashion designer to take Hollywood by storm, the second-wealthiest man in Italy, and he's lionised by everyone from Stefano Pilati and Kim Jones to Hedi Slimane.

Giorgio Armani's inventions are bafflingly timeless and so specific that they seem to come from — and make sense for — every era. And now more than ever. As menswear is U-turning from streetwear to tailoring, and nobody wants to ditch the comfort of a tracksuit, who else to go to than the man who radicalised and softened the traditional suit like no one before? Mr. Armani's clothes are outlandish and modest, modern and classic, uniform and deeply personal, familiar and weird all at once. Mostly, they're all very Armani, because at the

(193)

whopping age of 89, the designer still runs the ship with an unwavering eye for every detail. "While some people might accuse me of being dictatorial, my achievements show that I've always been right," he writes, with a modicum of irony.

But do we even know who Mr. Armani is? There was a time when people thought he lived a sort of monk-like existence, as he puts it in the following interview. They thought he was hiding out in his Milan headquarters like a hermit. How wrong the people were. Mr. Armani is in thrall to the magic of moviemaking, admires Jean Paul Gaultier and Dries Van Noten and scores his funkiest summer looks at local markets on indulgent holidays.

According to his book, Mr. Armani will one day leave his legacy to the two people he has tasked with the continuation of his empire: his niece Silvana, who runs the womenswear studios, and Leo Dell'Orco, his head of menswear for almost 40 years. "And that is how it will be," he writes. Not that Mr. Armani really wants to stop; he even struggles to finish his autobiography, taking two final chapters to try and put the story to an end. He just wants to go on. And indeed, look at what he's done, what he does, and where Giorgio Armani will take things next. And watch the world follow.

(194)

Giorgio Armani in *Fantastic Man*, no. 37 (Fall–Winter 2023–24).

276

QUESTION — Mr. Armani, you have a time machine to take you anywhere for 24 hours. Where would you go?

ARMANI — I would probably go back to my early days as a designer and give myself a lot of good advice. That's the practical answer. But for fun, I'd visit the pioneering days of Hollywood. When I was a kid I used to go to the cinema in Milan, which was the big city near where I grew up — in Piacenza — and it was a magical experience. I'd love to go see the formative era of moviemaking in action.

What's the craziest rumour you've ever heard about yourself?

There was a time when people thought I lived a monk-like existence. They thought I was holed up in my Milan headquarters like some sort of modern-day ascetic. That was never the case, but it played into a convenient narrative for the media, I suppose. In my experience, the media often deals in characterisations rather than nuanced reality.

Have you ever been lost for inspiration?

I can honestly say I've never suffered from creator's block. I have a very active imagination and creativity comes naturally to me. Inspiration comes from memories, from my observations of people and from research online and in books. I find it everywhere — in films I watch, in conversations I have and in my travels. The world is my inspiration. It never ceases to surprise and delight.

What is good design and what is bad design?

I consider good design to be essential, refined, simple, timeless. I consider bad design to be overwrought, unnecessarily fussy, or driven by passing trends. Where clothing and accessories are concerned, good design is also always comfortable and functional.

You emerged in the 1970s as part of a new wave of Italian ready-to-wear designers, with people like Walter Albini, Gianfranco Ferré, Gianni Versace. Was there a sense of camaraderie, or was it more a kind of rivalry?

We knew each other, of course, and it was an exciting time. There was definitely a sense of a new era of Italian fashion. We each had our own aesthetic and inevitably the press liked to play up rivalries. Gianni Versace and myself were often portrayed as being at different ends of the design spectrum: I was the minimalist and he the maximalist. It was a simplification, but it created a narrative that caught on.

Do you prefer day or night?

The daytime hours give me a sense of accomplishment and of being productive. I like to rise early, exercise for an hour, eat a healthy breakfast and then go to my design studio. I follow a routine that affords me the time and space to work in a concentrated way. And that's what makes me happy.

Your men's collections have famously influenced your womenswear, but have your women's collections ever influenced your menswear?

Of course. I've always been interested in blurring the lines where gender-specific design is concerned. In my menswear this expresses itself most evidently in my choice of fabrics, which are often fluid and drapey and perhaps of a type more often associated with womenswear. In contrast to traditional tailored menswear, my approach has been to let the wearer's physique define the form, which again might be said to be a characteristic of much womenswear. When I was starting out, I decided to introduce a kind of softness, aiming for a new harmony between the body and the garment, keeping in mind an essential point: clothing must bestow a sense of authority, elegance and dignity without disguising each person's individuality.

It seems like Chanel has been a significant influence on you. Are there any other designers who you respect or admire? Or are there designers who have been as impactful to your menswear?

Coco Chanel was a great talent, and her exploration of comfort and simplicity in clothing has always been a source of inspiration for me. This concept of comfort and simplicity extends to my menswear too. The body is both the point of departure and the point of arrival for everything I do. And then of course Nino Cerruti, who hired me and gave me confidence and taught me the basics of my work. It was from him that I learned the quest for a new classic style: soft, and anything but rigid. To me, he was an example of coherent style and intuition. And Jean Paul Gaultier, fashion's enfant terrible, who managed like no one else to retain his enthusiasm and innocence but also the ability to break rules and barriers using only his imagination. I also appreciate the work of Dries Van Noten, Hedi Slimane and Giambattista Valli. In general, I appreciate anyone who does his or her own thing at his or her own pace, not playing by the rulebook. That, too, is an attitude I admire.

(195)

Is there a collection or a garment that you regret designing, or one that you consider a mistake?

I don't believe in regret; it's a waste of time and energy. Inevitably you will create some things that work better than others, and occasionally you will go down a cul-de-sac as a designer. That is a necessary consequence of creativity. The trick is to recognise when this has happened and to get back on the right path.

"I've never suffered from creator's block. I have a very active imagination."

What's in your wardrobe that isn't Armani?

More than you would imagine, actually! During the summer, my ideal wardrobe is made up of simple pieces that I buy in local markets, or T-shirts from local places I like, worn with shorts and *friulane*, Friulian slippers. When I'm on holiday I love to wear colours, which may seem strange for someone who normally wears navy blue. I once got photographed in an Alanui cardigan, and that caused a bit of a stir. I also love watches, I own several vintage ones that I'm very fond of.

Do you wear jewellery?

I do, as a matter of fact: a wristwatch and a ring. Both were gifted to me by somebody very close to my heart.

Do you have any advice for a man who is struggling to dress himself?

Remember that the point of being well dressed is that you feel comfortable, because then you will feel confident. So don't try to disguise yourself. Go for simple elegance. Start with the basics and never overdo it. And always look in the mirror before you go out and ask yourself whether there is anything you can remove from your outfit to keep it essential.

Men's fashion has changed so much in the last couple of decades as a result of things like streetwear, extreme casualisation, gender fluidity, social media. What are the most surprising or important developments that you've observed?

These are all things I have been working on since the very beginning. I explored streetwear with Emporio Armani, which became a uniform for the *paninari* youth

movement in Italy and then reached the rest of the world. Gender fluidity has always been an aesthetic code for me, and casualisation is what I have pioneered in my collections through pursuing the idea of deconstruction in tailoring. So in many ways, the conversations that are now dominating the debate around menswear are ones I've been having with myself and my team for many years. Through social media, though, there is a genuine shift in how people engage with fashion, and with each other too. And that's new. My take on it is that while there are benefits to social media — undoubtedly, in the way that it promotes connectivity and can be used to get messages out there in a way that was unimaginable in the past — it also contributes to a worryingly frenetic pace of life. In particular, it feeds the notion that newness and passing trends are crucial to being stylish, which, in my opinion, is a fallacy.

You're famously involved in everything in your giant empire. How to delegate?

I've been asking myself that question for decades! I'm a perfectionist, and I need to be involved in all that is Armani. That said, my business is obviously far too large now for me to attend to all the decisions that need to be made on a daily basis, so I've gathered a great group of people around me. I oversee things and they action them. Where delegation is concerned, it's all about the people you have on your team, and I am careful to choose those who understand my vision and believe in it. But where design is concerned, I must confess I'm still very much involved in the minutiae. I simply don't know how else to do it.

And finally, do you believe in astrology or the supernatural?

I'm not a superstitious person, but I can't help but feel that fate has had a hand in my life and success.

→
Mr. Armani does not collect art; he thinks masterpieces should be kept in museums and not be owned by individuals for their egotistical pleasure. The only significant works of art he owns are a drawing by Matisse and a photo by Man Ray.

(196)

Giorgio Armani in *Fantastic Man*, no. 37 (Fall-Winter 2023-24).

278

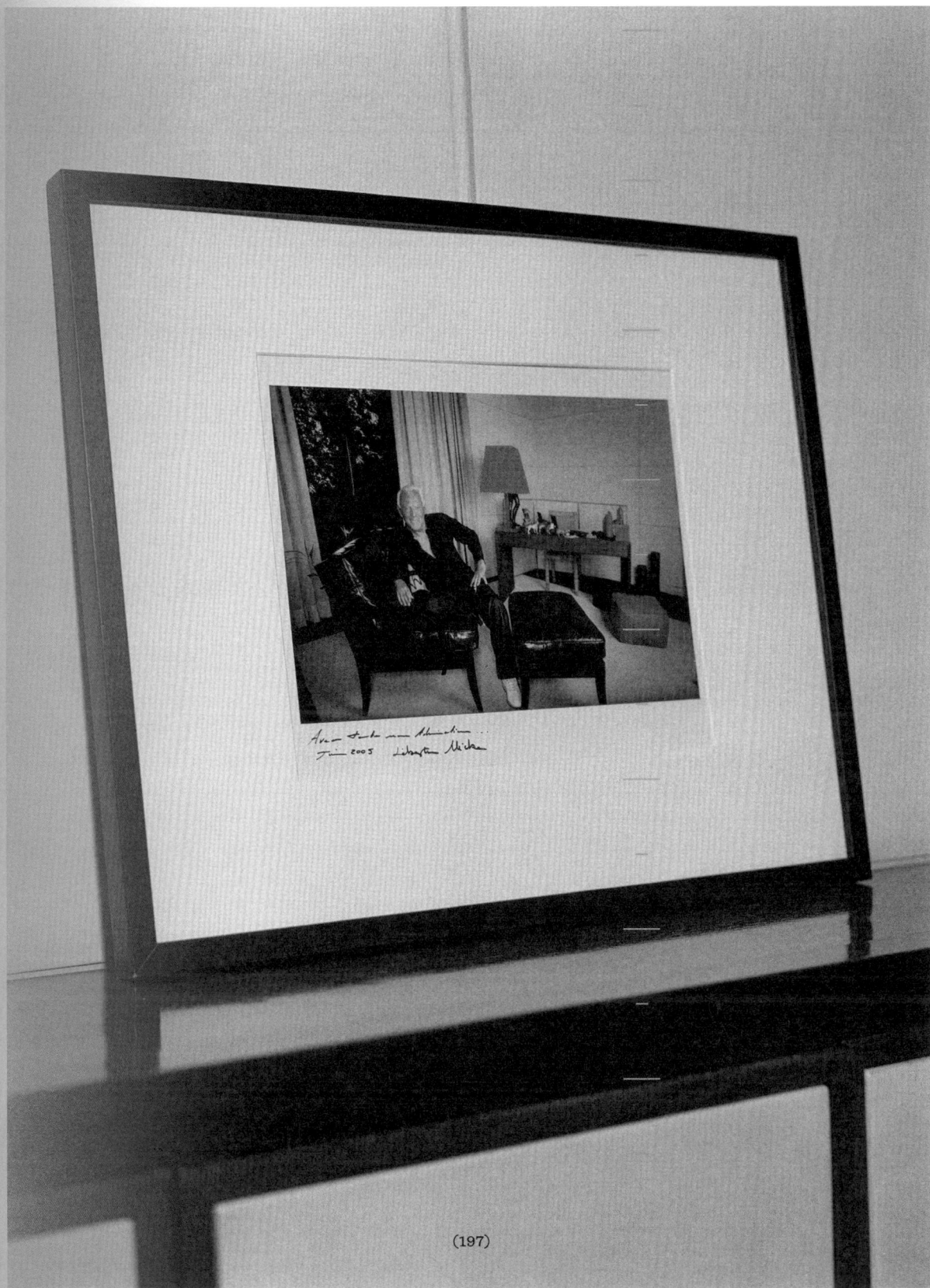

(197)

ADVENTURES OF ARMANI
by Jeremy Lewis

Why Mr. Armani got to be the superstar he is, featuring his youth, romance and his endeavours in the fields of fashion, hotels and everything else that bears his glittering name. Plus a surprising cameo from John Travolta. It's a story rich and full of spectacle.

RARE

Fashion has a tendency to self-mythologise and inflate its own importance. It hypes itself; it indulges in hyperbole and grandiose affectation. There is a concerted effort made by all actors and players in this great fashion conspiracy to disguise its commercial activities with pretensions of higher art. A particularly skilled designer is not merely a stylist or a savvy marketer but a visionary. A fashion collection is not just a coordinated assortment of merchandise but a triumphant creative expression of cultural importance. Or so they would have you believe. With perspective, one quickly realises that it's absurd to think that raising a hem length or popularising a fad could somehow carry weight in the broader scheme of things. But sometimes, well, actually, it can. Designers whose abilities and influence transcend clothing and commerce, reverberating into the world at large, do exist. They are, of course, exceptionally rare — rarer than the fashion cabal would have you believe. So, with that frank and unflattering truth laid bare, it is no exaggeration to say that Mr. Giorgio Armani is one of the most important designers of all time.

Here are a few concise background facts: Giorgio Armani was born on 11 July 1934 in Piacenza, Italy. After a false start studying medicine and a stint in the Italian army, he joined the Rinascente department store in Milan as an assistant merchandiser and later became a menswear buyer. In 1965, he segued over to the design studio of Nino Cerruti, where he learned and plied his skills in tailoring and creating clothing. He became a designer for hire, lending his talents to Krizia, Loewe, Ungaro, and Zegna (among many others). In 1975 he established Giorgio Armani S.p.A. and showed his first eponymous collection. Like Alexander in Rome before him, Giorgio Armani would go on to conquer the known world.

BLAZER REVOLUTION

In contrast to women's fashion, the evolution of menswear has been more conservative and has moved at a snail's pace. Its history is summarised in a handful of sweeping and expansive epochs rather than a rapid-fire cycling of seasonal trends. Menswear eschews sudden change in favour of cautious, creeping progress: a tightening of line in a silhouette, a subtle shift in shape and proportions. Innovation is not achieved through flagrant novelty but through the edging development of nuance in detail: the slope of a lapel, the curve of a shoulder, the break of a hem.

In the late 1960s, menswear was fussy and heavily constructed. Modernism gave way to dandyism to create what American writer Jay Cocks once described as "racetrack contours and crotch-cleaving pants that made any man, in profile, look like a bisected hourglass." Menswear was rigid and restrictive and at the same time stylised and prone to peacockery. The counterculture of the 1960s had chipped away at postwar conservatism. In the '70s, a new masculine identity emerged, one that was freer and more liberated. It required a new look, and Giorgio Armani had an idea of his own.

Armani's quiet revolution can be summed up in a single object: the unconstructed blazer. It was a rebuttal to traditional tailoring and, by default, conventional masculinity. Armani gutted the tailored jacket. He ripped out the lining and inner construction and replaced the heavy and inflexible fabrics with ones of a lighter hand and softer drape. His proposition was not entirely new: it was preceded by the Neapolitan jacket, an Italian innovation of the 1930s created by renowned tailor Vincenzo Attolini and famously sported by the then Duke of Windsor. But that had been 40 years earlier. In the time since, Italy had risen, fallen, lost a war, and was on the rise again, and menswear had shifted a world away. When Armani debuted the unconstructed blazer in 1975, the new soft look was nothing but startlingly contemporary.

Ease was the operative word. Armani proposed a sensual and relaxed look at a time when men's fashion was uptight and rigid. He advocated for a comfort and lightness that mirrored men's changing lifestyles and aspirations. Armani bestowed upon menswear a casual yet highly refined elegance. It was a runaway success.

The 1970s was the birth of Italian fashion as we know it today — an industry that rivals the quality, creativity, and market share of Paris. The era saw a new wave of eager ready-to-wear designers with something new to say — something that traditional tailoring or *alta moda*, in their ivory towers, could not. Included in Armani's cohort were Gianni Versace, Gianfranco Ferré, Fendi, Missoni and more. And while each of them enjoyed incredible success, it was Armani's arc, his quiet revolution, that would become most synonymous with this benchmark moment in fashion history.

(198)

Giorgio Armani in *Fantastic Man*, no. 37 (Fall-Winter 2023-24).

280

SERGIO

Hidden behind many great designers is a tenacious true believer—an individual whose faith and conviction is incorruptible and shatterproof. They are the fighters and cheerleaders and frequently also the backbone of the business. They toil behind the scenes to keep the fantasy flowing, negotiating with suppliers, coddling editors and journalists, signing cheques, balancing budgets. Yves Saint Laurent famously had Pierre Bergé. Calvin Klein had Barry Schwartz. Rei Kawakubo has Adrian Joffe and Rick Owens has Michèle Lamy. Giorgio Armani had Sergio Galeotti.

The pair were partners in work and life. They met in 1966 when Armani was still designing menswear for Nino Cerruti and moonlighting in womenswear in the still-burgeoning world of Italian ready-to-wear. They met at a nightclub, La Capannina. Galeotti was a hungry and ambitious 20-year-old architect and the two hit it off right away. Armani confided his hopes and ambitions to Galeotti and was rewarded with Galeotti's unwavering devotion.

"The more I spoke to him about my experiences, the goals I had achieved as well as my aspirations, the more he understood my potential," Armani divulges in 'Per Amore', his recent autobiography. "He lived in Versilia and yet wanted to move to Milan to test himself, but above all to experience this adventure together with me." Armani found him a job in Milan as a draughtsman at the architectural firm Peressutti and Rogers and the two decided to move in together, finding an apartment on Viale Lazio.

Eventually, the pair began working together, with Galeotti handling the business and administrative affairs of Armani's private design studio. Apparently, it was at Galeotti's insistence that Armani—who up until that time had only been designing for others—should produce and launch an eponymous collection. It was Galeotti who convinced Armani that he should sell his white Volkswagen to help raise $10,000 in start-up capital. They founded Giorgio Armani S.p.A. together in 1975. The 1980s saw a huge boom in fashion, as demand for conspicuous, status-enhancing clothing ballooned (along with the silhouette). Armani and Galeotti's business flourished. Italian fashion had arrived on the global stage, wrenching away the grip on power previously held by the French. It was against this backdrop of success and prosperity that the despair and devastation of the Aids epidemic unfolded. The first cases were reported in 1981, and the number quickly escalated around the world.

Knowledge about what caused the condition was scarce, stigma and fear ran high, and as the '80s went on, the casualties began to mount. The gay community was ravaged, as were the industries that gay men inhabited. Fashion was among the hardest hit. "Everything happened during the same year," Armani recalls in his autobiography. "The news of Sergio's illness, his immediate hospitalisation, the helplessness, the courage, on my part as well, to insist on talking about the future, as if nothing were wrong." At this point, the pair were no longer romantically involved, a fact that did nothing to ease the

"Sometimes if I want to look elegant, I'll put on a striped tie."

pain of saying goodbye and watching someone you love deteriorate before your eyes. Galeotti passed away in Milan on 14 August 1985, at the age of 40.

So crucial had Galeotti been to the business that it was presumed by the industry at large that Armani would call it quits and fold the company. He did not. "Some said a designer cannot be a businessman too," he would later tell Ingrid Sischy, in an interview in the catalogue for his early 2000s Guggenheim show. "It was very difficult, though. I didn't really know my firm. I had left a lot of the responsibility to Sergio." Slowly but surely Armani did learn, assuming all management duties. "I don't know how I did it, but I did it. And it is that, it is he [Galeotti] who gives me the strength even now to continue." Giorgio Armani triumphed over tragedy and emerged more fortified than before as a designer, chairman, and chief executive.

SEX & HOLLYWOOD

With the critical success of 1976's 'Taxi Driver' behind him, screenwriter Paul Schrader embarked on another ambitious and unsettling portrait of America, this time as director. His new film about a male prostitute framed for murder was set to star John Travolta. It was in fact Travolta's manager who had the idea to ask Giorgio Armani to provide the actor's wardrobe. Though Travolta would eventually drop the project, his Armani clothes remained in the film.

Starring Richard Gere and Lauren Hutton and released in 1980, 'American Gigolo' has become a case study in how cinematic storytelling and fashion can synergise to create a bona fide pop culture moment. The film is credited with launching Gere's career and introducing Armani to America. Part of the

(200)

Giorgio Armani in *Fantastic Man*, no. 37
(Fall–Winter 2023–24).

enduring appeal of 'American Gigolo' is that it is stylised but at the same time low-key and understated. The film's cinematography, location, architecture, set design and wardrobe combine to create a sweeping aesthetic statement despite none of the individual elements themselves being particularly vivid. Julian, played by Richard Gere, lives in a modernist bachelor pad in Los Angeles. He wears fine clothing in beautiful natural fabrics and drives a Mercedes-Benz 450 SL. His life is beautifully art-directed, a studied composi-

"Milan is a city that allows you to express yourself and respects you...if you have something to say."

tion. Though meant to contrast with sordid clandestine activities, the illusion is nonetheless solid. In one memorable scene, Julian is prepping for a job, sorting through what to wear, and there it is on labels peeking out from inside the collars of the shirts and jacket: Giorgio Armani.

From just a handful of shots, Armani's name became synonymous with beautiful people, beautiful worlds, affluence and means. And not only with these, but with sex appeal as well. Julian wears beautiful clothes and lives in a beautiful home, and he pays for all that by selling his beautiful body. Morality and ethics aside, it is a potent fantasy and perfect for selling clothes. The importance of 'American Gigolo' to Armani's success story cannot be overstated. Not only did it heighten the public's awareness of his designs, it marked the beginning of the designer's long and fruitful relationship with Hollywood.

CHANEL PARALLELS

Despite so often being reduced to nothing more than the flimsy flapper dress, the 1920s were in fact exceptional and radical. The world underwent an irrevocable change regarding aesthetic and stylistic innovations. This was the period that gave the world jazz, Bauhaus, Duchamp, Joséphine Baker, short hair on women, dresses without corsets, and, of course, Chanel.

Gabrielle 'Coco' Chanel founded a millinery practice in 1910 and eventually ascended to become one of France's greatest couturiers. She is closely associated with the boyish garçonne look. Indeed, Chanel took cues from

menswear and adapted them to women's fashion, allowing the fairer sex to finally dress with the ease and certainty of a man.

Her aesthetic was sober, but not plain. Buffering Chanel's spare sensibilities was an air of intellectual sophistication. She proposed that black be worn outside of mourning (and was mocked to her face for it by fellow fashion designer Paul Poiret). Chanel ran with the boys and dressed like them too. She designed her clothes accordingly: jersey, cardigans, sportswear and tweed. She spliced men's wardrobe staples into women's haute couture. Chanel's truest essence can be described with a single word: modernism. So, what does this all have to do with Armani?

If you were to ask Giorgio Armani who his favourite designer was, he would tell you it's Chanel. This can partly be explained by timing. In the early 1970s, as Armani was maturing as a designer and as Italian ready-to-wear was still burgeoning, a craze for art deco and the 1930s swept through fashion. It is from the '30s that the '70s derived the long, lean silhouette. Looking to the ease and sensual elegance of the past, designers adapted the period's soft dressing for their modern times. Chanel ruled the 1930s, and her work from this era would leave an indelible impression on Armani.

But one suspects his affinity for the designer is much more intrinsic and integral than that. There are many parallels between the two. Chanel and Armani both share a love of simplicity and luxurious austerity. They also revel in restraint and unflinching modernity. And even that iconic shade of Armani greige references Chanel's signature use of the colour beige.

Armani's masterstroke in womenswear was placing his men's unconstructed blazer on a female dress form. As alluring as his signature jacket was on a man, it was undeniably even more so on a woman — mannish but also feminine, powerful but also supremely elegant. Armani's "borrowing" from his men's collection synced with the emergence of a new fashion customer: an independent, well-paid woman who needed to navigate the business world of men. Enter Armani's soft power dressing.

From the 1980s onward, he would become the designer of choice for women in need of comfortable, modern clothing that could command authority in a room full of testosterone. What draws Chanel and Armani together is that Armani is ultimately a feminist: someone who believes that men and women are equal. If we look at the history of fashion as a whole and consider each designer in light of the values demonstrated in their clothes, it should be plainly evident to all that Giorgio Armani is Chanel's true spiritual heir.

(201)

EAST OF WEST

In 1933, Japanese author Jun'ichirō Tanizaki wrote 'In Praise of Shadows', an essay in which he compares and contrasts traditional Japanese and Western design. He ponders what modern utilities such as indoor bathrooms, electric lighting, plumbing, radiators, etcetera might look like had they been invented in Japan and informed by that country's unique aesthetic and cultural values. The same question could be asked about clothing, and not just that of Japan, but the clothing of any country whose traditional dress has ceded dominance to Western fashion over the last century. What would a suit look like today if Tokyo, Riyadh or Mumbai had been leading financial centres instead of London, Paris or New York? What would menswear have

"I've always insisted upon rigorous simplicity. I can't stand exhibitionism."

become had it not evolved out of Western hegemony over the last 200 years? Few designers have provided answers as compelling as Giorgio Armani's.

Armani's interest in the East began with his seminal collection for Autumn and Winter 1980/81. He was an ardent fan of Japanese director Akira Kurosawa and was taken by the splendour and scale of his 1980 feudal epic 'Kagemusha'. The film's period costumes, filled with samurai armour and traditional kimonos, left an indelible impression and catalysed a new approach in Armani's repertoire. He sampled and referenced their shapes and details and integrated them into the softly tailored silhouettes he'd pioneered only a few years earlier. The Japanese-inspired collection would turn out to be a huge commercial disaster, but it remains one of the designer's favourites and among his most influential.

Historically, Western clothing is based on the principle of imposing structured silhouettes onto the figure, i.e. tailoring. Tailored garments are rigid and restrictive, and they require rigorous construction not only to maintain shape but also to withstand the stress of the body's movements as it pulls and tugs on the garment's seams. In the East, both near and far, traditional clothes are based on the concept of joining loose expanses of cloth to create garments that rest softly on the body and allow for a full range of movement, not to mention comfort. Armani bridged that gap.

As costume historian Caroline Rennolds Milbank has aptly noted, "In his logical progression from the soft jacket, Armani has experimented with various elements and proportions that point east." Tunics, pyjamas, Nehru collars and Mao jackets are recurring favourites. Armani has blended East and West, reconciling the economical lines and relaxed volumes of the former with the workmanship and familiar tropes of the latter. From Armani's compelling amalgamation came a supremely elegant and cosmopolitan look.

NONSTOP

A cinematic flair pervades everything Giorgio Armani does. The scope of his vision is boundless. No idea is too big, no detail is too small. This distinct quality of his work is readily observed in his advertising — particularly in the epic and sweeping campaigns shot by Aldo Fallai and Peter Lindbergh from the 1970s through to the '90s. Together they created what is perhaps the greatest compendium of fashion imagery ever produced by a single brand. From the casting to the lighting to the locations to the poses and gestures to the clothes — the pictures are glorious, like stills from an impossibly beautiful movie screened only in one's dreams. And they underscore the fact that despite Armani's immense prowess and skill as a designer, the greatest expression of his ethos is not as clothing but as a lifestyle.

The Armani brand was founded to address the needs and dreams of a new way of life, and it has duly expanded as the world continues to evolve. In 1981 he launched Emporio Armani, Armani Junior, and Armani Jeans against the conventional wisdom of the fashion industry, which asserted that lower-priced diffusion labels diluted a designer's cachet. He released his first women's fragrance, Armani Femme by Giorgio Armani, in 1982 and his first men's fragrance, Armani Eau Pour Homme, in 1984. In '88 he introduced Giorgio Armani Occhiali (eyewear). In '91 he launched A/X Armani Exchange. The year 1997 saw the addition of watches, and in 2000 he expanded into beauty. Armani made a major entry into furniture and interiors with the art deco-inspired Armani/Casa in 2000. In 2005 he launched his Armani Privé haute couture collection. Why not?

Through his prolific success, Armani has accrued a fortune that has afforded him the most premium and luxurious of living arrangements. Of all the many things he's designed, the most telling and genuinely intriguing is his superyacht, Main, built in 2008 and named using one of his mother's nicknames. At 65 metres long and able to

Giorgio Armani in *Fantastic Man*, no. 37
(Fall–Winter 2023-24).

284

(Photographic assistance by Lex Kembery and Simon Mackinlay. Production by Partner Films.)

accommodate up to twelve guests, the vessel is, naturally, outfitted with custom Armani/Casa furniture and fixtures. Armani supervised the design himself, insisting on a tricky window and hull design to create the illusion that each deck is suspended weightlessly on top of the next. The pièce de résistance: the entire ship is painted a deep, murky green, making it nearly invisible on the horizon when at sea.

Armani's reach is far and wide; his label exists in as many permutations as the market can reasonably support. It is known throughout the industry that Mr. Armani personally approves every single style and stock-keeping unit (SKU) that bears his name. There are Armani hotels, bookstores, chocolates, jams, and even floral arrangements. Mr. Armani is the gravitational centre of a lifestyle universe, and no one exemplifies it better than him.

MYSTERIOUS SHORT

In 1990, Martin Scorsese premiered a documentary short at the Venice Film Festival called 'Made in Milan'—the same year as the release of his gangster smash 'GoodFellas'. It's proof of Armani's impressive global standing that a Hollywood hotshot like Scorsese would fix his directorial eye on the designer, even if the pair had become firm friends after Armani provided wardrobe for 'GoodFellas'.

The little-seen documentary is a series of fly-on-the-wall and fantasy montages, all accompanied by a hypnotic voiceover from Giorgio Armani, talking about his work, his clothes and his beloved adopted home. "Milan is my chosen city. It's a city that allows you to express yourself and respects you…if you have something to say." If the minotaur is part man, part bull and the centaur is part man, part horse, this film makes you search for a word for someone who's part man, part Milan. The exquisite shots of clinky dining rooms, silent interiors and chatty *aperitivi* offer a dreamy sense of the city's intimacy, exclusivity and privacy—the ideal setting for the world of Armani.

Armani's famous attention to detail is on full display throughout, as he throws and thumbs fabrics, considers hair and make-up and offers models pastoral instructions on how to walk. And there are useful directives on how to dress. "I've always insisted upon rigorous simplicity. I can't stand exhibitionism," for example, or "Sometimes if I want to look elegant, I'll put on a striped tie," or "Why blue? Because I think blue looks good on me," and perhaps most importantly for all: "Be faithful to yourself."

Scorsese went full throttle on this sub-30-minute documentary, pulling together an elite team of award-winning artists to make it. There's sensational cinematography from Néstor Almendros (Oscar winner for best cinematography in 1978), a transcendental score from Howard Shore (the proud owner of three Oscars, three Golden Globes and four Grammys) and Japanese drums by Kitaro (who has both a Grammy and a Golden Globe for his new age music). As a devoted film lover, Armani must have been honoured by the treatment he received as the subject of 'Made in Milan', but he also admits in the film that he wishes he'd made movies himself. "I would like to have been a director. This passion is still in my blood." In an Armani universe so total, it's surprising he never made one.

CONTRIBUTION
— Jeremy Lewis is a fashion writer and Armani fan who runs Lewis's, an Instagram account publishing a mix of acerbic present-day show reviews and archival appreciation for anything with a sumptuous, minimalist bent.

(205)

Italiques.

Maria Grazia Chiuri and Chimamanda Ngozi Adichie
in *F, l'art de vivre du Figaro*, no. 37 (November 21, 2023).

MARIA GRAZIA CHIURI & CHIMAMANDA NGOZI ADICHIE

"La mode a la responsabilité d'aider les femmes à prendre conscience de leur valeur"

L'une est directrice artistique chez Dior, l'autre une écrivain mondialement connue. Les deux sont des femmes puissantes qui font entendre la voix du féminin à travers leur vie et leurs œuvres Rencontre exclusive.

propos recueillis par Marie-Noëlle Demay et Anne-Sophie von Claer / photos Laura Stevens

L'entretien a lieu dans le bureau bibliothèque de Maria Grazia Chiuri, aux larges baies vitrées donnant sur les toits parisiens et la Seine, au lendemain du défilé Dior printemps-été 2024. On garde vivante à l'esprit la vibration de cette collection : silhouettes de rebelles, vêtements couleurs de cendre, animaux fantastiques, sensualité subtile et affirmée de celles qui revendiquent leurs différences. Car, pour Maria Grazia Chiuri, première femme nommée directrice artistique des collections féminines de Dior (haute couture, prêt-à-porter et accessoires), « *la mode ne se résume pas aux vêtements* ». Et cette collection n'échappe pas à la règle, qui sonde la signification du présent, sa coexistence avec le passé tout comme une exploration de la relation entre féminité et féminisme. Un message adressé aux femmes. Toutes les femmes. Une collection qui épouse parfaitement le fondement de l'œuvre engagée de l'écrivain nigériane Chimamanda Ngozi Adichie, star mondiale des lettres depuis la parution d'*Americanah*, et militante féministe respectée (Beyoncé a, dans sa chanson *Flawless* repris des extraits de son texte manifeste de 2014 *Nous sommes tous des féministes*). Un slogan en forme de profession de foi, qui a inspiré à Maria Grazia Chiuri un tee-shirt « We should all be feminists », pièce devenue culte de son tout premier défilé pour la maison Dior en 2017. Les deux femmes se connaissent et s'apprécient depuis longtemps. Chimamanda a fait spécialement le déplacement pour assister à ce défilé prêt-à-porter printemps-été 2024, dont la scénographie était signée de l'artiste italienne Elena Bellantoni : une installation vidéo reprenant des phrases battant en brèche les stéréotypes : « I am not your doll. I am not your game. Call me by my name », « Unlike my mother, I have a choice », « We want kids but we want roses too »… Une concordance de points de vue qui était l'occasion d'un échange exclusif.

Le féminisme n'est ni un virus, ni génétique… alors, comment devient-on aussi concernée par ces questions ?

C. N. A. – Moi je pense que c'est génétique *(Rires)* ! C'était le cas pour moi. J'étais féministe avant de connaître le mot. Petite, j'étais très observatrice, sans doute parce que j'ai toujours voulu écrire et que l'un des aspects de l'écriture est l'observation du monde. Enfant, je savais que les femmes étaient plus mal traitées que les hommes. Par exemple, j'ai grandi sur un campus *(son père enseignait à l'université du Nigeria, NDLR)* où il y avait très peu de femmes professeurs. Et les rares présentes étaient traitées très différemment. Je n'oublierai jamais l'une d'elles qu'on désignait comme arrogante. Et je me suis dit : « Attendez, elle est exactement comme les hommes ! » Mais personne ne faisait cette réflexion au sujet du genre masculin… J'étais donc féministe à l'époque, même si je ne connaissais pas ce mot. Je pense que je suis née féministe.

M. G. C. – J'ai grandi dans les années 1970, un moment historique très particulier en Italie. Ma mère et mon père étaient tous deux très libres. Je ne me souviens pas que quelqu'un m'ait rappelé que j'étais une fille. J'étais simplement Maria Grazia. Ils m'ont jamais donné l'idée que je ne pouvais pas ni ne devais faire quelque chose à cause de mon sexe.

Quelle est de nos jours la perception du mot féminisme qui, jadis, n'avait rien d'un compliment ?

C. N. A. – Ça ne l'est toujours pas aujourd'hui ! Je suis sûre qu'il y a beaucoup de gens qui sont réfractaires à l'avant-gardisme de Maria Grazia sur ce sujet. Tout simplement parce qu'il s'agit de féminisme. On entend des choses comme : « *Oh ! le féminisme est devenu cool.* » Mais moi, je pense que ce n'est pas le cas.

Qu'est ce qui distingue, selon vous Chimamanda Ngozi Adichie, Maria Grazia Chiuri de ses pairs, dans son approche de la mode ?

C. N. A. – Nous nous sommes rencontrées toutes les deux quand Maria Grazia a été nommée chez Dior en 2017 et m'a écrit une lettre adorable. Elle connaissait mon travail grâce aux conférences TED que j'avais données. J'ai assisté à son premier défilé et nous sommes restées en contact. J'ai toujours aimé les vêtements, mais je ne m'étais→

85

jamais vraiment intéressée à l'industrie de la mode. Maria Grazia a été mon introduction à ce secteur ! Ma mère était la femme la plus élégante du monde et elle essayait de faire de moi sa poupée. Je pensais, de façon stéréotypée, que l'industrie de la mode était en quelque sorte superficielle. Maintenant, que je connais mieux Maria Grazia, grâce à elle, je suis plus encline à lire des sujets qui concernent ce secteur. Je pense que ce qu'elle fait, elle le fait différemment… Je suis frappée par sa volonté et en même temps son humilité, bien que je n'aime pas ce mot lorsqu'il s'agit de femmes. Je me souviens lui avoir dit un jour : *« Vous n'avez vraiment pas un gros ego. »* Cela en dit long sur la manière dont elle aborde sa mission, en reconnaissant qu'un résultat magnifique est le fruit d'un travail d'équipe.

Quel est, en tant que femmes et féministes, votre rapport personnel au vêtement ?

M. G. C. – Je suis convaincue que la mode a la responsabilité d'aider les femmes à prendre conscience de leur valeur et à exprimer leurs différences. Chaque matin, je choisis des vêtements dans lesquels je me sens à l'aise. Je veux être confortable avec mon corps. Pour moi, c'est la priorité. Je ne porte pas beaucoup de talons hauts, parce qu'au bout d'une heure, c'est trop pour moi et parce que je veux pouvoir courir. Cela a à voir avec ma perception. J'aime aussi les belles pièces qui peuvent rester longtemps dans ma garde-robe. Les vêtements font partie de ma personnalité. Si j'utilise un manteau, c'est aussi parce que je me souviens de moi au moment précis où je l'ai acheté, où je l'ai porté. Les vêtements font partie de ma mémoire. J'ai une relation très spécifique avec eux. Je suis aussi une collectionneuse. Je conserve les vêtements de ma mère, un petit manteau que j'ai acheté jadis pour ma fille Rachele. J'espère qu'un jour, si elle a un bébé, elle le réutilisera. Je pense que les vêtements transmettent aussi des émotions. Pour moi, c'est vraiment un langage. Ils me rappellent un moment, un souvenir, ce ne sont pas seulement de belles pièces que je veux montrer. C'est quelque chose d'important pour moi. Mais pas nécessairement pour d'autres.

Si les vêtements sont un langage, portez-vous des vêtements pour transmettre un message ?

M. G. C. – Je ne sais pas ce que les gens perçoivent de mes collections. Mais quand j'y travaille, je pense d'abord à ce qu'elles représentent pour moi. Ce n'est pas seulement une question d'esthétique. Pour la dernière par exemple, j'étais obsédée par l'idée de la sensualité que l'on peut exprimer non pas nécessairement par la nudité, mais simplement par une petite partie du corps. Derrière chaque pièce, il y a une réflexion… Ce que vous ressentez lorsque vous mettez quelque chose sur votre corps est très important. Parfois, pour une occasion particulière, le bureau de presse me demande : *« Qu'aimeriez-vous porter pour cet événement ? »* Je ne sais pas ! Cela dépend de ce que je ressens au réveil. À mon avis, c'est pareil pour toutes les femmes, cela dépend de la journée, de ce que l'on ressent.

Et vous, Chimamanda ?

C. N. A. – Je pense que c'est encore plus pragmatique : mon corps de femme détermine ce que je porte. Si je suis en période hormonale et ballonnée, je ne

"Je pense que les vêtements transmettent aussi des émotions. Pour moi, c'est vraiment un langage"

MARIA GRAZIA CHIURI

veux pas de quelque chose de moulant. J'ai de plus en plus envie de parler de la façon dont le corps féminin façonne nos vies. Avant mes règles, je deviens « massive ». Il y a certaines pièces dont je ne veux pas et tout me paraît laid. Et puis mes règles passent et soudain tout va bien. Il ne s'agit pas seulement de l'expression, mais aussi des contraintes du corps féminin. Par exemple, il y a tellement de vêtements qui ne sont pas seyants parce que pas taillés pour les femmes qui ont des seins. Nous parlions de féminité. Maria Grazia fait des choses féminines. Et j'aime cela. La gamme de ses créations est assez large. Encore une fois, même si c'est un mot qui est trop souvent utilisé, j'ai l'impression qu'elle est assez inclusive, et c'est ce que je constate dans toutes les collections que j'ai vues d'elle. Une femme qui a des seins volumineux peut porter telle pièce ; une sans poitrine peut porter telle autre. Il y a une ouverture d'esprit. Parce qu'elle sait ce que c'est…

Vous parlez toutes les deux de combattre les clichés en tant que femmes. Quels sont ceux que vous avez dû combattre ?

M. G. C. – Le plus grand cliché est que, lorsque vous exprimez votre point de vue, vous êtes considérée comme étant en colère ou nerveuse. Ou qu'il y a quelque chose qui cloche dans votre vie, ou… que vous avez vos règles *(Rires)* !

C. N. A. – C'est intéressant parce que je pense que nous en avons déjà parlé dans le passé. Il y a ce cliché… Je me souviens que lorsque Hillary Clinton était candidate à la présidence, les gens disaient : *« Oh ! Mon Dieu, et si elle avait sa ménopause ou une bouffée de chaleur et qu'elle appuyait sur le bouton nucléaire ? C'est terrible ! »* C'est très insultant. On utilise la réalité féminine pour rabaisser les femmes. Et parfois, parce que nous répondons aux clichés, nous courons le risque d'aller dans la direction opposée, c'est-à-dire de ne pas en parler du tout. Mais la vérité, c'est que ces choses ont de l'importance. Il est terrible de dire qu'une femme fera quelque chose parce qu'elle est ménopausée. Il est également vrai que la ménopause entraîne des conséquences réelles pour les femmes. Je pense que pour moi, il s'agit de trouver l'équilibre. Combattre les clichés peut aussi signifier que vous ne laissez pas quelqu'un d'autre définir ce qui est important pour vous. Je ne veux pas dire que je ne parlerai jamais de mon syndrome prémenstruel parce qu'un homme ou une femme va l'utiliser contre moi. Je vais en parler de la manière dont je veux en parler. Toute cette idée de « rester à l'écart des choses qui ont à voir avec le corps féminin » n'est pas viable… Moi, cela m'intéresse de parler du corps féminin. Le cliché qui me dérange le plus est peut-être le fait que lorsque vous avez confiance en vous en tant que femme, on vous traite d'arrogante. Ou que lorsque vous ne voulez pas faire de compromis, on vous traite de difficile. Toute ma vie, j'ai dit ce que je pensais. Cela entraîne des conséquences. C'est un cliché que je combats. Je dois dire que, contrairement à Maria Grazia, j'adore les talons hauts et je suis très heureuse de me sentir mal à l'aise *(Rires)*. J'ai juste besoin d'être heureuse avec ce que je porte. L'inconfort, c'est bien. Je pense que c'est le prix à payer.

Vous avez toutes les deux des filles. Comment leur parlez-vous de ces sujets ?
M. G. C. – Je pense que nous ne nous en rendons pas souvent compte, mais le risque est de répéter une idée stéréotypée que l'on a reçue. Ma mère avait coutume de m'habiller comme une poupée et, d'une certaine manière, j'ai refait la même chose avec ma fille Rachele jusqu'au moment où elle m'a dit : *« Arrête ! Je ne suis pas ton jouet »*. Il faut être conscient que l'on reproduit les mêmes choses. Il faut y réfléchir.
C. N. A. – Ma fille vient d'avoir 8 ans, et jusqu'à ses 6 ans, je choisissais et lui disais quoi porter. Et à l'âge de 6 ans, elle a dit « Non ». J'ai appris à respecter cela. Aujourd'hui, elle veut arborer des choses que je trouve ridicules, mais je prends du recul et je dis *« Ok »*. Je pense qu'il est important de donner aux filles un sentiment d'autonomie très tôt dans la vie et je veille à le lui procurer.

Il n'en reste pas moins que les jeunes filles sont soumises au regard des hommes. Ce qui a évidemment une influence sur elles. Sont-elles aussi libres que cela ?
C. N. A. – Non, elles ne le sont pas. Il est d'ailleurs intéressant que Maria Grazia ait de l'espoir pour elles. Moi, je suis de plus en plus déprimée parce que je pense que les médias sociaux ont terriblement éloigné les femmes de la question de l'égalité. Il y a aujourd'hui tant de jeunes femmes qui, à cause des médias sociaux, n'ont plus confiance en elles, n'ont plus d'estime d'elles-mêmes, sont anxieuses, déprimées. Elles consultent ces médias et commencent à se sentir mal dans leur peau. Bien qu'elles soient magnifiques, elles ne le savent pas. Ce que j'essaie d'enseigner à ma fille, c'est qu'elle n'est pas un objet, mais un sujet. Si on lui dit : *« Les garçons n'aiment pas quand tu fais ça »*, je veux lui apprendre à répondre : *« Moi non plus, je n'aime pas ça. »* L'idée qu'une femme a le droit d'aimer quelque chose. Ou pas. On nous fait souvent croire que nous ne faisons que recevoir au lieu de donner. Nous devons apprendre aux filles à s'approprier davantage les choses. Quant au regard masculin… Pour moi, la mode est ce que j'aime. C'est ce qui me donne confiance en moi, ce qui me rend heureuse, qui rend ma vanité heureuse. Il y a des choses que je porte et qui font rire mon mari. Il me dit : *« Attends, c'est quoi ? »* Et je lui réponds : *« Moi, j'aime. »* Nous devrions davantage enseigner cela aux femmes : il ne s'agit pas de s'habiller d'une certaine façon parce que l'on pense que cela pourrait plaire à quelqu'un. Il faut que ce soit pour soi. Cela vous donne beaucoup plus d'assurance. Et peu importe que les gens critiquent. Ce n'est pas grave.

Le tee-shirt que vous avez créé dès votre première collection pour Dior, arborant le titre d'un ouvrage de Chimanda, « We should all be feminists »,

est devenu iconique. Comment vous est venue cette idée ?
M. G. C. – Je suis obsédée par les livres. La seule façon de changer les choses, c'est l'éducation. Pour moi, tout est possible. Nous pouvons promouvoir des ouvrages qui, d'une manière ou d'une autre, sont importants et les partager. Et, honnêtement, la mode

> "Il est important de donner aux filles un sentiment d'autonomie très tôt dans la vie"
> CHIMAMANDA NGOZI ADICHIE

peut faire beaucoup. Nous jouons un rôle important pour la nouvelle génération parce que la mode est populaire, c'est son pouvoir. J'ai tout de suite compris le rôle-clé de la plateforme Dior : il est essentiel d'avoir une communauté d'artistes avec des voix et des parcours différents, avec une créativité différente, qui peuvent l'utiliser. Avant même de signer le contrat avec Dior, je leur ai fait part de ma vision de la marque. J'ai dit que je voulais parler du féminisme, donner un point de vue différent, que Dior n'était pas une marque féminine dans la vision traditionnelle. Et la maison a accepté. Ils m'ont donné cette opportunité. Et puis il n'était pas si simple d'être la première femme à prendre ce poste dans une si grande marque à l'histoire très riche.

Écrivains, plasticiens, peintres, musiciens, danseurs… vous collaborez avec de nombreux talents.
M. G. C. – J'aime beaucoup travailler avec d'autres personnes créatives. Sinon, si vous restez seule dans votre chambre, c'est très ennuyeux. Chimamanda est une écrivain, elle doit s'isoler pour écrire. Moi, je deviendrais folle au bout de six mois !

La littérature, la mode : ces deux domaines sont encore majoritairement masculins…
M. G. C. – Il y a tout de même de grandes créatrices dans la mode : Elsa Schiaparelli, Gabrielle Chanel, Miuccia Prada… des femmes incroyables, propriétaires de leur marque. Aujourd'hui, la plupart sont des directeurs de création, c'est une approche complètement différente. Et, je remarque que le langage utilisé dans ce cas est différent : les directeurs créatifs masculins ont du succès parce qu'ils comprennent l'air du temps, les directeurs créatifs féminins parce qu'elles ont une fibre commerciale… Je ne sais pas s'il en va de même pour les livres, mais cette façon différente de parler du travail des hommes et des femmes perdure.

Maria Grazia, la mode que vous créez serait-elle très différente si vous le faisiez sous la marque Maria Grazia Chiuri et non sous le nom de Dior ?
M. G. C. – Je n'ai jamais pensé de ma vie à créer ma propre marque ! Je ne suis pas assez égocentrique pour cela *(Rires)*. S'exprimer différemment sous sa propre marque signifie que l'on veut vraiment se célébrer. Cela ne m'intéresse pas. C'est comme pour une maison. Préférez-vous en construire une nouvelle ou en restaurer une ancienne ? Pour ma part, je préfère restaurer une vieille maison. Je n'ai pas besoin d'en construire une autre.
C. N. A. – Moi, je construirais une nouvelle maison ! *(Rires)* Mais je pense que nous avons besoin des deux : de bâtisseurs et de restaurateurs. Si vous voulez restaurer, quelqu'un a dû construire à un moment donné. C'est ce que j'admire : Maria Grazia a beaucoup d'assurance, mais elle n'a pas un ego démesuré. Je pense que j'ai les deux ! Et il devrait y avoir de la place pour cela chez les femmes. Encore une fois, l'essentiel c'est la diversité.

87

memorabile
ipermoda

Selected Bibliography

Abloh, Virgil. *"Insert Complicated Title Here."* Berlin: Sternberg; Cambridge, MA: Harvard University Graduate School of Design, 2018.

Allen, Gwen, ed. *The Magazine*. London: Whitechapel Gallery; Cambridge, MA: MIT Press, 2016.

Bennett, Jane. *Vibrant Matter: A Political Ecology of Things*. Durham, NC: Duke University Press, 2010.

Bolton, Andrew, ed. *Camp: Notes on Fashion*, catalogue of the exhibition at the Metropolitan Museum of Art, New York, May 9–September 8, 2019. New York: Metropolitan Museum of Art, 2019.

Bonacina, Andrew, ed. *Disobedient Bodies: JW Anderson at The Hepworth Wakefield*, catalogue of the exhibition *Disobedient Bodies: JW Anderson Curates The Hepworth Wakefield* at The Hepworth Wakefield, Wakefield, March 18–June 18, 2017. London: InOtherWords, 2017.

Bourriaud, Nicolas, *Inclusions: Aesthetics of the Capitalocene*. London: Sternberg, 2022.

Butler, Judith, *Notes toward a Performative Theory of Assembly*. Cambridge, MA: Harvard University Press, 2015.

Coccia, Emanuele, and Alessandro Michele, *La vita delle forme: Filosofia del reincanto*. Milan: HarperCollins, 2024.

Darling, Michael. *Virgil Abloh: Figures of Speech*, catalogue of the traveling exhibition. New York: DelMonico Books; Munich: Prestel, 2019.

De Leo, Maya. *Queer: Storia culturale della comunità LGBT+*. Turin: Einaudi, 2021.

Frisa, Maria Luisa. *Le forme della moda*, 2nd ed. Bologna: il Mulino, 2022.

Frisa, Maria Luisa, ed. *Memos: On Fashion in This Millennium*, catalogue of the exhibition at the Museo Poldi Pezzoli, Milan, February 21–September 28, 2020. Venice: Marsilio, 2020.

Fury, Alexander, and Chris Moore. *Catwalking*. London: Laurence King, 2017.

Granata, Francesca. *Experimental Fashion: Performance Art, Carnival and the Grotesque Body*. London: I.B. Tauris, 2017.

Grechi, Giulia. *Decolonizzare il museo: Mostrazioni, pratiche artistiche, sguardi incarnati*. Milan: Mimesis, 2021.

Haraway, Donna J. *Staying with the Trouble: Making Kin in the Chthulucene*. Durham, NC: Duke University Press, 2016.

hooks, bell. *Teaching to Transgress: Education as the Practice of Freedom*. New York: Routledge, 1994.

Marcadent, Saul. *Publishing as Curating: Design and Imagery in Contemporary Fashion Magazines*. Venice: Marsilio, 2020.

McQuillan, Vésma Kontere, ed. *Fashion Spaces: A Theoretical View*. Amsterdam: Frame, 2020.

Molinari, Luca. *La meraviglia è di tutti: Corpi, città, architetture*. Turin: Einaudi, 2023.

Monti, Gabriele. *In posa: Modelle italiane dagli anni cinquanta a oggi*. Venice: Marsilio, 2016.

Morton, Timothy. *Hyperobjects: Philosophy and Ecology after the End of the World*. Minneapolis: University of Minnesota Press, 2013.

Nelson, Maggie. *The Argonauts*. Minneapolis: Graywolf, 2015.

Pignatti, Lorenza. *Cartografie radicali: Attivismo, esplorazioni artistiche, geofiction*. Milan: Meltemi, 2023.

Reilly, Andrew. *Introducing Fashion Theory: From Androgyny to Zeitgeist*, 2nd ed. London: Bloomsbury Visual Arts, 2020.

Rock, Michael, ed. *Pradasphere*. Milan: Prada, 2014.

Ruby, Sterling, and Raf Simons. *Beyond the Collaboration*. Berlin: Sternberg; Cambridge, MA: Harvard University Graduate School of Design, 2018.

Severi, Carlo. *Capturing Imagination: A Proposal for an Anthropology of Thought*. Chicago: Hau Books, 2020.

Severi, Carlo. *The Chimera Principle: An Anthropology of Memory and Imagination*. Chicago: Hau Books, 2015.

Sontag, Susan. *Against Interpretation and Other Essays*. New York: Farrar, Straus & Giroux, 1966.

Steyerl, Hito. *The Wretched of the Screen*. Berlin: Sternberg, 2012.

Sutcliffe, Jamie, ed. *Magic*. London: Whitechapel Gallery; Cambridge, MA: MIT Press, 2021.

Wales Bonner, Grace. *Dream in the Rhythm: Visions of Sound and Spirit in the MoMA Collection*. New York: Museum of Modern Art, 2023.

Authors' Biographies

Judith Clark

Judith Clark is professor of Fashion and Museology at the UAL, University of the Arts London, and a curator, exhibition maker, and art director based in London. Clark opened the first experimental gallery of fashion in London (1997–2002). Since then Clark has curated major exhibitions of dress for museums and galleries internationally, including the V&A (London), MoMu (Antwerp), Boijmans Van Beuningen (Rotterdam), Palais de Tokyo (Paris), Barbican Art Gallery (London), Fosun Foundation (Shanghai). Clark has recently opened a studio-space in which to create hypothetical exhibitions of dress in the form of 1:12 models and related "souvenir" artworks.

Emanuele Coccia

Emanuele Coccia teaches philosophy in Paris. He has written *The Life of Plants* (2019), *Metamorphoses* (2021), and *Philosophy of the Home* (2024), published in various languages. He has recently published a book on photographic theory with the Dutch photographer Viviane Sassen (*Modern Alchemy*, 2022), a philosophical correspondence on light with photographer Paolo Roversi (*Lettres sur la lumière*, 2024), and a book on the relationship between fashion and philosophy with the former creative director of Gucci Alessandro Michele (*La vita delle forme: Filosofia del reincanto*, 2024). He has codirected animation videos such as *Quercus* (with Formafantasma, 2020) and *Heaven in Matter* (with Faye Formisano, 2021). He has cocurated an exhibition on fashion (*The Many Lives of a Garment*, with Olivier Saillard, 2024–25).

Dylan Colussi

Dylan Colussi studied fashion design at the Università Iuav di Venezia, where he earned a PhD with a dissertation on the relationship between creative directors and archives. Recently he has collaborated on the exhibitions *Gucci Cosmos* (West Bund Art Center, Shanghai, and 180 Studios, London, 2023) and contributed to the book *Dior Scarves: Fashion Stories* (2024). Since 2018 he has curated the archive of Emilio Pucci Heritage in Florence.

Maria Luisa Frisa

Maria Luisa Frisa, fashion theorist and curator, is a professor at the Università Iuav di Venezia, where she founded the degree course in Fashion Design and Multimedia Arts. She is editor in chief of the academic journal *Dune*. Her most recent exhibitions: *Bellissima: Italy and High Fashion 1945–1968* (2014–16), *Italiana: Italy through the Lens of Fashion 1971–2001* (2018), *Memos: On Fashion in This Millennium* (2020). Her latest books: *Le forme della moda* (2022), *I racconti della moda* (2024).

Alexander Fury

Alexander Fury is an award-winning fashion journalist, author, and curator. He is the fashion director of *AnOther Magazine* and the men's critic of the *Financial Times*. He has curated a number of exhibitions, including *Forever Valentino* (2022–23) and *Swarovski: Masters of Light* (2023–24). He also acted as exhibition adviser to *NAOMI: In Fashion* at the V&A, London (2024–25), and provided narrative text for *Azzedine Alaïa: The Couturier* at the Design Museum, London (2018). He has written ten books on fashion, and is a passionate collector of vintage clothing.

Alessandro Giammei

Alessandro Giammei is assistant professor of Italian Studies at Yale University. Among his most recent books: *Giulia Nicolai* (with Marco Belpoliti and Nunzia Palmieri, 2023), *Heretical Aesthetics: Pasolini on Painting* (with Ara Merjian, 2023), *Gioventù degli antenati: Il Rinascimento è uno zombie* (2024), *Ariosto in the Machine Age* (2024, AAIS Book Prize). His writings and translations appeared in the *Paris Review*, *Vanity Fair*, and *The Nation*. His columns on masculinity for *Domani* and *Esquire* inspired the book *Cose da maschi* (2023).

Saul Marcadent

Saul Marcadent is a researcher at the Università Iuav di Venezia and curator. He focuses his research on the relationship between the world of publishing and a theoretical-critical perspective. He is the author of the book *Publishing as Curating: Design and Imagery in Contemporary Fashion Magazines* (2020) and managing editor of the academic journal *Dune*. He has collaborated, in the capacity of curator, with cultural institutions like the Istituto Svizzero and ICA Milano. He is currently a visiting researcher at the London College of Fashion (UAL, University of the Arts London).

Silvano Mendes

Silvano Mendes is a journalist at Radio France Internationale and associate professor of Fashion Communications at the Sorbonne Nouvelle University, Paris. In addition to his journalistic work on fashion he has contributed to the books *Fashion Cultures Revisited: Theories, Explorations and Analysis* (2013), *Fashion Heritage: Narrative and Knowledge Creation* (2022) and the journals *Luxury: History, Culture, Consumption* (2015), *International Journal of Fashion Studies* (2017), and *Fashion Theory* (2019). His research focuses principally on fashion, space, and communication.

Gabriele Monti

Gabriele Monti, PhD, is an associate professor at the Università Iuav di Venezia, where he teaches in the degree course of Fashion Design and Multimedia Arts. Among the focuses of his research are the relations between fashion and visual culture, fashion curating, and the links between fashion and the museum. He is a member of the advisory board of EFHA, the European Fashion Heritage Association. He was associate curator of the exhibitions *Bellissima: Italy and High Fashion 1945–1968* (2014–16) and *Italiana: Italy through the Lens of Fashion 1971–2001* (2018). He has published the monograph *In posa: Modelle italiane dagli anni cinquanta a oggi* (2016).

Nick Rees-Roberts

Nick Rees-Roberts is professor of Media and Cultural Studies at the Sorbonne Nouvelle University, Paris. He is the author of *French Queer Cinema* (2008) and *Fashion Film: Art and Advertising in the Digital Age* (2018), coauthor of *Homo exoticus: Race, classe et critique queer* (2010), and coeditor of *Alain Delon: Style, Stardom and Masculinity* (2015) and *Isabelle Huppert: Stardom, Performance, Authorship* (2021). He is currently writing a book on failure in fashion and coediting *The Elizabeth Wilson Reader: Feminism, Fashion and the Aesthetics of Modern Life*, both for Bloomsbury Visual Arts.

Marco Ricchetti

Marco Ricchetti is an economist and the CEO of Blumine, a consultancy dedicated to guiding textile and fashion companies toward sustainability. He serves as an advisor to the Camera Nazionale della Moda Italiana and Pitti Immagine. Over the past four years, Ricchetti has spearheaded the implementation of projects promoted by UNIDO, the United Nations Industrial Development Organization, on the circular economy in the fashion supply chain in Egypt, Morocco, and Tunisia. Additionally, he has held academic positions at various fashion schools and universities and has authored books and articles in scholarly journals.

Silvia Schirinzi

Silvia Schirinzi has been fashion director of *Rivista Studio* since 2021, where she is responsible for coordination of the editorial contents that concern fashion both in the magazine and on its website. Graduating with a degree in the history of medieval philosophy, over the years she has written about fashion for *Vogue Italia*, *L'uomo Vogue* and *D-la* Repubblica. She has also contributed to *Donna moderna*, writing about current affairs. She has a monthly newsletter in *Rivista Studio*, entitled *Industry* and devoted to the analysis of tendencies and movements in the sector, and has recently launched a podcast, *Glamorama*, which also focuses on fashion and its protagonists.

Luis Venegas

Luis Venegas is a creative director and the editor and publisher of *Fanzine137*, *EY! Magateen*, *C☆NDY Transversal*, *The Printed Dog*, *EY! Boy Collection*, *The Intim Mates News Paper*, and *Direct Booking*. His publications — always released as limited editions — are available only in a few selected bookstores around the world. Venegas is also a regular consultant, who has done projects with clients like Loewe, RIMOWA, the MOP Foundation, Rizzoli New York, and Acne Studios, among others.

Reproduction and Printing
Grafiche Antiga s.p.a., Crocetta del
Montello (TV)
for
Marsilio Arte® s.r.l., Venice